Working for Peace and Justice

Working for Peace and Justice

Memoirs of an Activist Intellectual

Lawrence S. Wittner

Legacies of War • G. Kurt Piehler, Series Editor

The University of Tennessee Press • Knoxville

The Legacies of War series presents a variety of works—from scholarly monographs to memoirs—that examine the impact of war on society, both in the United States and globally. The wide scope of the series might include war's effects on civilian populations, its lingering consequences for veterans, and the role of individual nations and the international community in confronting genocide and other injustices born of war.

Copyright © 2012 by The University of Tennessee Press / Knoxville.
All Rights Reserved. Manufactured in the United States of America.
First Edition.

Unless otherwise credited, all photographs are from the author's collection.

The paper in this book meets the requirements of American National Standards Institute / National Information Standards Organization specification Z39.48-1992 (Permanence of Paper). It contains 30 percent post-consumer waste and is certified by the Forest Stewardship Council.

Library of Congress Cataloging-in-Publication Data

Wittner, Lawrence S.
Working for peace and justice: memoirs of an activist intellectual / Lawrence S. Wittner. — 1st ed.
   p. cm. — (Legacies of war)
ISBN-13: 978-1-57233-857-9 (pbk.: alk. paper)
ISBN-10: 1-57233-857-1 (pbk.: alk. paper)
  1. Wittner, Lawrence S.
  2. Intellectuals—United States—Biography.
  3. Political activists—United States—Biography.
  4. Pacifists—United States—Biography.
  5. Scholars—United States—Biography.
  6. Historians—United States—Biography.
  7. Student movements—United States—History—20th century.
  8. Peace movements—History—20th century.
  9. Social justice—History—20th century.
 10. State University of New York at Albany—Faculty—Biography.
   I. Title.
CT275.W593A3 2012
305.5'52092—dc23
[B]
2011041685

To the many people who have made my heart sing

Contents

Foreword	xi
G. Kurt Piehler, Series Editor	
Preface	xv
1. Family Background	1
2. Brooklyn Boyhood, 1941–1958	13
3. College Days, 1958–1962	39
4. Graduate School, 1962–1967	69
5. A Young Faculty Member, 1967–1972	89
6. Overseas Exile, 1972–1974	113
7. Grappling with Issues of Work and Love, 1974–1980	127
8. An Activist Academic, 1981–1989	161
9. A National and International Figure, 1990–2001	191
10. Growing Old, but Not Gracefully, 2001–2011	221
11. In Retrospect	249
Other Books by Lawrence Wittner	253
Index	255

Illustrations

Following Page 147

Joseph Tzvi Barnatsky and Dvorah Barnatsky in Russian Poland, Late Nineteenth Century
Abraham Barnett and Rose Barnett, circa 1911
Leah and Joseph Wittner with Their Son, Jacob ("Jack") Wittner, circa 1911
Rose Barnett, circa 1928
Jack Wittner, February 1930
With Rose Wittner, August 1941
In the Playpen, June 1942
As a Young Boy, circa 1945
Alpha Phi Omega Visits McSorley's Old Ale House, Manhattan, Fall 1958
With Mike Weinberg on Brooklyn Streets, June 1962
Hampton Institute Convocation Ceremonies, 1967
Speaking with U.S. Sailors at Antiwar Coffeehouse in Japan, 1974
Marjie Wittner, Julia Wittner, and Jack Wittner, Late 1970s
DSOC Luncheon Talk by Michael Harrington
In Police Van Following Arrest during a Free South Africa Sit-In, 1985
Support Demonstration for ACTWU, Lorbrook Factory, Hudson, New York, 1987
With Ben Barker-Benfield on Cape Cod, 1988
At Peace Researcher Meeting in Moscow, 1990
Dorothy Tristman, Albany, New York, Late 1990s
Peace Historians at Dinner during Hague Appeal for Peace Conference, 1999
Interviewed by a TV Reporter amid Pro-Union Uprising, 2000
Solidarity Committee at Labor Day Picnic, 2000
Leading Singing of "Solidarity Forever" at Statewide UUP Convention, 2001
Solidarity Singers at Caffè Lena, 2003
Speaking at Georgian Court University, 2004
Leading Annual Nuclear Disarmament March through Streets of Hiroshima, 2004
Receiving Upper Hudson Peace Action's "Peacemaker" Award, 2007

Foreword

Working for Peace and Justice is the first memoir to be published in the Legacies of War series. It is especially fitting to include Larry Wittner's memoir in the series, given his life and career as one of America's leading academic experts on the peace movement and its impact on public policy. A prolific and internationally recognized scholar, Larry has lectured widely both in the United States and abroad, including a tour as a Fulbright Senior Lecturer in Japan. He has held a number of distinguished offices in major scholarly organizations, including a term as president of the Peace History Society. What is even more remarkable is that Larry has also been an activist in important social movements for most of his life, promoting the causes of peace and nonviolence, racial equality, and workers' rights.

Memoirs by their very nature are subjective, and a good one makes no pretense at objectivity. More important, a good memoirist must be brutally honest and draw upon his or her own experiences and recollections. It also helps if the memoir is well written. Larry Wittner's book meets all these essential criteria. *Working for Peace and Justice* offers important insights into the history of the second half of the twentieth century and the opening decade of the twenty-first century and underscores the profound legacies of World War II, the Cold War, the war in Vietnam, and the terrorist attacks of September 11, 2001, on American society. This era witnessed the rise of the national security state and the attendant military-industrial-academic complex, but it also gave birth to a vibrant, if often divided peace/nuclear disarmament movement.

This is also a memoir about a young man's coming of age and development in those tumultuous times. In many ways, Larry's career parallels the rise and expansion of American higher education in the postwar era and the broadening of access to higher education. Coming from a family of modest means, he attended Columbia University and the University of Wisconsin–Madison, then premier institutions for the study of history. His first full-time teaching position was at a small, historically black college in the late 1960s before he moved on to an elite women's liberal arts college north of New York City. Ultimately, Larry found a permanent academic home on the Albany campus of the State University of New York. In this book, Larry offers insights into not only the joys of academic life, especially the engagement with ideas, but also the mundane, sometimes difficult realities of finding and keeping a job, securing research grants, and serving on departmental and university committees.

But this memoir goes far beyond the academy. Indeed, it ranges over a broad sweep of history, from the bloody anti-Semitic pogroms of late-nineteenth-century Eastern Europe to the turbulent social struggles of the modern world. *Working for Peace and Justice* includes colorful vignettes in which Larry describes serving as a civil rights volunteer in Louisiana and Mississippi, organizing antiwar sailors in Japan, funneling money into the South African antiapartheid struggle, agitating among workers as a labor leader, being arrested as part of the Free South Africa movement, collaborating with peace-oriented intellectuals in Gorbachev's Soviet Union, participating in the heated controversy over the Smithsonian's exhibit on the atomic bombing, and leading thousands of antinuclear demonstrators through the streets of Hiroshima.

Despite Larry's long-term activism, his career and scholarship have been marked by a reluctance to embrace overriding theoretical models and a dismay over the sectarianism that has sometimes divided the peace and social justice movements. For instance, he honestly recounts an incident early in his career when his efforts to tackle the theoretical writings of Karl Marx put him to sleep. Never an ideologue, he managed to carve out useful roles in a variety of social struggles and, at the same time, develop a broad circle of friends. He also interacted with many interesting, prominent people, from top leaders of the peace and social justice movements to upper-echelon U.S. government officials. Indeed, Larry's memoir describes a remarkably successful career that combined serious, credible scholarship with political activism on behalf of peace, workers' rights, and racial justice. It also offers important personal insights into changing social mores, customs, and gender roles in the aftermath of the 1960s.

One of the legacies of war and modern weapons has been the rise of the peace movement. Beginning in the late nineteenth century, the peace movement had significant success in ameliorating the worst effects of war on POWs and civilians through the formation of the International Red Cross and the codification of the laws of war. Peace advocates succeeded in promoting a vision of international relations founded on the peaceful resolution of disputes through mediation and arbitration as well as through a world court and a League of Nations, later the United Nations. Even so, peace activists have also been among the ultimate outsiders and have gone against the grain in the world wars and the Cold War by condemning the resort to violence in international conflicts and by refusing to bear arms, even if that meant performing alternative service or enduring imprisonment.

Compared with the outpouring of memoirs by military personnel from soldiers to generals, we have precious few by peace activists. We hope this memoir will be followed by other works in the series that will examine the ways in which individuals, institutions, nations, and international organizations have sought to preserve peace as well as deal with the consequences of war. In publishing this memoir, the University of Tennessee Press will also be returning to its roots. During the 1970s and early 1980s, the press established a stellar reputation when it published several major and highly respected works in peace history.

G. KURT PIEHLER
FLORIDA STATE UNIVERSITY

Preface

On a cold night in mid-January 1985, the police in Albany, New York, placed me under arrest. Hustling me out the front door of the Leo O'Brien federal building—where I had been engaged in an anti-apartheid sit-in—they formed a sort of flying wedge to push their way through a crowd of several hundred angry demonstrators, mobilized by the local Coalition Against Apartheid and Racism. However, the crowd, about half of which was composed of African Americans, seemed determined to block our progress toward the police van. As a result, it began closing in on the police, while one of my friends in it led a chant: "Free Larry! Free Larry!" It was a tense moment—not only because this event was a protest against white racism, but also because it came on the heels of a highly controversial local killing of a black man by white police. Yet, somehow, the situation, broadcast live on local television, never got out of hand. I flashed a big smile, the demonstrators gave way, and the police managed to deposit me gently but securely in their waiting van. Then they returned to the federal building to arrest nine other troublemakers and drove us off to jail. It was my first arrest, but not my last.

Over the course of my life, I also have been tear-gassed, threatened by police with drawn guns, charged by soldiers with fixed bayonets, spied upon by U.S. government intelligence agencies, and purged from my job for political reasons. Although, in my opinion, I did nothing that merited this kind of treatment, it is certainly true that much of my behavior was quite unconventional. Indeed, throughout most of my life I worked diligently as a peace agitator, civil rights activist, socialist organizer, labor union militant, and subversive songwriter. My experiences ranged from challenging racism in the South, to building alliances with maquiladora workers in Mexico, to leading the annual antinuclear parade through the streets of Hiroshima. Like Wendell Phillips, the great abolitionist leader, I have been a consistent thorn in the side of complacency—or at least I hope so.

Ironically, if you were to take a superficial look at my past, you might think me fairly well integrated into American life. After all, I was a Boy Scout leader, a president of my college fraternity, a Fulbright scholar, a tenured university professor, a heavily published author, and an elected leader of professional associations, my union, and other organizations. I am even written up in *Who's*

Who in America and in *Who's Who in the World*. In June 1995, when I received an award from the Society for Historians of American Foreign Relations, it was at a banquet of about a thousand people, where I sat at the head table chatting with General Vernon Walters (a former deputy director of the Central Intelligence Agency) and other establishment figures. Some years later, in the course of my scholarly research, I was even granted lengthy interviews with three former U.S. secretaries of defense, two former U.S. national security advisers, a former U.S. secretary of state, and a former U.S. attorney general. To draw upon a phrase popular in my youth, you might even conclude that I was an "all-American boy."

But you would be wrong. More often than not, I was a marginal, alienated individual who lived in tension with the broader currents of his society. In short, an outsider.

Perhaps the single most important defining characteristic of my life is the fact that I stuttered. The stutter was never very severe, but it was noticeable enough to trigger alarm on the part of people I met for the first time, discomfort on the part of my friends, and a feeling of embarrassment on my part. According to what I've read, some stutterers become so mordantly shy that, like Marcel Proust, they abandon social situations and hide away in their homes. Plagued by stuttering since the age of five, I never adopted that kind of behavior. But I did become shy and withdrawn—personality traits I had to fight against all my life.

Although under most circumstances this would be isolating enough, other factors reinforced my marginality. From a fairly early age I was unusually bookish and sensitive—characteristics that have their advantages but do not necessarily contribute to broad social acceptance. Furthermore, my family was Jewish and secular in a society that, even when it was not anti-Semitic, was overwhelmingly Christian and religious. Finally, I developed a number of deeply held views that were not (and are not) in the mainstream of American life: beliefs in pacifism, social and economic equality, democratic socialism, and internationalism. And I acted upon these beliefs.

Looking back on it, I think I'm lucky I wasn't lynched—though, at times, I might have come close to it!

Anyway, here is my story.

1

Family Background

When I was growing up, none of my relatives from Europe ever discussed with me what their lives in the Old Country had been like, nor did they mention what had happened to the family members who remained there. Even in later years, when I discussed my family background with members of my parents' generation, all born in the United States, they came up with remarkably little information about life in Europe or even about the immigrant experience. In retrospect, it is easy enough to understand why.

During the late nineteenth century my great-grandparents on my mother's side, Joseph Tzvi Barnatsky and Dvorah Barnatsky, lived and worked in a rural region near Bialystok. Located about 105 miles northeast of Warsaw, Bialystok was a medium-sized city in Poland, a nation then under Russian rule. Both of these great-grandparents were Jewish. Joseph Tzvi, the son of Meyer Barnatsky, had a brother and a sister. Dvorah had three brothers—all of whom had adopted different last names as a means of staying out of the Russian army. Renting a water mill from a rich Polish landowner, Joseph Tzvi Barnatsky provided a good living for his family as a local grain miller. It was a successful business and, in fact, the Barnatsky family rented the mill for many generations. In addition to the mill, the site contained a *kretchma* (an inn, though perhaps just a saloon) and milk cows.

For most people residing in nineteenth-century Russia, life was difficult and sometimes quite brutal. Politically, Russia was a czarist autocracy, with the population kept in line by secret police, Cossack cavalry, a powerful Orthodox Church, prisons, near slavery (for peasants), and forced labor in Siberia (for political dissidents). Economically, Russia lagged far behind its West European counterparts, and—although industrialization gathered momentum in a few areas during the 1890s—the country remained largely characterized by a feudal agricultural system. Socially, Russia was also quite backward, with vast power in the hands of the tiny, wealthy nobility and the largest public constituency, the peasantry, bound to the land by serfdom. Even after the formal emancipation of the serfs in 1861, many Russian peasants endured lives of poverty, hunger, illiteracy, disease, and superstition.

Russia's Jewish population faced a particularly harsh existence. During the late eighteenth century, Russia annexed large portions of Poland and, thus, for the first time, acquired a substantial number of Jewish residents. Responding to this acquisition, the government of Czar Nicholas I (1825–1855) made anti-Semitism official policy by putting into place a broad range of anti-Jewish decrees and laws. Almost all Jews were officially confined to the Pale of Settlement in western Russia and barred from exercising many rights available to Christians, such as owning land. Jews became subject to compulsory military service, with the drafting of boys as young as eight and a term of service of twenty-five years. Although the status of Jews improved considerably under the liberalizing influence of Czar Alexander II, who came to power in 1855, their situation deteriorated dramatically after his assassination in 1881. Numerous bloody pogroms—outbreaks of Christian mob violence against Jewish communities—swept the Pale, often without hindrance by local authorities. Indeed, the new czar, Alexander III, was a staunch reactionary who battled against political or social liberalization and worked at fostering widespread "folk anti-Semitism," particularly the idea of the Jews as Christ-killers. His "May Laws" of 1882 banned Jews from all rural areas and towns of fewer than 10,000 people, even within the Pale, and set severe limits on the number of Jews allowed to enter secondary schools, higher educational institutions, and many professions.

Bialystok, the urban center near the home of the Barnatskys, was located within the Pale and had a heavily Jewish population. After Russia's incorporation of Poland, its new anti-Semitic laws brought about a marked deterioration in Bialystok's economic situation. Expelled from neighboring villages, masses of Jews, many of them homeless or unemployed, crowded into the city. Even so, Bialystok's economic conditions improved somewhat in the late nineteenth century, largely thanks to the development of the city's textile industry. Many of the new textile mills and other small business enterprises were owned by Jews, and their growing workforce was also heavily Jewish. By 1895 the Jewish population of the city had reached 47,783, 76 percent of its residents. During the 1890s, Bialystok was a thriving center of the Jewish labor movement and of the Bund, the Jewish socialist organization.

For a time, Joseph Tzvi and Dvorah Barnatsky remained largely untouched by these developments, for they continued to live successfully on the land. But their circumstances changed dramatically in the 1870s. Dvorah's brother, Selig Lifshitz, was jealous of their good fortune, so he secretly approached the Polish landowner and, offering him a substantial sum of money, sought to convince the landowner to rent the mill to him. The landowner, however, spurned the offer. But, upon the landowner's death, Selig and some wealthy friends contacted the landowner's son, who lived in Paris and had inherited the property, and offered him an even more substantial sum to transfer the rental rights to him. This time he succeeded.

Forced to abandon his prosperous business enterprise, Joseph Tzvi used his savings to build his own windmill on Cavalier Mountain. The new mill, considered a modern marvel, was an immediate success and, as such, threatened the livelihoods of other local grain millers. But it mysteriously burned down shortly after it opened. For many years thereafter, Dvorah remained convinced that Selig was the culprit and referred to him, grimly and sarcastically, as the *"gute Selige."*

The destruction of the mill brought financial ruin to the Barnatsky family. The mill was not insured, and the family was now penniless. Joseph Tzvi, an excellent mechanic, went to work for other millers, repairing their machinery. Once a year he would show up at the big local market to find a new job. But, in these circumstances—and also amid the deteriorating social and economic situation of Polish Jews in the 1880s and 1890s—he found it hard to make a decent living and to support his family. As the Barnatsky children grew up, the boys left for nearby towns in search of employment.

One of these children was Abraham Barnatsky, my grandfather. Born on January 5, 1878, Abraham left home at the age of fifteen and moved to the nearby town of Harodok, also in Russian Poland, to secure employment in a textile factory. Here he operated a cloth finishing machine (something like a giant lawnmower). His brother, Meyer, also worked at the factory, and lost two or three fingers on the job.

In Harodok, Abraham Barnatsky, a young worker, joined the Jewish socialist movement. As Enlightenment thought spread within the Jewish communities of Eastern Europe, it challenged the traditional religious orthodoxy and fostered a more secular culture and accompanying social movements, including socialism, Zionism, and Yiddishism. For Abraham and his young friends in the textile mills, socialism was particularly appealing. As he recalled many years later, "it was the time of the revolution in Russia against the Czar," and the struggle for socialism "drew in all the young people." He was arrested on several occasions for socialist activities, but each time his employer arranged to get him out of prison, as his operation of the factory's finishing machine made him indispensable.

Abraham's luck, however, soon ran out. Most Russian Jews, including the Barnatskys, dreaded the prospect that they would be drafted into the czar's army. Although the conscription age had been raised to twenty-one, they still resented providing the military muscle for a hated tyrant—one whom they would be forced to serve for decades, if they survived. Abraham's oldest brother, Aaron Lazer, was exempt from military duty because he was responsible for support of his parents. This meant that the second oldest, Meyer, would almost certainly be drafted when he came of age. To save Abraham from this fate, the Barnatskys reported that Abraham was older than he actually was, on the assumption that Meyer's military service would lead to Abraham's exemption. But this proved a faulty assumption. Meyer's loss of fingers in the factory meant that he was no longer eligible for the army and, consequently, Abraham was drafted prematurely, at the age of nineteen.

Abraham would have fled immediately to the United States were it not for the fact that in such circumstances his family would have been punished with a heavy fine. After induction, however, a new recruit's family no longer bore responsibility for his behavior. Consequently, Abraham tamely accepted induction and thereafter searched for some means to elude the armed soldiers guarding the unhappy recruits night and day. One night, when he noticed that his guard seemed preoccupied with looking at the moon, Abraham took a flying leap over a high fence and set off running at top speed. Although he could hear the panting of the pursuing soldier, he ultimately managed to outrun him. Hidden for a time by relatives, Abraham eventually set off for the German border. But he was captured by soldiers during the border crossing. As a result, he was savagely beaten by them and beaten by other soldiers in the barracks. He was then beaten again in prison, where it was customary for new prisoners to provide the older prisoners with money—money which, in this case, Abraham didn't have. Eventually, however, the Barnatsky family, working through agents, bribed Russian military officers sufficiently to facilitate Abraham's escape across the border into Proskin, Germany.

The way was now clear for Abraham's immigration to the United States. Leaving Bremen, Germany, onboard the *Stuttgart*, a freighter, he traveled the Atlantic for three weeks, during which he was constantly seasick. (Many years later, when Abraham set out for a day of recreational fishing off Brooklyn, he put one foot on board the rocking boat and then suddenly announced a change of plans. As he explained, he wasn't going to go through *that* again!) On January 12, 1897, he arrived at Ellis Island, a standard disembarkation point for immigrants, in New York City. Here he was met by Abraham Baskin, an older comrade from Poland's socialist movement. Arrested in Poland, Baskin had fled successfully to the United States the previous year.

Barnatsky and Baskin were part of a massive Jewish flight from Eastern Europe during the late nineteenth and early twentieth centuries. Starting with the terrible Russian pogroms of 1881, East European Jews poured into the United States in an effort to escape persecution or simply to find a better life. By 1914 some two million—about a third of the Jewish population of their homelands—had resettled in America. Flocking, for the most part, to big cities, they set to work creating new lives, although not without significant difficulties.

Certainly Abraham's life in North America was not an easy one. In West Hoboken (now Union City), New Jersey, Baskin found him a job as a weaver. But Abraham earned very little money and, living in an immigrant community, was slow to learn English. Five years later, as a handsome twenty-five-year-old, Abraham moved to Montreal, where he worked as a goldsmith, again at low wages. Discontented, he returned to the United States, where he opened a small and unsuccessful grocery store. For a time, he lived in Atlanta, Georgia, and Bridgeport, Connecticut. Eventually, he settled into a job as a loom-fixer in the silk mills of Paterson, New Jersey. To supplement his income, he rented out rooms in his house. Although considered very skillful at fixing looms, Abraham was ambitious and convinced that, through hard work, he would rise from these humble circumstances to riches. Consequently, several times he used his savings to establish his own silk mill—setting up all the looms there in the hours after his own workday. Each time, however, his business collapsed, due to the shifting market and prices for silk. As a result, he worked, lived, and—in August 1968—died at the age of ninety among poorly paid immigrant millworkers in New Jersey.

Along the way, Abraham funded the immigration of three of his siblings (Chaya Sarah, Anna Mary, and Meyer) to the United States. Aaron Lazer also bade farewell to Russia, but went to Palestine, instead. To enable his father to retire, Abraham sent him money, too. Meanwhile, he changed his last name to Barnett (probably around 1900) and finally learned to speak English. Discarding most of the socialist views he had held in Poland, he became a rather narrow, penny-pinching conservative who, faced with an array of Yiddish language newspapers—from Communist to socialist to conservative—chose to subscribe to the conservative one. About all he retained from his earlier beliefs was hostility toward religion. Having never received a decent education or a taste for culture, Abraham had no books or other signs of intellectual life in his household.

As Abraham put down roots in America, he married another Jewish immigrant from Poland, Anna Semiatitsky. Born in approximately 1881, she is a woman about whose past I know very little. On January 12, 1908, she gave birth to my mother, Rose Barnett. By this time, however, Abraham was a rather hard-driving, intolerant person, with few social skills. Not surprisingly, their marriage ended in divorce. Anna remarried, this time more successfully, wedding Samuel Rosen of Sea Gate—an appendage of Brooklyn, New York.

In 1913 Abraham also married again. His new wife, Lena, was young, pretty, and likeable. Born in Pamusi, Lithuania, in 1890 as Lipka Schiff, Lena was the widow of a childhood sweetheart whom she loved dearly. Unfortunately, shortly after their marriage he fell from a painter's scaffold and died. Caring for an infant child of that marriage (Louise, born in 1911) and lacking financial resources, Lena married Abraham largely out of necessity. Indeed, it was an arranged marriage and, as it turned out, an unhappy one. Although they produced three children—Fanny (who died in 1915), Harold (born in 1917), and Frances—Abraham, irascible and stingy, bullied Lena and made Louise's life miserable. Even so, Lena remained married to Abraham. According to Harold, "she felt trapped," with "small children, no money," and, probably, a weaker personality than Anna had. Also, she was committed to social propriety. When Harold suggested that she apply for a divorce, she replied that she could not, for it would shame her among her friends.

Some emerged from these unpromising circumstances more unscathed than did others. Harold Barnett grew into a handsome, brilliant, scholarship student, eventually earning his Ph.D. in economics from Harvard. During World War II he served as an OSS officer, narrowly escaping death when a transport plane he was taking to Europe crashed and the top brass—located in the front seats—were all killed when it went down nose first. After the war, Harold became one of the preeminent economists in the United States, working for Resources for the Future and, later, as a professor of economics and chair of his department at Washington University. Like Abraham, he was hard driving, ambitious, and, in his final years, rather conservative. Nevertheless, unlike his father, Harold possessed social skills and was conventionally successful. By contrast, Louise was crushed by her difficult childhood and pressured by Abraham into going to work after graduation from elementary school, at age fourteen. Frances, too, though a good student, received little encouragement from her family for schooling or career. She escaped into a marriage with a wise-cracking clothing salesman, Abe ("Algie") Goldstein.

My mother was also marked by her childhood experience. Born in 1908 in Paterson, New Jersey, Rose Barnett was often on the move. Shortly after Abraham and Anna divorced, she was sent to live for about two years with Abraham's sister, Anna Mary Murstein, and her family in Bridgeport, Connecticut. Here she became quite friendly with her two cousins, Frances and Rhyna Murstein. Upon her father's remarriage, she went to live with Abraham and Lena, encountering all the attendant problems, including poverty. Years later, she maintained that her feet had been ruined by the miserable shoes she wore and that she had been reduced to begging on the street—although I think these claims are exaggerated. After the remarriage of her mother, Anna, she moved to Sea Gate to live with the Rosens, who needed her help in caring for their two small children, Sylvia and Dorothy. Despite the constant moving about and changing of schools, Rose was an "A" student, receiving top grades right through her graduation from high school. But neither the Barnetts nor the Rosens, who had little money or education, saw much value in a girl attending college. And so she didn't.

Despite these difficult circumstances, my mother emerged as a very popular, attractive person. Possessing a pretty face, blue eyes, curly blond hair, and a curvaceous figure, she was regarded as a local beauty, sometimes compared to movie stars of the era. Years later, when my father was asked what drew him to her, he laughed with embarrassment and said: "She was the prettiest girl in the neighborhood!" I think she probably was. Furthermore, Rose was also a good-natured, unpretentious, affectionate, likeable person, and, during these years, at least, people were very fond of her. Decades later, her cousin Frances recalled her as "a darling person," a "favorite with our whole family." In addition, although culturally limited by her class background and stunted education, Rose was hardworking and bright. Given the norms for women of that era, she had a lot going for her. Mastering shorthand, she became a highly valued legal stenographer in New York City. Furthermore, as photos of the late 1920s and early 1930s reveal, she had plenty of girlfriends—and boyfriends, too, including my father.

Although my father's background was more stable than my mother's, it too was affected by the immigrant experience. During the late nineteenth century my great-grandfather, Abraham Wittner, and his wife, Sara, lived in Snyatyn, then a small city in the Galician region of Austria-Hungary (now part of the Ukraine), about 170 miles south-southeast of Lvov. Both were Jewish. In the mid-sixteenth century, when Snyatyn was ruled by Poland, a Jewish community began to develop there and to attain some success in commercial pursuits. Its economic and social advance, however, was cut short in 1648–1649, when a Ukrainian nationalist, Bogdan Chmielnicki, instigated a campaign that exterminated most of the Ukraine's Jewish population. In a frenzy of anti-Semitic cruelty and butchery, Chmielnicki's Cossack forces destroyed some 300 communities and massacred some 100,000 people. Survivors were raped or sold into slavery. Nevertheless, in the following centuries, Jewish settlements were reestablished in the region. By 1890 Snyatyn had a population of about 11,000—about 36 percent of it Jewish. The Jewish community was relatively pleased with the Austrian rulers of the time, for they helped to restrain the anti-Semitic Poles and the even more anti-Semitic Ukrainian peasants who inhabited the rural region outside the town.

Abraham Wittner was a manufacturer of fur hats in Snyatyn and an orthodox believer. Less is known about his wife, Sara, who died of typhoid fever at age twenty-two. Before her death she bore two children, Joseph Wittner (born around 1884) and Rose Wittner (born in 1886). Thanks to local pogroms and economic difficulties, an accelerating number of Jews left Snyatyn between the 1870s and the turn of the century to set out for the United States, Canada, and Palestine. Abraham became part of this current. Accompanied by Joseph and Rose, he immigrated in 1898 to the United States. As other Wittners left Snyatyn for America that same year, it seems likely that they were relatives. Indeed, the coincidence of their departure suggests that there might have been a Wittner family decision to abandon Snyatyn and move to the New World.

Arriving in the United States in 1898, Abraham Wittner established a fur business in New York City and a residence in Harlem. He also remarried and had three additional children. Subsequently, the Wittners lived in different parts of the New York City metropolitan area, where Abraham resided until his death at the age of ninety-four.

Joseph Wittner (my grandfather) worked in the family's New York City fur business and in 1906 became a U.S. citizen. In June 1907 he married Leah Heller (my grandmother), who was born in 1885 in Russia. On April 5, 1908, while she and Joseph were living at 144 East Houston Street, on Manhattan's Lower East Side, Leah gave birth to their first child, Jacob ("Jack") Wittner, my father. Two more children, both born in Brooklyn, followed: Murray Wittner (born in 1914) and Harold Wittner (born in 1918). Leah died in 1921, and thereafter Joseph Wittner remarried. His new wife, Estelle (or "Stella"), had one child (Marilyn) from a previous marriage, and together they had a son, Bernard, born in Brooklyn in 1934.

From 1914 to 1925, my father, Jack Wittner, attended Brooklyn's public schools, finishing up at New Utrecht High School, where he was captain of the tennis team. A fairly good-looking, easy-going, mild-mannered, and modest individual, with a knack for telling gentle jokes, he seems to have been well liked among his peers. Although years later he characterized himself as just an average American of his era, he received two cruel blows during his childhood. The first came when he contracted infantile paralysis (polio). This illness had at least one advantage, for it prevented his being put through the traditional bar mitzvah study and ritual required of Jewish boys, a fact that he never regretted. But the polio attack also left him bedridden for months and with a somewhat withered calf muscle. Although he did not seem self-conscious about his misshapen lower leg, I think it interfered with his tennis playing (which he dearly loved) and, during his final years, contributed to his crippled condition. The second blow was the death of his mother, Leah, when he was thirteen years of age. He rarely referred to her untimely death, but I am sure that it was painful.

After graduating from high school in 1925—and probably on a part-time basis before that—Jack worked in the family business (Wittner Furs), located at 345 Seventh Avenue, in Manhattan. Although he remained employed there until June 1931, it was not an entirely satisfactory arrangement. He did not particularly enjoy his job of marketing fur coats to retail stores (including, I believe, Bloomingdale's and Altman's). Furthermore, he recognized that this small business enterprise could not financially sustain his father, his stepmother, his brothers, and himself. Therefore, in September 1926 he began attending classes on the Washington Square campus of New York University. In September 1928, he enrolled at Brooklyn Law School. His usual schedule involved working at the fur business during the day, attending classes at night, and doing his homework during the wee hours of the morning. Although this was not an ideal learning situation, my father did well in his courses and became the first member of his family to receive a higher education and to study the classics of Western civilization. In June 1931 he graduated from law school, and in December 1932, after passing the bar exam on his first try (a rarity in the era of the Great Depression, when bar exam standards were kept high to protect the jobs of lawyers), he became a member of the New York Bar.

Nevertheless, as in the cases of Joseph Tzvi Barnatsky and Abraham Barnett, hard work did not necessarily produce economic success. During the 1930s, when he worked for a succession of four different law firms in New York City, Jack Wittner barely scraped by. His longest sojourn was with the law firm of Leopold K. Simon, located on Fifth Avenue. At this firm, he prepared cases for trial, tried some cases himself, and assisted with appeals. But his income there was only sixty-five dollars a month. With opportunities foreclosed by the depression and by his lack of "connections," my father found life as a lawyer difficult. Nor did the family fur business do much better. As it gradually crumbled, his brothers struck off on their own. Murray became a radio (and later TV) repairman, and Harold became a carpenter.

During these years, the bright side of the picture was provided by my mother and father's relationship. They probably first met in Sea Gate in the early

1920s, when Rose was living there with the Rosens (her mother's family) and my father was living there with the Wittners. A lengthy and happy courtship followed, marred primarily by the realization that they were too poor to support a family. The logical solution to the problem was to get married but delay having children, which is exactly what they (and millions of other young Americans of the time) did. Consequently, they were married in February 1934. Forgoing an out-of-town honeymoon, they celebrated by having their picture taken atop what was then the nation's tallest structure, New York City's Empire State Building.

Given the fact that they were the offspring of two families with some painful immigrant experiences and, furthermore, that they were forced to grapple with the ravages of the Great Depression, they constituted a remarkably attractive, happy couple from the mid-1920s through to the onset of the Second World War. Along with a group of friends much like themselves—young, Jewish, urban, upwardly mobile, second-generation Americans—they joked around, cavorted on the beach, and vacationed in the country. Although, like their parents, they could speak Yiddish, they rarely did. My father was even a member of a Masonic Lodge and became a lodge "Master" in 1937. Jack and Rose Wittner viewed themselves as wholesome, "modern" Americans, and in most respects were thoroughly assimilated.

Even their politics were not out of line with mainstream trends. The Wittners, at least, traditionally voted Republican—a protest against the rule of New York City by Tammany Hall, the corrupt Democratic Party "machine." But, like many urban Jews during the Great Depression, they began voting for Democratic candidates during the New Deal. Communists were noticeable in New York during the 1930s, but my father did not find them appealing. In later years he talked scornfully about a Communist lawyer he knew who, he said, behaved tyrannically toward his secretaries. To be sure, like many other New York City Jews, the Wittners joined the Arbeter Ring (the Workmen's Circle), a vaguely socialist organization founded by Jewish immigrants that provided mutual assistance programs and promoted Yiddish culture. But my parents never showed any particular interest in socialism (or, for that matter, in Judaism). Indeed, although they usually voted for liberal Democrats, they didn't discuss politics much at all.

And so—despite the economic hardship, arrests, and pogroms of their families' past—Jack and Rose Wittner put together a reasonably normal life in the United States. If they were not quite average Americans, they were not total outsiders, either. Indeed, their experience indicated the possibilities in America for some measure of social integration and social advance, at least in the relatively liberal, tolerant, and multiethnic climate of early twentieth-century New York City.

For my relatives who remained in Europe, the situation was much grimmer. The militance of the labor movement in Bialystok during the 1905–1906 revolution in Russia led to vicious acts of reprisal by the Russian authorities. The pogroms that occurred in that city in early June 1906 were the most violent of the mob attacks upon Jews throughout the czarist realm, with some 160 of Bialystok's Jewish inhabitants killed or gravely injured. Joseph and Dvorah Barnatsky survived, but during World War I they disappeared, probably slaughtered—along with so many other people—in that bloody conflict. After the war, Bialystok came under Polish, Soviet, and—beginning in June 1941—German rule. In dealing with the Jews of Bialystok, the German authorities began by murdering about 3,000 and herding the remaining 50,000 within a sealed ghetto. Here they were used for forced labor and systematically starved—at least until February 1943, when the Germans began the liquidation of the ghetto, killing another thousand on the spot and deporting 10,000 to the Treblinka death camp. Jewish resistance fighters, having painstakingly gathered small supplies of arms and munitions, fought heroically to halt the liquidation process, but the powerful German military forces, including tanks, crushed their efforts. Only small numbers of Jews escaped to the surrounding forests, where they joined the partisan movement. Within a month, the Germans deported 40,000 Jews from the city to the death camps at Treblinka and Majdanek. In the aftermath of the war, only about a thousand Jews remained alive in Bialystok.

Much the same pattern emerged in Snyatyn, the home town of the Wittners. After World War I, the city came under Polish rule, and the Jews living in it were severely affected by anti-Semitic agitation, including an economic boycott against them. In early July 1941, following Germany's invasion of the Soviet Union, troops from Germany's ally, Rumania, captured the city and began robbing Jews of their possessions, marking their homes for looting and forced labor, and—with the cooperation of the Ukrainians—murdering the Jewish population. Within two weeks, the Rumanians were supplanted by the Hungarians, who continued the forced labor policies but restrained the Ukrainians to some degree.

In September 1941, however, the administration of Snyatyn was transferred to the Germans, who proceeded to execute large numbers of Jews in the nearby Potoczek forest and to round up thousands of others in a local secondary school. There many died of thirst, some were trampled to death, and others were murdered, with the survivors shipped off to the Belzec death camp. Finally, in September 1942, the Snyatyn ghetto was liquidated, and the remaining Jewish population was shot or marched off to the train station, many with their hands chained. En route, the German and Ukrainian guards shot a number of Jewish women, throwing their bodies off a bridge into the river below. Those Jews who survived were shipped to Belzec for extermination. Some managed to leap off the train, but were shot by the German guards or were turned in to the police by the local population and quickly murdered. Snyatyn was declared *Judenrein* (free of Jews), and Jewish life there never revived.

Against this backdrop, the Barnatsky and Wittner families had little incentive to glorify or even remember their European past. And their American experience was just beginning.

2

Brooklyn Boyhood, 1941–1958

I entered the picture on the evening of May 5, 1941. Born in Brooklyn's Israel Zion Hospital, I was my parents' first child. In line with Jewish tradition, I was named after a deceased grandparent—in this case, my father's mother, Leah. Had I been a girl, that's probably the name I would have received. But, as a boy, I was named Lawrence and invariably called Larry. Initially, we resided in an apartment located at 2016 Avenue N, in central Brooklyn. But that July, probably for economic reasons—and perhaps also to give my mother a hand with childcare—we moved into the large house owned by my grandfather, Joseph Wittner, in Long Beach, New York. Here, among assorted members of the Wittner family, we resided until September 1942, when we moved into our own three-room apartment, located at 570 Westminster Road, in Flatbush, Brooklyn. Rented for a fairly modest sum, that one-bedroom apartment became our home for the next thirteen years.

During the 1940s and 1950s, Brooklyn—New York City's largest borough—had a population of about 2 million people. Most of them were blue collar, lower middle class, and middle class, usually of European origin. Many, in fact, were European immigrants or their children and predominantly Catholic or Jewish. Although left-wing—and particularly Communist—institutions collapsed after the late 1940s, as the Cold War progressed, New York City remained a bastion of liberal Democratic politics. In my region of Brooklyn, the tiny Liberal Party (which usually endorsed Democrats) regularly outpolled the Republicans. The city's public schools, public colleges, public radio station, public libraries, public parks, museums, powerful unions, and inexpensive mass transit system eased the difficulties of urban life and provided hardworking residents with opportunities to advance their economic and social status. Brooklyn was less urban and far less glamorous than the borough of Manhattan, which housed some of the city's richest (and poorest) people. Indeed, Brooklyn served as a bedroom community for many people who worked in Manhattan. Nevertheless, its crowded, bustling streets contained a very substantial number of small stores and other business enterprises.

Flatbush, at that time, had a lower middle-class to middle-class flavor. Like much of Brooklyn, the overwhelming majority of its residents were Jews and Catholics, with the latter predominantly of Italian or Irish background. Nearly everyone was white. Certainly that was true of the residents of the fairly large, aging red brick apartment complex in which we lived. Our apartment was located on the second floor of a six-story apartment house, where people of relatively modest means resided. This building was connected by hallways and basements to two others exactly like it that were under the same management and contained the same sort of constituency. Although there were some private houses on our block and across the street, on Westminster Road, a substantial portion of the people in the neighborhood lived in apartment houses much like these that were scattered about the area. On one side of our block, Newkirk Avenue, which fronted on Public School 217, there were small, unpretentious shops, including a candy store and a drug store. The grocery store was run by two Jewish grocers happy to slice a pound of cheese or fish out a garlic-drenched pickle from a barrel for their customers. Occasionally, a peddler came through the neighborhood with his horse and wagon, seeking to stir up sales of used clothing by crying out: "I cash clothes! I cash clothes!"

During my first few years, I seem to have been quite content, basking in lots of attention. My mother, who with my birth began her career as a housewife, breastfed me, although not without some difficulty. According to what I have been told, I would occasionally bite her in the process, leading her to wear a special device to protect her nipples from her overly assertive baby. Apparently, though, it denied me neither nourishment nor satisfaction, for I grew into a chubby, inquisitive, blond-haired toddler, doted on by parents and relatives. Both my head and my skin were very light—so much so that mosquitoes would move unerringly toward my head, apparently unable to distinguish between my hair and my scalp. Although my father continued his underpaid legal work on a full-time basis—in his own law practice (first established in 1940), for a law firm, and as a full-time lawyer for small businesses—off the job he was very much a family man. One of my favorite photos shows him sitting on the beach with a dismayed look on his face, as I (then about two years of age) placed in his hand some particularly disgusting object I had found in the sand.

Gradually, I shed my baby fat and turned into a little boy. Lithe and curly-haired, I played or rode my tricycle in front of our Brooklyn apartment house—

always under my mother's watchful eye. I also liked to wander along the edge of the sidewalk and pick up interesting things I found in the gutter. "Larry's going to grow up to be a garbage man," my mother would report to my father with amusement. Somewhere around the age of four, my parents enrolled me in a preschool program at the Yeshiva Rambam. I remember that I felt a certain amount of confusion there, largely because this was a new, unfamiliar locale, with rules that I never quite mastered concerning when we drank juice, ate cookies, and played. Even so, I don't remember encountering any major problems there, either. Somewhere around this time, my parents taught me how to read. At the age of five I began kindergarten classes at the nearby Public School 217. I must have been popular, for my kindergarten classmates elected me and Nessa—a pretty, dark-haired little girl (on whom I had a crush)—the class presidents.

Yet at the age of five my largely happy, uneventful childhood took a dramatic turn for the worse. I began to stutter. Never very severe, this speech impediment varied between a speech block and the repetitious struggle to produce words that people usually call stuttering. Why I started stuttering is anybody's guess. Despite thousands of years of theorizing about its causes, no single explanation is widely accepted today by specialists. In my case, its onset followed not long after I underwent a tonsillectomy, so it is possible that this operation was in some way the cause. But, of course, most children who have tonsillectomies do not begin to stutter. A better explanation, I believe, is that stuttering is genetically based. Afflicting about 1 percent of the world's population, stuttering seems to run in families (for example, my uncle Murray Wittner stuttered) and in other groups with a limited gene pool (for example, the British upper class). Whatever the cause, my parents were alarmed by the onset of my stutter and, fearing that I had a serious psychological problem, brought me to a psychologist for tests. Not surprisingly, the psychologist confirmed that I had a problem, although I never learned what it was. More to my parents' liking, he said that his tests revealed that I was an exceptionally bright child.

The upshot was that I embarked on years' of meetings with psychologists, speech therapists, and speech classes. Although I conversed at length with psychologists and took their Rorschach tests, these learned men and women didn't seem to know what to do with me. The speech classes, conducted in my elementary school and at Brooklyn College, did have the positive effect of letting me know that other children stuttered too, and therefore I was not totally abnormal. I also met a lot of friendly speech teachers. One of them, Morty Gunty, went on to become a well-known impersonator of celebrities in night clubs and on TV. But, as far as I can tell, the psychologists, speech therapists, and speech classes never produced any significant changes in my speech.

On a more immediate basis, the worst effect of the stuttering was that I began to shift from being a popular little boy to being a social outsider. The more I struggled to get words out, the stranger I seemed to my peers, teachers, and other acquaintances. Although I was one of the best students in my class, this did not save me from the marginality brought on by my stutter. Once, I recall, when all the students were lining up in front of the wardrobe for a spelling bee—part of a competition to identify the best speller in the school and, later, in the city—the teacher suggested that I stay seated rather than compete, lest my stutter lead to the conclusion that I was misspelling a word. Reading aloud in class proved particularly trying, especially because the teacher would call on us in the order of our seating, and I would feel my tension level building up as my turn to read approached. Well aware of my deviant status, I retreated from social situations.

Fortunately, in these circumstances, I discovered the joys of reading to myself. There were books and other publications around my house, but—reflecting my parents' limited education—they usually were of a popular, middle-brow nature. These consisted of plenty of second-rate novels, advice books, and old copies of popular magazines of the era (e.g., *Reader's Digest, Coronet, Ladies' Home Journal,* and *Saturday Evening Post*)—the magazines passed along to my mother by her half sisters, Sylvia and Dorothy Rosen. I devoured them all and also made attempts to read the few tiny, inexpensive pamphlets found around the house that contained essays by philosophers and other classic thinkers. Even better, I discovered the wonderful resources of the public library. Every few days I would take a hike there, borrow a stack of novels, and then sit hour after hour in our apartment reading them. Sometimes I sat in the same position so long that when I finally stood up I became dizzy.

I also began to write short stories. My first was composed at the age of five or six, when my father took me to his office one day and left me with the women in the "stenographic pool." Finding me a welcome change from the regular office routine, one stenographer gave me a pencil and asked me if I was strong enough to break it in two. Of *course* I was, I replied, and promptly did so. When I showed an interest in the typewriters, they set me up at one. For most of the day, I pecked laboriously at one key after another, typing up a story about a paragraph long. In subsequent years, I continued writing short stories. At one point I even suggested naively to my father that, as the writings really belonged in a book, he should buy me one with blank pages in which I could write them. Although rather disappointed that this suggestion produced only a loose-leaf book, I labored on.

Popular culture also kept me preoccupied, though in a passive way. At home I listened to radio programs about the adventures of the Lone Ranger, Tom Mix, and Jack Armstrong ("The All-American Boy"). On other occasions I watched the popular *Superman* films in special children's matinees at the Leader Theater, located just around the corner from our apartment house. Sometimes I gazed out of our apartment window at the large backyard, where "the big boys," dressed in colorful helmets and jerseys, played what I considered a glamorous game of football. I also avidly followed events in big league baseball, keeping track not only of the batting averages of the top players, but also of their doubles, triples, home runs, and RBIs. Although the Brooklyn Dodgers were the home team—rooted for fanatically by my peers—I became a Yankee fan. Why? I've forgotten. But my choice of team provided yet another factor that isolated me from the community.

Despite my tendency to withdraw into the world of books and fantasy, I was not entirely without friends. During my elementary school years, these friends came from among the boys in my public school class, in my apartment house, and from neighboring streets. We hung out together, flipped and traded baseball cards, played board games, read comic books, experimented with chemistry sets, begged for glasses of water at the candy store, squirted one another with water guns, and explored vaguely dangerous places, like apartment house basements. When I was five years old, I began having fun along these lines with my kindergarten chum Michael Nolan. The following year another friend and I were horror-struck when—throwing around a rubber ball in his room—we broke the window. Although we carefully hid the cracked glass with a pile of his toys, that very evening his parents phoned mine and told them the awful truth. I was certainly scolded for the action, including its cover-up, but there were no serious consequences. Sometimes I was even provoked by my playmates into wrestling with them. In this situation, which I heartily disliked, I would try to pin their arms to their sides, thus incapacitating them until they agreed to "cut it out."

My friends and I also played war. This might come as a shock to those who know me in more recent decades. But we grew up during and after the Second World War and, to us, that conflict was very much a morality play, with the virtuous Americans and British fighting the wicked Germans (usually referred to simply as "the Nazis"). So, as part of our own war games, we ran about in schoolyards, backyards, and basements, "shooting" at one another with sticks and crying out as we keeled over in combat. I had my own solitary version of these war games as well. I played hour after hour with small toy soldiers—supplemented by blocks and a tiny cannon that could fire a toothpick. As all my toy soldiers were male, I suggested one day to my father that he obtain for me some female soldiers as well. Unfortunately, he failed me on this score, turning up nothing more than a tiny female doll that had no resemblance whatsoever to a soldier. Nevertheless, I pressed her into military service. Furthermore, I often drew battle scenes that were composed of tiny infantrymen, tanks, and planes, all firing furiously upon one another.

Yet, despite some typically boyish behavior, I did not "fit in" with most of the children around me. As much as I could, I avoided bruising games like Johnny-on-a-pony and ring-a-levio. And, when it came to sports, vital for a boy in my neighborhood, I showed very little ability. Although I was tall and could run fast, I was pretty much a bust at the popular games of the time, such as baseball, stickball, punchball, football, and basketball. In baseball, I was a terrible fielder; in basketball, a rotten dribbler. When the boys chose up sides for a game, I was invariably one of the last chosen. Admittedly, my father taught me how to play tennis, and it became my best sport. But almost none of my peers played it, and I never played it very well. Also, the older boys in our neighborhood invariably bullied younger boys like me—threatening us, appropriating our athletic equipment for their own use, and, during the winter, pelting us with ice-packed snowballs. Even the younger boys tended to be "tough" (though by today's standards not particularly violent) and hang around in gangs. By contrast, I was a sensitive, withdrawn, bookish child—so much so that my father constantly urged me to go outside and "play with the other boys." I did as little of that as possible.

As things turned out, my isolation spared me a variety of difficulties. One day my father and mother confronted me and asked me if I'd been doing strange things in the basement with "Wesley and the other boys." "What do you mean?" I asked. Embarrassed, my father did his best to explain the lightweight homosexual behavior that Wesley—a tough, white South African kid in our building—had been discovered engaged in with other boys in his gang. I was rather astonished by the whole thing. ("Why would anyone want to do *that*?" I wondered.) Anyway, I had no trouble denying any connection to the culprits, for Wesley and his tough crowd were exactly the kind of kids I avoided. Wesley immediately dropped out of sight, having been "sent to reform school," or so I was told.

In fact, I was becoming increasingly interested in girls. As a very little boy, I had a number of female playmates, and I continued to find girls appealing. Gradually, I noticed that they did not seem as nasty and brutal as many of the boys I knew. In the sixth grade (age eleven), I also started to find them attractive physically. At school I daydreamed about a few of my female classmates and wondered what it would be like to kiss them. I soon learned. There were a number of birthday parties that year, and they often included the game of spin the bottle, in which one could (and sometimes did) end up kissing one of these fantasy girls. It was very exciting! The only disadvantage of knowing them better was that they sometimes shattered my vision of them as sweet, pure angels.

For example, I began to hear them use "dirty words." As a little prude, I was shocked and repelled by this behavior.

During these elementary school years, it became necessary to explain to me how babies were born. My mother consigned this task to my father, who with some embarrassment outlined the rudiments of human reproduction. I found the process difficult to understand, so I questioned him about the details. Although my father was a kindly, helpful person, he was—like much of his generation—rather reserved when it came to discussing sex, especially with his children, and I'm not sure he ever satisfactorily responded. For the most part, then, I learned about human sexuality in bits and pieces, based on reading and conversations with other boys. Naturally, I didn't learn very much.

The occasion for my father's little lecture on baby-making was probably the imminent arrival of my sister, Deborah Wittner. Born on September 18, 1948, in Brooklyn, Debbie grew up to be blond, attractive, and—luckily for her—fluent in speech. As I was more than seven years her senior, I was often expected to play the role of a mature big brother, which included tolerating her occasionally irritating behavior and babysitting for her. Also, the substantial gap between our ages meant that during our childhoods we never became playmates or peers. These factors, coupled with some sibling rivalry and my own shyness, prevented us from being as close as we ideally might have been. Nevertheless, we had fun together on occasion and usually avoided serious disagreements.

My family was fairly close-knit during these early years. With only one bedroom in our three-room apartment for all of us, I slept in a partitioned area of the kitchen and my sister slept in my parents' bedroom. My mother remained a model housewife and childcare provider. In the morning, before my father took the subway off to work and I ran off to school, she prepared our breakfast—a quartered orange, cheese sandwich, and coffee for him; a glass of milk and a peanut butter and jelly sandwich for me. When I came out of the school building in the afternoon, she was often sitting on a folding chair on that same street, enjoying the sunshine and rocking my sister in her baby carriage. I grew so used to seeing her there that one day I put my schoolbooks in the carriage before realizing, to my intense embarrassment, that I had picked the wrong mother and carriage. In the evening we always had dinner together, with my mother serving something like pot roast or potted chicken, accompanied by potted potatoes, onions, and tomatoes. We often had steak, too, but, given our family's straitened economic circumstances, it was the cheapest kind: chuck steak. My mother and father always took the tougher pieces and gave the softer cuts to the children.

In 1946 my father found a new and far steadier job, working as a field representative for the New York State Commission Against Discrimination, and this civil service position eased the anxiety he felt about employment and financial security. Even so, he never quite lost the Depression-era psychology that he and my mother shared. It's illustrated by a story he used to enjoy telling about how as a young child I told him I had discovered a dime while digging in the dirt. "What did you do with it?" he asked. "Oh," I said, "I threw it away." "Why?" he asked, a bit startled. I explained: "It was dirty." To my father, who didn't waste money, this was a great source of humor.

Although my father continued to take the subway to and from work, at some point he bought a secondhand car, an old Pontiac he used to drive us on weekends to visit my grandparents and sometimes the beach. Along the way, we would harmonize on songs like our own version of "Old Beer Bottle":

> There was a lonely beer bottle
> A-floating on the foam.
> There was a lonely beer bottle
> Many miles from home.
> And in it a piece of paper
> With this message written on:
> "Who finds this old beer bottle
> Finds the beer all gone."

My mother particularly liked to sing the pop songs of an earlier era, including "Bicycle Built for Two" and "The Man on the Flying Trapeze." I learned to belt them out, too, as well as more modern songs, such as the U.S. Army, Marine Corps, Navy, and Air Corps anthems. The pleasure in all of this was enhanced by the fact that I never stuttered while singing.

For the most part, this early, close relationship with my parents was a quite positive one. Although I certainly was not a spoiled child, I was never spanked or severely disciplined by them. My mother, who was home most of the time, was warm and encouraging. And on evenings and weekends, when my father was home, he often played board games and tennis with me. Of course, children sometimes have disagreements with their parents, and I apparently had mine. Feeling persecuted, I ran away from home on at least one occasion. But, after a few hours of walking up Coney Island Avenue, I forgot exactly what it was that I was angry about. So I headed home to my parents and never even bothered to tell them that I had run away.

After I turned seven, my parents began to pack me off to Workmen's Circle summer camps—the first year to Camp Hofnung (in Pennsylvania) and then the following two years to Camp Kinder Ring (in the Hudson Valley). The ostensible motive was to ease the childcare pressures on my mother, who in the summer of 1948 was very pregnant with my sister. But I think my parents were also anxious to facilitate my social integration, and summer camp seemed a good way to get me away from the apartment and my books and into a "healthy" environment with other boys. To some degree, this was successful. When the camp bus pulled out, I was not sobbing like some homesick children or waving frantically like others, but absorbed in reading a comic book. Once at camp, I proved a model camper, made some friends, and even played competitive sports. I can't say, however, that I particularly enjoyed the experience. I learned to swim when, heading across the camp dock to get my inner tube, I was caught up by a stampede of eager campers released by the starting whistle. They simply swept me into the water with them. Flailing about in desperation, I found—to my relief—that I was able to keep my head above water. Nor did I particularly enjoy sports. What I was really good at was reading. Recognizing this, the counselors soon had me reading stories to the other boys while they loafed contentedly on their cots.

About the best time I had at camp occurred one year on the final day of the season. Throughout the summer, one of the boys in my bunk—a big, overweight, nasty kid—bullied most of the others. In general, though, he kept away from me, as I was taller (albeit thinner) than he was and therefore potentially dangerous. However, I didn't mess with him, either. After all, I was a shy, sensitive child, and the authorities on the scene were the counselors—who did, in fact, sometimes call him to heel. But, as we were packing up our things to go home, the counselors decided that it would be a good idea to organize a boxing match between him and me. Characteristically, I was repelled by the idea. By contrast, he was eager to fight. So I had no realistic alternative. Reluctantly, I put on the boxing gloves and, after he punched me a few times, I proceeded to beat the hell out of him. The smaller children in the bunk, whom he had tormented all summer, were ecstatic. And, for me, it was a deeply satisfying experience. It also might have given me the first inkling that, although I was usually exceptionally "nice," I could, if necessary, become a very dangerous opponent.

Although political discussion was sparse around our house, the presidential election of 1948 brought me into its orbit—on the side of the Republicans. On Election Day, a friend and I were lounging around the schoolyard of P.S. 217, which was the local polling place. A couple of well-dressed political party operatives came by and asked us if we wanted to earn a dollar by distributing campaign literature to voters as they came down the street. That sounded like a good idea to us, so after the men departed, leaving us with stacks of palm cards and our dollar, we diligently worked at distributing the cards—at least until we grew tired of this and dumped the rest of them in the trash can. When I mentioned this political venture to my father, he asked me which party we had been working for, and I said that I thought it was for the Republicans. It turned out that he didn't mind this at all, as he had voted for the Republican candidate, Thomas E. Dewey, whom he thought had been a good governor of New York State. He believed that Truman had been "a terrible President." Apparently, he was not interested in Henry Wallace, the third party candidate who had drawn the fervent support of communists and some liberals.

As almost all my relatives lived in the New York City metropolitan region, there was a good deal of family interaction. I got to know the Rosens, in Seagate, particularly well. My Aunt Dorothy ("Dottie")—a rather coarse, heavy-set, aggressive woman—remained single. But my Aunt Sylvia—considerably more attractive but just as tough—married a handsome doctor, Sidney Kafka, and had two children with him, Reece and Mark. When pizza first became popular in the New York area, Sylvia and Dottie, who adored it, insisted on taking my mother, Reece, and me with them to a local Italian restaurant to introduce us to it. When what seemed to me like an enormous pan of pizza arrived—bubbling, oozing, and reeking of cheesy smells—my Aunt Sylvia ripped off a large piece, trailing long strings of cheese, and shoved it into my mouth. I immediately vomited.

Aunt Sylvia's husband, my Uncle Sidney, became our free family doctor, and, in turn, my father did free legal work for him. Always an operator, Sidney was never content with practicing medicine but kept trying to make a pile of money by establishing his own pharmaceutical companies. Children don't like doctors very much, and I confess that I didn't much like my Uncle Sidney, who had a way of jabbing me with an injection needle when I least expected it. To stanch my tears after these painful visits, my father used to take me to Nathan's—located right across the street from Sidney's office, in Coney Island—for hot dogs and a pineapple soda. On another occasion, Sidney came out to our house to stitch up my finger after I had accidentally slit it open on the hook of a kitchen cabinet. I cried and screamed plenty as Sidney sewed up the wound without anesthetic. Years later, worried that someday socialized medicine would cut into his income, Sidney decided to become a psychiatrist—the last medical field, he assumed, that would come under public control. Then, on the way to his training, he suddenly dropped dead of a heart attack.

Although I could never work up much enthusiasm for Sylvia, Dottie, and Sidney, my grandmother and grandfather, Samuel and Anna Rosen, were gentler souls. On one occasion, to amuse me, my grandfather asked me if I knew how to split an apple with my hands. Instantly attentive, I responded that I didn't. Taking an apple from the fruit bowl, he then placed it on the table, put one hand down on it at a right angle, and pounded his other hand into that one! Pieces of apple flew all over the room. I have no idea whether he really thought that he could split an apple properly or was just improvising for my benefit, but I do know that my grandmother expressed great annoyance with him for this stunt.

We also visited on occasion with the Barnett family. Although I do not remember my grandparents, Abraham and Lena Barnett, actually playing with me, they always treated me in a kindly fashion. Both were rather idiosyncratic. Abraham liked to eat stale bread and, for gifts, would present me with woven clothing labels. Lena went about nearly blind, keeping her eyes closed most of the time due to a nervous ailment. I also got on well, as did my parents, with my Uncle Harold and his wife, Mildred; Aunt Louise and her husband, Ben Lipkin; and Frances and Algie Goldstein. My mother's cousins, Frances and Rhyna Murstein, two quite intelligent and talented women, were now married—to David Zwanziger (an engineer) and Si Goldsmith (a commercial artist)—and though we saw them less (particularly the Zwanzigers, who spent three years in Belgium, where David worked for the Inter-Allied Reparations Agency), we liked them very much. I particularly enjoyed getting together with their children, Gary Goldsmith and Daniel and Eve Zwanziger, who were not only roughly my age, but bright, sensitive, and inquisitive.

We also saw a lot of my father's family. After a very brief marriage, my Uncle Murray became a confirmed bachelor, living with his father in Long Beach. He would exhibit for me the large stock of used radios and TV sets he was repairing. Always a jokester, he would tell me that I shouldn't clean them off, as their dust and other grime enhanced their reception. As for my Uncle Harold, he married an attractive woman, May Markman, moved to the Bronx, and had two children, Leonard and Joyce Wittner, whom we met on occasion. My father's youngest brother, Bernard Wittner, was only seven years older than I was, so we had some interests in common. I particularly liked a series of war novels he possessed, which recounted the imaginary adventures of Dave Dawson and Freddy Farmer, two teenagers who supposedly won World War II almost single-handedly for the Allies. I must have read all fifteen of them.

My grandfather, Joseph Wittner, then the patriarch of the Wittner family, was always treated with great respect by everyone. Consequently, I felt honored—and very happy—when he made plans to take me, by himself, to the Ringling Brothers, Barnum & Bailey Circus at Madison Square Garden. I enjoyed the circus immensely, but the trip back to Long Beach proved unexpectedly difficult. A snowstorm that night shut down the Long Island Railroad, forcing us to get off the train and walk, hand in hand, down the tracks to the next station.

Somehow we managed to get back to the Wittner house in Long Beach, much to the relief of the entire family, which fluttered about us as we marched in very late, but triumphantly, through the front door.

Although most of my parents' friends remained the same people they had been friendly with in the past, during these years a new and unique individual appeared on the scene: Fred Hoeing. "Uncle Fred," as I called him, met my father thanks to their employment by the New York State Commission, and his background differed dramatically from that of our circle. Descended from a wealthy, "distinguished" old WASP family in Rochester (where the University of Rochester boasted a Hoeing Hall), Fred had graduated from Harvard College and would have received a history Ph.D. from Harvard University had he ever gotten around to writing his dissertation. Living off a traveling fellowship from Harvard, he had gone to Venice to write about an aspect of that city's past glory, but had decided that he loved Venice too much to waste his time there on research and writing. ("I had a simply marvelous time," he told me.) This extraordinary individual, who lived in the swanky Gramercy Park section of Manhattan and had great upper-class charm, became a fast friend of my father's and seemed to like nothing better than to come to our very modest Brooklyn apartment for dinner and then sit down for a game of gin rummy with my parents and, eventually, me. Unmarried and childless, "Uncle Fred" apparently viewed me as a surrogate son. After Fred's death years later, my father discovered a framed picture of Fred and me that he displayed on his desk.

By the sixth grade, it was clear that I was one of the best students at P.S. 217. When a little genius named Norman skipped a year and was placed in my class, he and I would race to finish the assigned page of math problems first—glancing occasionally at one another's paper to see who had the lead. As a bookish child, I was also an above-average reader and writer. Some time that year an IQ test was administered to the entire class, and I did very well on it. Whatever my IQ was, it proved good enough to catapult me into the small stream of students earmarked for "rapid advance" junior high school, in which, together with other top students, one skipped the eighth grade. As a result, in 1953 I said farewell to most of my elementary school classmates and began classes at Walt Whitman Junior High School.

Unlike my elementary school, Walt Whitman was far away from my home, and I had to ride public trolley cars or buses to get there. Although this travel added a substantial amount of time to the school day, it was pleasant enough, for I rode to and from the school with a small number of friends—singing popular songs, discussing girls (a growing topic of conversation), and playing Geography (which added immensely to my knowledge of towns, cities, rivers, mountain ranges, and countries around the world). We also talked about and traded stamps, as many of us had become stamp collectors—a hobby facilitated by the fact that our families usually knew immigrants whose letters arrived covered with exotic foreign postage. Although my friends and I were in the rapid advance classes, most of the students at Walt Whitman were in regular classes, and they tended to be less academically oriented, tougher, and (by the ninth grade) older than we were.

For the most part, I enjoyed my junior high school experience. As a bright student, I felt a sense of intellectual exhilaration as we discussed literature, history, and other interesting subjects. Although I was less enthusiastic about the typing class, it did provide me with what would become a very useful skill. However, I remained a fairly shy student, and certainly not part of the inner social circle. One of my classmates, David, wore nice shirts, slicked back his hair, and went out on "dates." Alas, that was not part of my repertoire. But I was invited to a couple of parties at which I danced awkwardly with girls. I also became a member of the school glee club, where I sang with great enthusiasm "No Man Is an Island" and, from *The Pirates of Penzance,* "The Policemen's Chorus."

Despite my enjoyment of singing, I did not display any particular aptitude as a classical musician. My parents arranged for me to take piano lessons with a piano teacher living in our apartment house, but I never practiced very much or progressed very far. When my teacher organized a small recital by her students in her apartment, I was the only one who found it necessary to use sheet music. For a number of months my Aunt Sylvia brought me and her daughter Reece to classical music concerts for children at Carnegie Hall. Here I acquired a small bust of Beethoven, which I placed on our piano, but his talent never filtered through to me. And, if truth be told, I found the children's concerts rather boring.

As a junior high school student I was usually quite well behaved. But I remember that on one occasion I really tried the teacher's patience. David and I were sitting, side by side, in the back row, balancing ourselves on the rear legs of our chairs. First he tipped over, causing a commotion. Then I tipped over, causing even more tumult. And then—though not deliberately—we *both* tipped over simultaneously. You can imagine the class reaction—and the teacher's. In retrospect, I think it was only because we were such "nice" boys that we escaped from that incident without serious punishment.

The most memorable person at Walt Whitman was my ninth grade teacher, Leonard Saunders. To my delight, he had us read and talk about serious contemporary issues. At a time when *Robin Hood* was banned from school systems as a suspiciously "Communist" book, we read *The Little World of Don Camillo,* a comic novel in which a priest and a Communist leader vie for the allegiance of Italian villagers. Although the priest was clearly the hero of the book, we joked around about Communism in class, calling our teacher "Comrade Saunders." This was apparently too much for the school authorities, who, when they learned of it, ordered him to stop it immediately. Taking a more serious tack, he told us about the *Brown v. Board of Education* decision and about how its nonenforcement led him to join the NAACP. He also thought that we should learn to dance and, consequently, brought his very attractive wife to school so that they could demonstrate for us how to do the Lindy. On another occasion, he took the class on a Saturday to Steeplechase Park, in Brooklyn, where we cavorted about and went on the rides. In an era of frightened conformity, Leonard Saunders was a remarkably free spirit.

Although Comrade Saunders was our English and social studies teacher, he was also an aspiring guidance counselor. As a result, he practiced using the tools of his new trade by giving many of us a vocational preference test. I took the Kuder preference test with him at his home and turned up in the 99th percentile for "Literary." According to the official interest profile: "Literary interest shows that you like to read and write," with possible jobs including historian, teacher, and book reviewer. I also scored in the 94th percentile for "Computational" (bookkeeper, accountant, or bank teller) and in the 91st percentile for "Social Service" (social worker, nurse, or minister). Conversely, I showed a below average interest in mechanical, artistic, and clerical areas. As things turned out, the test—taken when I was only thirteen years old—predicted my future career fairly well.

At about this time, my parents and I passed several summers together at Fogel's, a small, Jewish bungalow colony in the Catskills. My mother, sister, and I spent the entire summer there—in what were considered salubrious, outdoor conditions—and my father drove up from New York City to join us on weekends and during his relatively brief vacation. I hung around, more or less, with the boys there of my age group, playing baseball, swimming in the pool, and building a ramshackle "clubhouse." Although this was supposed to be fun, I didn't enjoy it. By contrast, the women in the bungalow colony had an active, happy social life, and I remember my mother meeting with other women to write and produce a musical comedy based on their lives there. In the performance they danced around in hula skirts and sang songs, including their own seductive version of "Diamonds Are a Girl's Best Friend." As the men were not around very much, they played a less important role. But sometimes our fathers engaged in baseball games with the men of neighboring bungalow colonies.

It was during one of these games that I had my first run-in with the law. Growing bored as our fathers huffed and puffed around the base paths at a nearby bungalow colony, the other boys and I headed off to explore the locality. In one apparently empty field, we were delighted to discover golf balls lying about. As we jabbered away and filled our pockets with these unexpected treasures, a tough-looking man suddenly appeared, confronted us, and ordered us to march up to his office. He informed us that this was a driving range (whatever that was), that we had been caught stealing golf balls, and that the police had been called. It was an unpleasant turnabout, and a local policeman actually did grill us about what had happened. Ultimately, our fathers saved the situation, and I never did any time for golf ball theft.

In another attempt to provide me with a "healthy" social life, my parents arranged for me, at the age of twelve, to join Boy Scout Troop 193, which met across the street at P.S. 217. This turned out to be a rather insensitive group of boys who, under the direction of an adult scoutmaster, would march about in military-style flag drills (which I disliked), take rope-tying, fire-building, and other tests to advance their rank (which was okay), and go on overnight hikes (which I more or less enjoyed). I quickly noticed a high level of sadism, particularly during a game we invariably played that separated us into two teams whose members, standing on opposite sides of the gymnasium, threw a basketball as hard as they could at their counterparts on the other team. I was taller—though certainly not tougher—than most of the other boys, and this spared me some degree of bullying and humiliation. Indeed, I eventually rose through the ranks to become a Patrol Leader, a Junior Assistant Scoutmaster, and a Life Scout. But, outside scout meetings and events, I rarely hung around with members of the troop. I still spent most of my free time at home, curled up in a chair, reading books.

As my thirteenth birthday approached, my father asked me if I would like to take bar mitzvah lessons. Nearly all the Jewish boys I knew were then taking such lessons in preparation for the traditional religious ceremony that, upon becoming thirteen, certified in Jewish culture that a boy had become a man. This carried some weight in my mind, for I assumed, based on my immediate environment, that most Americans were Jewish. On the other hand, I had no particular interest in religion and viewed the bar mitzvah lessons, conducted at Hebrew School, as a waste of time. After all, instead of spending my afternoons learning to pronounce the Hebrew words in an undecipherable passage from the Torah, I could be reading novels. So I plucked up my courage and told my father that I wasn't interested in taking the lessons. As he was not religious himself, he did not object. However, this choice had some important ramifications. Although I enjoyed the free time it preserved for me, my rejection of the lessons and the bar mitzvah ceremony meant that I became ever more the odd man out.

In fact, I was never enthusiastic about any religion and increasingly viewed myself as an atheist. Of course, Jews—having been attacked, murdered, and otherwise oppressed for 2,000 years by Christian fanatics—have become stubborn and do not easily abandon Judaism, for such a renunciation would grant the anti-Semitic *goyim* (Christians) the victory they have sought so ardently. On the other hand, like my parents, I was very much a freethinker, with no belief in God. Nor was I at all interested in the traditional religious ceremonies. Every once in while, my family, upon invitation, did attend a seder, usually at the Rosens' house. But I found seders pretty dull events, with the only consolation available in drinking the glasses of sweet Manischewitz wine that made me giddy. Fortunately, we did not attend religious services at the local synagogue, and therefore I never had to sit through them. We remained secular Jews.

Having completed junior high school in the spring of 1955, I entered Erasmus Hall High School that fall. As Brooklyn's oldest public school, Erasmus had seen better days by the mid-1950s and was not the most welcoming environment for an entering sophomore, especially one who—having skipped the eighth grade—was a year younger than most of his classmates. Suddenly I was no longer in a special class composed of the school's brightest kids, but instead sitting alongside many average and below-average students who were sometimes tough, alienated, and threatening. However, after one semester at Erasmus, before I could even learn where most things were located, my parents bought their first house, in another area of Brooklyn. Located near the corner of East 24 Street and Quentin Road, the home was modest and not far from where I had passed my first months in Brooklyn. Unlike our previous neighborhood, which was dominated by apartment houses, the Midwood section was composed of single-family homes. And my new school, James Madison High School, located just around the corner from our house, had a somewhat more middle-class flavor than did Erasmus.

The student body at Madison, composed of more than 5,000 students, was very white (although it contained a few black middle-class students) and divided. The better students, usually Jewish and middle class, were enrolled in the academic program, were often drawn into the honors classes, and were college-bound. Other students, usually Catholic, were enrolled in the general or commercial programs, often ended up in the regular or modified classes (the latter for "slow" students), and were en route to jobs as secretaries, clerks, hairdressers, and nurses. People did not say much about this intellectual, religious, and vocational stratification, but the students recognized it, more or less. Although I was clearly destined for the "good student" stream, it took the school authorities a while to channel me into it, as I started classes at Madison relatively late, in my fourth semester of high school. This meant that, initially, I got to know some of the school's "slow" students, who on occasion were happy to have me around, for I sometimes helped them with their homework assignments. But, by my junior year I found myself in honors classes and, by my senior year, in an English HB class—the site for the crème-de-la-crème of the student body.

Despite my advance through the school's intellectual ranks, I remained socially isolated—a relatively solitary, sometimes brooding individual without any real friends in my new neighborhood. Those few friends I did have were located in the old one. Occasionally, when the weather warmed up, I would join friends from my former neighborhood, such as Freddy Mirer, on bicycle trips to Coney Island or to even more remote areas of Brooklyn or Queens. Sometimes a friend and I rode on the subway to Brighton Beach. There, at the ocean, we set up our towels in the garbage-strewn sand and rode the waves, stopping only to buy knishes and sodas for lunch. During the colder months, we occasionally took a subway to the Hotel St. George, where one could rent a locker for the day and go swimming in the large hotel pool.

At Madison I did not join any of the school clubs or other extracurricular activities and, in fact, never socialized with any of its students outside of school. Within the school's confines, of course, I did speak up in class and sometimes chatted with other students. Once, upon the invitation of an attractive girl sitting across from me in French class, I even worked up the nerve to slide over and join her in her seat. Building on a mild flirtation we had with one another, the incident ended badly. The French teacher, spotting our little tryst, went bananas and ordered me back to my assigned seat. But, when it came to a pretty girl, I possessed more gumption than usual. So I bought two tickets to a school football game and invited her to attend it with me. Alas, she said that she had another commitment that weekend. And that, unfortunately, ended that.

Throughout the rest of my high school years, my relations with the opposite sex were minimal. Although a party was arranged that brought together the older boys in my scout troop with a group of girls, it did not lead to any follow-up, at least on my part. Thus, it was not until my senior year at Madison that I went out on my first "date." My cousin Reece had suggested that I accompany her to a dance in Brooklyn, organized by her high school. Once there, we would split up and see whom we met. Somehow or other, overcoming my shyness, I did manage to meet someone: a cute, dark-haired Italian-American girl. I even went so far as to ask her for her phone number—considered a major step in those days—and she, in turn, was willing enough to give it to me. For a while, I didn't have the nerve to phone her and ask for a date. But, ultimately, I did and—at the age of sixteen—went out on a date for the first time.

A far more momentous development in my life came at the age of thirteen, when my mother began to undergo serious changes. She put on weight rapidly, particularly on her torso and face. The mental changes were even more dramatic. For days she would sit around the house in her robe, deeply depressed. Then she would enter a manic phase, typified by great enthusiasm for odd, crackpot schemes. While riding on a crowded subway, she suddenly conceived a plan for sharing subway seats on a first-come, first-served basis, and—enthusiastic about her conceptual breakthrough—mentioned it to the stranger sitting next to her. Thereafter, terrified that he would steal the credit from her, she insisted that my father hire a private detective to track him down. Another of her schemes involved writing to the parents of all my friends—not that there were that many of them, of course—and inviting them to a public meeting to discuss "Our Troubled Youth" (or something like that). In both cases, my father defused the situation, asking the detective to play along with her and canceling the meeting. Meanwhile, my mother repeatedly painted and reorganized our wooden furniture until I never knew what color it would be, or even where it would be, when I came home from school. Increasingly housebound, she sent my father out food shopping every Sunday, with long lists of items on sale at stores scattered throughout Brooklyn.

It was clear to everyone who knew her that something was wrong. But what was it? Eventually, the doctors concluded that she had Cushing's Syndrome, a disturbance of the adrenal glands that led to overproduction of adrenalin. But this conclusion came after a long period of confusion in which the doctors—and our family and friends—did not know what to do. The doctors even prescribed for her a favorite panacea of that era for psychological problems—electric shock therapy. Of course, this terribly painful treatment did not help her at all. Even after they diagnosed her illness correctly, nothing seemed to work. The doctors removed one adrenal gland, but after a short time the other gland compensated for it and left her as demented as before.

My mother's illness, from which she never recovered, came as a crushing blow to our family. Previously, Jack and Rose Wittner had made an attractive, charming couple, drawing family and friends into their orbit. Now that situation had ended, and relationships with family and friends gradually began to deteriorate and grow more distant. My sister, who was only six or seven years old at the time my mother began unraveling, was probably hit the hardest by her deterioration. But my father was seriously affected by it as well. Although he dutifully took care of my mother, almost never challenging her directly, his normal, good-natured style gave way when she wasn't around to grumbling and irritation.

In my case, my mother's illness ranked alongside stuttering as the worst thing ever to befall me. Exacerbating the situation was the fact that as I was then undergoing puberty and developing into a somewhat rebellious, precocious teenager, I had little patience for her madness. Indeed, I could barely understand how my father put up with it. Thus, as my mother went through her manic depression cycles, with the attendant insanity, I clashed repeatedly with her. Our conversations deteriorated into ugly shouting matches. Embarrassed by my mother's use of my short stories to brag about me to her friends, I deliberately destroyed them—a pretty clear act of passive aggression. Although I am embarrassed to confess it, I developed an aversion to her. From my perspective, my beautiful, warm, vivacious mother had turned into an ugly, untrustworthy madwoman.

Meanwhile, life continued, though not very happily. Summers, at least, I managed to escape from the newfound misery of family life. During the summer of 1956, at the age of fifteen, I worked as a counselor-in-training at a summer camp, operated by my scoutmaster, near Diamond Point, New York. In this woodsy setting I gained some welcome competence at canoeing, aquatic lifesaving, and chopping down trees. During the summer of 1957, I worked as a relief counselor at one of the camps I had attended years before, Camp Kinder Ring, filling in for other counselors on their days off. This was not an enjoyable job, for—as a substitute—I did not have the control over the campers that a "regular" counselor had; as a result, the kids tended to be boisterous and unruly. Even worse, I resided in a small bunk with three unusually nasty teenage boys only a year or so younger than I was. They took great delight in making my life as miserable as possible. After a day's work, I frequently came back to my bed at night to find the sheets or other vital items missing. My protests to the camp director were unavailing. One night, when I walked into the bunk I found an enormous, dirt-covered boulder lying in the middle of my bed, with my tormenters lined up laughing hysterically. I must have been enraged, for I somehow picked up the boulder and hurled it into one of their beds. This ended my problems with them, for—having barely managed to lift the boulder with all three of them on the job— they were suddenly enormously impressed with me. I was not at all impressed with them, but I was certainly glad that their harassment came to an end.

Another reason for my taking these jobs—and also working occasionally as a caddy at golf courses—was that my parents, and particularly my mother, felt hard-pressed financially. Worried about our limited income, she insisted upon stocking up on grocery items that were on sale. When she bought clothing for me, she often purchased "seconds"—clothing that had been reduced in price because the buttonholes weren't quite lined up with the buttons or because one sleeve was a little longer than the other. Drawing upon relatives for hand-me-down clothing, she also repaired the clothing we had—sewing patches on our shirts or pants and darning the holes in our socks. Actually, I didn't mind any of this, as I hated going shopping, barely knew that fashions existed, and considered reuse of commodities (what we today call recycling) simply common sense. Yet, in retrospect, I wonder how much of it was really caused by our financial circumstances.

During my final years of high school, as I grew more sophisticated and analytical, I became a critical observer of its curious social mores. The smoothest, most popular students formed a clique and moved about the school and local streets wearing fraternity or sorority sweaters. In general, they dominated Madison's extracurricular activities. An even larger group hung out on afternoons and on weekends along Kings Highway, the major commercial thoroughfare in the neighborhood. Here and elsewhere they discussed cars, television programs, sports, and the new rock-and-roll songs. With the exception of sports, none of this interested me, and I didn't hang out with them at all.

Even in the midst of this largely insipid, middle-class culture, there was some degree of student violence. Some of the boys were clearly "hoods," or aspiring hoods, and went about with their hair slicked back in a D.A. (duck's ass), their collars turned up, and cigarette packs stuffed in their rolled-up shirtsleeves. They particularly liked to build up their biceps, on which they occasionally sported tattoos. To control these kids, who sometimes assaulted other students or extorted money from them, the school administration employed some of them as school "guards." It was a system very much like using the fox to guard the henhouse or employing the Nazis to protect Europe. One day while eating in the cafeteria, I saw at a distance some of the guards beating a student so badly that a gusher of blood spurted from his nose. Upset by this incident, I spoke about it that evening with my father, and he convinced me that it had to be reported to the school authorities. So the two of us went to meet with an assistant principal, who promised us that action would be taken. And it was, at least in that case.

Much of the schoolwork was pretty mundane, and for the most part I learned more from my undisciplined reading at home than from my formal education at school. It was soon clear to me that I had no particular knack for science—at least compared to some of the other students who were busy building computers or conducting scientific experiments at home. I did reasonably well in languages—French and then German, after Uncle Fred convinced my father that a second language (preferably German) would be useful for me in graduate school. On numerous evenings, while I conjugated French verbs, my father sat staring at my grammar book, sometimes dozing off along the way. Although I never enjoyed math very much, I had considerable talent for it and was placed in a math honors course. Symptomatic of the era, there was only one girl in the class, Jane Brody. Then clearly a math/science whiz, she ultimately became a writer on science and nutrition for the *New York Times*. I also did very well in history and, of course, in English. My father, given his fixation on secure jobs, spotted my excellent grades in math and thought I should study to become an engineer, accountant, or actuary. However, I had a more romantic view of my future and planned to become a novelist.

Philip Roddman's class confirmed my literary aspirations. Teaching the very select English HB class that I took throughout my senior year, Roddman stood out from the other teachers at Madison because he assumed (or acted like he assumed) that we students cared passionately about literature and about the great writers of the past. Never talking down to us, he often spoke of these writers in a way that was far above our heads. Suddenly, we were discussing symbolism and surrealism. Much of what he said was beyond me, but there was something intellectually exciting about it that made me want to reach past the limitations of my life to a deeper level of ideas and of civilization. And, of course, I had already gotten some flavor of intellectual transcendence from the books that I had been reading. I knew that I did well in that class, but lots of the other students, many of whom went on to brilliant careers in the arts and sciences, also did well. Therefore, it was with surprise and pleasure that I watched him write in my graduation yearbook: "To Lawrence—the best and the brightest." Roddman's high opinion of me probably was also the reason that at graduation I received Madison's top prize in English.

Alongside my intellectual awakening, I was undergoing a political awakening. My father's employment by the New York State Commission Against Discrimination played an important part in this process. In 1945 New York became the first state since the Reconstruction era to pass antidiscrimination legislation. This legislation banned discrimination in employment on the basis of race, creed, color, or national origin. Beginning his work with the commission in 1946 as a field representative, my father would take complaints of discrimination from aggrieved individuals, investigate them, and write up determinations for the commissioners. To my father, scraping by for years as a lawyer, this was a good job with a regular income, and he did not approach it as an ideological zealot. Nevertheless, like many Jews, he recognized the unfairness and dangers of racial, religious, and nationality prejudices. Therefore, he was in total sympathy with New York's pioneering antidiscrimination legislation, which over the years was expanded to cover public accommodations and housing. As a result, our dinner table conversation often focused on outrageous examples of prejudice and discrimination and sometimes on ways in which my father had outfoxed discriminatory employers or hotel managers and brought their biased practices to an end. Furthermore, at a time when black people were still largely "invisible" to whites or depicted in a demeaning fashion—for example, on television's *Amos and Andy* show—my father not only had black colleagues, but also a very dignified African American boss, Commissioner Elmer H. Carter III.

Thus, gradually I obtained a much better idea than did most white Americans of the seamy underside of American life—of the dirty secrets, dating back to slavery, that lay hidden behind the constant blather of the American Celebration. I began to understand that, despite all the talk of equality and justice, these were not built-in realities in my nation or any other, but ideals for which people continued to struggle.

Furthermore, understanding the nature of prejudice, I began to spot it in other areas, too, some of them closer to home. Within my extended family's all-Jewish ranks there was considerable bad-mouthing of the *goyim*. Although, of course, I could appreciate opposition to Christian anti-Semitism, I thought the more general denigration of Christians (who were depicted by some of my relatives as stupid, cruel, and vicious) quite narrow-minded and intolerant. Certainly, my Christian friends—one of whom was even a *German* Christian (a gentle immigrant boy named Peter)—did not fit these stereotypes. Nor did Uncle Fred.

There were other consciousness-raisers during these years as well. One day, when my father and I were walking down the street to our car, I asked him: "What's Communism, Dad?" "Be quiet, Larry," he warned me. Young and irrepressible, I continued: "But why is Communism such a bad thing? It doesn't sound so bad to me." "Larry, be quiet!" he demanded, in a much harsher tone than he ordinarily used. I got the point. Despite all the rhetoric about free speech in America, you'd better watch what you say.

I also discovered deception by the powerful. Spotting a newspaper advertisement for some sort of gadget, I suggested to my father that he run out and buy it. "Larry, it's just an ad," he said, smiling. "What do you mean?" I asked, in confusion. "They're just trying to sell that product," he explained. "It's not necessarily as good as they claim it is." I was beginning to understand. "You mean they're lying?" I asked. "Well," said my father, "not exactly. They're just not telling you the complete truth." To a boy trained in honesty, this seemed a rather dubious distinction. And, increasingly, I was skeptical of business practices and of the mass communications media.

In addition, I experienced some chilling preparations for nuclear war. During elementary school there were "take cover" drills, during which—upon hearing that command from our teacher—we would scramble to hide under our desks. At some other point in my schooling, students were issued metal dog tags bearing our names and addresses and told to wear them night and day, even in the shower. We were told that after a nuclear war the dog tags would help to identify what was left of our bodies. This was not a particularly reassuring future for children, or a very pretty picture of what the governments of the world were preparing to do to them. My father might have thought so, as well. One day, when he noticed the dog tag I was wearing, he asked me about it and I told him its purpose. Irritated, he told me: "Throw it away!" As a dutiful son, that's what I did.

Another influence on me was the *New York Post,* then a solidly liberal newspaper. Each day on my father's way to work in lower Manhattan, he would read the *New York Times* on the subway; then, on the return trip, would read the *Post.* Both newspapers ended up in our house, where I began reading them as a teenager. The *Post,* featuring powerful columns by James Wechsler and Murray Kempton and political cartoons by Herblock, hammered away at McCarthyism, racial segregation, and the unwillingness of the Eisenhower administration to fund social programs. One day I remarked to my father that in my classes I was almost always sitting on radiators rather than on chairs. In these overcrowded classes, seating was either based on height or on the alphabet. As one of the tallest students whose last name began with *W,* I was invariably among the last seated. He suggested that I write a letter about school overcrowding to the *Post.* I did, and a few days later the letter was printed! It was my first publication.

I also began to observe that although my family and I considered my views quite reasonable, others found them dangerous, even subversive. As I sat in a barber chair, precociously expounding on some political issue, the barber suddenly stopped shaving my sideburns and remarked, testily: "Where did you get *that* from?" "From the *Post,*" I responded glibly. With a nasty glint in his eye, he slowly stated: "There's some that say the *Post*'s a Communist newspaper!" As the barber was then holding his straight razor about two inches from my throat, I decided it would be a good time to retreat. "Is that so?" I said, benignly.

My home room teacher, Miss Herlehy, was also losing patience with my increasingly unorthodox thought. Assigned to write an essay on a utopian civilization of the future, I included a sentence stating that its residents could choose when they wanted to die by taking a painless poison pill. Horrified, she snapped:

"That sounds like a terrible idea to me!" On another, more dramatic occasion, in preparation for our graduation, she passed out an official loyalty oath for us to sign. I raised my hand and asked as innocently as I could: "What does pledging not to overthrow the New York State and federal governments have to do with certifying that we've satisfactorily completed our course requirements?" As her face turned red, she yelled: "Wittner, you're always bucking me! Your diploma is based not only on your academic work, but on your moral character. Now sign it!" And so I did. Years later, I learned that a few students at Madison refused to sign the oath and thus did not graduate. But by that point they had been accepted at colleges, and this official retribution failed to harm them.

When most people in those days read George Orwell's popular novel *1984*, they thought of the Soviet Union. I did, too, but I *also* thought of the United States and its disturbing signs of intolerance, media manipulation, suppression of civil liberties, and preparations for full-scale war. The novel's tormented hero, Winston Smith, escaped the televised propaganda in his apartment and, consequently, was able to think independently, discover the realities of his society, and reject power (i.e., Big Brother). This perspective did not necessarily put me in a left-wing frame of mind. During high school gym class—when ten boys played basketball and hundreds of others lounged around the outskirts of the court, occasionally trying out the parallel bars but mostly doing nothing—I sometimes had interesting conversations with Gene, another deviant student. One day he said to me that he'd discovered what this country really needed: democratic socialism! I quickly brushed off the idea, saying that that would simply contribute to statism and thus to more McCarthyism. Yet, at the same time, I was definitely developing the mind-set of a dissident. I was starting to view myself less as GI Joe and more as Winston Smith.

As a teenager I increasingly felt the desire to engage in great and noble deeds. This romantic impulse—what is sometimes called youthful idealism—was certainly fed by the books I read, with their tales of heroic, selfless actions. Unfortunately, nothing in my rather provincial environment bore any obvious connection to this world of bravery and daring. Nor, in my uncomfortable relationships with girls, was I swept up in a great love—though I certainly would have welcomed that. Instead, life, when not painful, appeared mundane and mired in dull, petty, and irrational customs.

During my senior year at Madison, many of the students focused on admission to college. Having secured good grades and done well on the College Board exams, I seemed like a strong candidate for acceptance at first-rate schools. Accordingly, I applied to a number of colleges recommended by the school guidance staff and by Uncle Fred, including Harvard, Columbia, Cornell, Colgate,

Union, the University of Rochester, and Brooklyn—the last considered a fallback in the event that I was rejected elsewhere. My Harvard interview, conducted by two of its alumni at an apartment in New York City, got off to a terrible start because I arrived late—a consequence of my taking the wrong subway train. The Columbia interview went better. At its conclusion, the interviewer—the school soccer coach—eyeing my lean, athletic-looking six-foot frame, asked me if I would consider trying out for the soccer team. "Sure," I said, avoiding any mention of the fact that I was a disaster at sports. As things turned out, Harvard rejected me and at Colgate and Union my admission was fouled up because the Madison guidance staff inexplicably neglected to mail in my applications. The other schools accepted me, with Rochester even offering me a small scholarship.

As my family did not have much money, it looked like the decision as to which college I would attend would boil down to its affordability. Brooklyn College was tuition-free at the time and, therefore, that school loomed as a very live possibility. But it was not a particularly desirable one, for its intellectual standards were relatively low, it would draw many of the mediocre students from my neighborhood, and it was a commuter school, thus guaranteeing that I would live with my parents. One day, however, when I arrived home from Madison, I found my mother sobbing. "What's wrong, Ma?" I asked. "You've won a Regents Scholarship," she said, handing me the notification letter. And, indeed, I had. Awarded on the basis of a competitive test, these New York State scholarships provided between $250 and $750 per year—then a lot of money, at least relative to the tuition at many colleges. Based on our family income, I would receive $534 annually. Within a short time, however, my mother decided that I should attend Brooklyn College and pocket the guaranteed minimum, $250 a year. My father, though, stood up to her this time and insisted that Columbia was a better school. I think he also believed that I would be better off away from her. In any case, it was finally agreed that I would attend Columbia.

Ironically, yet another stream of income—this one generated by the Cold War—led to my attending Columbia. In the late 1950s, the Soviet Union shocked Americans by rocketing *Sputnik,* a Soviet satellite, into orbit around the earth. This event convinced pundits and government officials alike that the United States was falling behind in the race to develop guided missiles that, fitted with nuclear warheads, could annihilate rival nations. And this lag, in turn, convinced many that it was vital to the national defense to encourage American students to pursue a higher education, thus enabling them to compete more effectively with their Soviet counterparts. Consequently, Congress enacted the National Defense Education Act, which provided interest-free loans to U.S. college students. In my case, an NDEA loan provided a welcome supplement to my other sources of income, though I cannot say that it ever did very much for the national defense.

My impatience to leave home and carve out a new life was spurred along in the summer of 1958, following graduation, when I worked as a counselor at Pioneer Youth Camp. Replete with social workers, racially integrated, and directed by a woman (whose husband was in charge of the garbage disposal), it was a very different sort of institution than the other camps I had attended. In place of competitive sports, there was an emphasis on arts and crafts, woodlore, singing, and plays. The counselors were particularly interesting, and we hung out a lot together, sometimes piling into the back of the garbage truck for a trip to town to see a film. I particularly liked Ann, my co-counselor's girlfriend. Bright and attractive, she had just finished her first year of college and liked to talk about literature. "Have you read Jack Kerouac's *On the Road*?" she asked. "No? You'd love it!" She also told me that I'd really enjoy college—and I believed it, especially if the students were like her. When she broke up with my co-counselor, she asked me one evening to walk her back to her bunk, and I did so. But I was too shy to seize what might have been my big moment and within days she was going out with someone else.

Thus, by the summer of 1958, at the age of seventeen, I was ready to break out of what I considered the provincial confines of my life in Brooklyn. Chafing at the limits of my family, my relatives, my school, and my society, I was developing an intellectual, cosmopolitan, romantic worldview. Not surprisingly, it clashed increasingly with my parents' limited cultural background, as well as with the irrationality of my mother's manic depression. It also meshed poorly with the narrow-mindedness of some of my relatives, the pop culture and cruelty of many teenagers, the simple-minded consumerism of the era, the authoritarian measures of government officials, and the racism and Cold War fanaticism of the broader public. Where was that glorious realm suggested by the books I had read and by bits and pieces of my own experience—the world of literature, of challenging ideas, of adventure, and of romance? I was longing to find it.

3

College Days, 1958–1962

Founded in 1754 as Kings College and renamed thanks to the American Revolution, Columbia College was one of the prestigious Ivy League schools. Over the next two centuries, it gradually relocated from its original home in lower Manhattan to permanent headquarters on Manhattan's Upper West Side. Along the way, it attracted other colleges and graduate schools—including Barnard College (for women), the College of Physicians and Surgeons, the School of Law, and the Graduate Faculties—which together comprised Columbia University. As the oldest component of this conglomerate, Columbia College viewed itself as the heart of the university, most of which sprawled between West 114th Street on the south and West 122nd Street on the north, and Morningside Drive on the east and Riverside Drive on the west. In 1958, when I began attending Columbia College, it had about 2,000 students (including some 600 in my class)—100 percent male, 99 percent white, and, for the most part, very intelligent. Despite these distorted (in retrospect, quite weird) aspects of the place, it played a key role in opening up new and exciting intellectual, social, and political horizons for me.

In September 1958, I moved into the Columbia dorms, along with the other members of the Class of 1962, to begin Freshman Week. Wide-eyed and sporting freshman beanies, we underwent a dizzying barrage of exams (e.g., placement for language courses), socializing, registration information, and rah-rah activities. To familiarize us with the campus mores, we were assigned sophomore advisers. I still recall mine solemnly warning me never to talk with women about politics, religion, or sex—a rule that I broke repeatedly. As we lined up for meals or other events, cigarette companies helpfully passed out free samples of their cancer-causing products. After choking on one or two cigarettes, I gave that up. Many of these students were remarkably like me—bright, socially awkward, and bursting with energy—and my roommates and I stayed up late at night gabbing about everything that popped into our heads. School spirit was lathered on thick, and we were quickly introduced to the raucous singing of assorted songs (e.g., "Who Owns New York?" and "Sans Souci") that have stuck in my brain to this day. Mixed among these were some pretty ribald ditties, as well as a variety of hearty male chants. Yet despite the atmosphere of traditional masculine fun and games, the contemporary world occasionally broke through. One of the chants, I remember, moved gradually from "1962" to "1984."

Columbia had a dormitory room shortage that year, so a substantial number of us were assigned to rooms in an old Upper West Side apartment house, the Arizona, located right across West 114th Street from John Jay Hall. After the excitement of Freshman Week, in which we'd been scattered about randomly in the dorms, I was looking forward to meeting my regular roommate. Therefore, it came as a shock when he showed up to announce that he planned to have a friend reside with him and that, to accommodate this, I should move out of the room and move in with his friend's roommate. Annoyed and personally offended, I said I wasn't planning to change rooms and that, if he wanted to switch things around, *he* could move out. He did, and that evening his friend's roommate—a fellow named Michael Weinberg—arrived in my room and began moving in.

Mike was a tall (six-foot-two), skinny, sixteen-year-old from the Bensonhurst area of Brooklyn. In a number of ways, he was very much like me. Jewish (though not religious), he was lower middle class and nearly as socially maladroit as I was. In addition, he had attended Brooklyn's public schools, had been a very good student, skipped a year via "rapid advance" junior high school, and had parents who were fairly conventional and not very well educated. On the other hand, unlike me, he did not have much use for literature, the humanities, and politics. Instead, he was a math/science whiz who had received a New York State engineering scholarship and seemed perfectly content to become a civil engineer. Furthermore, he quickly pledged a social fraternity and joined the freshman crew team. These early interests and activities—so different from mine—gave us a somewhat divergent lifestyle that year. I would be studying in the room after dinner when he would arrive exhausted after an afternoon's workout and dinner with the crew and would sometimes just doze off at his desk or in our only easy chair. Nevertheless, perhaps because we had similarly offbeat values and ideas, we quickly became fast friends.

Actually, despite the similarity of Mike's social background to mine, Columbia provided me with a more diverse social experience than I had had previously. The student body, to be sure, was composed almost entirely of white males, while the faculty was all-male and all-white. But within the student body there was substantial geographical diversity, with students drawn from all over the country and the world. Furthermore, although the number of students with working-class or impoverished backgrounds was small to nonexistent, for the first time in my life I met substantial numbers of people with upper-class backgrounds. Many, in fact, had attended fancy private schools. I recall attending one "stag dance," in which I chatted with a young man to pass away the time as we checked out the women. "Say," he asked companionably, "where did you prep out?" I ended the conversation by reporting that I had "prepped out" at James Madison High School in Brooklyn.

Although a large number of Columbia students were Jewish, the administration was embarrassed about this fact, and—continuing a policy in place for decades—made yeoman efforts to provide the student body with a public image that was stereotypically upper-class WASP: tall, blond, well-dressed, gentlemanly, and athletic. In this fashion, the administration ignored the typical student at Columbia and displayed a wistful longing for the typical student at Princeton. The ideal was what the administration referred to as the "well-rounded man." But the reality was that many of us were Jewish, unconventional, and not well-rounded at all. Thus, large numbers of Columbia students felt some degree of contempt for the administration and for its genteel Princeton model.

For me, these college years were enormously exciting. Having lived all my life at home in fairly conventional circumstances, I found it liberating to stay up until any hour reading, talking to bright people, and pondering the riddles of existence. If Mike and I, after hours of conversing about the meaning of civilization, felt hungry at 2:00 A.M., we simply trotted off to Take-Home Foods to pick up enormous meatball or sausage hero sandwiches. Then, returning to our room, we devoured them as we continued our discussion. The tenant next door, unhappy about our late night conversations, would sometimes pound on the walls to silence us, but eventually we lost patience and simply pounded back.

Repeatedly, I was caught up in laughing jags. In part, this reflected the fact that I was having a good time. But there was also something zany and irreverent about aspects of Columbia life. I found *Jester*, the campus humor magazine, very appealing and quickly submitted a story to it. The story was never published, though it did earn me a token position on the *Jester* staff. Years later, one of the editors commented on the fact that he had once received a bizarre story about how a student had sacrificed his roommate to a chicken. He didn't mention that it was my story—one that I didn't discuss at the time with Mike. The campus newspaper, *Spectator*, also had a droll style, and every April 1 it came out with an April Fool's issue bearing articles that always left me in stitches. I remember one tiny article, buried away on the last page, was headlined "WORLD TO END TODAY."

Sometimes the joyous irreverence had a thoughtful basis. Many of us read *Growing Up Absurd,* in which Paul Goodman, the anarchist intellectual, argued that in a crazy society the only sane thing to do was to refuse to adjust to it. Some of us found this a perfectly reasonable position. At other times we were attracted by the bizarre. Standing on the corner of West 116th Street and Broadway, an elderly fellow whom we called "the Emsch" preached on a regular basis. Totally out of his mind, he conducted lively and wonderful conversations with crowds of adoring students. No one I knew smoked pot at that time, but we didn't need it to bring on gales of laughter. All sorts of things served as sources of amusement.

This taste for the irreverent, even for the outrageous, seemed fairly widespread at Columbia. Residing in a room adjoining ours, Artie Garfunkel, who had given up his early singing career (with Paul Simon) to become a college student, borrowed my copy of *Job*—one of the books of the Bible that we read for the freshman Humanities course—and, when he returned it, the title on the cover had been transformed into *Get a Job!* (the title of a popular song, which we sang on occasion). One night, during the tense period of finals week, someone in the dorms turned on his record player at a blasting volume, thereby leading growing numbers of unruly students to pour out into 114th Street. Suddenly, Artie pounded on our door, telling us to shine our gooseneck lamps out of our window and onto his balcony. When we did so, he strode into the spotlight, raised his hand for silence, and began playing a song for the mob on his guitar. At this point, police cars roared onto the scene, lights flashing and sirens wailing, only to be met by a hail of toilet paper rolls and other objects flung upon them from the dorms. Thus began an exciting, broadly based riot—less popular, of course, with the administration, which placed Artie and other ringleaders on probation.

In many cases, these youthful high jinks were accompanied (and sometimes undergirded) by an intellectual transformation. Columbia had a system of core courses taken by all students. In the first year of the Humanities sequence, we read the classics—portions of the Bible, the Greek philosophers and playwrights, Rabelais, Shakespeare, the great nineteenth-century poets and novelists, and many more. During the second year of Humanities, we took a semester's course on the history of art and also a semester's course on the history of music. Simultaneously, we went through two years of Contemporary Civilization, a combination of history and philosophy, the latter beginning with early Christian theologians and moving on through Spinoza, Erasmus, the Enlightenment *philosophes,* Locke, the utilitarian philosophers, Mill, Marx, and Freud. In later years, critics pointed out the white, male, Western bias of these courses. And they were correct about that. Nevertheless, for us Humanities and Contemporary Civilization provided a sweeping challenge to much of what we had previously been taught or taken for granted. Immersed in a clash of some of the world's most important ideas over the broad sweep of history, many of us underwent an intellectual revolution.

Certainly, for me, the experience was mind-boggling. Of course, during my childhood I had had inklings of the profound intellectual, social, and political currents that ran far deeper than my petty, provincial Brooklyn life. But now I had finally plunged into their turmoil and excitement, and they bowled me over. I explored with Plato the possibilities for creating a just society, I roared at Aristophanes' lampooning of war and gender relations, I grappled with Augustine's bleak view of human nature, and I was swept away by the Enlightenment's attempt to use reason to carve out a better world. Voltaire especially delighted me as he employed his sharp wit to lash out at ignorance, superstition, and folly. My new watchwords became: "Ecrasez l'infâme!" Ideas, I could see, were not abstractions, for they had wrenched the world free of the grim muck of the past and propelled it toward dramatic and liberating changes. Pondering the history of intellectual and social upheaval, I began to believe that the dead hand of the past did not necessarily determine the future, and that intellectuals—activist intellectuals—could play an important role in charting a better life for humanity.

Of course, I identified with these intellectuals and was eager to join their ranks. On my bad days at Columbia, when I felt plunged into gloom by some quarrel or other depressing event, I would wander out at night to the sundial, in the middle of the campus. Here I would sit alone, facing the frieze on Butler Library, pondering the daring lives of my new heroes: Socrates, Erasmus, Spinoza, Voltaire, and other intellectual giants. And I would gain inspiration from their example. Socrates, after all, had been murdered as a dangerous dissident. Erasmus had skated on thin ice with the Catholic Church. Spinoza had been excommunicated. Voltaire had been driven into exile. Who was I to complain about some piddling misfortune? Squaring my shoulders, I headed back to my room, determined to continue and ultimately to prevail.

I don't know if the intellectual revolution experienced by other students was quite as profound, but I do know that a surprising number of them became intellectually unhinged. Cut loose from his moorings by what he had read in his Contemporary Civilization and Humanities courses, Mike dropped his math course (thereby forfeiting his scholarship), scrapped his plan to become an engineer, and started dabbling in psychology. Many a night thereafter we sat up discussing B. F. Skinner's *Walden Two,* in which that behavioral psychologist spun out his schemes for creating a utopian society. Another friend, Charlie Nadler, who, thanks to pressure from his father, had started college as a physics major, suddenly rebelled and deliberately failed his only physics course. Plunging into the field of philosophy, Charlie set out to help clarify human thinking by becoming a philosopher.

Yet another friend, Bill, who had grown up in a small-town Christian environment, found his early views shattered by the startling exchanges of ideas in his early Columbia courses. Late one night as we were staggering back to our rooms after a drinking spree at the West End Bar, a few blocks from the Columbia campus, Bill lurched to a stop in front of a church on Broadway. "Fuck God!" he shouted at the top of his lungs. "Fuck God!" I was amused but also worried, for I wondered if this wild display of sacrilege might be too much for local residents, even on the relatively tolerant Upper West Side. "Come on, Bill," I implored, "let's get back to the dorm." But Bill, bolstered by his newfound freethinking and a few beers, was immovable and irrepressible. "Fuck God!" he continued shouting, raising his middle finger high in the air. *"Fuck God!"*

Despite my increasingly iconoclastic, avant-garde views, I continued to identify with the Democratic Party. The 1958 Democratic sweep of U.S. senatorial races delighted me, and I hoped that it augured a serious challenge to the humdrum conservatism of the Eisenhower administration. In 1960 I rooted for the liberal Hubert Humphrey in the Democratic presidential primaries. Even when the more centrist John F. Kennedy secured the Democratic nod, I had no qualms about backing him. In the final days of the presidential campaign, I stood for hours in a vast welcoming crowd on Broadway, bordering the Columbia campus, awaiting his campaign motorcade. Although I was not overly impressed with what Kennedy had to say—and found his opening citation of a Greek philosopher rather pretentious—I still considered him far preferable to the Republican candidate, Richard Nixon (then packaging himself as "the new Nixon," for, by this point, the old version was considered too McCarthyite and right-wing to sell to the nation).

There were Columbia students, a *very* few students, who went beyond electoral politics—publicizing the southern lunch counter sit-ins, putting up posters about a mysterious worldwide General Strike for Peace, courting arrest by boarding nuclear submarines, and (like young Eric Foner, later to become a very prominent historian) promoting Student SANE (the youth group of the National Committee for a Sane Nuclear Policy). Although I was not among them, I felt sympathetic to their efforts. Not surprisingly, I was totally committed to the burgeoning civil rights movement. In addition, I was increasingly skeptical about the nuclear arms race. One day my father and I joined Uncle Fred as his lunch guests at a swanky Manhattan restaurant, and a crowd of demonstrators surged by the restaurant window, carrying antinuclear signs and banners. When Fred made a derisive comment about them, I launched into a passionate defense of their cause. Taken aback by my remarks, Fred—always the upper-class charmer—reversed gears and launched into an anecdote about his youthful life in London during the early 1920s, when his father had been stationed there as a high-ranking U.S. diplomat. He remembered, he said, joining a mass protest demonstration and carrying a sign reading "Free Sacco and Vanzetti!" We laughed, as our relationship was restored.

On campus, too, I sometimes found myself on the fringe, politically. One day, in Professor Joseph Rothschild's political science class, he casually remarked that although in the past people were concerned about economic equality, it was now a bygone issue. In response, I spoke up and said that I cared about economic equality and thought that it was disgraceful that poverty existed in the midst of so much wealth. This immediately sparked a debate. In another class, taught by Professor Richard Neustadt, then a rising star among political scientists, we explored the thesis of C. Wright Mills's new book, *The Power Elite*. I found Mills's argument that the United States was dominated by a military-industrial cabal a persuasive one, as did some others in the class. But Neustadt brushed it off, claiming that although that situation existed during periods of Republican rule, like our own, Democratic administrations were different. Just wait and see what Kennedy would do. Right after that, he headed off to Washington to serve as an adviser to the new Kennedy administration.

Although Columbia had a vaguely liberal Democratic tone, such values were certainly not hegemonic. When the right-wing Ayn Rand spoke on campus, she drew a substantial crowd. There was also a very noticeable Naval ROTC unit that paraded on the campus. In one of *Spectator*'s April Fool issues, the newspaper lampooned student peace and civil rights activists, twenty-three of whom had supposedly turned out for "a massive all-cause protest." As such articles indicated, not everyone favored efforts to foster racial equality. Deeply resentful of my role in bringing an African American student into my fraternity, a southern white member resigned in disgust and made sure to communicate that fact to me. Indeed, even a friend of mine—then in a conservative, libertarian phase—condemned the civil rights movement and argued vehemently against civil rights legislation.

On much rarer occasions, I also encountered ideas to my left. In an economics course, where my eyes often glazed over with the boredom of learning about abstract concepts like marginal utility and marginal revenue, the instructor finished up an opaque lecture on the business cycle by asking students what it all meant. The football players in the class, taking the course because they planned to "go into business," hadn't a clue. But something clicked for me. "It means that capitalism is inherently unstable," I said. "That's right, Mr. Wittner," he responded happily. "That's *right!*" I remembered the gleam in his eye on that occasion when, some time later, I learned that he had traveled to Cuba to advise the Castro government on economic policy.

Probably the most impressive political speaker I heard during these years was young Michael Harrington, whose powerful study of poverty, *The Other America,* would soon challenge the widespread notion that the United States was a contented "Affluent Society." Dazzled by his oratorical skill, as well as by his cogent analysis, I noted with interest that he was not a liberal or a Communist, but a socialist. Those socialists, I thought, made a lot of sense!

Even so, for the first three years of college I spent less time on politics than on my social life, which, miraculously, began to take off. Columbia's social fraternities were too cliquish for my tastes, and it's possible that I was too socially awkward for theirs. But by October 1958 I had found a congenial organization to join, or rather "pledge"—Alpha Phi Omega, a service fraternity. Unlike the social fraternities, Alpha Phi Omega did not maintain a fraternity house. Instead, it sponsored a number of campus activities, including a used-book exchange and an Ugliest Man on Campus contest. But there also was plenty of socializing, with members accompanying the new pledges down to McSorley's Old Ale House, an early nineteenth-century, males-only tavern in lower Manhattan, where we drank, swapped stories, and sang raucous songs. Somewhat to my surprise, I found that my newfound fraternity brothers—a mixture of smooth operators and socially maladroit individuals—actually liked me.

They also needed me. In the spring of 1959, when one of Alpha Phi Omega's good old boys dropped the ball in running our fraternity's Ugliest Man on Campus (UMOC) contest, they pressed me to fill in for him, which I did. Yet another of Columbia's offbeat ventures, UMOC entailed students "voting" to elect one of six faculty members to this exalted position by placing coins in a jar next to a bizarre picture of him. All the proceeds went to the Columbia scholarship fund. UMOC proved a lot of work, but also a lot of fun. That May, *Spectator* reported with its usual tongue-in-cheek humor that Larry Wittner, "the little Boss Tweed of Alpha Phi Omega," had announced the Ugliest Man on Campus (Professor H. Dustin Rice of the Fine Arts Department) and that $187 had been raised. In a testament to my surprising social acceptability and obvious efficiency, I was elected to serve, beginning in the fall of 1959, as the fraternity's second vice president, with the job of pledge master.

This admittance to a congenial social circle was certainly a remarkable turnabout from my lonely high school years. As Mike made plans to move into his fraternity house that fall, I teamed up with Paul Gilbert, Alpha Phi Omega's incoming first vice president, to share a suite that fall in Livingston Hall, one of the campus dorms. Living catty-corner to us was the incoming president, Bob Morgan. Paul grew up in Queens and, like me, had a certain social clumsiness. But he was a year older and spent more time than I did preparing for classes. Bob, a WASP from Danvers, Massachusetts, home of the Salem witchcraft trials, was a much more colorful character—in fact, almost off the charts. Always flamboyant, he liked to portray himself as a confirmed monarchist, scornful of the masses. But it was hard to take him seriously about this role or about much else, for most of the time he seemed to be joking, lampooning everything and everyone, including himself. Indeed, we—and a number of other friends—got on wonderfully.

Unfortunately, the good feelings did not last. In November 1959 Alpha Phi Omega had a role at a Columbia alumni association Homecoming Day event at Baker Field, Columbia's athletic facility on the upper tip of Manhattan. On that cold, rainy, and muddy occasion, our fraternity pledges had the job, I very vaguely recall, of serving beer, and I was in charge of them. After hours of this, we decided that in those difficult conditions it was time to pack up and go back to campus. But Bob, who was also on hand, argued that this would constitute abandonment of our post and that we should remain on the job. When we didn't, he became apoplectic. I was sorry about that, but—cold and wet—we just didn't have the stamina to continue. In fact, when I got back to my dorm room, I became sick and spent the rest of the day in bed. At the next fraternity meeting, which he chaired, Bob denounced us in harsh, theatrical terms and then, resigning the fraternity presidency, stormed out of the room.

This provided us with quite a mess, and it soon became worse. Given a heavy course load and other commitments, Paul could not attend our fraternity meetings, which meant that I—at the age of eighteen, after only a year of college, and with minimal social skills—had to take charge of the organization as acting president. I did my best, but it was difficult. Bob showed up at the next meeting and harangued us at every turn. Enraged, I retorted that, given his abrupt and irresponsible resignation, he had forfeited the right to be taken seriously. This was not a tactful or a useful approach on my part, and it led to Bob's storming off again and not speaking to me thereafter. Over time, with considerable effort, I managed to get fraternity affairs on track once more. And the organization even began to thrive, particularly during my junior year, when—after having been tossed, in accordance with Alpha Phi Omega tradition, into one of the campus fountains—I served as the elected president. But the schism with Bob was painful, and it continued to provide a fault line in the fraternity and in my personal life.

Although I developed a circle of good friends at Columbia, it did not include some noticeable groups. One was composed of the campus jocks, especially the wrestlers and football players. Two of them lived next door to Paul and me, and sometimes at two or three in the morning there would be enormous thuds against the wall that shook our rooms. When Paul, who knew them slightly, knocked on their door once to find out what was happening, he discovered that these behemoths liked to wrestle off their surplus energy by smashing one another's bodies against the walls. Another group that I had little to do with were the campus smoothies—the students who emulated the Princeton model by sporting ties, white shirts, sport jackets, and big phony smiles. One of them earnestly told me that he could never bear the thought of not putting on a freshly starched white shirt in the morning. These smooth operators tended to be concentrated in the Van Am and Blue Key societies, two very exclusive organizations that provided the bulk of the students tapped by the college administration to serve public roles. Articulate and conventional, they dominated the student government until the student body, in an act of rebellion, voted to abolish it. In later years, many of them went on to become corporate executives, stockbrokers, corporate lawyers, and leaders of the alumni association.

Despite my burgeoning social life, I remained a relatively shy person, especially in situations in which I first met people. And this, in turn, was based primarily on the fact that, although my stutter tapered off somewhat during these years, it was still noticeable and capable of giving people a negative impression of me. My occasional withdrawal from social situations, however, did have some positive aspects. It continued to channel me toward reading and writing. Furthermore, it gave me a lot more time to analyze other people's behavior—often as an outsider—and thus become more thoughtful about it. For example, one summer, as the counselors (mostly new) clustered together on one of the first days of camp, I spoke up a bit but mostly watched, fascinated, as they competed in displaying their verbal wit in an attempt to score points and attain popularity. Perhaps because I had so little facility at this, it struck me that we would all be much better off if we scrapped this competitive game and found a more rational way to develop friendships.

Overall, I genuinely enjoyed my classes at Columbia. Oddly, though, I never signed up for courses taught by three of Columbia's most famous faculty members of the era: the sociologist C. Wright Mills, the literary critic Lionel Trilling, and the historian Richard Hofstadter. Mike, though, took a course with Mills, whom he recalled would show up for only about a third of his class sessions. A colorful figure, Mills would roar up to campus on his motorcycle, read a powerful section from one of his new books and then depart, leaving students uncertain about when they would see him again. Preoccupied as I sometimes was with fraternity affairs, I did not do as well in courses as I might have if I had devoted more time to studying. Even so, over the years I compiled an overall B+ average (placing me in the top seventh of my class) and an A- average in my major.

The story of my major is a curious one. As an aspiring novelist, I began Columbia with a major in English. And nothing in the freshman Humanities course or English course led me to think that this was a bad choice. But Columbia had a required course sequence for English majors, and, accordingly, I signed up in the fall of 1959 for the first step in the sequence, Seventeenth Century Prose and Poetry, taught by a young instructor, Charles Van Doren. Although Van Doren was an excellent teacher, I found the readings very tedious, particularly given the obscure, dated, and opaque language. Therefore, I impulsively dropped the course. And without it, of course, I could not be an English major. I had to major in something, but what? I decided that, as I was enjoying the American history course I was taking, I might as well major in history. It was a lightly considered but fateful choice. Meanwhile, that November, after my departure from his course, Van Doren confessed that his success on the popular TV quiz show "Twenty-One" was based on being provided with the questions in advance. He soon abandoned Columbia in disgrace, though not before a demonstration supporting him broke out among his loyal students.

As things turned out, the history major suited me very nicely. I liked the history courses that I took, particularly the U.S. survey (taught by Henry Graff) and another on the French revolution (taught by Peter Gay). In addition, I did very well in such courses. Possessing a knack for quickly discerning the thesis of a history reading, I also had a good memory for detail and could write well. At the same time, there was plenty of room in my schedule for courses in other areas that I enjoyed, such as political science (a field in which I minored) and literature. Thus, I ended up reading many modern novels, particularly by Russian and British writers. One of the courses I found most interesting focused on the modern drama. Taught by Eric Bentley, it covered a stunning array of playwrights, from Henrik Ibsen to Bentley's own specialty, Bertolt Brecht.

My respect for literature and the arts meshed nicely with Alpha Phi Omega's sponsorship of the Columbia Arts Festival. Begun in the spring of 1959 with readings, organ, choral, and jazz concerts, and several dramatic performances, the Arts Festival soon developed into my fraternity's most ambitious project. In the spring of 1960, when I served as acting fraternity president, it included an all-Vivaldi concert by the New York Sinfonietta, a visual arts exhibit, premier performances of four Chekhov farces, a concert of electronic music by its faculty composer, performances of John Gay's *Beggar's Opera,* a modern dance performance, and a jazz festival. The Arts Festival was enormously exhilarating but also exhausting, and I began to recognize that the success of voluntary organizations rests heavily on the shoulders of a very small number of committed activists.

I also needed time for remunerative employment. By today's standards, Columbia's yearly tuition and fees were remarkably low: $1,200 a year when I began and $1,450 during my last two years there. But there were additional expenses for room, board, books, and incidentals. Despite my state scholarship and NDEA loan, there remained a substantial gap, and it was imperative to close it. In theory, I could find a paying job during late May and June and then move on to camp counselor employment during July and August. But no one, it seemed, wanted to hire students for only the first period or even for the whole summer. With classes concluded, I spent weeks in the stifling heat getting up in the morning, donning my only suit, and taking the subway to commercial sections of Brooklyn and Manhattan in a desperate search for a job. As the big businesses to which I applied would only hire people willing to work on a long-term basis, I began to say that I was dropping out of college to earn enough money to put me through it.

One day I received word that a vice president of a giant life insurance company to which I had applied wanted to speak with me. Taking the elevator to the top of the company's skyscraper, I entered the plushest office I had ever seen, surrounded by windows that gave him a magnificent view of Manhattan. These people, I thought, really do rule the world! As the air-conditioning hit my clothes, drenched with sweat from the crowded subways and city streets, I grew more comfortable and then chilly. "Sit down, sit down," he told me. "You know, you knocked the top off our test," he said. "And I notice that you received an 'A' in your freshman math course at Columbia." Excited, I began to think I had the job. But actually I didn't. "Stay in college," he urged me. "Finish your coursework. There will always be a place for you here." I used my argument that I needed money to *attend* college, but to no avail. After all, they could wait and see what happened. As I hit the sweltering streets again, I vowed that I'd never enter a career that involved working for a bunch of complacent, callous businessmen.

When I finally found a job in June 1959, it was as a stock boy for E. J. Korvette & Company, a department store in downtown Brooklyn. Here I worked a fifty-hour week, breaking up and flattening clothing cartons for ninety cents an hour, a subminimum wage without time-and-a-half for overtime. The only enjoyable period during the day came during my lunch break, when I'd gobble down a sandwich in ten minutes and spend the rest of the half hour reading Erich

Auerbach's *Mimesis: The Representation of Reality in Western Literature.* Fortunately, the summer camp job that followed relieved the tedium somewhat.

The next year I was hired for the best post-college-year employment I ever had: working for the New York State Commission Against Discrimination. Using his influence at the Commission, my father landed me a job indexing the transcripts of its meetings. I enjoyed the work, completing it so quickly that the commissioners, somewhat dismayed, had to scramble to find something else for me to do.

During college, one of the most dramatic changes from my past was taking young women out on dates. Often on a Friday or Saturday night we went to dinner at one of Manhattan's small foreign restaurants, attended an art film, or found something interesting to do around Greenwich Village. Sometimes, Mike and a date of his would join us. Once, in fact, thinking that it would be really hip, Mike and I buried a bottle of brandy in Greenwich Village's Washington Square Park, and then during an outing with two young women we proceeded to dig it up for our use. Although I was definitely interested in broadening my sexual experience, which was virtually nonexistent, things never went very far along these lines. I remained shy and my dates inhibited; the most we managed was a brief kiss goodnight. Ironically, I think that their mothers, whom I met when I stopped by their homes to pick them up, were impressed with me. After all, I was a polite, rather quiet, intelligent student attending a prestigious college. But these same characteristics did not sweep young women off their feet.

Another drawback of my dating scene was that I often spent six hours on an evening's transportation: taking a subway out to Queens, catching a bus to my date's house, taking a bus with her back to the subway station, taking a subway with her to Manhattan, taking the subway with her back to Queens, taking the bus with her back to her house, taking the bus back to the subway station, and taking the subway back to Columbia. If it's exhausting to read this, imagine how exhausting it was to *do* it—especially late at night, when the subways and buses ran very infrequently. Sometimes I wouldn't fall into bed until three or four in the morning.

There was also the widespread assumption by college administrators that their institutions should act *in loco parentis*. Columbia's sister college, Barnard, was situated right across the street and could have provided a rich source of dating and amorous activity for Columbia students. But official squadrons of matrons patrolled the Barnard dorms, and they made sure that Barnard students—like Cinderella—met a curfew, which was something like 10 P.M. on weekdays, 11 P.M. on Fridays, and midnight on Saturdays. Also, men were barred at all times from entering their rooms. Chastity was the norm—to such an extent that when one unmarried Barnard student publicly proclaimed that that norm was ridiculous and that she was pregnant, the Barnard administration promptly expelled her.

Things were a bit looser at Columbia, but not much. Although we did not have any official curfew or chastity policing, women were formally barred from our rooms. As there was no place for Columbia students (aside from those who lived off campus) to be alone with their dates or girlfriends, banning women from the dorms provoked constant protests. A *Spectator* editorial remarked that if the administration was worried that allowing women in the dorms would lead to pregnancies, it should simply distribute condoms. Eventually, a besieged administration made what it considered an important concession to student opinion: on one day a month, for one hour in the afternoon, women would be allowed to enter Columbia dorm rooms. But the room doors had to remain open. How open? By at least the width of a book, we were told. One campus wag suggested that we should use match books, which we did.

I grew more serious about women in the summer of 1960, when I worked again as a counselor, this time at Camp Greylock, in the Berkshires. During the camp's opening days, I spotted a short, cute counselor, Patricia ("Patty") Sheinblatt, two years younger than I was and a high school senior. She seemed to have spotted me, too, for—observing me engaged in a chess game with one of my campers—she suggested that I teach her how to play. I did and thus began a romantic summer, during (and after) which we never played chess again. The daughter of a suburban New Jersey dentist, Patty was intelligent, well-read, and cuddly, and we got on very well. I believe, though, that she was both attracted and frightened by my iconoclasm. One night, as we lay on a blanket in the big field behind the recreation hall, looking at the stars, we had a discussion about God. I told her that it was obvious that no God existed and, to prove this, drew upon a demonstration suggested by George Bernard Shaw. If God existed, I said aloud, he should strike me dead with a bolt of lightning. In fact, I dared him to do so. Although no lightning flashed from the heavens, Patty did not—in these eerie, isolated circumstances—particularly like this little demonstration.

During the 1960–61 academic year (when I was a junior), Patty and I went out on numerous dates, meanwhile preparing to see one another again at camp during the summer of 1961. But the plan for another two idyllic months at camp eventually turned sour, at least for me. Having been accepted for admission at Douglass College, the women's school of Rutgers, Patty decided that a relationship with me would unnecessarily limit her college social life. Thus, shortly after we arrived at camp, she broke up with me. As she was my first serious girlfriend, I felt devastated. That night, I placed a package of razor blades under my pillow with the intention of slitting my wrists in the early morning hours. But, lying there in bed, I dozed off, and when I woke up suicide no longer seemed a very good idea. Leaving Patty and the camp behind, however, seemed necessary. So I had my father, bewildered by the whole thing, pick me up by car and bring me back to Brooklyn. Ultimately, I found another camp job—one that turned out reasonably well, for my co-counselor had a guitar and taught me how to play simple chords on it. Ultimately, I began memorizing folk songs and learned a great deal from them about working-class life. But at the time the breakup left me tearful and gloomy.

At the end of my junior year, with Paul graduating and Mike anxious to move out of his fraternity house, Mike and I decided to room together once again, this time during our senior year. For a rental of only eight dollars a week each, we found a room just a half block off campus, on West 116th Street between Broadway and Riverside Drive. It was part of an old West Side apartment, with a bathroom at one end of the hall, a small kitchen at the other end, and six separately rented rooms in between. Only one of the rooms—ours—was occupied by students. For Mike and me, it was a perfect arrangement, and our friendship flourished.

Quite accidentally, I discovered what he was planning to do after college. Ever since he had dropped out of the engineering program, this had been a mystery. He had taken courses in a wide range of fields that didn't seem to add up to anything—among them psychology (his major), primitive religions, and accounting. But when asked about his plans he remained elusive, claiming that I should be able to guess his future career. One day, when I picked up our mail from our joint mailbox, I noticed that he was a subscriber to a couple of nudist colony magazines. At first I thought he might have subscribed because they were titillating. But, in fact, nudist colony magazines are not especially erotic. When I entered the room, I started joking with him about the magazines and then noticed a strange smile on his face. Suddenly, it hit me. "Mike, you're not planning to manage a nudist colony, are you?" "Yes," he said. "It should be an interesting career!" And it certainly would have been—had he pursued it.

Meanwhile, I commenced another round of dating, with the usual limited experience of women's charms and extensive experience of late-night subway rides. The most memorable relationship developed in connection with my fraternity's Intersession Orgy. For some time, my fraternity brothers and I had joked around about holding such an event, but, for obvious reasons, it proved impossible to arrange—at least for us. Finally, though, one of them did manage to launch a reasonable facsimile. In early January 1961 we were supposed to meet a group of girls one night for a wild party up in Westchester—though I am not sure that the women knew that this was supposed to be an orgy. As a budding historian, I did research for a speech on the history of orgies, turning up information on all sorts of fascinating sexual rites. On the appointed evening, Mike (whom I invited to attend) and I piled into a fraternity brother's car, picking up other participants along the way. When we arrived, around midnight, the party didn't look very much like an Intersession Orgy—or any kind of orgy. Even worse, all the women seemed to be paired off with the men. Convinced that this was going to be a disappointing evening, Mike and I began to consume copious quantities of rye whiskey.

But things took a turn for the better. Through a gathering alcoholic haze, I noticed an attractive, dark-haired young woman walking into the room. I asked her to dance and soon found that she was pressing herself so tightly against me that it was hard to tell where she began and I ended. We did take a little break, during which someone made a speech about our fraternity and I gave my talk on the history of the orgy, the latter to appreciative applause. At one point my arm seemed surprisingly wet, which—upon examination—resulted from my squeezing a cup of rye until it overflowed. Back we went to dancing and passionate kissing, steering around a body on the floor that turned out to be Mike, blissfully polishing off another drink. Hours later, still locked together in what passed for a dance, the young woman and I noticed someone tapping me on the shoulder. It was Mike, now on his feet, who commented that he and I had better leave, for we were supposed to be heading off in a few hours for an out-of-town trip. However, as Mike and I wove our way to the door, he had a sudden inspiration: "Kiss her goodnight!" So I returned to my dance partner for a lengthy, passionate reunion, at the end of which I asked her for her phone number. Named Linda, she was the daughter of a U.S. diplomat who resided in a fancy section of Westchester. In the following months, we went out a few times but never quite recaptured the passion sparked by the Intersession Orgy.

Actually, Mike and I embarked on something even more bizarre that year: the formation of the Society of Orpheus. The immediate cause, I think, was an incident at a stag dance. To avoid paying the admission fee, Mike and I decided to enter by following two other students through a short, unguarded passageway that led to the dance floor. As we entered, Proctor Walter Mohr—who served as Columbia's elderly chaperone at these kinds of events—realizing that students were gaining entry in this fashion, came puffing forward from the dance-floor end of the passageway. As the people closest to the door, Mike and I quickly and easily ducked out. Then, to my surprise, Mike locked the door, trapping the other students with Proctor Mohr, the guardian of campus propriety. "Come on," said Mike, laughing, "it's a good bit." And so we raced off.

Back in our room, Mike and I got into one of our many late-night discussions—this one focused on how to shake things up through the formation of a secret organization. Calling it, for want of a better name, the Society of Orpheus, we decided that its professed guiding principles would be Radicalism, Skepticism, Bestiality, and Hedonism. By this point, we were in hysterics. When we finally calmed down, we had to decide what would be our first project. Faced with this issue, we made a fairly rational decision. The apartment's only telephone, a pay phone, sat in the middle of the hallway, and as Mike and I occupied the room nearest to it, we usually ended up answering it when it rang. With calls coming in for everyone, clearly this was an unjust procedure—and certainly a pain in the neck for us. Consequently, that night, drawing upon my knowledge of French revolutionary rhetoric, we drafted our first revolutionary manifesto, the "Decree Establishing a More Equitable System for the Answering of the Telephone." Posted that night in the hall and embossed only with the great seal of the Society of Orpheus, it commanded the residents of the apartment to sign up for hours during which they would be responsible for answering the telephone. To our astonishment, everyone did.

This rapid success convinced us that even somewhat normal people (i.e., nonstudents) were pretty malleable and, if encouraged by the Society of Orpheus, might fall into line. Thus, some weeks later, we listened with considerable interest as our landlady, Mrs. Raskin, who sometimes cleaned the apartment, presented us with several rolls of toilet paper and asked us to use them to stock the apartment bathroom. After her departure, Mike and I began a long conversation about toilet paper, including a discussion of the hysterical chapter on the "arse-wipe" in Rabelais's classic, *Gargantua and Pantagruel*. Such considerations were now important because, after all, we now had control of the apartment's toilet paper supply! Seizing the opportunity, we entered the bathroom late that night with our second revolutionary manifesto, the "Decree Establishing a More Equitable System for the Distribution of the Toilet Paper." We removed the toilet paper roll and, in its place, taped up six envelopes, each marked with a tenant's name and containing twenty-five squares of toilet paper. Explaining that this new system "represents the latest advance in scatological research," the decree went on to state that "all suggestions for improvements in this service may be left in your envelopes."

For a time, this system worked just fine. Every night, at about midnight, Mike and I would enter the bathroom and replenish the toilet paper squares in the envelopes. However, as we were interested in learning how far people could be pushed along by the Society of Orpheus, we cut the ration for the second day to twenty-four, for the third day to twenty-three, and so on. When would they revolt, we wondered. Would they *ever* revolt? Of course, the declining ration of toilet paper did not inconvenience us personally, as we kept possession of the rolls.

Alas, after seven days, there came a fierce pounding on our door. It was Mrs. Raskin, who apparently did not welcome the new system. "What is this? What is this?" she shrieked, holding aloft our crumpled manifesto in her fist. Mike, contending that he was a major in scatology, did his best to explain the new system to her. And he pointed out, with some justice, that she had left us in charge of replenishing the toilet paper supply. As for me, I worked valiantly at keeping a straight face, though not with complete success. Nevertheless, despite our pleas to continue the new system, she made it unmistakably clear that she wanted the toilet paper roll back in place.

Even so, we were young, determined, and a bit off our rockers. Also, we did not easily submit to authority, even to the authority of a shrieking landlady. We would rally the masses against her. Consequently, that night we returned to the bathroom with yet another manifesto, designed—as it said—"to determine whether the tenants prefer this clean, egalitarian, democratic, scientifically proven system, or the old, unsanitary, communistic, outmoded system." Polling the tenants, the manifesto encouraged them to check a box next to their names, either in favor of the "new, up-to-date, efficient system" or of the "old, primitive, inequitable system." To assist the tenants, we provided a pencil on a string tacked to the wall. It would be difficult for them to vote for the old system, however, as the string was only long enough for the pencil to reach the boxes favoring the new system. Before leaving the bathroom, Mike and I, eager to create a bandwagon effect, kicked things off by casting our votes for the new system.

Perhaps because the toilet paper rations of the other tenants were beginning to reach a crisis level, there was not a surge of support for the new system. One cheated by drawing his own box, which he checked off and captioned "old fashioned tried & true method," adding: "All users are not born equal." Another drew an arrow toward the old system. Still, hope remained alive, for two tenants had not yet voted. One was a fierce-looking Arab, and we decided that, in his case, discretion might be the better part of valor. So, instead of approaching him, we focused our persuasive efforts on Russell. A *very* strange individual, Russell seemed to go out only at night. When he spotted us in the hall, he invariably froze, much like the apartment's many cockroaches. Cornering him one night in the kitchen, we pointed out that he had not yet voted. Didn't he like the new system, we asked. "Oh, yes, I do!" he explained. But he also argued that he didn't want to impose it on others.

Russell's unfortunate response brought us to the final round of the toilet paper saga. Yes, the Society of Orpheus had failed to rally the masses. But it would not abandon the field without exposing the disruptors of progress. Consequently, we posted our last manifesto. "Citizens!" we proclaimed, "The forces of reaction have triumphed." We explained that, although only a minority of the tenants had indicated their preference for the old system—true enough!—in a democratic society it was necessary to respect the rights of those few people with greater needs. To provide readers of the manifesto with additional information on just who those persons with the greater needs were, we suggested that they "See below." And there, indeed, we provided a chart graphing everyone's daily toilet paper consumption over a nine-day period. Overall, these and other ventures of the Society of Orpheus left us with the impression that other people—"normal" people—might be just as crazy as we were.

Actually, in some ways my life seemed to be taking a more conventional turn. Well into the second semester of my senior year, Patty, now attending Douglass College, wrote me a friendly—though not a romantic—letter. I could have written back to her or perhaps given her a phone call. But I concluded that the most interesting thing to do after the hiatus in our relationship was to just drop in on her unexpectedly, which I did. Entering her dorm lounge one afternoon, I convinced a young woman sitting there to run upstairs and tell Patty that a mysterious man wanted to speak with her. As I sat waiting, I listened to singers on a record, like the chorus in a Greek tragedy, wailing: "Marry the man today, rather than die of sorrow. Marry the man today and change his ways . . . tomorrow!" It was a telling prediction of our future, but I ignored it. Instead, I was pleased to find that Patty was suitably startled and that our relationship could be restored. We began going out once again.

I also needed to make a decision about my post-college years. As a first-rate student in history, I concluded that the obvious thing to do—indeed, just about the only thing to do—would be to go on to study it some more, in graduate school. Then perhaps I would become a college teacher, an *engagé* intellectual like my heroes of past centuries. At that time, Columbia students applying to graduate history programs were urged to speak with Professor James Shenton, one of the most popular, colorful faculty members at the college. In response to his request, I provided him with draft copies of my graduate school applications and returned to meet with him the following week. "Larry," he began, "you can't submit these." "Why not?" I asked. He then proceeded to explain that what I had written—outlining how I planned to become a historian to help transform the world—might well torpedo my chances for admission. I was astonished and countered that colleges and universities provided sanctuaries where scholars pursued ideas freely, without the corruption of wealth and power. A smile crossed his face. "I want to loan you a book," he said, handing me a copy of *The Academic Marketplace* by Theodore Caplow and Reece McGee. "Oh, and you might also find these of interest," Shenton added, digging out two copies of a new journal, *Studies on the Left*.

Shenton set me thinking. Just what were my politics, anyway? From my standpoint, key elements of modern society didn't make much sense. Why should some people starve while others were fantastically rich? (Wasn't there enough for all?) Why were people on different sides of national boundaries slaughtering one another in wars and preparing to do so in nuclear wars? (Wasn't this a ridiculous way to settle their quarrels?) Why were racial, religious, and other prejudices so powerful? (Couldn't people see that these biases were irrational?) I was certainly a social critic and favored the building of a more humane future. But where did that leave me politically?

By giving me copies of *Studies on the Left* to read, Shenton had implied that my views were left-wing. By contrast, I had always thought of them as liberal. And I certainly had no particular affection for Communism, dogmatic Marxism, or most other things that I identified with the Old Left. But maybe he was correct, I concluded, especially after reading one of the journal articles written by C. Wright Mills. In this "Letter to the New Left," Mills lauded the young intelligentsia (students involved in civil rights and other contemporary protest campaigns) as the new agency of social change. Moreover, *The Academic Marketplace* certainly didn't make faculty at colleges and universities look like proponents of cutting-edge political thought. Emphasizing academia's capitulation to McCarthyism, the book reported that in surveys faculty members around the nation—neutered and homogenized—indicated that the most pressing issue on their minds was campus parking. Clearly, I didn't share their values. Ultimately, I followed Shenton's advice, dropping some—but not all—of the political discussion in my graduate school applications.

Naturally, I didn't mention in them that in the fall of 1961 I had participated in my first political demonstration. In late August, the Soviet government had announced that it was withdrawing from the great power moratorium on nuclear testing, and it seemed only a matter of time before the U.S. government resumed its own atmospheric nuclear tests. Spotting a leaflet announcing a student bus trip to Washington to oppose U.S. test resumption, Mike and I decided that the time had come to get out in the streets and protest. Early the next morning, dressed in our suits (to impress government officials), we boarded the one bus making the trip, along with a rather bohemian looking group of students—guys sporting sandals and beards and girls wearing fishnet stockings and long braids—and headed off to our confrontation with power. Picking up what I considered a very clever sign ("Kennedy, Don't Mimic the Russians!"), I joined the others (supplemented by a second busload of students from a Quaker college in the Midwest) circling around a couple of trees outside the White House. Mike and I—as new and zealous recruits—circled all day without taking a lunch or dinner break.

For decades I looked back on this venture as a trifle ridiculous. After all, we and other small bands of protesters couldn't have had any impact on U.S. policy, could we? Then in the mid-1990s, while doing research at the Kennedy Library on the history of the world nuclear disarmament movement, I stumbled onto an oral history interview with Adrian Fisher, deputy director of the U.S. Arms Control and Disarmament Agency. He was explaining why Kennedy delayed resuming atmospheric nuclear tests until April 1962. Kennedy personally wanted to resume such tests, Fisher recalled, "but he also recognized that there were a lot of people that were going to be deeply offended by the United States resuming atmospheric testing. We had people picketing the White House, and there was a lot of excitement about it—just because the Russians do it, why do we have to do it?" Fisher concluded: "And that's the reason we didn't resume atmospheric testing." In politics, I ultimately learned, you never know how effective you are until long afterward—and sometimes not even then.

Not surprisingly, I was also drawn into the battle for racial justice. That same fall, galvanized by the heightening civil rights struggle, Mike and I turned up at a meeting to help establish a Columbia chapter of CORE, the Congress of Racial Equality. Today, it is assumed that most decent Americans rallied behind such organizations. But at the time our early CORE gatherings on campus drew only about a dozen people, many of them drifting in or out of the meetings. Our major project turned out to be testing the racial integration of Manhattan restaurants by sending in white, African American, and mixed race teams to dine there and then report on whether the service was affected by the racial composition of the team. Sometimes, it was. But we also served as a northern support group for the much larger, more endangered southern freedom struggle.

In this connection, one of CORE's southern black activists, Ronnie Moore, addressed our Columbia CORE chapter one evening in the spring of 1962. Having headed up a voter registration campaign in his hometown of Baton Rouge, Louisiana, Ronnie—and three other students at Southern University, an African American school which they had all attended—was out on bail on "criminal anarchy" charges, which carried a penalty of ten years at hard labor. Only nineteen years old, Ronnie also had been expelled from Southern University and now was touring northern campuses to stir up student support for the southern struggle. He certainly stirred us. Coming up to Ronnie after his talk, Mike and I asked him how we could help the cause. Looking us in the eyes, he said, smiling: "What are you boys doing this summer?" In reply, we explained that we were going to be driving around the country. "Any chance that you'll get to Baton Rouge?" he asked. "We could manage it," we said. "Well, do it, then," he remarked. "Maybe we can arrange to get you arrested!" We all had a good laugh about that. Then, intrepid as ever, we said we'd be there. And that summer we were.

For some time, Mike and I, chafing at our confinement in New York City, had been toying with the idea of emulating Jack Kerouac's bohemian characters in his classic novel *On the Road*. Ultimately, we concluded that the best time to hit the highway was right after graduation, during the summer of 1962. Gradually, things began to fall into place. Mike somehow convinced his father to loan him his car for this purpose. To compensate for the loss of my usual summer income, I found imaginative ways to save money, forgoing desserts and sometimes whole meals. I also took an extremely boring part-time job in the spring of 1962 as a file clerk in the Columbia contracts office. There was no longer any doubt about it. That summer we were going "On the Road"!

During that last semester at Columbia, Mike and I were both enrolled in an international education course, and we wondered if there was something outrageous that we could contribute to it. The answer came to us when, the night before the final exam, we decided to forget about further studying and go out to see a French movie. In the film, a crusty old codger repeatedly declared: "Education is a rat-hole for public funds." This struck us as a wonderfully appropriate statement for an education course. So we resolved that both of us somehow would work this declaration into our essay answers on the final exam. Our mission proved easy to accomplish, and we used our exams to transmit this cheering message to the course instructor. Like our fellow tenants, he made no comment on our bizarre behavior, though maybe it provided him with an unexpected source of amusement during the ordeal of exam-grading.

As graduation approached, I had to decide what to do about graduate school. On the aptitude test section of the Graduate Record Exam, which I took in January 1962, I scored within the top 1 percent of would-be graduate students on the quantitative section and within the top 4 percent on the verbal section. This very high-level ranking, coming on top of my solid academic performance at Columbia College, made me a strong candidate for admission to a number of high-powered graduate history programs. It also led to my receipt of a New York State Regents Teaching Fellowship, whose winners would receive $2,500 a year for study in a university doctoral program in New York State. But tuition at Columbia or another New York State school would eat up most of that fellowship, while the University of Wisconsin—on the basis of my college grades—offered me admission on a tuition-free basis. Furthermore, I liked the idea of leaving my New York life behind and was intrigued by the possibility of studying at Wisconsin with Merle Curti, a very prominent historian whose field—U.S. intellectual history—seemed a natural for me. Thus, I ultimately chose to begin attending classes at Wisconsin in the fall.

Columbia's graduation brought a strange congeries of events. I invited Patty to attend the ceremonies, and it was arranged that she would stay over the preceding night, in my room, which Mike would conveniently vacate by sleeping in his fraternity house. But on the afternoon of Patty's arrival the three of us arrived at the room to find that a large portion of the ceiling had collapsed into it. By that night Mike and I had gotten the debris out of the way and contacted our landlady about the cave-in (which she suspected us of instigating, in this case unfairly). Very early in the morning there came a light rapping on the door. It was Mike, who—failing to find a spare bed in his fraternity house—had been sleeping next door, having entered and appropriated (without asking, of course) the room of one of our fellow tenants for this purpose. Worried that the tenant might arrive and find him sleeping in his bed, Mike arose particularly early to warn us that the Wittner and Weinberg families would be arriving in a few hours for the graduation ceremonies. As a result, by the time they did arrive, we had eaten breakfast and were all dressed up like proper students. After that, the official ceremonies provided a calm respite, during which I graduated with honors and tried not to doze off.

The denouement to our college experience was going "On the Road" that summer. In the weeks right after graduation, Mike and I worked to put the last details in place. Partially to appease our parents, who wanted to know just where we would be and when, we drew up a reasonably detailed itinerary, based on a route that wound clockwise around the country. Unfortunately, my parents were beginning to have second thoughts about the venture. My mother, particularly, began to argue that the whole idea was ridiculous, for I should be working to earn money to pay for graduate school. In the final days before our departure, this led to some bitter fights with her and, at her instigation, with my father. But having denied myself food and having put in extra hours to accumulate money for just this purpose—plus having dreamed about this venture for so long—I was implacable. Thus, as planned, on the morning of June 29 Mike pulled up in front of my house in his father's car. We loaded my gear into it, had a picture taken of us wearing odd hats that Mike had dug up somewhere, and then took off on our adventure.

In a little less than ten weeks we drove some 13,000 miles around the United States and Canada, covering many of the spots we had marked on our itinerary, but also branching off to others just for the hell of it. Determined to keep the trip low budget and bohemian, we almost never took a room in a hotel. Instead, we slept by the side of the road, in campsites, in the car, and—to a lesser extent—in the homes of friends and relatives. On two occasions we were awakened in the middle of the night by police who, training their guns on us, told us to get moving! Most of our washing and shaving (when we bothered with it) took place in the men's rooms of gas stations. When we needed a bath—and driving in a car without air-conditioning, sometimes we *really* did—we would appropriate a gas station men's room, lock the door, and wash off as best we could in the sink. Packing our own food in the car, we spent little money on meals. At lunch time we often stopped at a grocery store, picked up a quart of buttermilk each, and used them to wash down a couple of apple butter sandwiches that we prepared from our stock of food. Once, as we sat on the curb of a small town street, gobbling down our lunch, a small child—apparently intrigued by these two hoboes—wandered over to us. Yanking him away, his mother warned him: "Come along, Johnny. If you don't watch out, you'll grow up like *them!*"

We loved our new and varied activities. We caught trout and devoured them for dinner in national parks, attended a bull fight in Tijuana, reeled in tuna on a boat trip off Santa Monica, visited the City Lights bookstore in San Francisco, guzzled free beer and cheese at the Pabst brewery in Milwaukee, and played pool with ghetto dwellers in Detroit. Refusing to pay admission to a tourist site with segregated facilities, we sneaked in to see the Natural Bridge in Virginia. Our guide book warned people against visiting Death Valley in the summer, and thus we made a point of spending two days there. One evening we located a Death Valley pay phone and, using the operator to place a person-to-person collect call to Friedrich Nietzsche, dialed up Patty, who, alert to this scam of ours, reported to the operator that he was out. On the outskirts of the Seattle World's Fair, we used our guitar and bongo drums to entertain a crowd, and this led to our performing at a downtown café, as well as to finding a free place to sleep for the night in someone's attic. In New Orleans we somehow managed to pick up two teenaged girls with whom we got along swimmingly—at least until I tried my trusty demonstration of God's nonexistence, which triggered a half hour's fervent avowal of Christian faith from one of the girls and a very dirty look from Mike.

Not far from Yakima, Washington, with the assistance of the government's farm labor service, we finally located a paying job—as prune pickers. We spent the preceding night sleeping in our car on a city street—at least until the local police awakened us and threatened to run us in as vagrants. ("We're not vagrants," we explained. "Then why aren't you sleeping in a hotel?" they demanded.) Having reluctantly followed their orders to "move along," we grabbed breakfast at a diner and then joined a crowd of poor, bedraggled people at the hiring shape-up outside a large farm. Here we were taken on to climb ladders into the trees and pick purple plums. First we tossed the plums into the large sacks draped around our necks; then, when the sacks grew too heavy to bear, we dumped their contents into large crates. Although the farmer hired us at thirty-five cents a crate, he raised our pay to forty cents a crate after it began raining and most of the work crew decided to leave. Like the fools we were, we continued to pick, stopping only to stuff our bellies with plums. After a twelve-hour day, I came away with nearly four dollars, though Mike—a superior prune picker—topped that. Exhausted and famished, we blew our day's pay on dinner.

One particularly dramatic incident occurred in the Grand Canyon. After a night's sleep in our car, we decided to hike down to the bottom of the canyon via a trail on the South Rim and then climb on out again. Normally, people took mules on the trail, or if they did hike it made arrangements to stay overnight at the bottom. But, in our characteristically insouciant fashion, we decided to make the trip (6.8 miles each way) all in one day. Our walk down the canyon wasn't so bad, for it was marred only by the blisters that developed on our feet (caused by the necessary braking action on the steep trail) and by the necessity to jump off the trail a few times to let a thundering herd of mules (then in training) pass. At the bottom of the canyon it was possible to eat our lunch, replenish our water supply, and take a nap. But the trip up the canyon was a disaster. Setting off on the climb at 5 P.M., we at first moved up the trail at a brisk pace. Yet it soon slackened. As the trail grew steeper, our breath came shorter, and our hearts pounded faster, we realized that we were going to have to make a forced march. We decided that we would walk 200 paces and then stop, repeating this again and again until we climbed out of the canyon. On the third round, Mike simply collapsed along the way. I sat down near him, and for a time neither of us had enough energy to speak. Mike declared that he couldn't and wouldn't go any further. I pointed out that we had no choice, for the trail was now devoid of people and—trapped there in the desert—we had no additional food and only about half a canteen of water each. Unless we kept going, we weren't getting out. Finally, it was agreed that Mike would stay there and I would continue, however slowly, making progress toward the top. Once there, I would rest up a bit and then head back down the trail with a good supply of food and water.

So we split up. I wandered alone, hour after hour, up the canyon trail, occasionally passing out. Eventually, at about 2 A.M., I reached the canyon rim and the lot where our car was parked. Helping myself to water and food from the car, I decided that I just didn't have the strength left to set off down the canyon again and then climb out of it. So I drove to a park ranger station to explain to the rangers the imperative need to get Mike out of there. To my astonishment, they replied that this sort of thing happened a lot and they didn't have the resources to handle it. "When he gets hungry and thirsty enough," they remarked confidently, "he'll climb out." I didn't find this encouraging, so I fell back on a plan to pay the mule-skinner to transport food and water down to Mike. But the mule train wasn't leaving until 8 A.M., so I drove first to the park's cafeteria for breakfast. As I was going out the cafeteria door, a bizarre-looking, dirt-covered individual staggered up the front steps. It was Mike. Looking at me in a crazed fashion, he asked: "Where was the car?"

After I set Mike up at a cafeteria table with breakfast and about twelve glasses of water, he told me what had happened. Following my departure, he had dozed off and then dreamed deliriously of fountains, rivers, and thirst-quenching libations. Awakening, he decided to drink his remaining water (after all, Larry would be back soon, wouldn't he?) and then start up the trail again. Refreshed by his sleep and his water, he made good progress. But inevitably he began to tire once more. At this point, however, he began to forget about me. He reasoned that if he could only get to the canyon rim, there he would find the car and our large water jugs. On he went, until exhausted he reached the canyon rim. But there was no car, nor any sign of Larry. Dazed, he began to wander about until, following the sound of some bells, he came to a trough where mules were feeding—and drinking. The situation posed a tough choice. Should he force his way in among the mules to drink at the filthy, dung-strewn trough, or should he delay quenching his thirst. He chose delay. Staggering over to the canyon rim road and gesturing at his open canteen, he sought to flag down cars. None would stop for him, not even when he lay down by the side of the road. Eventually, he considered lying down in the middle of the road. But, before he embarked on this last, desperate measure, a truck driver pulled over, gave him a drink, and drove him to the cafeteria. "When I saw you, Larry," Mike remarked, "I was ready to kill you. But I was too weak."

More than three decades later, I read in a newspaper story that in 1994 the Grand Canyon search and rescue team (presumably formed since our visit) handled 474 calls—11 of them involving deaths—which made this national park one of America's most hazardous wilderness areas. More than three-quarters of the calls involved hikers, and 90 percent of the incidents occurred on the South Rim trail during the summer. Park rangers reportedly had a saying about summer hiking there: "It's for fools and rangers making rescues."

Another memorable experience resulted from our plan to visit Ronnie Moore, CORE's Baton Rouge field secretary. In July, as we moved into the lower South, the weather turned unbearably hot and steamy. Perspiring profusely, we kept the car windows rolled down and stopped frequently at gas stations to buy bottles of soda, which in that region meant Dr. Pepper, "The Perky Picker-Upper." Although eventually bloated with the sweet fluid, we remained just as sweat-drenched and miserable as before, if not more so. We also met some of the local white folks. Conversing with one southern white hitchhiker we picked up, Mike asked him: "Why does there seem to be so much hostility around here to people from the North?" He looked at Mike and slowly replied: "I guess it's because you Yankees kiss the nigger's ass." Well, that was a showstopper! We got him out of the car as soon as we could.

Arriving in Baton Rouge, we couldn't find the Congress of Racial Equality listed in the phone book. But we did spot a Committee on Registration Education, and figured that, with the same acronym, that must be it. It was. The state authorities had gotten a court order to shut down the former group, so Ronnie and his friends had created the latter. When we arrived at their tiny office, Ronnie was delighted to see us and, together with his coworkers, took us out for coffee at a local all-black establishment. In his view—and ours, too—the only safe people in the South were black. As for the local whites, we considered them all actual or potential Nazis, and we scrupulously stayed clear of them and their institutions.

At dinner time, Ronnie suggested that we drive over to Southern University, from which he had been expelled. As we entered the dining hall, students started yelling: "It's Ronnie! It's Ronnie!" Hundreds of black students swiveled around and cheers rent the air. Leaping onto one of the tables, Ronnie made an impassioned speech about the freedom struggle and then announced that he had brought with him two movement supporters from the North. "Get up here, Larry and Mike!" So we jumped up there, too, and—facing a sea of black faces (a new experience for us)—did our best to deliver strong messages of solidarity. We had just about finished when a student rushed in to warn that the campus security police were on their way and that we had better get out of there fast! While students ran interference for us, we ducked out the back door, raced to our car, and roared away. That night, Mike and I slept on the Moore family's hall floor—a relative luxury, albeit a source of some anxiety, as local racists had been known to fire bullets into the hall through the front screen door.

In the following days, we did voter registration work in Baton Rouge and then moved on to Jackson, Mississippi. Ronnie had convinced us that our earlier plan, to visit the places where the Freedom Riders had been attacked and firebombed, would be far less interesting than accompanying him to Jackson, where a regionwide CORE-SNCC (Student Nonviolent Coordinating Committee) gathering would be held at the local Freedom House. Thus, after dinner the three of us piled our gear into our car and headed north.

As we got to northern Louisiana, however, we had to stop for gas. So, spotting a gas station with gas advertised at a relatively low price (27.9 cents a gallon), we pulled into it. The gas station attendant—a big, heavy-set blond guy with a crew cut—walked slowly out to the car and asked in an unfriendly fashion: "Whad y'all wahnt?" From the driver's seat, Mike said: "Fill 'er up!" While the gas station operator did just that, Mike noticed that the gas price on the pump said 29.9. As ours was a very low-budget trip, Mike decided to press the issue: "Hey, fella, why does your street sign say 27.9 and your pump say 29.9 for gas?" Looking coldly at Mike, he replied: "It's mah gas station; ah charge whad I wahnt!" In response, Mike—an uppity New Yorker more than adequately trained at Columbia to catch such flaws in logic—said: "It might be your gas station, but that doesn't give you the right to lie about your gas prices!" That did it. Enraged, the attendant announced that he was going to kill Mike. But, as he sought to pull open Mike's door and drag him out of the car, Mike held onto the door from the inside, and I—sitting in the back seat—slid over to the driver's side of the car, slammed down the button repeatedly, locking the door, and sought to cool the situation with a lot of fast talk. Ronnie, sitting in the front seat (where in the South black people were definitely not supposed to be), didn't move a muscle or say a thing. In the midst of northern Louisiana's Klan country—with two Jewish civil rights workers in a car bearing New York license plates, accompanied by a black CORE activist out on bail on criminal anarchy charges—it was definitely a bad scene.

And it got worse. When our Defender of the Southern Way of Life—ruefully giving up on dragging Mike out of the car—headed back to the gas station office to get us our change, Ronnie turned to Mike and said: "Mike, this is the South. You gotta watch what you say to white folks." Somehow, our gas station attendant picked up on this, for he wheeled around, stormed up to Ronnie's side of the car, and yelled at him: "What did you say, you black bastard?!!" We now went through a repeat performance on Ronnie's side of the car, with our blond beast pulling on his door, Ronnie hanging onto it from the inside, and my sliding over to pound on Ronnie's door lock and fast-talk the snarling attendant. Ultimately, frustrated, he again headed for the gas station office. Looking at the gas pump, I saw that our bill was $2.48. "Mike, how much did you give him?" I asked. He answered: "$2.50." "Drive!" I commanded. Tearing out of that gas station, we didn't stop again until we hit Jackson.

In Jackson, things were very interesting, although—after our gas station confrontation—a bit anticlimactic. At the Freedom House—an abandoned building taken over by the movement and around which local police cars circled menacingly—we joined dozens of CORE and SNCC activists from the Deep South, among them Dave Dennis, Lawrence Guyot, and Bob Moses. At night, they had lengthy political discussions, and I was struck by the anger they expressed toward the Kennedy administration for its failure to back civil rights legislation or to protect movement activists from southern racist violence. In the day, after washing and shaving in the bathtub (the only source of running water), Mike and I went out with a local black activist, LaVaughn Brown, just released from the county work farm, to go door to door in a black Jackson neighborhood and encourage its residents to register to vote. This was a tough job. The chance of a southern white official registering a local black voter approached zero. Also, Mike and I were, of course, white, and we wondered how local black people could take anything we said seriously. Plus, there was a constant danger of violence. The following summer, Medgar Evers, head of the local NAACP, was murdered in Jackson for doing just what we were doing. In these circumstances—and also because Mike was rather shell-shocked by his experience in northern Louisiana—we did not remain long in Mississippi, but instead moved on with relief to other parts of the nation.

That summer's experience "On the Road" provided a fitting culmination to my college years. To my delight, life at Columbia College had been packed with exciting and sometimes joyous experiences. Furthermore, through my reading and coursework, I had deepened my understanding of world civilization and my growing identification with its humane, liberating currents. At the same time, I came out of my socially isolated shell, seizing the opportunities for developing close personal relationships and for building a life of challenge and adventure. Going on the road meshed nicely with this new mode of existence. Overall, my college life—though apparently dominated by classes and irreverent escapades—gave me a heady whiff of possibilities for the future.

4

Graduate School, 1962–1967

My choice of the University of Wisconsin for graduate work was designed, in part, to provide me with a different sort of life than I had experienced in New York City. And it did. The university maintained a big, sprawling campus right in the middle of Madison. Although it was a fairly liberal, sophisticated city, as well as the state capital, for me it exemplified small town life with curious customs. Striding across an intersection one day when there were no cars in sight in either direction, I received a warning ticket from a local policeman, who pointed out that I had crossed against the light. (I was accustomed to the ways of the New York City police, who apparently had more dangerous things to worry about.) As sales of beer were restricted by law to people twenty-one and older, younger persons (including almost all undergraduates) drank a near-beer with a low alcoholic content. Bucky Badger, the university's mascot, was ubiquitous, with Bucky Burgers and related delights on sale everywhere. "Brat" (bratwurst) was also popular, although margarine was nonexistent—effectively banned by a state law (put into place by the powerful dairy farmers) that decreed that margarine had to be dyed a disgusting color.

Many Wisconsin students—and especially the undergraduates—displayed a lack of intellectual sophistication that I had not encountered at Columbia. The reason, I think, was that Columbia College was extremely selective in its admissions process, whereas Wisconsin simply accepted all students who graduated from state high schools and then flunked out large numbers of them during their freshman year. School football games drew enormous crowds, which were stirred up by cheerleading, band-marching extravaganzas. In the off-campus private home where I rented a single room, I socialized with three undergraduates who also roomed there, and was struck by what I saw as their small-town, provincial mind-sets. In the case of two of them, I had difficulty getting them to understand what a labor union was. Another student, about thirty years old, was a mild-mannered, innocent fellow exceptionally proud of the fact that he grew up in Appleton, Wisconsin, Joe McCarthy's home town. When I made a critical comment about McCarthy, he had no idea what I was talking about. After a month or so, when he realized that I was Jewish, he was astonished, never having met a Jew before. In fact, it presented him with a real dilemma, for although he sought to encourage my belief in God, he recognized, as he glumly told me, that if I did turn to religion, it probably would be to Judaism.

Portions of the student body, however, were considerably more sophisticated, especially those from out of state. Among Wisconsin's undergraduates, students from big cities like New York and Chicago tended to be better educated, more liberal in politics, and more likely to harbor unconventional ideas. And the graduate students were as sharp and politically conscious as any in the country. Certainly, this was true of the students enrolled in Merle Curti's graduate seminar in U.S. intellectual history. Meeting every week during the 1962–63 academic year, the Curtisians (as we called ourselves) developed friendships with one another and some degree of group cohesion. For the most part, I found them a bright, intriguing lot and hung out with a number of them. Although my friendships with them never went very deep, this reflected my brief tenure at Wisconsin rather than any sense of alienation on my part. Our discussions inside and outside of class were often interesting and lively.

At the center of the Curtisians was our teacher. In a number of ways, Curti, then sixty-five years old and nearing retirement, proved a surprise to me. Although an eminent American historian—a past president of the American Historical Association and the Organization of American Historians—he did not seem to exercise much authority in our seminar sessions. This seemed to fit his personality, for he appeared rather ethereal. In addition, having read one of his early books, *The Social Ideas of American Educators*, which had a decidedly left-wing flavor, I expected him to be politically *engagé*. But he did not seem to be. In one seminar session, when I reported on Richard Hofstadter's new book, *Anti-Intellectualism in American Life*, I criticized it for its elitist, antidemocratic thesis. Yet Curti seemed to overlook the book's annoyingly conservative tone. On another occasion, when the Curtisians gathered for a party at his home, a young woman and I, both from his seminar, sat down beside him and sought to draw him out on the reason for studying history. "Because it's interesting," he responded. "But don't you think it can help change the world?" she persisted. "No," he said, to our dismay. "It's just interesting."

Even so, I didn't fully understand or appreciate Curti at the time. Although there was certainly something detached about him, he set a tone for class discussion that allowed students to speak up and take their own ideas seriously. Furthermore, at times he did express strong opinions on current political issues—for example, on civil rights—and I am not at all sure that he studied history only because it was interesting. Having seen the nation's academic life ravaged by McCarthyism, Curti very likely had learned to be circumspect when commenting on what his profession could do to transform the world—especially when that issue was broached by a couple of graduate students he barely knew. Nevertheless, Curti directed our seminar's attention to a number of unusual issues that cried out for research by historians. During one session he pointed out that, since the publication of his book *Peace or War* in 1936, no one had written a history of the American peace movement.

Other courses I took included one with E. David Cronin on twentieth-century U.S. history, another with William Taylor on U.S. intellectual and cultural history, and yet another with William Appleman Williams on the history of U.S. foreign relations. At the time, Williams was considered one of the most controversial historians in the country, for he condemned not only the U.S. role in the Cold War, but also the entire sweep of U.S. foreign policy, which he argued was based on a drive for U.S. economic expansion. In October 1962, on the day after President Kennedy made the Cuban missile crisis public by going on television and talking of nuclear war, students poured into Williams's class to learn what he would say about it. Williams did not disappoint us, for he launched into a devastating critique of the U.S. government's position. After the class, another graduate student and I wandered over to the student union building to get a cup of coffee. Looking out at the lake, we discussed what we should be doing at this moment, when the world teetered on the brink of nuclear war. Was there some way to stop these lunatics who ruled the United States and the Soviet Union? Should we be phoning our families for final conversations? Or should we just trot off to the campus library and take care of our reading assignment? Ultimately, we headed for the library.

There were small political groups on the Wisconsin campus. *Studies on the Left* had a close association with members of the university community. In addition, a student socialist club existed, and I went to hear one or two of the talks it sponsored. There was also a conservative group on campus, and one night—when it hosted a speech by L. Brent Bozell, the son-in-law of William F. Buckley Jr. and a darling of campus conservatives—I decided to attend its meeting. After his talk, Bozell took questions, and the socialists in the crowd, smart and articulate, used this opportunity to give him a tough time. I also raised my hand, with a similar intention. Looking around a bit desperately, Bozell called on me in what I assume was the expectation of a friendlier reception, for—unlike most of the socialists—I was clean-cut and wearing a navy blazer. As I rattled off yet another hostile question, I could see the irritation wash over his face.

During my first semester at Wisconsin I missed my Columbia friends, particularly Patty. A relatively shy individual, I had plunged into a situation in which I knew no one, and although I did begin to develop friendships none was yet very strong. Nor had I worked up the nerve to ask any women out on dates—though I would have liked to. By contrast, my relationship with Patty had been flourishing by the time of my departure for Madison—and not only in terms of romance. We had many cultural tastes in common, including classical music, foreign films, art, and literature. I also found her family attractive. There was a certain charm to the relationship she had with her two sisters and to the close-knit family life she enjoyed. So, in lonely moments I often thought of her.

When I flew back to New York City in December 1962, at the beginning of the Christmas break, I saw Patty as much as I could. On a cold wintry night in early January 1963, after dinner at her house, she asked me to take the garbage out to the garage. That proved easy enough, but on my way back to the house I slipped on a patch of ice and badly twisted my ankle. I spent the night downstairs on the couch, with my ankle propped up on a pillow. The next morning a local doctor, who had initially analyzed the injury as a sprain, reported that the ankle—very badly swollen by this time—was probably broken. I was immediately rushed to the hospital, where the bone was set and a cast installed.

This new situation dramatically transformed my life in Madison. Hobbling along on crutches, with a heavy plaster cast running from my toes to the top of my thigh, I could not possibly traverse the mile or so to campus from my rented room, especially with snow on the ground and a temperature that dropped at times to thirty degrees below zero. In fact, I had a hard enough time just going up the flight of stairs to my room and went tumbling down the stairs on my first night back in Madison. As a result, I moved into the University Club—a dowdy alumni-faculty building just off campus where I could share a room and have meals in its dining room. Even so, my new life on crutches was difficult, especially on snowy days, as I trudged up the long, icy path on Bascomb Hill to my classes. I worked up such body heat in this process that eventually, despite the snow and bitter weather, I didn't bother wearing a coat. The limitations imposed by six weeks on crutches and another two weeks with a cane also cut me off from doing things with other people, and during that spring semester my life grew more solitary. The only advantage to this enforced isolation was that it gave me a lot more time to focus on writing my M.A. thesis.

As a participant in the civil rights movement, I was intrigued by the development of nonviolent resistance, a subject that thus far had received little attention from historians. Consequently, for my M.A. thesis I decided to write on nonviolent civil disobedience in the United States. The thesis focused on three incidents: the seventeenth-century Quaker "invasion" of the Puritans' Massachusetts Bay Colony, William Lloyd Garrison's championing of nonviolent resistance in the antislavery movement, and the modern civil rights struggle. With lots of extra time on my hands, I researched and wrote it that spring in about two or three months—probably a local record. On the other hand, it was not a first-rate work of scholarship. Its major importance, I think, lay in familiarizing me with the process of research in primary sources, with the preparation of a lengthy manuscript, and with past efforts to link peaceful behavior to social struggle. Curti and other faculty seemed pleased with it, and the way lay open for the receipt of my M.A. degree that June.

That same spring, Patty and I decided to get married. In April 1963 she spent a week visiting me in Madison, and we greatly enjoyed our time together. Thoughtful, intelligent, and attractive, she struck me as an ideal partner. Although I had nothing to measure my feelings for her against, I certainly believed that I was in love. Consequently, I proposed marriage—and she accepted. In retrospect, I think we rushed into things, for we were both very young and quite inexperienced with relationships. Perhaps we should have decided to try just living together. But in those days that was a very uncommon practice. Marriage was the norm, and—young and foolish—we easily slipped into it.

The marriage decision put us face to face with the problem of where to live the following academic year. Patty was inclined to have us move to New York City, where she could finish up her last two undergraduate years at Barnard College and I could study for my Ph.D. at Columbia. But by this point I was beginning to enjoy my life in Madison, so I had a slight preference for staying there, where she could finish up in the college and I could begin studying for the Ph.D. The issue was decided when the Wisconsin history department failed to award me a teaching assistantship for the following year, thus pulling the rug out from under me financially. The explanation for the department's action was that in my first semester there I had received a B in two courses. Although my other six grades were As, these first two grades, which were the only ones that appeared on my transcript in the fall, apparently counted heavily against me when it came time to distribute assistantships. Curti recognized that in my case the department was making a mistake, but there was little that he could do about it. Consequently, Patty and I chose the Barnard-Columbia option, and when I received the M.A. from Wisconsin that June, I was already back in Brooklyn, living with my parents.

Although residing in New York in the summer of 1963 enabled me to resume seeing Patty on a regular basis, it was not a pleasant time. According to the doctor who set my broken ankle, it had not healed satisfactorily, and—after hours of our waiting in his office on numerous occasions—he suggested that he break it open again and start anew. Furthermore, to earn money to support us when we returned to school in the fall, I took a job as a salesman for the All-Rite Pen Company. It turned out to be exceptionally sweaty, distasteful work. Although the pens were of a high quality, they were also relatively expensive, and I spent exhausting days trudging to a vast number of stationery stores, candy stores, drug stores, department stores, and beauty parlors in Brooklyn and Queens in a usually futile effort to convince the owners to stock them. But this experience was educational. During one of our sales meetings, our leading salesman explained that his success was based on assuring store owners that these ballpoint pens would never need a refill. I assumed that the sales manager would be horrified by this fraudulent claim. But instead he praised his salesman's cleverness. Nor were the store owners exempt from the pervasive corruption. One told me proudly how he would install a new pen refill for a customer, drop the old one on the floor, and then pick it up later for return to the company—demanding a free replacement. After a summer of this, it became pretty clear to me that the dominant business ethos was "Screw you, Mack!"

That summer, as Patty and I prepared for our wedding in late August, I began to realize that I was also acquiring a slew of relatives with whom I was not entirely comfortable. Patty's parents, for example, voted Republican. And although they were usually middle of the road in their politics, my father's employment by the New York State Commission Against Discrimination convinced them that he must be some kind of Communist. Patty's father, Joseph Sheinblatt, spent much of his time with me engaging in sophomoric jokes, such as introducing me to his relatives as "a *goy*." Her mother, Molly, though far more tactful, was quite conventional and could be domineering at times. When our families had a little get-together at the Sheinblatt home in suburban Elizabeth, New Jersey, it proved an awkward occasion. At one point, Patty's sister, Carol, broke into gales of laughter when she discovered a tiny patch on my shirt sleeve, embarrassing my mother. And most of Molly's Baltimore relatives, whom we began to see frequently, were firmly committed to the maintenance of racial segregation.

Although I noticed these disconcerting features of Patty's family, I assumed that she did not share their values. After all, in conversations with me she seemed happy enough with my opinions. But it turned out that she was deeply attached to her family members and therefore was unwilling to challenge them. Furthermore, sometimes she agreed with them. Thus, Patty usually went along with their priorities and expected me to do the same. This became clear as plans went ahead for the wedding. I soon learned that Patty's family members were planning to give us remarkably expensive sets of traditional silverware and china, which, of course, had been registered with the appropriate swanky stores. When I suggested to her that they might instead provide us with monetary gifts that would enable us to cover our next year's expenses as students, she brushed this idea aside as thoroughly unreasonable. When I suggested that we dispense with a rabbi at the wedding, she responded that her family insisted upon it.

Despite these early intimations of trouble, the wedding took place in late August 1963 in Newark. Patty's father had died a few weeks before, and for this reason, the event was almost canceled. But a local rabbi ruled that a death in the family did not preclude a marriage, so the wedding went forward. Reduced in size and splendor thanks to the death, it nonetheless went off fairly well. Mike drove us from the wedding celebration to Newark Airport, where we hopped a helicopter to a New York airport. From New York, we flew to Bermuda for our honeymoon. This provided a rather unreal, albeit pleasant, escape before returning to the New York area to begin our lives as Columbia students.

Prior to leaving, we had arranged to rent a tiny one-room apartment on West 113th Street between Broadway and Riverside Drive. In early September 1963 we moved in and set up housekeeping. For a very brief time I was the better cook, as Patty—who had grown up with a full-time maid in her family home—had never learned to prepare food. Once, when I suggested that the toast she had made seemed rather hard, she laughed at this notion, bit into it, and broke her tooth. But Patty dearly loved food and soon was turning out succulent meals that surpassed anything that I could prepare. Of course, we could not accommodate the masses of wedding gifts we had received. They included enormously expensive silverware, silver trays, china, vases, and other useless bric-a-brac—most of which was stored, for years, in her mother's attic. Patty and her family insisted that it was absolutely essential to take out heavy insurance on these and other expensive items we acquired, as well as on my life. So I did. After all, I was now married. And, as I began to realize, it was a lot easier to get married than to get unmarried.

Starting that September, I plunged into Ph.D. classes at Columbia. I took a colloquium on American social history with Carl Degler (then moonlighting from Vassar College), a course on mid-nineteenth century America with Jim Shenton, and a course on modern American political history with William Leuchtenburg, as well as two political science courses taught by the prominent scholars Wallace Sayre and Malcolm Moos. I did very well and went on to pass a written qualifying exam in March 1964 and an oral exam in December 1964. The oral exam proved the more memorable. At one point Shenton asked me a question about what U.S. legislation I considered the most important of the late nineteenth century. Taking what I thought was a clever tack, I responded that I believed it was the Pendleton Act, for that law established the civil service system and thus undermined the basis for patronage-based political parties. Later, another questioner came back to that issue, suggested another law, and commented: "That's what you meant, Jim, wasn't it?" Shenton said nothing but continued staring at the bookshelves in the room. The bewildered faculty member tried again: "I said, that's what you meant, Jim, wasn't it?" Finally, Shenton awakened abruptly from his trance (or perhaps his nap), remarking distractedly: "Yes. . . . Uh, yes."

The only exception to my smooth advance through Columbia's history Ph.D. program came in the area of languages. Faced with the requirement of passing two foreign language exams, I began with the German test—and failed it. German, with its accumulation of verbs at the end of sentences, is a difficult language, and I had taken only two years of it in high school and a summer refresher course at Columbia. Even so, this test failure came as a shock, particularly because failing the German language exam for a second time would mean being dropped from the Ph.D. program. Consequently, I went through arduous preparation for the second exam and, to my enormous relief, passed it. I also took the French language exam. Given the simpler structure of that language and the additional years I had studied it, I sailed through the test with relative ease.

Like many Columbia graduate students, I worked hard and read diligently. Along the way, I became acquainted with numerous first-rate classmates, including Gerda Lerner, then on the cusp of her brilliant career as a pioneer in the field of women's history. Perhaps because I sought to blend political concerns with my historical interests, I gravitated toward recent American political history, with Leuchtenburg as my natural adviser. At the time, Leuchtenburg was certainly one of America's most respected scholars in this area. A forthright New Deal–style liberal active in Americans for Democratic Action during his youth, he was also an impressive lecturer and a fluent, widely respected writer. Because he was a very busy person, then at the top of his profession, he did not waste much time on idle chitchat with students. But he proved to be a hardworking, tough-minded, first-rate adviser, and I learned a great deal from him.

Given the expenses of tuition at Columbia and life in New York City, I immediately cast about for part-time employment. Ultimately, during the spring of 1964, I managed to obtain my first teaching job: team-teaching a philosophy course at Adelphi University on Long Island. This proved a bizarre experience. In this "Topical Investigations Seminar," the philosophy department chair (who had hired me) engaged in a virtually nonstop, often incoherent monologue, leaving the other part-time instructor and me to listen aghast to this travesty of higher education. After a few class sessions, no longer able to bear it, I tried to intervene at points to get a genuine intellectual discussion going. But this effort was to no avail. The department chair just wouldn't stop talking, and, of course, I lacked the authority and power to tell him off. For me, it was a discouraging introduction to college teaching.

Fortunately, starting in the fall of 1964 a series of fellowships freed me from the necessity of seeking off-campus employment. Based on a competitive exam, I was awarded a New York State Regents Teaching Fellowship ($2,500 a year) from 1964 to 1966. The following year I received a Herbert Lehman Fellowship in the Social Sciences and International Affairs. Newly instituted by New York State, the Lehman fellowship was exceptionally lucrative ($5,000 a year) and exceptionally competitive. But I did extremely well on the fellowship examination, ranking among the top 1 percent of those taking the history test.

To top off the Regents Teaching Fellowship, I also worked as a reader in history for Shenton from 1964 to 1966. Perhaps because he had recommended me for a teaching position at the Manhattan School of Music that had fallen through, Shenton felt some responsibility for my economic welfare. Although the reader position did not pay very much ($500 a year), it was easy enough, for all it entailed was grading exam papers for his undergraduate course on mid-nineteenth century America. Also, I hoped it would provide a way to become better acquainted with this colorful, popular Columbia figure. Although Shenton occasionally invited me to lunch or to some other campus event, he would invariably pick up a host of friends and admirers along the way, thus diluting my contact with him. As a result, I never got to know him very well.

Despite my absorption in graduate work, I continued my keen interest in politics. Never enamored of Kennedy, I was less shaken up than were most people at Columbia by his assassination in November 1963. Indeed, I reasoned that Lyndon Johnson, as a southern Democrat with little credibility in the northern wing of the party, was more likely than Kennedy to put himself on the line for vital liberal legislation, including a civil rights bill. And I guessed right about this. In 1964, when I cast my first ballot for president, I had no hesitation voting for Johnson against the very conservative Barry Goldwater. I also began sending letters to the *Columbia Spectator* about the university's conservative policies, including its granting of an honorary degree to Greece's Queen Frederika and its embrace of CIA recruiting on campus.

Many of my political concerns focused on domestic issues. My job interview at the Manhattan School of Music brought me into East Harlem, and as I walked through its streets I found the slum conditions there deeply disturbing. Like many other New Yorkers, I was also becoming sensitized to the issue of police brutality. A citizens' review board had recently been established to investigate complaints of police violence, but the police had counterattacked by putting a proposition on the ballot to eliminate the board. Thus, one evening shortly after midnight, my sister and I—equipped with a large pot of homemade paste, a large brush, and posters—set out to plaster the walls and storefronts of the Upper East and West Side of Manhattan with the "Vote NO" message. Given the likelihood that we would receive very unfriendly treatment by the police if caught doing this, it was dangerous and exciting work. But it was not successful, for the police managed to frighten much of the city's white population into voting to abolish the review board. I also took part in my first union picket line. Having found employment as a New York City social worker, Mike suggested that I join him for his union's contract picketing outside a downtown office building. I did so and, to my amusement, my father encountered me there when he arrived at the building to begin work at his own, unrelated office.

But the Vietnam War gradually became all-absorbing. Considering U.S. policy in that conflict outrageously brutal, arrogant, and unnecessary, I was opposed to it from the start. In December 1964, I participated in a Greenwich Village rally against the war that had been called by pacifist groups and the Socialist Party. At the event I was impressed by the antiwar speeches of three aged political crusaders: pacifist leader A. J. Muste, socialist leader Norman Thomas, and civil rights leader A. Philip Randolph. In February 1965, when Johnson began the U.S. bombing of North Vietnam, Mike and I joined other antiwar protesters in picketing outside the United Nations. In the ensuing months and years, I took part in a blizzard of antiwar meetings and demonstrations. These ranged from the first Fifth Avenue Vietnam Peace Parade (an exciting venture, as we finally had enough credibility and participants to fill a street) to the massive New York City demonstration of April 15, 1967, when 125,000 peace demonstrators surged through the driving rain to the United Nations. On the latter occasion, the huge crowd, packing the broad streets from building to building, felt a sense of enormous power, for it seemed to have taken control of the city, and its antiwar chants echoed off the surrounding skyscrapers, dotted with waving and cheering bystanders.

Opposition to the war was also building up on the Columbia campus. In the spring of 1965, an all-night teach-in drew a large crowd. Even so, for a time there remained substantial numbers of prowar students at Columbia, especially among the school's athletes (the "jocks") and military men. When other antiwar activists and I went into John Jay Hall to confront the military recruiters who had set up tables there, a tough gang of military enthusiasts physically assaulted some members of our group. Some days later, in a follow-up action designed to show our determination to persist, activists organized a large peace march around Van Am Quadrangle, with appropriate antiwar chants. It was soon surrounded by a substantial number of jeering, cursing, threatening prowar students, many of them jocks. Although the Columbia authorities managed to keep the two groups apart, it was a tense situation. As I passed a group of red-faced football players, then loudly cursing us as "pukes," "commies," and "queers," I deliberately blew one of them a kiss. Flabbergasted and enraged, he almost broke through the security cordon to attack me. But time was on our side, and by 1967 campus antiwar sentiment was overwhelming.

Of course, the draft was a particular concern for antiwar activists. Although as a graduate student I was deferred from military service, I decided that if drafted I would simply go to prison. Eventually, however, I concluded that it was Lyndon Johnson and not me who should be imprisoned. Therefore, I made up my mind that if drafted I would flee to Canada. Mike, who was not shielded by a student deferment, decided that the best way for him to keep out of the war was to join the U.S. Army National Guard, which put you through six months of basic training but then left you on the home front in the reserves. This worked for him, but at a cost. When, along with Patty and Mike's mother, I visited Mike in 1964, during his basic training at Fort Dix, he looked horribly skinny and miserable. This merely confirmed for me that there was no way that I was going to serve in the armed forces.

The situation was considerably more dire for Jim, one of Mike's friends whom he met during basic training. A concert pianist, Jim recognized that reserve meetings were interfering with his career and simply stopped attending them. As a result, he was drafted. With about a month to go before his physical exam, Jim managed to get a sympathetic psychiatrist to write a letter saying that he was mentally ill. He also avoided washing, wore the same clothes every day, spilled copious quantities of food and drink on his clothing, and went without sleep for several days before the dreaded exam. Quite by accident, I called Jim the night before his exam and learned of this situation. Unwilling to abandon him in his hour of crisis, I volunteered to drive him to his draft board the next morning. When we got there, we both sat down to wait until Jim was marched off with other draftees to his physical. I waited for him hour after hour, but he didn't return. Finally, concluding that all signs pointed to his induction, I was about to leave when suddenly Jim came staggering down the stairs. With a wild look in his eyes, he simply announced "4F" (rejected for physical reasons), and we strode off for a breakfast celebration. It seems that somehow

Jim had managed to pass all the military's tests until he reached the room with the psychiatrist. Here, as the psychiatrist read his letter about mental illness, Jim really *did* start to feel sick and seemed about to vomit. That did it.

Although I was a political activist, I didn't have any specific political affiliation. Marxist-Leninist groups—with their rigid ideologies, sectarianism, and overall nastiness—had no allure for me. Increasingly attracted by the idea of democratic socialism and by the programs of European social democratic parties, I did subscribe to the Socialist Party's newspaper, *New America*. But I found it obsessed with left-wing conflicts of an earlier era and, even worse, hostile to the growing peace movement. Nor did I join Students for a Democratic Society (SDS), then the rising radical student organization. When SDS held an organizing meeting on the Columbia campus, Mike and I attended it, along with a substantial number of other students. Attempting to decide on a single project for the group, participants talked on endlessly, delivering lengthy proposals and long-winded speeches. Finally, we took a vote and, to my relief, a hefty majority agreed upon a project: opposing South African apartheid. "At last we know where we're going," someone observed. "No, quite the contrary," remarked one of the meeting's organizers. "We decide things on the basis of consensus—everyone has to agree upon it!" For many of us, this was the final straw, and we left the meeting, never to return.

Even so, given our political activism we were not exactly mainstream. This was driven home to me when in 1966, after receiving an M.A. in educational psychology, Mike became a Peace Corps volunteer. In connection with his application, a U.S. government investigator arranged to interview me. After the government agent buzzed downstairs for entry into the apartment building, I glanced rapidly around our living room to make sure that there was nothing to be seen that might give him a negative impression. And there, lying on the coffee table, lay a copy of *The Communist Manifesto!* Patty had left it there because it was an assigned course reading at the high school where she taught English. I realized that it had to go, and just as the investigator knocked on the apartment door, I tossed it behind some books on the bookshelf. During the ensuing interview, the investigator focused his questions on Mike's civil rights work, which I discussed in the blandest, most acceptable way possible. Very cautious by this point, I didn't say anything about Mike's role as an antiwar activist.

What would government officials have thought if they had known more about us? They certainly would have been startled if they had seen me, not long after this, at the play *Paradise Now!* Performed by Julian Beck and Judith Malina's Living Theatre and staged at the Brooklyn Academy of Music, this was definitely the most avant-garde piece of theater I had ever seen or, more accurately, participated in. In this work of revolutionary art, the actors and actresses quickly drew the entire audience into a tumultuous upheaval. Sometimes, in fact, the play got quite out of hand, with women screaming that they had been sexually assaulted—though it was impossible to tell whether such claims were real or merely part of the performance. When the directors needed to cool things off, they herded the frenzied crowd into a few piles, where we chanted "Ommmmmmmmmmm" and gradually quieted down. *Paradise Now!* concluded as the actors and audience, stirred to action, surged into the streets, presumably to make a revolution.

During these years, a number of my old friendships continued. After two years as a naval officer, Charlie Nadler returned to Columbia, along with his rather strange, spacey wife, Susan, as a philosophy graduate student. Discarding his earlier conservative views, Charlie was swept up in the tide of New Left thought and protest, and, not surprisingly, we got on better than in the past. My cousin, Daniel Zwanziger, also returned to New York, where he took up a postdoctoral fellowship in physics at New York University after living abroad in France and elsewhere. I had always liked Daniel, and during my college years, when he was a Columbia graduate student, we had socialized on occasion. Now his new, bearded, sandal-wearing, cosmopolitan ambiance was particularly attractive to me. Shortly after the two of us attended one of the massive protest marches against the war, Daniel phoned to tell me to pick up the *New York Times*. There in the magazine section was a photo of us—Daniel looking a bit like Leon Trotsky and I more clean-cut—waiting for the march to begin.

Mike also joined me for demonstrations, as well as for zanier ventures. Before his departure for the Peace Corps, we decided to go off on a camping trip and, drawing on a book about edible wild plants, survive by living off the land. On our first afternoon in the woods, we grew increasingly desperate, for almost none of the plants could be found. But in a local pond we did spot water lilies, and our book assured us that water lily roots, once properly cooked, made excellent food. So, plunging into the water, we swam out to them, knives in our teeth, on our foraging mission. Tearing them up from the mucky pond bottom, we noticed that they had a disgusting smell. But hope remained as we grilled them over our camp fire and placed a pat of margarine (our one concession to civilization) on their crispy brown exteriors. Alas, they tasted just as bad as they smelled. Spitting out our first bites, we went to bed hungry, and the next day we returned to civilization for a good meal.

I also made some new friends. Thanks to a study group formed to prepare for the History Department's qualifying exams, I became acquainted with Sydney Weinberg, a very bright, savvy young woman who somehow had managed to give birth to two children during her college years at Barnard. Another member of the study group with whom I became friendly was Steve Klein. An intellectually sophisticated graduate student, he married Sue Yakubian, who, like Steve, had a very respectable style. Typically, nothing stopped Sydney, who wrote her dissertation, received her Ph.D., and went on to become a college history teacher. But for some reason Steve found it impossible to write his dissertation. To everyone's surprise, he ended up without the Ph.D. and eventually prepared exams for Educational Testing Service.

My friendship with Derek and Barbara Wittner had a strange genesis. There weren't many Wittners in the United States, so when Patty and I spotted the name Wittner on a mailbox in our apartment building, we took note of it. One day we met them at the building's mailboxes, and it proved an eerie experience. Derek, who attended Columbia Law School, had, like me, been born and raised in New York City. Six feet tall, slender, and brown haired, he also looked something like me and enjoyed playing folk songs on the guitar. Although he was two years younger than I was, he had a brother named Loren, who was approximately my age. Both our fathers were lawyers, though neither practiced law at the time, and both lived and worked in New York. Furthermore, both Patty and Barbara were then Barnard students, having transferred into the college. Given the fact that Derek and Barbara lived in #23 and Patty and I lived in #43, we sometimes received one another's mail, and, as Derek noted with amusement, it often came from the same political groups. Although we never managed to figure out whether or not we were related, we did have a lot in common, and sometimes we went out to dinner or attended antiwar demonstrations together.

I also kept in touch with Mike, then serving as a Peace Corps volunteer in Chile, and managed once more to get him into trouble. Acquainting him with political and other developments in the United States, I sent him some materials about Negotiations Now!, a moderate antiwar venture headed by Martin Luther King Jr. that called for a negotiated settlement of the Vietnam War. One of its early projects was a newspaper advertisement that was scheduled to appear in the *New York Times,* signed by thousands of Americans. Beginning in the spring of 1967, Mike and twelve other Peace Corps workers mailed out the ad proposal to every Peace Corps volunteer in Chile in an effort to obtain signatures. As a result, the organizers were called in by U.S. Ambassador Ralph Dungan, and—as Mike recalled—told that the ambassador "had just gotten off the phone with LBJ, who was livid with anger that *his* Peace Corps volunteers should be protesting his war! Then he told us that, as U.S. government employees, we had no right to protest U.S. policy" and "threatened us with expulsion from the Peace

Corps." The organizers stood their ground, though, pointing out that they had not given up their rights as U.S. citizens, and if there were 100 or more signers they would submit the Peace Corps names for publication. Ultimately, despite the efforts of Peace Corps staffers to intimidate the volunteers, some 120 of them signed the advertisement, although their rebellion drew less public attention than they would have liked.

Other political developments affected my family. As the civil rights movement progressed and new antidiscrimination legislation was enacted, my father's career moved forward. After all, he was one of a small number of people in the nation who had some practical experience in handling complaints of discrimination and resolving them. In recognition of his expertise, he had been named a senior field representative at the New York State Commission Against Discrimination in 1958. But this was only a modest promotion. His experience and abilities received more appropriate recognition in August 1963, when he was hired as director of investigations at the New York City Commission on Human Rights, headed by Eleanor Holmes Norton. Here he directed a staff of nine persons who enforced the municipal code forbidding discrimination in employment, public accommodations, education, and housing. During these same years, the New School for Social Research suggested that he teach a course on the enforcement of civil rights law, and he spent considerable time preparing for it. Unfortunately, however, an insufficient number of students signed up for the course and it was canceled.

Meanwhile, on February 28, 1964, my mother suddenly died of a heart attack. Recognizing the first symptoms, she had phoned my father at his Manhattan office and he had succeeded in getting her regular doctor, located nearby, to race to their house. But the doctor proved unable to revive her. Given her fragile health, caused by her lengthy bout with Cushing's Syndrome, her death did not come as a total surprise. From my standpoint—and perhaps the standpoint of others as well—it was even something of a relief. The real tragedy lay in the illness that struck her a decade before, blighting her existence and, indirectly, ours. Although undereducated and limited to the roles of stenographer and housewife by the prevalent assumptions about women, she was regarded for most of her life as an intelligent and very likeable person. In later years, relatives would tell me how shocked they were when they met her after the onset of the sickness, particularly because in the past they had always found her so beautiful, sweet-tempered, and charming. I remember her that way, too, but, alas, also in her later, far less attractive and more difficult incarnation.

Somewhat to my surprise, in July 1965, at the age of fifty-seven, my father remarried. His new wife, Marjorie Levy, was a fifty-four-year-old widow whom he had met in the spring of 1964 as he sought to arrange for my sixteen-year-old sister, Debbie, to attend a summer camp run by the Ethical Culture Society. After my father left the room, Marjie turned to her colleagues and told them: "That's the man for me!" With this in mind, Algernon Black, the leader of the New York Ethical Culture Society, arranged for my father to speak about intergroup relations at a committee meeting of the organization, and he saw to it that Marjie was the only committee member present. After that, everything fell into place.

Marjie turned out to be a terrific person, and—particularly after my mother's long, depressing illness—just what my father needed. Short, dark-haired, and attractive, she was an exceptionally good-natured, dynamic individual who quickly drew my relatively sedate father into everything from folk dancing to the social concerns committee of the New York Ethical Culture Society. Often eccentric, she liked to mix together leftovers, so that you never knew when she would serve you a weird concoction of chopped green beans, meat, and nuts or of peaches and spinach. ("That's not bad, is it?" she would ask with a wacky smile.) She was also a classic fellow-traveler—a person who, while not a member of the Communist Party, thought the Soviet Union was in the vanguard of world progress and that capitalism (especially of the U.S. variety) lay behind most significant problems. Yet, she was such a likeable, bubbly person that even this political quirk was more amusing than annoying.

After their marriage, Marjie moved in with my father in Brooklyn. But within a short time they sold that house and relocated to a large cooperative apartment on the West Side of Manhattan, on West 90th Street, off Riverside Drive. I was happy for them and enjoyed visiting with them at their new residence, which was only about a mile and a half away from mine. My sister, who lived with them in the apartment, clashed repeatedly with Marjie. Hard hit by my mother's illness, Debbie was also a rebellious teenager. In addition, she harbored resentment toward Marjie, who tried to exercise some authority over her. Although bright and attractive, Debbie was often sullen, filled with complaints, and dissatisfied with her studies at Brooklyn College. At one point Marjie and my father suggested that I speak with her, but I didn't make much headway. To some degree Debbie idolized me as an academically successful big brother, but she also felt jealous and resentful of me.

Debbie might have envied me less if she had realized how badly my marriage was going. Just as I was becoming more alienated from the mainstream, Patty was becoming more conventional. When she insisted that I wear nothing less than a suit on an airplane flight, I refused to do so and she threw a fit. When she and her mother bought dining room chairs for our apartment, they turned out to be amazingly uncomfortable, spindly little things. She insisted that they were wonderful antiques, to which I countered that I wanted chairs on which I could sit comfortably. Although she lost on this issue, too, she didn't let me forget it. Also, despite my long-term loathing for television (dating back to my reading of *1984*), she secretly conspired with my father and Marjie to install their old television set in our apartment. When I came home after classes one evening, there it was, to my intense irritation.

Furthermore, Patty's family continued to pull her—and through her, tug me—toward their view of success. As I reached the verge of being awarded a Ph.D., her mother suggested that she would be happy to fund my attendance at medical school. I did not miss the fact that this offer devalued all my graduate studies, as well as my clear preferences. Visits to Baltimore were a particular ordeal. I would hardly get through the door before her southern relatives would begin baiting me about civil rights. During these discussions, Patty remained aloof; after them, she complained to me that I was arguing too much with her family. Sometimes the situations approached the surreal. To show us a good time, her Baltimore relatives would take us to their posh country club—where the membership was confined to white people and the service to African Americans. Occasionally, I would lose sight of my car in the club's parking lot, for it was a small, unwashed, foreign model buried by glittering Cadillacs.

Clearly, our priorities were diverging. In my case, my childhood as an outsider, my extensive reading, and my interaction with the contemporary crises of race and war were turning me into a rebel. In Patty's case, her comfortable background, rooted in her family, was pulling her in the opposite direction. Beyond this, I think, lay the fact that in a society rigged to the advantage of the wealthy and of men, Patty based her personal success on acquiring property, gaining luster from associating with the powerful, and making a "good" marriage. For a short time, I seemed like a reasonably good catch: a clean-cut Ivy League student on his way to becoming a renowned college professor at one of the "best" universities. But as my dissident, unconventional qualities emerged, our relationship grew more problematic.

My choice of dissertation topic provided yet one more sign of my unorthodox nature. For a time, I floundered about, exploring a number of possibilities. But none seemed especially interesting or new. Then suddenly I remembered Curti's remark about the absence of a history of the U.S. peace movement since 1936. And he was right. Although scholars had written about a few specific aspects of the movement's history—for example, the treatment of conscientious objectors during World War II—none had put things together into a comprehensive account. Furthermore, in the midst of an escalating anti–Vietnam War movement, here was a subject that was genuinely exciting—one that melded historical scholarship with a hot contemporary political issue. In addition, the files of numerous peace groups—many of them never examined—were available at the Swarthmore College Peace Collection. When I suggested to Leuchtenburg that I write my dissertation on the American peace movement from 1941 to 1960, he replied that that sounded like an excellent idea. By the spring of 1965, I was off and running.

I loved doing the research. Life at Swarthmore College was a bit of a dream. Unlike noisy, grimy New York City, Swarthmore was a quiet, verdant oasis. Leaving my quaint housing on the campus, I strolled across the ample lawns, glancing at the ancient trees and beautiful female students on my way to the campus library. Here I settled down to plowing through the records of groups like the War Resisters League, the Fellowship of Reconciliation, the Women's International League for Peace and Freedom, and SANE, as well as their periodicals. At first I had no context for the masses of material, for there were no published accounts of the movement's history and few published descriptions of its leaders. Gradually, however, the pieces of the puzzle began to fall into place. I saw that what I was working on was nothing less than the missing link between the mass peace movement of the 1930s and its revival in the 1960s. Two factors struck me as particularly important in this connection (and still do): the development of nonviolent resistance and the advent of nuclear weapons.

Conducting interviews was also a delight. Although I had a very poor sense of what questions to ask, I spoke with some very interesting people. They included the brilliant and radical A. J. Muste, then the senior leader of American pacifism and a key figure in the burgeoning antiwar movement. Given my democratic socialist inclinations, it was also a thrill to have the opportunity to interview Norman Thomas. Unfortunately, however, he was then in his eighties, and when I entered his office I was disconcerted to find this once handsome, urbane, and dignified hero of mine snoring at his desk with his mouth hanging open. Another interview I conducted was with Dave Dellinger, a leading radical pacifist since World War II. After meeting at the office of the War Resisters League in a seedy area of Manhattan, we decided to grab some dinner at a nearby Chinese restaurant. On our walk there, a panhandler stopped us and Dellinger gave him some money. Continuing our stroll, I told Dellinger, rather smugly, that I hadn't done the same because I believed in justice rather than in charity. Dellinger replied that over the years he had come around to believing in both. Gradually, so have I.

At Leuchtenburg's suggestion, I also interviewed Mercedes Randall, one of the founders of the Women's International League for Peace and Freedom

(WILPF). While her husband, John Herman Randall Jr., a distinguished philosopher at Columbia, worked away on a manuscript in an adjoining room, she regaled me with stories of opposition to World War I and of WILPF's ensuing history. Near the end of our discussion, she turned the tables. "Why aren't students doing more to protest the Vietnam War?" she demanded. "Why aren't they out there in the streets?" I replied that there was growing student resistance to the war, especially around Columbia, but she remained dissatisfied with the extent of student protest. Walking back to my apartment, I could not help but admire her pluck and steadfast determination, as I generally did the attributes of the older generation of peace activists. They were very inspiring people.

As I pulled my research together, it seemed that if I made a supreme effort I might finish writing the dissertation in time to graduate in May 1967, after which I could begin full-time teaching. Overly confident that my writing would require no alteration, I typed up the first two chapters for Leuchtenburg using the official university format. When he returned them to me, I was crestfallen, for his red-penned corrections covered nearly every page. Even so, I bounced back from this rebuff to my youthful hubris and worked at a frantic pace. At one point that spring, I completed five chapters in four weeks. Greatly impressed, Leuchtenburg later remarked upon my ability to produce high quality work at an extraordinarily rapid pace. In fact, I managed to turn in the completed dissertation in time for its successful defense—an exam by its faculty readers—in early May.

The only problem I had was filing the dissertation with the university. Holding the required five copies of it in my arms, I entered an enormous room in Low Library, to which I had been directed. I went up to a secretary, then chewing gum and chatting with a friend of hers on the telephone, and asked where I should deposit them. Barely glancing at me, she waved vaguely in the direction of one of the walls. There I saw enormous piles of dissertations. However, as this was my last step before getting the degree, I wanted to make sure I did the right thing. So I went back to the secretary, still chatting on the phone, and asked, pointing toward the wall: "Over there?" "Yes," she shouted, "over there!" And so, in my parting gesture after eight years at Columbia and twenty-two years at educational institutions, I dumped the copies of my dissertation onto one of the piles. I was done!

Well, not quite. I also needed to find a job. Writing nonstop that spring, I did not have much time to devote to job hunting. But I did learn that a position as an assistant professor of history was open at Hampton Institute, an African American college in Virginia. Unlike most colleges, Hampton did not seem to interview job applicants at the conventions of the major historical organizations or on its campus. Instead, its president, Jerome Holland, met with candidates at his hotel room in New York City. I was interviewed that spring and, to my delight, was offered the position. To me, as a former civil rights activist, teaching at a school with a largely black faculty and an almost entirely black student body was perfectly in line with my values. And the salary ($8,500 a year) was quite reasonable. Patty's family members, I think, were less pleased with this position, and once they realized the racial composition of the college they avoided mentioning it. I later learned that an uncle of hers in Baltimore boasted to one of his African American store employees that I was about to become a professor at Hampton Institute, only to have his employee tell him, to his dismay, that his nephew was a student there.

In June 1967 Columbia's graduation ceremonies brought together these disparate currents. To celebrate my receipt of the Ph.D., both Patty's family and mine were on hand. And it proved a large, impressive event, full of the traditional pomp that marked centuries of academic life. However, by this time outside issues like the Vietnam War, racism, and urban poverty had become so salient that they could no longer be ignored. SDS leafleted the ceremonies. Parents openly worried that their sons would be drafted. Even Columbia's aloof, establishment-oriented president, Grayson Kirk, called attention to the costs of the war and to the unraveling of American life. Yet the exceptionally timid nature of Kirk's remarks, coming on top of his earlier scolding of faculty and students for their outspoken criticism of the war, merely reinforced my conviction that the university president was a hypocritical, pompous ass. Attending Columbia had been immensely liberating. But I was convinced that the people who ran it—like the people who governed the United States—were basically elitists unwilling to come to grips with deep-seated problems of war and privilege.

As I departed from Columbia, I had a different agenda. For years I had been drawn toward the idea of changing the world. But as the 1960s progressed two social movements added appreciably to this commitment: the campaign for racial equality and the revolt against the Vietnam War. Deeply stirred by these struggles, as well as by their leaders and supporters, I increasingly felt part of a community of heroic, wonderful people. Intellectually interesting, morally beautiful, and intensely alive, they had won my heart.

5

A Young Faculty Member, 1967–1972

In September 1967 I began my first full-time college teaching position at Hampton Institute in Hampton, Virginia. Founded in 1868 by U.S. General Samuel Chapman Armstrong, whose troops garrisoned the Virginia Tidewater region during Reconstruction, Hampton began as a school for newly freed slaves. Over the years, Booker T. Washington and many other prominent African Americans attended Hampton. When I started teaching there, it had a student body of more than 2,000 (99 percent of it black) and a faculty of over 300 (about two-thirds of it black). The campus was large and fairly modern. Nevertheless, although Hampton was one of the nation's top black colleges, it reminded me of the Southern black campus portrayed so devastatingly in Ralph Ellison's *Invisible Man*. Its black administrators and many of its senior black faculty were very cautious and prided themselves on their respectability and social conservatism. Its black students were often restless with this accommodation to white southern and white American mores but not quite sure what to do about it. And there was a significant third constituency, comprised of young white (and a few black) faculty—new Ph.D.s from northern and western universities, where they had often been in the vanguard of civil rights and antiwar protests.

Of course, I was part of the third group, which proved an interesting one. As veterans of campus and other protest campaigns, we had gravitated easily to jobs at a southern black college. But it was not easy to figure out what, aside from teaching, we should be doing there. After all, we were almost entirely white and did not want to offend more conservative black faculty or increasingly separatist, Black Power–oriented students. For the most part, we found ourselves allied with the students, but race did serve sometimes as a dividing line, especially for them. Meeting on numerous occasions, we tied ourselves up in theoretical and practical knots over what we should do. Ultimately, like the Columbia SDS group, we failed to make any decision along these lines but simply drifted into things on an ad hoc basis.

Given our common values, we got along well. There was Sandy Hughes, one of the few southern whites, who had taught at Hampton longer than the rest of us and clearly had left-wing politics. Another was Bob Heifitz (a son of the famed violinist), who had just arrived in Hampton and who hosted our early meetings. I also became friendly with Norman Hodges, a young black history Ph.D. from Detroit who probably had the most upper-class background among us. And there was also young Mike Hillinger, a new political scientist on the faculty. But Howie Schonberger soon topped the list of my new friends. A tall, somewhat awkward, gangly-looking fellow, Howie grew up in a left-wing Jewish family in Chicago and had studied history at Wisconsin with William Appleman Williams. Newly arrived at Hampton—along with his Wisconsin-born wife (Ann), one small child, and another on the way—Howie was good-natured, unpretentious, and laughed easily. I could not have found a better friend in this novel and rather strange environment.

The city of Hampton was particularly odd and in certain ways threatening. Billing itself as the "Oldest Continuous Anglo-Saxon Settlement in America," Hampton was a white-dominated, racially segregated city that had little respect for Hampton Institute. Patty and I became well aware of that during the summer of 1967, when we drove down there to line up housing for the coming fall. After a real estate agent showed us an apartment in a small development right across the Hampton River from campus, we decided to take it and returned to his office to handle the paperwork. I was checking out the lease while the agent looked over my completed questionnaire. Suddenly he stopped me. "Oh, I see you'll be teaching at Hampton Institute," he said with a troubled note in his voice. "We've never rented before to anyone from Hampton." "Well, you will now," I said, rapidly losing confidence in that statement even as I made it. "Do you think you'll have colored guests?" he asked. "That's a good possibility," I responded, pointing out the heavily black composition of the place. "Well," he said, "I'd better call the owner to make sure it's still available." With his departure, Patty—her eyes wide—asked me what was going on. I explained that, for racist reasons, it looked like we were about to be told that it was already rented. And when the agent returned, that's what happened. "Are you rejecting us on racial grounds?" asked Patty, still incredulous. "Oh *no*," he said. "We'll be glad to keep you on the list for the next apartment that opens up." "Don't bother," I said, and we walked out.

Eventually, we did find housing in the city, but not because local whites wanted to make it available. Robert McNamara, as U.S. secretary of defense, had issued an order designating segregated housing facilities as off-limits to U.S. military personnel. This meant that in the Tidewater region of Virginia, where there were several large military bases, the bigger housing developments had to drop the color bar if they were going to continue to rent to military employees. Thus, Patty and I managed to rent an apartment in one of these developments. Even there, however, my teaching at Hampton Institute continued to provide a source of bewilderment. The white woman who staffed the front office of the development once said to Patty: "Doctah Wittnah seems lahk such a nahs mayan. Wah'd he evuh take a jahb at Haampton Instahtute?"

Everywhere we turned it seemed racism permeated the local culture. Applying for secondary school teaching jobs, Patty learned at the interview stage that in a segregated society she was the wrong color. Indeed, an administrator of one black school to which she applied was very nervous about her presence and got her out of the building as quickly as he could. Once, as she waited in an automobile showroom for our car, then being serviced in another section of the building, she overheard a particularly striking conversation between a black army sergeant and a white auto salesman. Buying a car partially on credit, the sergeant filled out the appropriate form until he came to the question of color. "Which color do you want," the sergeant asked, "mine or the car's?" "Yours," replied the salesman. Then he added with an awkward laugh: "I guess they don't ask your color in Vietnam, do they?" The sergeant just scowled and went back to the form.

Patty adapted the best she could to the circumstances. Giving up on finding a teaching job, she enrolled in Hampton Institute's graduate program in guidance and counseling. This turned out to be an excellent choice, for by the end of the following summer she had her M.A. degree in that field, thereby giving her the necessary credentials for her subsequent career as a guidance counselor. Even so, life at Hampton Institute and in Hampton, Virginia, was not quite what she had in mind when she married me, and she felt frustrated by it. When was I going to live up to my potential and get us both out of there, perhaps to Harvard? During this time, she acquired printed stationery, some of it headed "Dr. and Mrs. Lawrence Wittner" and the balance headed "Mrs. Lawrence S. Wittner." But it wasn't getting her very far.

Like other Hampton faculty members, I taught four courses in the fall and another four in the spring. As I had never taught a history course before, preparing for classes kept me pretty busy. Yet for the most part I enjoyed teaching at Hampton. Although many of the students—having attended segregated southern schools or inferior northern ones—had limited educational backgrounds, there was something exciting about the fact that for many of them I was opening up new areas of knowledge. Conversing with a student in my office, I suddenly realized that he had never heard of Freud, and I had the pleasure of outlining that pioneering psychiatrist's life and theories for him. It was also interesting to talk with African American students about racism. As one of my courses progressed, it must have become clear that I was one of the least threatening whites they would encounter. Consequently, one female student suddenly raised her hand in the middle of a class session and asked me: "Professor Wittner, why are white people so uptight about race?" It was a tough question to answer, but it was good to be confronting it.

Meanwhile, I began revising my dissertation for publication as a book by Columbia University Press. Writing to me, Leuchtenburg—who had a great deal of influence with this publisher—first suggested the book possibility. Naturally, I leaped at the opportunity. Book publication would give me a way to get the results of my pioneering research on the American peace movement out to historians and to the broader public. And it would also bolster my academic credentials—though I think the administration at Hampton was already happy enough with me to continue my employment there. Thus in my spare time I worked at putting additional material into the dissertation, particularly in the form of an epilogue that would bring the story of the peace movement up to the tumultuous present. And I also sought to sharpen the manuscript's theoretical and political framework.

Another scholarly project began when I learned that a MacArthur memorial, housing many of General Douglas MacArthur's papers, had just opened up in nearby Norfolk, Virginia. As Howie Schonberger was Hampton's U.S. foreign policy historian and I was its twentieth-century U.S. historian, this material sounded appealing to us, so we piled into Howie's old jalopy and set off to see what we could find. The memorial, located in Norfolk's former city hall, had been built to celebrate this famous military officer, and there one could view his staff car, his "scrambled eggs" cap, and other MacArthur memorabilia. MacArthur's papers were not as interesting, at least in terms of public policy. One reason—as we learned years later—was that members of the Bataan Gang (the general's World War II cronies), who dominated the board of the memorial, had insisted that the archivist remove any controversial material and hide it in his safe. Even so, amid the mass of fan mail available I found interesting correspondence regarding the role of religion in the occupation of Japan. And this led in later years to several publications of mine on the occupation and on MacArthur. Howie, too, became intrigued by what he found, and for decades he painstakingly added to it until in 1988 he finally came out with his very incisive study of the occupation, *Aftermath of War*.

My scholarly research, particularly on the peace movement, was especially germane as the Vietnam War and accompanying draft calls escalated. In the fall semester I wrote a short article, "On Conscientious Objection," for the campus newspaper, the *Hampton Script*. Discussing the history of war and conscientious objection, it mentioned that Martin Luther King Jr. and Julian Bond had recently urged black college students to apply for C.O. status. I added my own recommendation to theirs, concluding: "By becoming a C.O., you will be signifying to the military and political rulers of all nations that you are pulling out of history's age-old death march, and that you have made your peace with mankind." That spring the editors reprinted the article.

In March 1968, when plans were announced for representatives of the U.S. Army, Navy, Air Force, and the local draft board to speak to a campus assembly, students demanded that I address it as well. So I did. It was a tense evening, with an audience of about 150 students. Howie later told me that seeing me seated at the speakers' table, surrounded by military officers, he felt a stomach ache coming on. But he needn't have worried, for the students gave the military recruiters a remarkably tough time of it. The *Hampton Script* reported in apparent amusement that there had been "a very interesting discussion, to say the least." Lots of questions were directed to me and to the panel about C.O. status and about other forms of resistance to the military.

As nationwide protest against the Vietnam War surged, so did activism among students and the younger faculty. In the fall of 1967 a group of us traveled north to participate in the tumultuous march on the Pentagon. Waving banners and chanting slogans, tens of thousands of us poured onto the Pentagon grounds and surrounded the nerve center of the U.S. military command, guarded by U.S. troops with fixed bayonets. The vast sweep of the scene provided a stunningly eerie panorama symbolic of the war then tearing the nation apart.

The thought of Johnson, director of the war and betrayer of Great Society promises, running again for president in 1968—accompanied by the loathsome Nixon for the Republicans and the racist George Wallace on a third-party ticket—was deeply repulsive to me, as it was to many Americans of the time. Consequently, some of us picked up the idea, voiced in peace and social justice movement circles, of backing a Martin Luther King Jr.–Benjamin Spock ticket for the presidency and vice presidency. As a Peace and Freedom Party (PFP) was emerging to make this campaign a reality, Howie and I and a couple of other young Hampton faculty decided to get the PFP organized in Virginia. This was not an easy task. According to state law, to get on the ballot we needed not only 1,000 signatures from registered voters, but also persons willing to serve as PFP electors from every county in Virginia. And some of these counties were solid

Ku Klux Klan country. Nevertheless, through patient travels around the state, we built local PFP chapters, found persons willing to serve as electors, and laid plans for our petition drive.

Then, in April 1968 King was assassinated. I learned of it during a dinner with friends at our apartment, when I received a frantic phone call from Mike Hillinger. Greatly agitated, he began: "Martin Luther is dead." I started to make a joke about the sixteenth-century Protestant leader but suddenly realized what had happened. The news immediately cast a pall over the gathering, which quickly dissolved as people headed home to brood. Early the next morning, when we learned that Hampton students planned a protest march through the city that same day, Patty and I decided to join them. Although we had no idea what kind of reception we—as whites—would have from this crowd of angry black students, in a nation swept by black rioting all across the country, we were relieved to find that we were welcomed to the ranks of the march. Composed of thousands of black students and a handful of whites, it wound its way through the streets of Hampton, deserted (apparently in fear) by the local white populace.

King's last project had been the Poor People's Campaign—an effort to mobilize thousands of the nation's poorest people, of all colors—to march on Washington and then camp out there in full display of their misery, thus symbolizing the nation's disgraceful treatment of its most impoverished citizens. With one feeder march of the Poor People's campaign slated to come through our region in May 1968, our group of campus activists worked on local preparations for it. Ironically, this often meant that young white faculty prodded some of the more complacent, older black faculty to assume leadership roles. Howie and I did this in the case of the black chair of the college's social science division, and he later thanked us profusely when his mother, informed of his newfound activist status, told him tearfully that she always knew he would live up to her hopes for him. We whites took on lowlier tasks, such as serving as marshals for the march when it came through Norfolk. Although our job was to see to it that gangs of white racists were prevented from attacking the march, everything, in fact, went smoothly and colorfully as thousands of southern poor people, many wearing raggedy clothes and driving mules, poured through the downtown streets. I can still remember the fried chicken, mashed potato, and cornbread dinner served to delighted marchers and marshals alike that evening in a local black church.

That June U.S. government agencies began spying on me. Chester Goldstein, a student at Brandeis University, had returned for the summer to his hometown of Newport News and had asked me to accompany him to the nearby Selective Service office in downtown Hampton. Chester wanted some help copying down the names of young men who had been classified 1A—which under the draft law had to be publicly posted—so that he could mail them information about that law's provisions for conscientious objector status. Accordingly, on June 18 we went to the draft board office and asked the clerk where the 1A lists were posted. She directed us to the hallway, where we began copying down the names. Within a short time, a well-dressed man came up to us and, claiming to be a local postal worker, asked us what we were doing. When we explained, he professed to be delighted, for, he said, he was a Quaker. Growing chatty, he drew us out on where we lived and what our occupations were. At the time, I didn't pay much attention to this colloquy, as our actions were perfectly legal and I thought beyond reproach. Nonetheless, years later, when I obtained portions of my FBI file under the Freedom of Information Act, I learned that our new friend actually worked for U.S. Army Intelligence and had been alerted by the draft board clerk.

He filed an extensive report on us with the FBI, which, among other things, made me sound much bigger (and thus more threatening) than I was: possibly, he warned, six foot four and 190 pounds. Thereafter, the local FBI office assumed major responsibility for my case—gathering information about me from its "source" at Hampton Institute, producing a garbled version of my article in the *Hampton Script,* and then turning the ongoing investigation over to the FBI office in Poughkeepsie, where I would be moving that fall to begin teaching at Vassar College.

The Vassar job emerged thanks to the fact that Carl Degler, chair of the history department at that institution, was looking for a twentieth-century U.S. historian and remembered me from the seminar at Columbia that he had taught a few years before. In the spring of 1968, when I drove up to the Vassar campus for an interview, Degler asked me if I found it unsettling to be at a women's college. I responded that I was more unsettled by the fact that almost everyone seemed to be white. In fact, though, I was impressed by the school's bucolic charm, by its relative closeness to New York City (which I still viewed as the center of the universe), and (I confess) by its academic prestige. By contrast, Hampton Institute was a fairly homely place, located in the small-town, racist, reactionary South. How long did I really want to live there? Moreover, in the context of the growing demand within the African American community for Black Power, I wondered whether there was still a useful role for white faculty to play on black campuses. Thus, when I was offered the Vassar job, I accepted it.

When I mentioned my plan to leave Hampton to Sandy Hughes, he reproached me, asking: "Why do you want to go teach rich white women?" At the time, I was taken aback by his implicit rebuke. In retrospect, though, I think that I should have given more thought to my decision.

During the summer of 1968, as Patty and I laid plans for our return to the North, I had no teaching responsibilities, but I found plenty to do. This included lots of writing and putting our PFP venture over the top. King's tragic death disheartened and disorganized our small group of activists for a time. But gradually we regrouped behind a Dick Gregory–Benjamin Spock ticket and began petitioning for ballot status.

Fortunately, a wonderful contingent of lively young American Friends Service Committee work campers, both black and white, had arrived in the area and volunteered to help out with the petitioning in their spare time. As we were very grateful, I suggested that in the late afternoon, after they finished the petition work, they come over to our apartment development, where they could swim in the lake and dig into a steak dinner that we would prepare for them. However, local realities intervened. While Patty and I were upstairs in our apartment preparing the dinner, one of the work campers tore in to tell us that the police were about to arrest them at the lake. I raced downstairs to find that the situation was even worse than he reported. There was not only a fully armed policeman on the scene, barely restraining a vicious German shepherd on a chain, but also a mob of local white people looking on in a very ugly fashion. I did my best to explain to the policeman that these were my guests and that I had set them up at the lakefront (which I had). However, this explanation went nowhere in the startling context of an interracial group of high school boys and girls having a good time together on the beach. Although the policeman could point to the fact that there was a little sign at the site saying "No Swimming," everyone knew that this inexplicable prohibition was ignored every day by residents of the development (including me). With a very bad scene shaping up, the kids and I made a rapid decision to get off the beach and up to my apartment. And we had a good dinner together, with a lot of joking around about our confrontation with southern justice.

In the fall of 1968 I began teaching at Vassar College. Founded in 1861 as one of the first women's colleges in the United States, Vassar began as an avant-garde institution. By the late 1960s, however, it seemed rather old-fashioned. Most women preferred to attend coeducational institutions. Furthermore, the campus was located in the small, somewhat depressed city of Poughkeepsie, New York, where very little of a cultural or intellectual nature occurred. The politics of surrounding Dutchess County were of a humdrum, Republican nature, although in recent years they had been enlivened by a right-wing, law-and-order, gun-toting assistant district attorney named G. Gordon Liddy, who headed up Nixon's 1968 campaign in the county and was rewarded with a job in Washington. Also, Vassar's traditions had acquired a dated, genteel, upper-class quality and weighed heavily against innovations in teaching and research. Before I arrived there, Alan Simpson, an English historian brought in as president, sought to modernize the place along fairly conventional lines, but his first great venture—merging Vassar with Yale—was blocked by the irate alumnae.

Even so, Vassar had a number of things going for it. The campus was quite beautiful, with lots of trees, shaded lawns, and old, interesting buildings. And many of the people were beautiful and interesting as well. The nation's upper class and the upper middle class that emulated it—two constituencies from which most of Vassar's student body was drawn—received the best dental care, health care, food, cosmetics, and education that money could buy, and their clothing, even when quite casual, invariably enhanced their appearance. It was quite pleasant—although a bit surreal—to join these handsome, charming, intelligent students in the Gold, Silver, or Diamond Room after dinner, as we sprawled on Victorian furniture or on the Oriental rug and sipped demitasse from gold-rimmed cups.

Though this seemed cloying at times, there *was* a new excitement to the place. Some of this excitement came from the admission of the first male students on a transfer basis and in 1969 as part of the general admissions process. This resulted in a collapse of the old parietal rules and a great surge of student sexual activity. Marijuana and other mild drugs also became prevalent at Vassar. Given the law-and-order propensity of the Dutchess County sheriff, Lawrence Quinlan (whose troopers had American flags sewn on their sleeves), there were constant panics on campus about drug busts, with students desperately flushing their pot supplies down their toilets. But most of the new excitement was generated by the shocks that the tumult of the civil rights movement, the discovery of poverty, and the rise of the antiwar movement administered to higher education. Even America's traditional ruling class institutions were becoming unhinged. By the time I arrived at Vassar, radical and countercultural students had made their appearance on the campus, organizing an SDS chapter and demonstrating against the war. They were also beginning to make common cause with the new faculty members who, like me, were veterans of movement activism.

Sharing liberal-Left values and some measure of political experience, the new faculty—joined by a group of holdovers from earlier years—proved a very congenial lot. There was Paul Metzger, a lugubrious radical sociologist; David

Novack, a witty, immensely literate economist; Linda Nochlin Pommer and Dick Pommer, good-natured art historians; George Berger, an eccentric bohemian philosopher; Judy Kroll, a thoughtful, irreverent poet; David Schalk, a shy, mild-mannered historian; Mel Rosenthal, an outrageous, provocative English teacher; Lilo Stern, a moody, rebellious anthropologist; Howard Cohn, a literary whiz who looked like Rasputin; George Frangos, an outgoing, urbane historian; Joachim von der Thüsen, a specialist in German literature; and lots of other interesting academics. Like President Simpson, we looked forward to changing Vassar, but we wanted to do it in considerably more fundamental ways. Clustering together, we hung out during the afternoons in the Retreat (a campus coffee shop) or during the evenings in one another's homes or off-campus bistros.

As in my earlier jobs, I was conscientious about my teaching. I began with two sections of twentieth-century American history and another of Western civilization in one semester, and two sections of the history of American foreign policy and another of the American history survey during the other. Given my 4–4 course load at Hampton, this 3–3 load was relatively light. The problem was the Western civilization course, which covered European history from the Middle Ages until just before the French revolution. As I knew extraordinarily little about this subject, I did what many college teachers did in similar situations: stayed one chapter ahead of the students. Remarkably, this seemed to work, although I stumbled pretty awkwardly through the theological dispute between advocates of transubstantiation and consubstantiation. In the following years, I worked a few new courses into the mix: one on African American history (necessitated by the rising demand for it on the part of students) and another on the history of American radicalism (yet another course with growing relevance). Given my speech difficulties, I was never a spectacular teacher, but I did well enough, and my courses were soon among the most heavily enrolled in the Vassar history department.

My scholarly record was particularly impressive. My first book, *Rebels Against War*, appeared in the spring of 1969 and quickly drew widespread positive reviews and substantial sales. Columbia followed up with a paperback version in 1970. Awarded a research grant by the National Endowment for the Humanities for the summer of 1969, I headed down to the Schomburg Library in Harlem, plowed through the files of a neglected but important civil rights organization (the National Negro Congress), and by late 1970 had a major article in print on the subject in the *American Quarterly*. My research on Douglas MacArthur was also bearing fruit, for I wrote another important article ("MacArthur and the Missionaries") that was published in the *Pacific Historical*

Review in February 1971 and—with the research assistance of one of my students, Ted Lieverman—edited a book, *MacArthur,* that was published by Prentice-Hall later that year. Together with Julie Thayer, another of my students, I also wrote a lengthy article on student activism at Columbia University during the 1930s, which appeared in Columbia's alumni magazine that summer.

This scholarly efflorescence, usually linked to issues of war and peace, led to my ever-closer association with an unusual organization, the Conference on Peace Research in History (CPRH). Founded in 1964 by Merle Curti, Frederick B. Tolles, Charles Barker, and other eminent scholars as an affiliate of the American Historical Association, CPRH began with the assumption that historians and other intellectuals could contribute, through their research, to the development of a peaceful world. In 1970, when I first presented a paper at a CPRH-sponsored conference and was elected to the CPRH executive board, I began friendships with numerous remarkable people. They included a few members of the CPRH older generation—Peter Brock of the University of Toronto and Hilary Conroy of the University of Pennsylvania—and some members of the new: Charles Chatfield, a Wittenberg University faculty member who had contacted me during my Columbia graduate school days about our overlapping dissertation work; Blanche Cook, a Johns Hopkins University graduate student who wrote a rave review of my *Rebels Against War;* Sandi Cooper, a faculty member at Richmond College of the City University of New York; and Berenice Carroll, a political scientist at the University of Illinois. Their personal encouragement and organizational sponsorship of a range of professional ventures—a CPRH newsletter, panels at scholarly conferences, joint publishing projects, and, starting in 1973, a scholarly journal (*Peace and Change*)—did a great deal to sustain my own activities as a peace-oriented historian.

But my life was not all teaching and scholarship. In the spring of 1969, when I was still a relative unknown on the campus, Mel Rosenthal and I launched one of the more bizarre activities of my career: a campaign for Vassar sheriff. The goal was to lampoon Sheriff Quinlan and satirize national political trends. That April, Mel campaigned across the campus as the complete hippie—the Love Candidate—on a FEEL (Federation for the Ecstatic Elevation of Love) platform. "Feel good with Mel" ran one of his key slogans. I was his antithesis, "Mr. Law & Order," dressed in my old Boy Scout uniform, beret, and combat boots. In photos I stood poised with one booted foot in the air, about to stomp Mel's prone body. With the assistance of a dedicated corps of daffy students who on my behalf marched about singing "Freedom Isn't Free" and "Up with People," signs sprouted around the campus declaring "Wittner Lives Clean" and "Just How Far (Left) Will Mel Go?" My favorite campaign material, though, was a leaflet we put together declaring "Larry Wittner Says: 'America is ripe for moral rearmament. Do your part!'" It went on to urge stamping out Obscenity, Disloyalty, Comsymps, Sex, Gun Controls, Music, Hippies, Love, Pseudo-Intellectuals, Intellectuals, and Literacy, while urging support of Mom, Our Boys in Vietnam, Patriotism, Clean-Living, Our Boys in South Africa, Free Enterprise, Americanism, Our Boys in Santo Domingo, the Home, God, Our Boys in Bolivia, and Your Local Police. The campaign ended with a showdown on the lawn in front of Main Hall, where I employed a giant can of Mace (a covered waste basket) to gas Mel, only to be overcome myself by the chemicals. When I arose from the grass, transformed by the experience, I threw off my military gear and joined Mel and a crowd of delighted students in a giant circle dance celebrating Love.

Of course, Vassar campus activism was not all fun and games. In early October 1969 I accompanied a group of Vassar students to an antiwar rally at the Fort Dix army base in New Jersey, where—along with thousands of others—we were tear-gassed and driven off the premises by bayonet-wielding soldiers. That same month, I played a key role in circulating a petition, signed by over 150 of the 200 Vassar faculty members, calling for the suspension of classes on October 15 as part of a nationwide protest against the war. Near the end of the month, thirty-five black students seized a portion of Main Hall demanding, among other things, the establishment of a Black Studies program and the hiring of more African American faculty. In November, I was the key organizer of Vassar participation in the nationwide Vietnam moratorium effort in which numerous Vassar faculty members announced plans to suspend their classes on November 13 and 14, called on others to do so, and urged participation in a massive antiwar demonstration in Washington on November 15. The Vassar administration was losing control of things and didn't like that at all. President Simpson, scapegoating the dean of the college, Nell Eurich, for his difficulties with the black students (and perhaps much else), fired her forthwith, and she departed from the campus the following day in tears.

By contrast, my friends and I found this upsurge of activism quite exhilarating. Vassar was indeed changing. Antiwar sentiment was rife on campus, and the administration—or what was left of it—had acceded to virtually all the black student demands. Meanwhile, the campus's sleepy, elitist ambiance was fast disappearing. During the much-publicized black takeover of Main Hall, a corps of faculty members was formed to safeguard it from a raid by Sheriff Quinlan or angry local whites. The younger, more sympathetic faculty formed a substantial portion of this defense corps and took on the most dangerous shift—from midnight to 6 A.M. As we patrolled the entrances to Main, we comprised an interesting-looking group: young, mostly bearded, and dressed in dungarees, black turtleneck sweaters, and combat boots. When a carload of local citizens drove up to Main, I stopped them, inquiring what they were doing on campus. "We just wanted to find out whether there's been any trouble here," a woman said. "Everything's fine," I said. "Don't worry about it." But she persisted: "How long do you plan to stay in the building?" Then it hit me. She assumed that *we* were the students. "Ma'am," I said, "we're the *faculty*." Bewildered, they looked at one another, turned around their car, and drove off into the night.

Actually, the faculty was increasingly divided by the new atmosphere of social protest. Within my department things were very "civilized," polite, and superficially friendly. But just as some of us (particularly the newer, untenured faculty) were caught up in the spirit of the era, others (particularly within the tenured ranks) were horrified by this phenomenon. Tony Wohl, a British expatriate who named his daughter Tory, astonished me one day by confiding that he thought my gentle colleague David Schalk was a potential Robespierre. Another senior department member, Don Olsen, made a great show of preserving departmental traditions. Alma Molin, our department chair, secretly reassured the Vassar administration that the "Silent Majority" (a Nixonian term for backers of the Vietnam War) would prevail. Meanwhile (as I later learned through a FOIA request), she sent reports on campus dissidents to the FBI. Carl Degler, the most eminent department member, was a mainstream liberal with little use for pettifoggery and might have offset their influence to some degree. But, unfortunately, he left Vassar for a job at Stanford just as I was arriving.

Indeed, there existed a different Vassar—championed by the people one of my colleagues jokingly termed "the Mossbacks"—that I couldn't begin to understand. There was, for example, the History Department's "Note Topic," developed in the early twentieth century, which required students to take notes for a research paper that they never actually wrote. Curiously, the notes had to be written on a specially sized notepaper, arranged in the order of one's outline, and placed in a specially sized envelope—with the materials custom made for Vassar and available only at the Vassar bookstore. One morning one of my students arrived at my office crying and near hysteria. The night before, it seemed, she had completed her note-taking and outlining, but there were too many notes to fit into the little envelope. Try as she might, she—and eventually her supportive roommate—couldn't force them in. As they worked at it, the envelope began to tear, bringing her to a state of desperation. As I watched her sobbing away in my office, I wondered: Should students really be worrying about this sort of thing?

Other strange developments surfaced around hiring decisions. Through the connivance of the Mossbacks, my department hired an immaculately groomed young man who appeared for classes every day decked out in a white shirt, dark tie, and a dark tweed suit. This formality was matched by his speaking style, which was so upper-class English that it could have passed for that of the British royal family. Referring endlessly to his glorious days as a student at Oxford, he sat about the department lounge, drinking tea, smoking his pipe, and opening boxes of his special tobacco that, he assured us, had been dispatched to him by his "tobacconist" in Britain. Eventually, I was stunned to learn that the poor sod had been born and raised in the Bronx and had spent only two years abroad. But in the context of the senior faculty who controlled my department, he clearly knew which side his bread was buttered on. Of course, when my friends and I suggested hiring someone, the idea fell on barren soil. To fill a three-year opening in U.S. history, I proposed taking a look at Staughton Lynd, then in the process of being fired at Yale (apparently because of his prominent role in the peace movement). Naturally, the Old Guard found numerous reasons why that was out of the question. The most creative explanation was produced by my "English" colleague, who argued that if Lynd was as good a teacher as portrayed we'd never be able to fire him.

The same polarization was evident at the December 1969 convention of the American Historical Association. At the business meeting antiwar forces led by Lynd proposed a resolution condemning the Vietnam War. As I stood just inside the entrance to the large meeting hall, distributing leaflets urging a full debate on the war, one of the young historians pouring into the room, looking very much like the stereotype of an anarchist (thus clearly one of "my" people), stopped and called out: "Larry!" It turned out to be my old friend Gene, whom I hadn't seen since high school. As I suspected, he was going to vote for the antiwar resolution. But lots of other historians were not going to, either because they supported the war or because (as some preferred to say) they didn't think the organization should become involved in political controversies. The most offensive of the resolution's opponents was Eugene Genovese—only recently a public champion of a Communist victory, but now on the way to ingratiating himself with the historical establishment by denouncing us. Rocking on his toes, Genovese pounded his fist into his hand while screaming into the microphone: "We must put them down! We must put them down hard! We must put them down once and for all!" Thanks to bad parliamentary maneuvering, critics of the war failed to get a resolution through that meeting. But the following year they succeeded.

By contrast, life at Vassar still remained relatively pleasant. Lacking a formal framework to discuss our research, a group of the younger faculty got together at one another's homes, making brief research presentations, fielding questions, and then socializing with friends and family members. At other times, we'd pile into a car to go to the movies in nearby New Paltz or to go swimming at a local pond. Because the school was quite small and also because I wasn't that much older than the students, I became friendly with a number of them. Julie Thayer, a descendant of the founder of West Point and of the infamous judge in the Sacco and Vanzetti trial, proved a warm-hearted, politically active person. She told me that one day she sat sobbing in the campus library while reading the biography of Eugene Debs that I had assigned her class. Erika Franke, one of the early Vassar SDSers, horrified the local authorities by organizing local high school students against the war. Ted Lieverman, active in Senator Eugene McCarthy's 1968 antiwar campaign, was a terrific political speechmaker and writer, and, accordingly, served as a key mobilizer of campus peace activism. He also had a wonderfully dry wit, which led to many hours of humorous conversations with him.

One of the most highly charged situations I stumbled into at Vassar was a growing confrontation with the IBM corporation, which had numerous facilities in the Hudson Valley and was a major U.S. defense contractor. The situation began innocently enough when Glen Johnson, the assistant to President Simpson, suggested to us that if we wanted to take practical action to end the Vietnam War, we should contact Thomas J. Watson Jr., chairman of the board of IBM, to see if he—as an ostensibly liberal, antiwar businessman—would help with such a project. Although we had our doubts that dealing with Watson would lead to his participation in antiwar ventures, we decided that it might have some educational value. Thus in early December 1969 Ted (then a representative of the Vassar Committee to End the War in Vietnam), Sara Ridgway (vice president of the student body), David Novack, and I wrote to Watson, asking him to meet with us to discuss the possibility of IBM taking two actions to pressure the U.S. government to halt the war: ceasing to accept defense contracts and refusing to service Defense Department computers. Not surprisingly, Watson said he could not find a time to meet with us and added that "if one wants to stop the war," this was not the way to go about it. When we suggested that we meet at other times or sponsor an address by him on the Vassar campus (in which he could discuss corporate responsibility in time of war), he rejected any discussion and declared tartly that our action proposal "seems to advocate anarchy, and I do not advocate anarchy." In our response to him, we pointed to his refusal to speak to those with whom he disagreed, to the longstanding corporate defense of "freedom of contract," to "the unfortunate alliance that has developed between business and the military," and—in the context of the bloody war—to "your own corporation's moral bankruptcy."

This might have passed over fairly quietly, except for the fact that we put together a special supplement to the student newspaper, the *Vassar Miscellany News*. Appearing on February 6, 1970, the supplement had a cover page headlined "The Profits of Death" and—through a computer printout made up of the letters I, B, and M—showed a large bomb falling. Ted, who produced this creative bomb design, was pleased to have turned it out on a computer that had been donated to Vassar by IBM. The second page, entitled "The Responsibility of Corporations," carried a brilliant article by Ted that compared the heinous military projects of corporations in the United States to those of Nazi Germany. The third page, entitled "IBM and the War," was written by me and explored IBM's growing military role, including its key work on the much-heralded "Electronic Battlefield," then being put into place to kill anything that moved in Vietnam's "free fire zones." On the fourth page there appeared the "Vassar-Watson Correspondence." Given the close relationship between the Vassar administration and IBM—including millions of dollars in IBM stocks held by Vassar, large IBM financial contributions to the institution in past years (including Vassar's "Watson Apartments"), and, most recently, an IBM proposal to establish a technology center on campus—all hell broke loose. At the next faculty meeting, President Simpson read aloud a formal statement adopted by the Vassar board of trustees condemning us for our action.

Although campus events often preoccupied me, I became drawn into other kinds of activities as well. In May 1969, for example, I joined Mike Weinberg in the most daring of our outdoor adventures. Our plan was to take a weeklong canoe trip along a 130-mile chain of lakes, streams, and rivers located in northwestern Maine, a vast, largely uninhabited wilderness region. The route we mapped out was shaped like a giant lollipop, with the nearly circular Allagash River at its head. Driving up to Greenville, Maine, we rented a canoe, augmented our food supplies, and pushed on along a lengthy dirt road to Lake Chesuncook, where we set out by canoe into the wilderness. It was quite an experience. The paddling and occasional portaging were not bad at all, at least compared to the rainstorms, which occurred on a daily basis. Moreover, during the day clouds of black flies would descend upon us, biting us fiercely, drawing blood, and leaving us covered with itchy, bloody scabs wherever they could get at our flesh. At sundown, the black flies would depart, only to be replaced by squadrons of hungry mosquitoes eager to supplement their regular diet of coyote and bear blood with ours. A few times we came upon giant moose towering over us in the streams, and we tactfully avoided them. Thankfully, Mike and I were both healthy and reasonably good at canoeing, and I also retained my Boy Scout knowledge of starting cooking fires in the rain—a particularly useful skill on this trip.

As the days passed, the wilderness began wearing us down. One morning, awakening in our tiny pup tent, I noticed that my feet were unusually cold. Checking this out, I saw that the tarp closing off that end of the tent had fallen away, thus allowing the rain to drench the bottom of my sleeping bag. As it was fruitless to plunge out into the rain and onto the stormy lake, I simply put on my boots and lay there, shivering. Finding himself in the same circumstances, Mike followed my example. All day, as it rained, we lay there without the will or energy to move. It was impossible to cook—and, indeed, we were growing short on food—so we just nibbled some cookies. As night came on, I began to think of a Jack London story I had read in which the hero, trapped in the icy Alaskan wilderness, finally gave up, sank into the snow, and died. Was something similar happening to us? By early the next afternoon, when it was still raining and we remained immobile in our sodden sleeping bags, Mike and I began to take this danger seriously. Consequently, we forced ourselves to rise, break camp in the rain, and launch our canoe once again. To our delight, it stopped raining and, for a time, we felt a sense of exhilaration.

But when we reached the Allagash River, we discovered that we were paddling against the current. In fact, the farther we went upstream, the faster the river flowed and the more difficult it was to make any headway. As Mike had brought along a fisherman's rubber wading suit, he volunteered to put it on, walk in the water, and pull the canoe upstream while I paddled or poled from the rear. And so in the dark, as the rain began to descend once more, we proceeded laboriously up the Allagash. Exhausted, I felt myself losing consciousness every once in a while. But I awoke with a start when Mike lost his footing, threw himself over the bow, and the canoe went swirling downstream. Somehow I steered us to the riverbank, where we confronted our predicament. Could we continue? Conversely, on our ninth day out, with most of our food gone and half the distance to go, could we afford *not* to continue? The answer was obvious. Once again we plunged into the current, Mike pulling the canoe by a rope and I paddling in the rear. For a time, we made some progress. But then once more Mike lost his footing. And this time he didn't manage to hold onto the canoe. Shrouded by the blackest of night, he stayed upstream as I went swirling downstream. It was not a good situation. Even so, I managed to work the canoe over to a riverbank, and Mike waded downstream to where I was located. As it seemed senseless to go any farther, we pulled out as best we could on the riverbank, cooked our last dinner in a light rain, and waited for daylight.

By dawn we had concocted a plan. A canoeist we had passed a few days before had mentioned that there was a ranger station somewhere in the vicinity, at the end of an old, abandoned tram line—whatever a tram line was. If we could find it, that seemed our best bet. So we paddled down the Allagash—which was considerably easier—swept onto the adjoining lake, and somehow located the tram line. Leaving our canoe on the shore, we hiked through the woods along the rusted tram line, wondering all the while if this was a will o' the wisp. Then, just as it started to rain again (would nature never stop tormenting us?), we broke into a large clearing, at the bottom of which stood a sturdy wooden house with a big American flag flying next to it. As the rain poured down, we raced for the door, which was conveniently held open for us by a pleasant-looking, gray-haired woman. As we stood there, puffing and panting, she proceeded to ask us: "Well, what are you boys doing here?" We told her the whole story and asked her to radio out to Greenville to see if she could get our canoe rental store, Holt's Flying Service, to send in a plane to pick us up. "No, sorry boys, can't do it," she said, explaining that the radio had to stay free for fire-related messages. Finally, though, she agreed to use Morse code to contact a hermit in the hills, who—if he would do her a favor—would transmit our message to Holt. We held our breath as she acted upon this flimsy plan. After what seemed like a very long time, including numerous difficulties with the hermit, she turned to us with a little smile: "You boys had better hurry back to the lake. Holt's on his way." We hurried! Within a remarkably short time, we were out of the wilderness and back in our car.

Meanwhile, my relations with the Wittner family continued on a fairly even keel. In 1969 my father left the New York City Commission on Human Rights to accept a position as an equal opportunity specialist with the Defense Supply Agency of the U.S. Defense Department. Given my antiwar activism, Marjie's disdain for the war, and, by this point, my father's own opposition to the conflict, this new job generated a lot of joking around on our part. Told by my father that federal investigators might be coming around to question me about him, I urged him not to worry: "I'll tell them that you wouldn't do anything I wouldn't do!" Actually, my father, who continued to live and work in New York City, didn't perform military tasks of any kind. Instead, he reviewed the affirmative action programs of government contractors, which he did until his retirement at the end of 1974. Meanwhile, I continued to get on well with Marjie and acquired a new brother-in-law, Steve Solomon, who married Marjie's daughter, Jane. My sister, Debbie, also married during this period and moved to Belgium with her Brooklyn-born husband, Eddie Golembe, so that he could attend medical school there. Although Debbie's departure eased her relationship with Marjie, both she and Eddie seemed to harbor some lingering resentment against her and against my father.

My relations with Patty—who was then working as a guidance counselor in a local high school—were considerably more problematic. As before, we had similar cultural tastes and could get on well enough superficially. But on a deeper level we didn't make much sense to one another. She didn't take very well to my more political, bohemian friends, and she seemed primarily interested in acquiring new furniture and bric-a-brac for our apartment, holding dinner parties, furthering my career, and proving to her family that she lived an ideal upper-middle-class life. Given the widening gap between her conventionality and my unconventionality, plus the accelerating number of marriage break-ups occurring all around us, I suggested several times that it might be a good idea for us to separate or simply get divorced. She fiercely resisted this proposition—mostly, I think, because she felt she couldn't bear the embarrassment of a "failed" marriage.

In these circumstances, I made plans for a cross-country trip to the San Francisco Bay area in the summer of 1970. Originally, it was to be a journey with Mike Weinberg, who was moving there to start a new life. The idea of joining him in his small Volkswagen camper bus—packed with all his personal effects and his dog, Granny—was appealing. So was the plan for a reunion in the bay area with some of my Vassar friends, including Mel Rosenthal, George Berger, and Artie Bierman (an offbeat philosopher I met at Vassar during his work leave from San Francisco State). In the context of my growing marital difficulties, it was also appealing to have a break—in my view, a trial separation—from Patty. In the context of the massive upheaval on campuses and elsewhere caused by the Vietnam War, the invasion of Cambodia, and the murder of students at Kent and Jackson State, taking a separate vacation did not strike me as outlandish. But Patty was horrified by the idea, and ultimately I couldn't resist her entreaties to come along. So Mike, Patty, Granny, and I piled into the camper bus and headed across country. It proved to be an enjoyable trip, at least in part because Patty, apparently determined to save her marriage, adapted to our rather grubby, bohemian existence. But it didn't resolve the issue of our relationship.

What did resolve it, at least temporarily, was her pregnancy, which she announced that fall. Like millions of other young men, I now had some tough decisions to make. In my case, I decided to stick with the marriage. Why? My image of myself was of a nice guy (like my father) and, accordingly, it was difficult for me to abandon Patty in these circumstances. Also, she and I had gotten on better that summer, so I thought that maybe the marriage could work after all. Finally, it seems to be much easier to continue a behavior pattern in one's life, even if it's unsatisfactory, than to make a radical break with it.

So Patty and I stayed together, and by the beginning of June 1971, when the baby was due, she was swollen like a seed pod ready to burst. But for some reason nothing happened. Having been displaced from our apartment thanks to a three-year limit on residing in Vassar housing, we had made plans to move to a picturesque coach house late that month, weeks after the expected birth. But now, with the baby refusing to be born, the birth date edged dangerously close to the moving date. Then, on June 27, as Patty, her mother (who had been living with us, waiting for the childbirth), and I sat one evening on the patio of a small café near our apartment, Patty's water suddenly broke. This was it! I raced her to the local hospital, spent the night and morning with her as she drew upon her Lamaze breathing technique (which didn't seem to work), and had my first glimpse that morning of my baby daughter: Julia Rachel Wittner. It was very exciting. And there was more to come. When I returned, without having slept that night, from the hospital to our apartment, the two moving men had already arrived. June 28, it turned out, was not only the day of my child's birth but also our moving day. And I was supposed to be working with the movers, carrying our furniture and books. By late that afternoon, when we finished the job, I was drenched with sweat and exhausted. But Patty and I did have a new home, as well as a new daughter.

Despite these absorbing events, including the clear signs of hostility from the administration and trustees, I continued my role as an activist on the Vassar campus. In the fall of 1970, President Simpson made the tactical mistake of announcing that the plan for the IBM-funded technology center on the campus (written up by a consultant under the wonderful title of *An Engineered, Engineering Education*) would be voted upon by the students and faculty. Conducting an unrelenting campaign against it, my friends and I staged a wild, costumed student/faculty invasion of the campus dining halls in which we leaped on the tables and performed some guerrilla theater, singing (to the tune of the antiwar Country Joe and the Fish song "I'm Fixing to Die Rag"):

> Well, it's one, two, three
> Who are we working for?
> Don't ask me, I don't give a damn.
> We're paid by IBM
> Well, it's five, six, seven,
> Who do we educate?
> Well, that's not our job to figure out.
> Whoopie! We're all selling out!

When 90 percent of the Vassar students followed our lead by voting against the IBM plan, Simpson suddenly announced that this vote was not binding and turned in desperation to the faculty. But we gave him a very rough time on this front, as well, for a faculty meeting voted to dramatically alter the plan and then nearly voted down this revised version entirely. Ultimately, IBM, reeling from repeated rebuffs, simply withdrew its proposal.

Nor were these the only waves I made at Vassar. Taking the lead in protesting the growing number of faculty firings, I stirred up a major petition campaign among faculty members when my friend David Novack was denied tenure. Eventually, the issue of faculty firings—usually from the ranks of the dissident faculty members—became a major issue on the campus, with protesting students holding a lengthy sit-in at Main Hall in the spring of 1971. Although the administration hesitated to fire dissidents among the tenured faculty—presumably because that would bring lawsuits as well as negative publicity from an AAUP investigation—it did take measures against them, including freezing their salaries. Some got the message and left for other jobs. In this context, I wrote an article for the *Vassar Miscellany News* that called attention to the emergence of colleges and universities as academic marketplaces and urged faculty unionization. In the next issue, a senior faculty member produced a stinging rejoinder, arguing that Vassar faculty most certainly did not need a union, for their employer had their best interests at heart. He explained that originally the response to my article was going to be written by the chair of the Vassar board of trustees, but it was thought more appropriate to have a faculty member write it.

In these incidents and others, my political activism (like that of many other young people) was undergirded by the idea of authenticity. Disgusted with the conduct of the "good Germans" of the Nazi era and with the shabby moral and political compromises of more recent decades, we were determined above all not to sell out. Of course, this flinty refusal to compromise or to remain silent in the face of war and injustice could lead activists off into arrogance, self-righteousness, and ever-escalating radicalism. And sometimes it did. On occasion, young New Leftists could be just as obnoxious and pig-headed as Old Rightists. But I think that I largely escaped these traps thanks to a combination of a fairly benign personality and a Gandhian (or perhaps merely romantic) belief in human potentialities. Also, of course, I was fundamentally a reformer, feeling the same impatience with revolutionary fantasies of armed struggle that I felt for reactionary visions of social hierarchy. Although I enjoyed Leon Trotsky's history of the Russian revolution, I felt a much greater sense of personal identification when reading *The Autobiography of Bertrand Russell*.

Nevertheless, given my prominence as a dissident, my days at Vassar were numbered. On paper, I was an excellent candidate for tenure, as I had published additional articles, received an advance contract for yet another book, and drawn positive student evaluations. For this reason—and also because my allies in the history department hoped to avoid a logjam of candidates the next year and to see if my conservative colleagues would raise any objections to me—they put me up for tenure a year early. Everything went along smoothly until mid-March

1972, when at a meeting of the department's senior-level faculty (the only ones with voting rights in tenure cases), the conservatives outvoted the liberals 4–3 to reject my tenure. The next day the department chair, Don Olsen, presented me with the grounds for the negative verdict, which he claimed was my biased behavior as a teacher. In response, I pointed out that my syllabi were balanced, that most of my students had rated me "superior" or "excellent" on official course evaluations, and that charges of teaching bias had never been voiced by students or faculty during my nearly four years at Vassar. But this response had no impact, largely because it did not address the real motive for denying me tenure, which was that I had made waves on campus. In a final, bizarre touch, Olsen concluded his remarks by saying that serving as a department chair was a difficult job, as I would see when I became one.

Of course, it did not seem likely that I would become one at Vassar. Nor—despite the fact that there would be another vote on me by the same people and by the administration, which made the final decision, the following year—did it seem likely that I would continue teaching there after my contract ran out in May 1974. In short, like many of my friends at Vassar, I was on the road to being fired. Naturally, I was furious at the smooth political purge that had been initiated, both for its flagrant dishonesty and for its clear contempt for intellectual freedom. Realistically, I probably should have recognized that being forced out of Vassar was inevitable. But, as indicated by my political views, I was always a bit of a romantic and believed that somehow justice would prevail. And it does, at times. But from this point on it was pretty clear that justice was not going to prevail in *my* case.

Fortunately, I had some resources I could fall back upon. I notified dozens of friends of what had happened and of my desire to find another job. Two of my sympathetic senior colleagues in the Vassar history department—Clyde Griffen and David Schalk—also did their best to explain my imminent departure from the college and to smooth the path for my being hired elsewhere. Meanwhile, thanks to a very generous provision in the second contract Vassar granted at the time to junior faculty—which provided for a year's leave at full pay—I didn't have to live near the campus, alongside my hypocritical conservative colleagues, during the forthcoming academic year. Instead, I was free to go anywhere in the world and write my new book. Patty, too, could reside anywhere, as she had left her guidance counselor job to stay home and care for Julia. As a result, we located a cottage that we could rent inexpensively in Amalfi, Italy—a picturesque town on the Mediterranean Sea that we had visited previously—and made plans to live there during 1972–73. After five years as a college teacher, I was down but far from out.

I could also comfort myself with the fact that during my years at Vassar I had had a significant impact on the place. Numerous students wrote to me in later years telling me how important an influence I had been in their lives. Some remained friendly with me, as did a substantial number of Vassar faculty. I was even invited back to campus once as a guest speaker. There were also some unexpected consequences of my teaching there. Perhaps the most amusing began when I served as a volunteer one afternoon, interviewing candidates for admission to the college. During my interview with one young applicant, I discovered a really nasty recommendation letter in his file from his prep school headmaster denouncing him for lacking in masculinity. As he seemed a very bright, talented fellow, I told him about the letter and assured him that I was going to write up a favorable report on him. I did so, and he was admitted. Years later, I was amused to discover, through an article in *Esquire*, that he had become famous as "Jackie St. James." Wearing a flashy dress, heels, and a boa, he swept into Vassar dances proclaiming coyly: "Aren't I a vision?" Well, I thought, at least I had provided a nice departing gift for the Vassar administration.

6

Overseas Exile, 1972–1974

Arriving in Amalfi at the beginning of September 1972, we were struck by its beauty. Patty, Julia, and I lived in the small, marble Villa Lara, one of several upgraded peasant cottages on a mountainside estate overlooking the town and the Mediterranean. The estate was owned by the Duchess of Amalfi, who bewailed the fact that it was the only thing left to her by the duke, who on his deathbed, she said, had been convinced by "the priests" to leave his money to the Catholic church. Opening our front door, we walked a few feet through the sparkling sunshine to pick trellised lemons. Later in the day we wandered down the street to the market to buy fresh vegetables and fruit. Other food was locally grown as well. Alerted to the availability of fresh pork from a newly slaughtered *swino* (a pig), Patty went to the butcher shop one day, only to discover—to her horror—that she was leaning on a counter right next to the pig's bloody head. Often we dined out quite cheaply in local restaurants. I enjoyed swimming in the Mediterranean, as well as carrying Julia around in a backpack. One day, the three of us took a long hike up into the mountains. Patty decided to stop off at a village school while I continued up the mountain trail, whistling old partisan tunes and carrying Julia, now dozing, on my back. When I reached the top, the air was cool and the view of the rocky coastline against the blue water was spectacular. I thought: "This is fantastic!"

Not everything, of course, was quite as glorious. Buying a car in Italy proved a hassle, and obtaining a typewriter in Amalfi also presented difficulties. With the assistance of the duchess's live-in French lover, who handled business matters for her, I finally managed to purchase a new Olivetti typewriter at a remarkably open black market area in Naples and thus get going on my writing. We had considerably greater troubles when in October the weather started turning cold and rainy. Suddenly, the restaurants began closing, swimming in the

Mediterranean lost its appeal, and our charming little cottage turned cold and wet. Thanks to Julia's use of cloth diapers, substantial portions of our rooms were soon devoted to clotheslines full of dripping cloth, which in the cold, wet weather dried very, very slowly. Our helpful Frenchman installed a small woodburning ceramic stove in our living room, but it did little to counter the cold, gray, wet gloom descending upon us.

As this slippage in our living conditions was occurring, however, I was corresponding with George Berger, who—disgusted with Vassar—had moved to Amsterdam, where he taught philosophy at the university. Things were cold, gray, and wet in Amsterdam, too, he pointed out. But it had warm, dry apartments and lots of things to do. Why not move there? It was an appealing suggestion, and we took it. At the end of October we loaded our gear in our car, said farewell to the duchess, and wended our way up through France to Amsterdam.

Amsterdam proved urbane, civilized, and—as I quickly discovered—infinitely groovy. Pulling my car over beside one of the city's long-haired policemen, I asked him where I could find Beethovenstraat, the street on which our apartment—secured in advance of our arrival—was located. "Beethoven," said the policeman with a deadpan expression on his face. "Wasn't he a composer?" From my standpoint, life in Amsterdam was ideal. I'd roll out of bed in the morning, run across the street to a bakery to pick up a loaf of warm, freshly baked rye or pumpernickel bread, and return to the apartment for a leisurely breakfast. Then, if it was a nice day (i.e., a lighter shade of gray), I'd take Julia to the local park to watch the ducks and ride the swings. In the afternoon, I'd buckle down to research and writing, and then on many an evening I'd join George and his Dutch friends at the Literaire Café, where we drank beer, read newspapers and magazines, and listened to jazz bands. In the early hours of the morning we staggered home along the canals, laughing and singing. Although I don't think Patty had as good a time as I did, she made friends of her own—usually more conventional than mine—and joined me at dinners, concerts, movies, and performances by the Netherlands Dance Theater.

Throughout 1972–73, life in Amsterdam was gripped not only by aspects of the counterculture—marijuana cigarettes passed freely from hand to hand at bars, a church painted in wild Day-Glo stripes, and a park with sleeping sites and lockers provided for hippies—but also by political activism. The Vietnam War was a constant source of agitation, with large antiwar demonstrations sweeping through its streets. One day I witnessed about a thousand grade school children surging down Beethovenstraat, chanting *"Nixon moordenaar!"* (Nixon murderer!). Given Amsterdam's adoption of Hanoi as a sister city, an enormous Amsterdam Helpt Hanoi (Amsterdam Helps Hanoi) campaign emerged, including the exhibit of a piece of antiwar sculpture a couple of stories high in the Dam Square and a major fund-raising project in which citizens went door to door collecting coins and putting little stickers on doors attesting to public generosity. As the Watergate scandal unraveled, every evening Dutch television carried hours of videotaped broadcasts of the congressional hearings in English. In the aftermath of George McGovern's sad defeat for the presidency, what a joy it was to sit with friends, Dutch and American, and watch the downfall of the Nixon administration.

We also had some visitors from the United States. Ted Lieverman came and stayed with us for at least a month, doing a masterful job of research for the book I was writing, *Cold War America*. On one memorable day, Ted, George, and I took a train to Utrecht to participate in an exceptionally large antiwar demonstration. Uneasy about being spotted as Americans, we conversed as best we could in French. During his visit, Ted told me that although my heart was invariably in the right place when it came to politics, he thought I should engage in a more rigorous reading of the left-wing classics. As I had never read more than snippets from the writings of Karl Marx, I thought this might not be a bad idea. Thus, I picked up an abridged version of Marx's writings and, on those evenings when I wasn't gadding about downtown, sat down to plow through it. What a job! After a page or two the print would begin swimming and I would doze off. After considerable repetition of this phenomenon, I decided to save my reading of Marx for those nights when I had trouble falling asleep. And as I rarely had trouble doing that, the book ended up gathering dust on my shelf.

Julie Thayer also spent a short time with us. Unfortunately, within days she broke her ankle on a sand dune at the beach, thus becoming one of the few people in the history of the Netherlands who was ever hurt falling down a hill. Before she fell, however, Julie, Ted, and I had what I considered a hilarious confrontation with some Christian evangelists dispatched from the United States to spread the gospel of Jesus to the benighted, decadent people of Europe. Wandering around downtown Amsterdam after having had a bit too much to drink, the three of us were suddenly accosted by these earnest young preachers, who seemed determined to save us from the fires of hell, or at least to reach their daily quota of souls they had saved. Invariably polite, I tried to keep a straight face and not say anything provocative, but it was a struggle. Finally, my religious assailant, winding up his sales pitch, asked: "You do know Jesus, don't you?" Alas, he had pushed me over the edge. "Yes," I said, "but he's no friend of mine!" And that ended that.

Ted had worked for a while at the left-leaning Institute for Policy Studies (IPS) and was contacted when IPS sent Eqbal Ahmed to explore the possibility of setting up a Transnational Institute in Amsterdam. Eqbal was a Pakistani who had played a role in the bloody Algerian revolution against French colonial control. Since then he had acquired a reputation as a fierce academic critic of Western exploitation of the Third World. During Eqbal's visit, Ted arranged a dinner that brought us together, along with an Algerian woman married to an old friend of his, a well-known leader of the Algerian revolution. It was fascinating to hear the two of them reminisce about who had been arrested, tortured, or executed in the Algerian struggle and after it. By contrast, my own problem of looming unemployment seemed quite petty. Nevertheless, I eventually mentioned it, and Eqbal responded reassuringly that he was sure that I would find another job, even if it was only at one of America's lowly community colleges. Growing more grandiloquent, he predicted that, given the current purge of young faculty activists from prestigious colleges and universities in the United States, the community colleges might well produce the country's next great wave of social upheaval.

I had my doubts about that, especially as I wasn't finding a job at a community college or anywhere else. I applied for all sorts of positions—mostly at colleges and universities, but also with the American Friends Service Committee, IPS, and with Congressman John Conyers. But I had no luck. The bottom was dropping out of the academic job market and, with the assistance of my department chair at Vassar—to whom interested employers eventually turned for the scoop on me—I was being blacklisted. Some chairs of search committees told me, sympathetically, that I was *over*qualified for the junior-level positions they were seeking to fill.

And I *did* need a job, for in March 1973 Olsen informed me that the vote had once more gone against me in the senior ranks of the department. Though Olsen didn't mention it, all the conservatives had voted against me and all the liberals for me. This time, there was no talk of my alleged bias—a tricky issue for my critics, as a historian is supposedly free to adopt any historical interpretation he desires. Instead, at the key meeting new and ingenious justifications were seized upon for disposing of me. For example, it was said that I seemed alienated by the earlier decision to reject me; therefore, if tenured, I might not prove collegial. None of this was broached in Olsen's letter, which remained silent about the reasons for their negative decision. President Simpson could have reversed it, if he had desired to do so. Indeed, he had reversed a departmental decision a few years before, when the vote went against a conservative. But, of course, in my case, Simpson was happy enough to go along with the recommendation of my conservative colleagues.

Their actions against me prompted a story splashed across the top of the front page in the *Vassar Miscellany News,* along with a very sympathetic editorial ("Academic Freedom"). Noting that my scholarship had been "highly praised by historians around the country" and that "the majority of students in his courses have evaluated his teaching as 'excellent,'" the editorial asked "why a professor as eminently qualified as Wittner is forced to leave a college that is already academically undernourished" and "that has too few first-rate scholars and too few 'excellent' teachers." Needless to say, no explanation was forthcoming, at least from the department or the administration. Quoted in that same issue, I burned any bridges I had left to the institution by calling attention to the faculty who had already been purged and declaring that their "intellectual daring and distinction ... will surely bring recognition among free people and ideas long after the craven servants of thought control have moldered away."

In June 1973 I sent a resignation letter to Olsen, with copies to other senior members of the department. Referring to their decision to deny me tenure, I stated that "I understand ... that you cannot reveal your true motives. Outside the confines of your authority, it is no longer as popular as it once was to preserve the society of the faithful by ousting the unorthodox. Once you could have had the satisfaction of publicly burning a heretic; now you are reduced to inventing wretched excuses to explain why he fails to meet 'standards.'" Then I announced that I would not return to teach at Vassar in 1973–74, the final year of my contract. Concluding the letter, I declared: "Be of good cheer. . . . I shall not be back to introduce an unsettling element of doubt into your tidy sinecure. It is even possible that you can shield the faithful from heresy for years to come. (The Church managed this for centuries; your counterparts in the Soviet Union for decades.) Surely this knowledge will be a great comfort in your long and tireless struggle against intellectual freedom."

Fortunately, by this point I had managed to find a job, at least for 1973–74, as a senior lecturer in Japan under the Fulbright program. Casting my net far and wide for employment, I came up with the Fulbright possibility—a very attractive one, for it provided not only a chance for me to escape from Vassar, but also a salary about 50 percent higher than the one I currently had. But the Fulbright position, aside from being quite competitive, had an apparently insuperable obstacle: a requirement for a recommendation letter from a college or university administrator. How was I going to get *that*? The solution emerged during the previous summer, when Olsen's departure for vacation led him to pass on the position of department chair temporarily to Molin (the trusty FBI agent), who—when she in turn went on vacation—found no one else at the full professorial rank to pass it on to except Don Gillin. Don was one of my supporters in the department, so during his one week as department chair he wrote the recommendation letter for me. Then, sure enough, free from the usual blacklisting by my department chair, I was offered the job.

The blacklist that operated in my case reflected the limited tolerance for political dissent in American academic life of the era. Despite the strong political stands I had taken, I was not—on a personal level—abrasive, but instead a rather polite, pleasant, inoffensive individual. Furthermore, unlike some young activists of the era, I was not a flaming radical or revolutionary. To be sure, I spoke out frequently and acted upon my beliefs. But my beliefs were peace oriented and social democratic, and I would have fit pretty well into most socialist, social democratic, and labor parties around the world. Ignoring the revolutionary fantasies of the time, I happily backed McGovern's Democratic presidential campaign of 1972, which focused on peace and social justice. Although my residence overseas limited my participation in that campaign, I did send it a very substantial financial contribution.

My distance from "revolutionary" politics also surfaced during the summer of 1973, when I returned to the United States before beginning my Fulbright year in Japan. After being purged from Vassar, David Novack found a job with the Allen Center, a small experimental college at the State University of New York in Albany. Although David was basically an outspoken liberal, when I drove up to Albany in the hope of landing a job there I discovered that a number of his colleagues were ivory tower Marxist-Leninists. As we sat around over lunch, in what David told me was a job interview he had arranged, they spent most of the time discussing the latest developments in sectarian left politics, including the recent formation of new Communist parties. Along the way, they mentioned that out of the ruins of the old Socialist Party, Michael Harrington was forging a Democratic Socialist Organizing Committee to bring social democratic values into the Democratic Party—an effort they ridiculed but which sounded good to me.

In October 1973, still without long-term employment, I flew off to Japan to find a house in Tokyo and begin teaching at three Japanese universities in that city: the University of Tokyo, Sophia University, and St. Paul's University. With the groundwork laid for the arrival of Patty and Julia, they flew in not long after that. The biggest problem we faced was the language barrier, for fairly few Japanese spoke English and we could not manage more than a small number of key phrases in Japanese. Furthermore, there was no way we could read the many street, building, and subway station signs, or the writing on cans of food, menus, newspapers, books, and other products, for almost all of it was comprised of the thousands of bewildering characters that make up the Japanese language. We had been plunged into illiteracy. Fortunately, I soon learned to adapt. Instead of reading menus, I looked at the wax models in restaurant windows and copied down the Japanese characters accompanying the appealing-looking prospects for meals. Instead of reading subway station signs, I kept track of the number of stops I had to make before I reached my destination. Also, in the three courses I taught—America since 1945, the history of U.S. peace and social protest movements, and international relations in the Pacific—I had interpreters in two of them. In the third course, at the University of Tokyo (Japan's premier educational institution), the students could understand my English—or at least that's what they claimed.

One of the stranger aspects of my job was that, although I was hardly a typical American, I was in certain respects a representative of the United States. Even though the Fulbright program was formally separate from U.S. foreign policy, it was linked to the U.S. government in numerous ways, including its funding. Shortly after we arrived, in fact, Patty and I were invited to a large U.S. embassy cocktail party, held on the embassy's grounds: a mountainside in the middle of downtown Tokyo. Chatting at this lavish event with an assortment of well-dressed U.S. government officials, I felt acutely uncomfortable and wondered what I was doing there. Moreover, even Japanese who didn't know me at all easily spotted me as an American, with all the baggage accompanying that. This was exemplified when, eating lunch at a campus cafeteria, I was approached by a Japanese student who told me earnestly that he wanted to assure me how much he supported the U.S war in Vietnam. Actually, most Japanese students were bitterly hostile to the war. Indeed, many were members of revolutionary Marxist-Leninist student groups and stood fiercely at campus entrances, masked, dressed in military fatigues, and proudly bearing red banners on bamboo poles. Fortunately, caught up in sectarian disputes, they hated one another far more than they hated me, and I never had any difficulties with them.

In the midst of this strange, rather alienating situation, where was I going to find friends? My Japanese colleagues were pleasant enough, but our relations were usually rather formal, confined to welcoming dinners at local restaurants, in which Patty and I would be feted by a group of male faculty. (Given traditional views about women in Japan, there were very few women faculty members. Furthermore, faculty wives were not invited—though an exception was made for Patty, the Western woman.) Furthermore, most of the Fulbright faculty members were scattered about throughout Japan. Fortunately, however, I stumbled upon a group of very compatible people—members of the Committee of Concerned Asian Scholars (CCAS), a dissident antiwar group that had emerged in the Asian Studies Association. Ironically, I met one of its members at the embassy party, and he soon steered me to meetings of the group in Tokyo. Composed of activist graduate students and young faculty members, they were people much like me. Thus, although I was certainly not an Asian studies specialist, I easily fell in with them, becoming friendly with Mark Selden, Angus McDonald, and others. At one of the CCAS meetings, I gave a talk on U.S. foreign policy. At another, I brought along my guitar and led them in singing labor and other protest songs.

Some of the most memorable CCAS activities in which I participated occurred in the winter of 1973–74. Japanese antiwar activists had asked the CCAS group to help out with the GI coffee houses in Japanese cities with U.S. naval bases. As we were Americans and they were Japanese, it was easier for us to "reach" American soldiers with an antiwar message than for them to do so. Thus, we spent one day chatting with GIs at a coffeehouse near the naval base in Yokusuka, where the aircraft carrier *Midway* was homeported. That evening, when the sailors had to return to the ship, they suggested that three of us accompany them. Would we be allowed to do so? After all, there recently had been massive Japanese demonstrations protesting the *Midway*'s presence, thanks to charges that, in contravention of an official Japanese government ban on bringing nuclear weapons to Japan, the ship carried them. But our new GI cronies—including at least two huge black guys with big afros—insisted that there would be no problem. So that evening we strode up to the dock with them and were promptly challenged by an armed U.S. Marine Corps guard in a watchtower. The GIs identified themselves as sailors, said we were their friends, and—to our astonishment—we were told to proceed. So we ended up strolling about the decks of the *Midway,* snapping pictures of one another leaning on the planes, and then going below, where one sailor casually remarked: "There's where the nukes are stored."

To follow up on these and other contacts with American GIs, the CCAS group arranged to take them on a tour of Tokyo. We began by visiting well-known shrines and tourist sites. But that afternoon we made a visit to Sanya—an exceptionally grim, day laborer section of the city. To me it looked much like the Bowery, with the addition of masses of miserably destitute people bedded down in the parks and other open spaces, where they lived on dirty mattresses, huddled around fires made of garbage, passed the bottle, and commiserated about the snow that was falling upon them. We received a good introduction to the area from a saintly Japanese fellow who ran a kind of flophouse and soup kitchen designed to mobilize these people politically by dealing with their immediate problems. As we sat huddled in his tiny rooms, he explained how the Japanese were lured to Sanya from the countryside in the hope of getting day laborer jobs. Once there, they were exploited and intermittently employed by labor contractors—corporate middlemen who, in fact, were gangsters that would maim or kill anyone who caused them labor difficulties. They had already threatened our host. He added that the laborers—desperate to raise money for food and shelter—would sell their none-too-healthy blood, which would then be sold to cosmetic companies to put into makeup for "rich, white Western women."

It was a pretty heavy afternoon, even for me, and the GIs—politically unsophisticated but good-hearted guys—looked devastated. As we walked back to the subway station through Sanya's streets, littered with garbage and bedraggled human beings lying about on the icy ground, we were suddenly stopped by two sinister-looking Japanese men standing in front of us in the middle of the road. Wearing suits and fancy, pointy shoes, they didn't look like anyone else around there. Like most of the GIs, I couldn't understand what they were saying. But our CCAS guides translated and explained that these were two of the more notorious labor contractors, members of the Japanese mafia, and were telling us to get out of Sanya *now*. It was a tense moment. The GIs, wigged out by what they had heard and seen that day of exploitation, were ready to take the two labor contractors apart. And, unlike the rest of us, they knew what to do and had some chance of doing it. But what would happen after that—for example, when their gangs were mobilized and all hell broke loose—was anybody's guess. Ultimately, cooler heads prevailed, and—after some exchanges of insults—our group gradually withdrew from the scene.

It is sometimes very difficult to trace what impact one has on other people. But that July, when I read in the newspaper that a substantial number of American GIs had refused to board the *Midway* for a mission to South Korea, then swept by popular protest against the U.S.-backed dictatorship, it occurred to me that I might have played some small role in inspiring their mutiny.

Ironically, at about that same time the U.S. Information Agency (USIA) also drew upon my services. When I first received a call from an official of this U.S. government body suggesting that I give USIA-sponsored lectures on U.S. foreign policy, I explained that this might not be a good idea, as I was a critic of that policy. "Oh, that's OK," he replied, "we accept up to 70 percent criticism." Although I pointed out that I had never quantified my criticism, he continued unfazed and, as a result, I finally agreed to do the lectures he suggested in Nagoya, Hokkaido, and elsewhere. Arriving in Nagoya at the end of February 1974, I gave my talk at the American Center in that city, alongside a talk by a rising Japanese political scientist, then being hailed as "the Japanese Kissinger." I must have gone beyond the 70-percent limit, for at dinner that evening—served by a Japanese waitress whose eyes had been widened through an operation (to Westernize them), in a lavish restaurant (taking up an entire floor of a skyscraper) in which we were the only customers—the local cultural officer handling my visit grew very agitated. Finally, he burst out with: "Well,

Professor Wittner, just what *is* wrong with U.S. foreign policy, anyway?" So I told him, after which there was a long period of silence.

The following morning, I did an encore before a luncheon meeting of the Japan-America Society in downtown Nagoya. My official host was again horrified by my talk. When, just to provoke him, I asked what he thought of it, he replied: "You know I'm going to have to report this, don't you?" "That's fine with me," I said with a smile. Then, as I stood outside the building, chatting with a couple of Japanese historians who had attended, something truly startling occurred. Thousands of Japanese workers surged forward sporting slogans such as "Down with Capitalism!" and "Smash American Imperialism!" on their chests, foreheads, and banners. When I asked the Japanese historians what was going on, they replied that this was the beginning of the "Spring Offensive" of Sohyo, one of the two Japanese labor federations. My USIA talk had been delivered at the protest site: the Japanese Chamber of Commerce building. The Japanese historians and I went off together to have a very pleasant lunch, during which we chatted about the history of the Industrial Workers of the World and other protest groups. The USIA, however, was less pleased. A staff member eventually phoned and canceled my Hokkaido speaking trip. Nor did the other USIA speaking commitments materialize.

Of course, I had plenty of other things to keep me busy. In early April we moved down to Kyoto, where I taught recent American history courses at Doshisha University, Ritsumeikan University, and Kyoto Sangyo University. Despite the rebuff from the USIA, many other organizations invited me to give lectures, including the Japanese Association for American Studies. Also, *Cold War America*, a textbook with a New Left interpretation that I had written on American foreign and domestic policy since 1945, was in its final stages. I had turned in a first draft to my editor at Praeger Publishers, only to be told that, given its substantial length, the manuscript should be cut by 25 percent. As a result, while still in Tokyo, I sat up late at night in a tiny unheated room separated from the rest of the house typing up a revised version. It was so cold in the room that the typewriter keys often stuck, so I kept at hand a Q-tip in a cup of Wesson oil to periodically lubricate them. Although I typed wearing my overcoat and scarf, my fingertips invariably turned blue. Fortunately, the weather was milder in Kyoto and the book work, accordingly, easier.

In Kyoto I also became good friends with one of my "closest colleagues" (the Japanese faculty members whose courses I taught), Toyoomi Nagata. Unlike many Japanese professionals, Toyoomi was an outgoing, jolly fellow, and he had staunch antiwar, democratic socialist beliefs. We got on very well and often socialized. Once he invited me to his brother-in-law's home for dinner, and I regaled the family with American folk songs. When they requested "My Old Kentucky Home," I explained, with some embarrassment, that I never played that one, thanks to the racist lyrics. "What do you mean?" they asked. "Well, there's the line saying 'Tis summer, the darkies are gay.' That implies that black people were happy under slavery." "Duckies are gay," persisted Toyoomi, still confused. "No, no, *darkies* are gay," I explained. They suddenly understood and were shocked. During "Golden Week," a traditional time of Japanese vacationing, Toyoomi suggested that our families travel together to a place outside Hiroshima, where his wife's father had a large house that could accommodate us. En route we crossed the Japan Inland Sea on a large ferry boat. Standing on the upper deck, we looked out at our children playing together and at the sparkling water beyond them. "You know," he said, "if we were born somewhat earlier, we would have ended up fighting and killing one another. And now, here we are, together, friends." "Yes," I said. It was a very poignant moment.

Patty also enjoyed our life in Japan. Although she was initially hesitant about moving so far away from her relatives, she enjoyed visiting ancient temples and other tourist sites, made a number of friends, and even found herself a part-time job teaching English to Japanese businessmen, who were always eager to practice their English with a "native speaker." In both Tokyo and Kyoto, she found plenty of girls who enjoyed babysitting for Julia, thus freeing her up to go out shopping during the day. Sometimes, of course, she found Japanese customs strange. Once, entering the famous Takashimaya department store, she was knocked to the ground by a well-dressed man as she tried to enter through the front door. She had assumed that he would give way before a woman, while he apparently assumed that she, as woman, should give way before a man. Even so, she concluded that that year in Japan was the best in her life.

Julia, too, seemed to thrive. Although it was the third continent on which she had lived in the first three years of her life, she adapted reasonably well to it. She romped around with other children (despite the language barrier), rode ponies in the park, and dressed up in Japanese clothing. In Kyoto, just like us, she slept on a futon that we laid out on the tatami floors of our house in the evening and rolled up for storage in the morning. Now a very curly-haired, blond, blue-eyed child, she became a magnet for curious Japanese onlookers. As I shopped in a market, with her in my backpack, crowds of Japanese admirers would cluster around her, chattering and touching her, sometimes to her annoyance. I couldn't entirely blame them, however, for she was an exceptionally cute little girl, and a very charming one as well.

Despite the fact that I was regarded in Japan as an eminent scholar and academic, as my Fulbright grant drew to a close it looked increasingly unlikely that I would be able to remain in academic life. Although I had applied for numerous jobs in the United States, I remained unable to secure a teaching position or anything else. By July 1974 nearly all of the academic jobs beginning that September had been filled. Part of my problem lay in the dwindling job market, part in the fact that I was out of the loop—unable to attend the professional conventions or to be interviewed by colleges and universities in the United States. Furthermore, with American academic life increasingly polarized, my writings on the American peace movement and other subjects branded me as social critic, one of the new and dangerous crop of campus rebels. Worst of all, I was blacklisted. If a history department did have an interest in hiring me, its chair would ultimately contact Vassar's chair to find out why I—a well-qualified historian—had not received tenure at Vassar. And the Vassar chair (Olsen) would inform him (or her) that I was a dangerous radical. With only a little more than a month to go before the start of the fall semester, it seemed that my luck was finally running out.

Fortunately, almost at the last minute, I was thrown a lifeline. In the middle of the night I received a phone call from Patty, who had already returned to the United States. Very excited, she said that Arthur Ekirch, whom I had met through the Conference on Peace Research in History, was trying to contact me about a job opening in the history department at the State University of New York in Albany. Arthur was a colorful character—a C.O. during World War II who thereafter had given up his early liberalism for rugged individualism and libertarianism. Now he was a heavily published scholar, professor of history, and chair of the search committee for the position at SUNY/Albany. Although he was not comfortable with my left-wing political views, my guess is that he viewed me as much like himself: a peace-oriented historian and a highly productive scholar. Furthermore, scornful of intrusions upon intellectual freedom, he was disgusted by the way Vassar had treated me. Within days of returning to the United States in early August, I was driving up to Albany to be interviewed for the job.

Arriving at the SUNY/Albany history department, I met with the search committee, members of the department, and with Kendall Birr, who was completing his final weeks as department chair. Superficially, all went very well. Thanks to a last-minute resignation, the department needed someone to teach the two-semester history of U.S. foreign policy course, plus assorted other courses, including the U.S. history survey. Authorization for the position—a three-year associate professorship with tenure consideration in the second year—had been received from the administration, and the search committee decided that I filled the bill. Although Birr pointed out that the terms of my contract still had to be negotiated with the administration, it was clear that I was going to be hired. Driving back on the New York State Thruway to Elizabeth, New Jersey, where Patty and I were staying temporarily at her mother's house, I was elated. With only two weeks to go before the onset of classes, and after two and a half years in the wilderness and hundreds of fruitless job applications, I finally had managed to return to American academic life. Furthermore, as I listened to the radio I learned that Richard Nixon, on the verge of impeachment, had resigned from the presidency and flown off, in disgrace, to San Clemente. It was certainly a day for celebration.

Below the surface, however, swirled darker currents. Both Birr and the incoming chair, Joseph Zacek, fretted about my left-wing reputation and, to check up on me, phoned the chair at Vassar. Fortunately, though, the Vassar history department had just elected a new chair. Although the tenure process at Vassar was limited to senior faculty (who in history were predominantly conservative), both senior *and* junior faculty voted for a department chair, and this broader electorate produced a new, considerably more liberal chair: my friend David Schalk. Queried by Birr and Zacek about that dangerous New Leftist Wittner, David responded that it was a great shame that I had chosen to leave Vassar, for I was a wonderful teacher, a superb scholar, and a great colleague. Even so, Birr and Zacek remained wary. Furthermore, one of Birr's protégés, Richard Kendall—a staunch conservative and war hawk—was dean of the Social Science College and thus the administrator with whom Birr would negotiate my contract. Aside from his political disdain for me, Kendall had a vested interest in preventing anyone with my heavyweight academic credentials from becoming the department's specialist on U.S. foreign policy, for that was his field. If he ever returned to the department, it would be embarrassing to have someone with superior qualifications teaching it. Thus they decided, as Birr told a friend, that they would put me on "a very slow track."

This meant that when the formal job offer was made to me a few days later, the post had dwindled to that of a visiting lecturer. It would be a temporary position, limited to one year, on a nontenure line (i.e., without any future consideration for tenure), at a salary roughly half of that authorized by the administration. I objected, pointing out that a lecturer position was invariably reserved for someone who lacked a Ph.D. or substantial academic credentials. (By this point, I had had the Ph.D. for more than seven years, had taught on a full-time basis since that time, and had a long list of publications.) Of course, I desperately needed a job and my bargaining power was limited. The best I could do was to get Birr to agree that, although my contract would run for only a year, the line (that is, the teaching position) would become permanent, and

I would be considered for it. Justifying his stance, Birr explained to me that I had a reputation as a New Leftist and, as the department and campus had been plagued with the evils of radical politics in recent years, the department needed time to look me over. I was less astonished by this viewpoint than by his outspoken expression of it. Did these people feel no embarrassment at limiting intellectual freedom?

Thus, as Patty, Julia, and I moved up to Albany in late August 1974, it was clear enough that, although I had managed to hang on to my teaching career, it was only by my fingertips. For a dissenting intellectual like me, academic life continued to be precarious.

7

Grappling with Issues of Work and Love, 1974–1980

In the fall of 1974, when I began teaching at SUNY/Albany, the school had had a long, rather uninspiring history. Founded in 1844 as the New York State Normal School—a two-year training college for grade school teachers—it evolved over time into the four-year New York State College for Teachers and in 1962 into one of four University Centers of the newly established State University of New York. (The other three were located at Binghamton, Buffalo, and Stony Brook.) To live up to its University Center status, SUNY/Albany expanded rapidly between 1962 and 1974. New graduate programs quickly emerged, and the student body grew from 2,500 students to some 14,000—10,000 undergraduates and another 4,000 graduate students.

Although the old campus remained in operation in downtown Albany, in 1966 a new one was added on the western outskirts of the city. Designed by the architect Edward Durrell Stone, the new campus was a super-modern, alienating one in which all the buildings looked alike. With the exception of a small section of hills and trees, retained from the original site, the rest of the campus was a flat, bulldozed slab of concrete and grass, dotted mostly with small trees (all exactly the same size) and some larger ones (also all the same size). Within a perimeter road and vast parking lots sprawled four perfectly identical and symmetrical dormitory complexes (each surrounding a twenty-three-story high-rise dorm). At the center of it all stood the grandly named Academic Podium—whose look-alike buildings could only be differentiated by their identifying signs. Toyoomi Nagata, visiting me shortly after I settled in on the new campus, remarked in amusement: "Larry, this is where you belong! Right in the middle of modern capitalism!"

I was less amused. Not only did the new campus have an inhuman quality, but it also lacked the political and intellectual liveliness to which I was accustomed. Although SUNY/Albany had been swept by waves of protest against racism and the Vietnam War, especially in 1969–70, the insurgent tide had almost entirely receded by the fall of 1974, when I began teaching there. About all I found that recalled the earlier era was a little card, abandoned in my desk drawer, headed "Demonstration Alert Plan" and offering guidelines for contacting the "Security Office." Nor was the professoriat particularly scintillating. Hired to work at a middle-rank state teachers college, many faculty members had not done any significant scholarly research since they had written their doctoral dissertations. Although the advent of Ph.D. programs should have led to the recruitment of faculty members doing cutting-edge work, and therefore capable of supervising scholarly research by their students, many of the carry-overs from the teachers college—particularly in the History Department—were rather lackadaisical about this. Instead, they often hired people much like themselves: competent in the classroom but weak in scholarly credentials. For the most part, the campus had very little intellectual interaction. After teaching, faculty simply went home—sometimes to do writing, but more often to cultivate their hobbies or to watch television.

My disaffection for the place was heightened by my tenuous job status. As a lecturer, I was the lowest of the low in my department and treated as such. Joseph Zacek, the department chair, scheduled the second semester of my bread and butter course—History of U.S. Foreign Policy—from eight to ten on Saturday mornings. It was an unheard-of time slot, which as a faculty member aspiring to be rehired I found troubling, for it naturally led to a dramatic falling off in my course enrollment. The students were ready to stage a protest rally, but—worried that this would be a red flag to my back-lashing colleagues—I convinced them that it would be a better idea to simply petition for a better time. Nonetheless, Zacek resented the petition, which he told me indicated my dangerously subversive orientation. A deeply committed Cold Warrior, Zacek viewed himself as a bulwark against radicalism. A few years before, he reportedly had swaggered around the hall of the Social Science building, loudly proclaiming that he was going to keep a gun in his office, and if student troublemakers tried to enter it, "blood will flow!" In addition, Zacek had a nasty, bullying style that he displayed in his dealings with the relatively powerless untenured faculty. Junior faculty, he told one of them contemptuously, should be cleaning the toilets. When the young man objected to that, Zacek, enraged, sent the items atop his desk crashing to the floor.

Nor was my morale improved by the search conducted in the fall of 1974 to fill the History of U.S. Foreign Policy position after my lectureship concluded in May 1975. At the request of the dean, the right-wing Richard Kendall, a full-scale recruitment effort was made to fill this job—my job—at the assistant professor level. Hundreds of applications were secured, dozens of candidates were interviewed at the American Historical Association convention, and three candidates were flown to the campus for lectures and meetings with the history department. Eventually, the department search committee unanimously recommended hiring me at the associate professor level. The department then voted unanimously to reappoint me and split three ways on rank, with the plurality favoring associate professor. Zacek, as the chair, recommended offering me a two-year contract as an assistant professor. This lower rank, he explained to me, would at least lift me out of my absurd lecturer status and onto a tenure line. Finally, in the spring of 1975, after the official deadline, Kendall offered me another one-year lecturer contract. To top this off, Kendall vetoed a salary raise for me—recommended by the department on the basis of the publication that academic year of my new book, *Cold War America*.

People reacted in different ways to this situation. Curiously, my departmental colleagues seemed largely oblivious or indifferent to my lowly and inappropriate job status. To be sure, when it came down to acting on my contract, a good number (though hardly all) of them exhibited professional standards in their voting behavior. But for the most part they seemed unconcerned about my plight or thoroughly ignorant of it. Frequently, they were surprised when I told them that my new contract merely continued my status as lecturer. Even Arthur Ekirch, though contemptuous of the old boy network that controlled the campus and the department, was not particularly helpful, for he was an isolated, otherworldly individualist who lacked the bureaucratic savvy and contacts necessary to overcome the dean's obstructionism. By contrast, many of my friends elsewhere were simply outraged—particularly Howie Schonberger, who sent me letters of commiseration and notices about other jobs. But some were more philosophical. Commenting on my mistreatment at SUNY, my former Vassar pal Paul Metzger opined that in the past my insurgent views were cerebrally based. Now, at least, they had an objective basis rooted in labor exploitation.

Actually, there was plenty of academic labor exploitation during these years. Not only were there people like me, pushed to the margins because of their avant-garde politics, but many other young Ph.D.s who were left unemployed, underemployed, or mistreated thanks to a crisis in the academic job market. The "good days" of the 1960s—fueled by the dramatic expansion of higher education—had come to an end and were succeeded by a desperate scramble among young people for a dwindling number of academic positions. Moreover, as in my department, there was a smug indifference to this desperate situation on the part of many faculty members in the tenured ranks. Visiting my friend Toyoomi down in Princeton, where he had gone to study with Arthur Link—a very celebrated historian at Princeton University—I had the opportunity to meet the great man when he stopped by Toyoomi's apartment to arrange for the purchase of an expensive wristwatch from Japan. Conversing with Link, I lamented the current job crisis, to which he replied coolly: "Well, at least it will separate the sheep from the goats."

As for me, I felt a strong sense of bitterness. On the surface, I remained polite, friendly, and "civilized" with my SUNY/Albany colleagues. Underneath, however, I was seething with anger. How dare these comfortable, securely tenured faculty members and administrators (and their counterparts at Vassar)—many of whom, I believed, had pedestrian minds and academic qualifications inferior to mine—push me around and destroy my career? How dare they deprive me, my wife, and my little daughter of the income needed for survival? To me, their behavior illustrated the corruption I had discovered, so painfully, in academic life. When, during my student days, I had looked out at the names of the great intellectuals on the frieze of Butler Library, it had never occurred to me that almost none were academics. Now, after years of mistreatment, I was all too aware of the gap between academia's intellectual pretensions—its breezy talk of "the life of the mind"—and the petty, self-serving reality. And perhaps because I saw this bigger picture, my marginalization did not inspire in me a sense of self-doubt and defeat. Rather, I felt a fierce anger and a determination to prevail.

This attitude was exemplified by my decision to continue doing scholarly research and writing. In the context of my inability to land a job in which my scholarship was valued, it was tempting to just drop it. And, for a brief time that first year at SUNY/Albany, I did set it aside, turning instead to write the opening chapters of a novel. But soon this struck me as self-defeating. After all, I was a first-rate, prominent historian. My three books (*Rebels Against War, Cold War America,* and the edited *MacArthur*) were selling by the thousands, and I had numerous articles in print (including one already reprinted in an anthology and another that introduced a book written by Bertrand Russell during World War I). Back at Vassar, George Frangos and I had toyed with the idea of doing a joint study of U.S. intervention in the Greek civil war of the 1940s, and we now decided to begin that project, with George handling the Greek side of it and I the American. With this in mind, I applied for a research grant from the Truman Library in Independence, Missouri, and secured it. Consequently, accompanied by Patty and Julia, I departed in the summer of 1975 for a month of intensive research there. With the help of a friend, we found a place to live in Lawrence, Kansas, and every day I set out by car across the Great Plains to do the necessary research. Once I drove back to Lawrence during a gathering tornado, with lightning flashing dangerously across a blackened sky. Nothing was going to stop me.

Although George, facing his own job crisis, abandoned his part of the study, in the following years I continued my research on U.S. policy toward Greece, which led to yet another book contract with Columbia University Press. As this research progressed, I became acquainted with a number of interesting people who assisted my efforts. Among them were Elias Vlanton (a young Greek-American journalist working on the mysterious murder of CBS reporter George Polk), Marion Sarafis (widow of an assassinated leader of the World War II Greek resistance), and John Iatrides (a distinguished Greek-American historian). One of the more colorful of these new acquaintances was Harry Cliadakis, whom I met while we were both doing research in State Department records at the National Archives. Harry had been a Greek-American high school dropout with a job loading garbage trucks in Queens when a fellow worker, also Greek-American, told him about his experience with EAM (Greece's National Liberation Front) during the Second World War. Harry was stunned to learn of this hidden left-wing history and shocked when his coworker told him: "Harry, you're an idiot. With your brains, you shouldn't be out here loading garbage." Thinking it over, Harry concluded that his coworker was right. Accordingly, he returned to school, earned his Ph.D. in history, and set out to write the story of the Greek revolution.

Meanwhile, my sense of alienation from SUNY/Albany was softened by growing campus friendships. Although relationships with students were far more distant at SUNY/Albany than at Vassar, I did become friendly with some interesting young academics. Within the History Department's tenured ranks, Don Birn—whom I had originally met through CPRH—shared my social democratic political perspective and regaled me with amusing, colorful anecdotes. I also got on well with three other junior faculty members in the department or in its affiliated American Studies program: the countercultural Kay Reinartz (a Nebraska farm girl who knew how to summon pigs); the more conventional Joe Giovinco (a gentle transplanted Californian); and the witty, bohemian Ben Barker-Benfield (a Briton whose iconoclastic sense of humor meshed remarkably well with mine). George Frangos, it turned out, was also on campus, at the downtown Allen Center, having been hired for the teaching position I had been hoping to get. Given the Allen Center's Left sectarian tone, George and I used to joke that both of us would be better off if I stored my left-wing books at his Allen Center office and he stored his establishment books at my History Department office. Actually, I had a number of things in common with the young, bohemian faculty at the Allen Center, and late on Friday afternoons I would head down there to join them in playing guitar and singing folk songs.

I was also sustained by longer-term friendships. Although my Vassar cronies had been scattered far and wide by faculty firings, I kept in touch with some of them, particularly Paul Metzger (at SUNY/New Paltz), David Novack (at SUNY/Utica/Rome), Ted Lieverman (attending Northeastern law school), and David Schalk (who, thanks to his tenure, had managed to survive at Vassar). I also visited with Mike Weinberg in Florida and got together with Howie Schonberger (now at the University of Maine) during conventions of the major historical associations. As a member of the national board of the Conference on Peace Research in History, I became increasingly friendly with other board members, especially when we gathered for meetings in New York City, usually hosted by Sandi Cooper in her Upper West Side apartment. I remember hanging around after one meeting, singing Joe Hill's "The Rebel Girl" to a delighted Blanche Cook, as Charles Chatfield looked on in amusement.

But battling my way into a regular appointment at SUNY/Albany remained crucial. Fortunately, in this connection I had two breaks. The first was a bitter split in the ranks of the department conservatives. Although Zacek could be charming on occasion, he could also be quite belligerent. As a result, his behavior during his first years as department chair deeply alienated people who previously had been his close allies, including Kendall and Birr. Powered by their resentment, a genuine conspiracy developed against Zacek, and this served in turn to raise his level of anger and paranoia. Thus, as Kendall, in his role as dean, consistently blocked my advancement, Zacek began to rally to my side. As the enemy of one of his enemies, I had become—in his eyes—his friend.

Even more important to my future was the fact that acquiring scholarly credentials became a priority for the history department. In the fall of 1974 a report by a group of outside consultants (the May Committee), commissioned by the New York State Education Department, put the department on notice that the state was planning to strip it of its Ph.D. program for insufficient scholarship. "What percentage of your history faculty has written two or more books?" Harvard Professor Ernest R. May demanded of Dean Kendall. In the face of this attack, the dean and the department dithered, vainly attempting to justify the program that existed. But this simply wouldn't wash. The State Education Department remained determined to scuttle the Ph.D. program. In the fall of 1975, another group of consultants (the Ferrell Committee)—this time commissioned by the new university president, Emmett Fields—sought to determine what it would take to restore the department's Ph.D. program. Much like the May Committee, the Ferrell Committee emphasized the department's lack of publishing scholars and named me as one of only two department members (out of some twenty-five) who had written two or more books. (The other was Ekirch.) Meeting with the department and the dean, President Fields stated that the department's first priority was to attain a "critical mass" of scholarship. Thus, in an effort to attract publishing scholars, a major recruitment campaign began.

In this context, my fortunes were bound to improve, and did—at least somewhat. In late 1975 the department voted overwhelmingly to offer me a three-year contract as assistant professor. (Many preferred the associate rank but were deterred from supporting it by Zacek's argument—which seemed amply justified—that such an appointment would be blocked by the dean.) As chair, Zacek recommended me for a three-year assistant professor contract. Hemmed in by the department and the president, Kendall nevertheless reduced the contract to two years and, once again, vetoed a recommended salary raise. That spring, numerous outside candidates with credentials inferior to mine were offered tenured full professorships at salaries approximately twice mine. Several even commented on this anomaly. Naturally, I was still smoldering. But I also recognized that the tide was turning and that—at last—I was now on a line that could lead to tenure.

Indeed, the case for granting me tenure acquired enormous momentum. The department's outside recruitment efforts in the spring of 1976 proved disastrous, for none of the candidates accepted the offers, probably because SUNY/Albany—which had undergone state budget cuts—had retrenched whole departments and schools (including the Allen Center) and thus fired tenured faculty members. Increasingly desperate, President Fields appointed a new department search committee in the fall of 1976, with instructions to get publishing scholars on board at all costs. At the same time, taking note of my three books in print (with two more under contract) and twenty-one published articles and reviews, five senior faculty members nominated me for promotion to associate professor and for tenure. They could also point to the fact that the previous summer, thanks to Jim Shenton, I had taught at Columbia as visiting associate professor of history. Furthermore, my *Rebels Against War* had sold some 7,000 copies (an extraordinarily large number for a scholarly monograph) and my *Cold War America* had been adopted as a text at some ninety colleges and universities. At the SUNY/Albany history department's October 1976 meeting, the faculty voted 24–0 for promotion and 20–2 for tenure, with the negatives in the latter case reflecting the last ditch stand of hardcore conservatives. Zacek, relishing his battle with the dean, strongly supported my case, which now moved on to higher levels.

At this point, however, things became considerably more problematic. Although the personnel committee of the College of Social and Behavioral Sciences voted unanimously for my promotion and tenure, the dean employed a tricky maneuver that had the potential to derail things. In his official letter, Kendall concurred with the earlier recommendations. But he gave no reasons for concurrence and, at the same time, expressed unstated reservations. In this fashion, the dean established himself in a position to testify against me without making his charges part of the formal record or enabling me to respond to them. And, sure enough, there soon was trouble at the level of the university review committee, which—ostensibly because my tenure consideration was not yet mandatory (i.e., I had been on a tenure line for only a few months)—decided to make "no recommendation." So the focus now shifted to President Fields, who could go either way on this. Yes, to restore the history Ph.D. program he needed publishing scholars in the history department, even an ostensibly dangerous radical like me. But I was already in the department. Why "rush" to grant me promotion and tenure? If I were a nail biter, I would have been hard at work.

In February 1977, I learned of Fields's decision. George Frangos, who after the demise of the Allen Center had managed to find a job in the campus administration, had told me that he would keep his ear to the ground. And he did. Late on a cold afternoon I was working in my office when George appeared, flushed and panting, at my door. "Larry," he said, looking me in the eyes, "you've got it!" We embraced. My long battle for secure academic employment was finally over.

Actually, there was a curious irony in George's delivery of this news. Having been hired at the Allen Center while I was desperately looking for a job there and elsewhere, George seemed for a time to have received much the better deal. Also, Paul Raskin, a key figure at the Allen Center, later told me, to my astonishment, that he suspected George's receipt of the job that I coveted had been finessed by my friend David Novack, who, Paul said, had never told him and the other Allen Center faculty who "interviewed" me in the summer of 1973 that I was interested in a position there. By contrast, David campaigned for hiring George, who was offered the job. Why, I wondered, would David do that? It might well have been because George—also a friend of David's from our Vassar days—struck David as superior to me as a teacher (which he almost certainly was). But Paul suspected that David's decision to back George was political—flowing from his preference for a somewhat less left-wing colleague. I'll never know, for not long after I was hired by the SUNY/Albany History Department, David succumbed to a heart attack. He was a brilliant, playful intellectual whose tenuous job status and long commutes to far-flung SUNY campuses probably hastened his untimely death.

In any case, my situation and George's had now been reversed. I had secured a tenured faculty position while George—flung to the winds, along with the rest of the Allen Center faculty—kept his academic career alive only by moving into an administrative position at SUNY/Albany and later at SUNY/Central and Downstate Medical Center. By contrast, a group of the other Allen Center faculty, including Paul, formed an energy consulting firm. This seemed like a harebrained scheme to me, largely because none of them had any training or background in this field. But, to my astonishment, they set up an office in Boston and were soon raking in lucrative contracts from corporations and governments alike. A few years later, I ran into one of these leftists-turned-businessmen at a party and asked him how they had managed to succeed so brilliantly, given the fact that they had started without knowing anything about energy. "Larry," he replied, "in academic life there are lots of very bright people chasing a few jobs. In the business world, there's lots of money and not many bright people. How could we fail?" It was a shrewd observation. In later years, it occurred to me that if I, instead of George, had been hired by the Allen Center, I might have ended up as an academic administrator or a businessman. Thank God—or maybe David—I didn't get that Allen Center job.

Another sign of the upturn in my career was my election in 1977 to a two-year term as president of the Conference on Peace Research in History (CPRH). In numerous ways, this was a very flattering development—a sign of the respect I had acquired in the ranks of peace researchers. On the other hand, as I soon discovered, the organization was far more of a fly-by-night operation than I had realized. John Chambers, the outgoing president—who then taught at Barnard College—was a very likeable, talented fellow and had done the best he could with the job. But in the aftermath of the Vietnam War, CPRH—like the peace movement—was on the wane, down to a few hundred members. When, after a meeting in New York City, John reached into his car trunk to hand me the box housing the organization's records over the past two years, the bottom fell out and papers scattered along Broadway. Although I put the records together as best I could, the combination of dwindling membership and my lack of experience at running a professional organization limited opportunities for a comeback. Even so, under my stewardship CPRH continued to sponsor panels at the historical conventions, publish its own newsletter (which I wrote) and journal (*Peace and Change*), and develop close, supportive ties among peace researchers. We also secured nongovernmental organization status at the United Nations. Most of the CPRH constituency seemed to think that was good enough, and after my term as president concluded in 1979 I was reelected to the CPRH board for decades.

I also resumed my role as a local political activist. For a time, it was difficult to locate any political activism around Albany, where it had almost disappeared by the mid-1970s. But gradually I began to meet people with similar political approaches to mine. And this led to the formation of a group focused on *In These Times*. Founded during these years by the historian James Weinstein, *In These Times* was a democratic socialist newspaper that rejected both corporate capitalism and authoritarian socialism. I found this idea appealing, and starting in 1977 I worked with Peter Pollak and Gene Damm, two veterans of the student protest movement at SUNY/Albany, and Susi Kaplow, a young faculty member at SUNY/Albany, to promote local interest in the newspaper. Ultimately, we set up monthly *In These Times* discussion group gatherings at the Albany Friends Meeting House. Usually drawing from twenty to thirty people, these meetings featured speakers on everything from health care to labor rights. The difference between our perspective and that of Marxist-Leninists was highlighted one evening when a group of local Trotskyites arrived and berated our speaker—an organizer for the J. P. Stevens campaign—so persistently that he left the event fuming. I also hosted a fund-raising party for the newspaper at my house, with Weinstein doing the sales pitch.

In addition, during the late 1970s I was gradually drawn into the campus leadership of SUNY's statewide academic and professional staff union, United University Professions (UUP). Noting my peace-oriented, pro-labor views, one of my graduate students introduced me to John ("Tim") Reilly, a faculty member in the English Department who had been a leading campus activist against the Vietnam War. Tim had been elected vice president of the Albany UUP chapter, and when the president resigned to accept an administrative post he inherited the presidency. Tim encouraged me—and a few other young faculty members—to become active in UUP. Initially I was hesitant, for my knowledge of unions was based entirely on books rather than on direct experience. Also, UUP seemed to be such a placid organization, almost a company union. However, in 1978, when the National Education Association (NEA) challenged the American Federation of Teachers (AFT, with which UUP was affiliated) for collective bargaining rights on the campus, things livened up considerably. Repelled by NEA's appeal to "professionalism" and corresponding criticism of AFT as part of a labor movement composed of blue collar workers, I came out strongly for AFT and sent a letter along these lines to as many of my colleagues as I could reach. In the balloting, AFT (and thus UUP) won a substantial victory. I was delighted, as was Tim, who had campaigned ferociously for AFT. He now pressed me to run for the post of Albany UUP delegate to statewide UUP conventions, which would also place me on the Albany UUP executive committee. I did and won. As a result, starting in 1979 I served as an elected leader of our campus union.

In my official union capacity, I also started attending the meetings of the Albany Labor Council (the Albany County Central Federation of Labor, AFL-CIO). The Labor Council was a rather somnolent organization, and for a time Albany UUP leaders weren't sure that such an organization existed. But Jim McClellan, another new Albany UUP executive board member—one with a strong left-wing orientation—finally located it. Accordingly, a few of us were appointed Albany UUP delegates to the Labor Council and began attending its meetings in the Albany Labor Temple. Looking forward to a whiff of the class struggle, I was sorely disappointed. Ralph, the Labor Council president from the Laborers Union, chaired the monthly gatherings and was about as sour and uninspiring an individual as I had ever met. Although delegates came to the meetings from a variety of unions, the organization was controlled by the relatively conservative building trades and, as far as I could see, did virtually nothing. Occasionally, a delegate would make a proposal for activity, but Ralph invariably cast cold water upon the project.

On the other hand, through my attendance at Labor Council meetings, I became acquainted with a sprinkling of young, rebellious labor activists. Among them was Fred Pfeiffer, a left-wing machinist who was active with the Capital District Anti-Nuclear Alliance. On one occasion I joined him in leafleting the workers at a National Lead Industries plant, which was polluting midtown Albany with low-level nuclear waste. Ultimately, the situation at the plant became such a public scandal that the New York State government shut it down. I also met the rambunctious Bob Redlo—who headed up the regional office of the Amalgamated Clothing and Textile Workers Union. Bob first came to my attention when he got up at a Labor Council meeting and asked delegates if they wanted to join him in traveling to Pennsylvania to participate in a protest demonstration at the Three Mile Island nuclear power plant site after the near meltdown of March 1979. When a group of young, heavyset, bearded representatives from the Public Employees Federation, headed by Mike Keenan and Stan Byer, were sworn in as new delegates, Bob whispered to me: "Look at those guys. They're going to be ours." He was right.

At about this same time, I also became involved in a byzantine intrigue connected with the evaluation of my former nemesis, Dean Richard Kendall. It all began when Fields left SUNY/Albany to accept a post elsewhere and was succeeded as campus president by Vincent O'Leary, a canny academician with the style of an old-fashioned big city Irish politician. O'Leary promptly instituted a policy of evaluating administrators, with a key role to be played by the faculty. By this point, Zacek was no longer History Department chair, for Fields had removed him from that position after Zacek had engaged him in an angry shouting match. Thus, in the context of the evaluation process, it was the new chair,

Kendall Birr, who came to see me and ask me if I would like to nominate Sung Bok Kim, one of my tenured colleagues, for the College Council. The council would choose the evaluation committee for the dean—Birr's friend and former student—and Birr struck me as anxious to elect a person to this key body who would be sympathetic to him. However, Kim—as I knew but Birr did not—was quite disgusted with Kendall's behavior, which he considered harmful to the department. Therefore, I said I'd be happy to make the nomination. Kim, in turn, was elected by the department to the College Council and saw to it that an appropriate person from our department was selected by the council for the dean's evaluation committee: me!

Although a number of faculty members told me that Kendall, thanks to his administrative connections, was untouchable, I was not so sure about this. When our evaluation committee met, it became clear that although he had a couple of friends on it, most of the committee members either disliked him or were ready to give his record a thorough scrutiny. Furthermore, even I was startled by the data we gathered about him. The written comments of faculty were overwhelmingly negative. Asked to evaluate his record as dean on a scale from 1 (the lowest) to 10 (the highest), more than half the college faculty rated his record as 1. For a time, Kendall resisted providing the evaluation committee with a copy of his vita—the résumé of professional accomplishments required of all faculty and administrators. But we insisted upon it, and eventually he gave way, handing us a vita that was startlingly brief and bereft of achievements. His total scholarly work consisted of one five-page coauthored article in a debate society journal. Here was a man who lacked the credentials to be hired for the lowliest job in my department and now was a tenured associate professor of history and dean of the Social Science College at a University Center. Drawing up a negative report, we sent it upstairs and held our breath. In the end, O'Leary did the right thing. He removed Kendall from the position. Even so, like many an administrator or corporate executive, Kendall had a soft landing, for he simply returned to his tenured post in the History Department, at a salary substantially larger than mine. And the evaluations of administrators came to an end.

Despite my rising status on the campus, in the community, and in the historical profession, I did not have much clout in my department. In the late 1970s, nearly all of its members were much more conservative in their views than I was, and almost none of them were political activists. Although most of my colleagues had come around, reluctantly, to voting for my promotion and tenure, it had only been in the context of the department's urgent need for publishing scholars. Relatively few of them genuinely wanted me in the department or had much respect for my intellectual or political concerns. For the most part, I was tolerated rather than enthusiastically welcomed into their ranks.

The department's chilly response to deviant ideas became particularly clear during the 1978–79 academic year, when Ben Barker-Benfield came up for promotion and tenure. Born in Britain to a working-class mother and upper-class father, Ben had graduated from Cambridge and come to America to escape the prejudices of a class society. But while doing graduate work at UCLA, he began to lose his starry-eyed view of the United States. In 1968, disgusted with the Vietnam War and with American racism, he threw himself into Eugene McCarthy's presidential campaign. Arriving at SUNY in 1974, Ben began as the protégé and pawn of the Birr-Kendall faction in the department. And he did not share my social democratic, pro-labor perspective. Indeed, he was a bit of an anarchist. Nevertheless, I was charmed by his intellect, his wit, and his irreverence. I was also impressed by his cutting-edge scholarly research, which focused on male attitudes toward sexuality and how these were expressed in the history of the medical profession. Many of my departmental colleagues, however, were much less impressed by Ben and his work. Without any appreciation of avant-garde ideas or recognition that such ideas might lead to hostile reviews of his first book, they moved to purge him. At the crucial department meeting, I was shocked and stunned by their assault. Somehow I kept my cool, and I made the case for him. For the rest of that year, I worked closely with Ben to formulate a strategy for getting him through the university evaluation process. Ultimately, on a last-minute appeal to the university chancellor, Ben was granted tenure and promotion. But it was an extremely close call, as well as another sign that academia did not always welcome unorthodox ideas.

Another dismaying pattern of events emerged in connection with my sister, Debbie. During the mid-1970s, not long after she and her husband, Eddie, returned to the United States and had a child (Andrea), Debbie began to have very severe asthmatic attacks. Eddie, by this time an intern, saw to it that their apartment was cleared of the obvious allergens, including their cat, but the attacks persisted. To enable her to breathe, Debbie began taking heavy doses of steroids. The hope was that she would be able to stop using them once her condition cleared up. But, by and large, it did not. Accordingly, she remained on the steroids year after year, with horrible consequences. Once slender and attractive, she grew bloated and misshapen. Furthermore, the heavy medications warped her mind, and she became manic depressive. Indeed, she now looked and acted much like my mother after *her* illness began.

By November 1978, when I stayed with Debbie and Eddie at their apartment in the Washington suburbs before heading off to give a paper at a scholarly conference in that city, the situation was almost unbearable. After Eddie left for work, Debbie—clearly deranged—ranted on nonstop, denouncing Eddie and others. Although I did not have a close relationship with Eddie, I did not consider him nearly as bad a person as she depicted him. Instead, then and often subsequently, Debbie struck me as mentally unbalanced. The steroids had pushed her over the edge.

Patty, by contrast, was thriving. Obtaining a job as a high school guidance counselor in a local suburban school system, she specialized on working with "the gifted," a group she especially enjoyed counseling. Long horrified at my plummeting professional career, she was delighted at the turnabout that began with my appointment as an assistant professor. Consequently, she pressed hard for the accoutrements of what she considered a normal life, among them a large suburban house. As usual when it came to acquisitions, we differed, with my interest in a house—which was minimal—running toward one in the city or in the country. Eventually we compromised, buying a large, handsome house in suburban Niskayuna, with nothing but woods and the Mohawk River in back of it. We started living there in 1976, and immediately Patty occupied herself with the task of buying furniture and other bric-a-brac with which to fill its spacious rooms. The hiring of a housekeeper, lavish dinner parties, and good china and silver on display followed in due course. For me, the new house and its amenities provided a comfortable—albeit out of character—existence, and I particularly enjoyed biking in the warmer months or skiing in the colder ones on a newly built bike path along the river.

I also enjoyed caring for Julia. While still in Albany we enrolled her in the Temple Beth Emeth nursery school, and I was one of a group of parents (except for me, all mothers) who took turns carpooling our children there. Although these three- and four-year-olds were very cute, they had a dismaying tendency to tease or poke one another. Casting about for a way to control their behavior during the drive to nursery school, I found that the easiest thing to do was to get them all singing together. And so we belted out many a song. Our favorite chorus began: "O' the ocean waves may roll; let 'em roll! And the stormy winds may blow; let 'em blow-o-o!"

After we moved to Niskayuna, Julia started attending kindergarten, and it gave me a jolt when this little girl got on the school bus all by herself and headed off to elementary school. Although a sensitive and shy child, Julia seemed to enjoy going to school and participating in extracurricular activities. As a result, I ended up attending lots of school concerts, ballets, and plays, with most of the students displaying a great deal of charm but considerably less talent.

Julia continued to be a very well-behaved child and was quite attached to us. At night, Patty and I would alternate getting her to sleep, with one of us performing that task and the other cleaning the dinner dishes. After sitting on Julia's bed and reading her a "good night story," I would sing her soothing, monotonous songs—such as "Kumbaya"—to lull her to sleep. Then, making sure she had nodded off, I would depart on tiptoes from her bedroom. This kind of performance often stretched on and on, as neither Patty nor I had the heart to insist that she go to sleep on her own. Sometimes, sprawled out on her bed, I would be the first to doze off, only to have Julia, clinging to wakefulness, rouse me with: "Dad, you're sleeping!" Arising very early in the morning, she would climb in between us in our double bed and then continue her slumbers. Sometimes she would end up at right angles to us, and I would wake up with her foot pressed uncomfortably into my back.

Given the flexible schedule I had as a college teacher, I took care of Julia during parts of the day as well. Sometimes we went for short walks together. At other times, she drew pictures; if I appeared in them, I would invariably be portrayed with my head encircled by a wide wreath of curly hair. On still other occasions, I would put a classical music record on the stereo and watch her twirl about in her ballerina costume, which included a wand, a crown, and a slip she chose to wear upon her head. The slip, omnipresent, apparently had something to do with being a princess. Characteristically, Patty considered the slip an embarrassment when she went out in public with Julia, but I just found it amusing. When our housekeeper, who doubled as a babysitter, was on the job, I usually would retreat to my study to write. Yet the demands of scholarship were hard for a young child to understand. Therefore, on such occasions Julia invariably gravitated to my study to show me pictures she had drawn or to converse with me. Once she even slipped little crudely lettered notes to me under my study door.

Even so, in this unusual household, Julia did pick up some understanding of what it meant to be a writer. One weekend afternoon, she and I sat at the dining room table as I gave her a little lesson on how to draw the letters of the alphabet. She did a good job of copying them but occasionally made errors. After one such mistake, she suddenly threw down her pencil, burst into tears, and declared: "I can't *do* it!" "But Julia," I said, "you're doing fine. Even I make mistakes sometimes and then correct them. I'm always writing things and then crossing some of those things out." "That's all right for you," she retorted, tears still streaming down her cheeks. "You've got a publisher!"

Alas, my time with Patty was far less enjoyable, for our marital incompatibility remained. Patty gloried in a bourgeois life, and I did not. I threw myself into intellectual and political pursuits, and she did not. Her orientation was conventional, mine was bohemian. Much of the time, of course, we would just go our own ways. She would spend the day shopping while I would hole up in my study and write. She would visit with her comfortable friends and I would participate in demonstrations. Sometimes, of course, we would go together to a concert or a film that we'd both enjoy. But other joint ventures were more problematic, such as spending a long weekend with her family. Still trying to work out an amicable marital separation, I suggested it again in the late 1970s. But, once more, Patty couldn't bear the idea of it. Furthermore, from her standpoint, things were going well enough—and would go better yet if I would just grow up and accept what she considered our proper role in society.

In early 1976, as the storm clouds over my marriage persisted, I met Dorothy Tristman. Enrolled in the graduate course I taught on Cold War America, she had just begun taking classes at SUNY/Albany. Lively, intelligent, and articulate, she was soon one of the most active participants in the course. Sometimes Dorothy hung around after class or stopped by my office to chat, and it became clear that we were on the same political wavelength—indeed, knew and admired some of the same people. Born Dorothy Axelrad, she was a child of Holocaust survivors who had fled Czechoslovakia and Austria after the Nazi takeover in the late 1930s. As an undergraduate at Hunter College from 1959 to 1963, she was the head of the Anvil Club—a front for the Young People's Socialist League, the youth group of the old Socialist Party. In this capacity, she knew Michael Harrington, Bayard Rustin, and other democratic socialist luminaries, although she was put off by the political disputes and sectarian wrangles within the organization. A bit later, she fell in with Paul Goodman's small anarchist bohemian circle. Throughout, she was a participant in the civil rights and peace movements. Good natured, free spirited, attractive, and knowledgeable about things ranging from Reichian therapy to modern jazz, she was a very appealing person. Not surprisingly, we became good friends.

Ironically, as I later learned, this friendship came as a surprise to her. While a graduate student in art history at Columbia, she had felt very alienated from her teachers, for they seemed all too content to focus narrowly on their courses and ignore the U.S. military destruction of Vietnam. Sometimes, impatiently, she would speak up in class and demand to know how they could go on with their comfortable lives as if nothing was happening. Therefore, it was with some relief that she left Columbia and the tense atmosphere of New York City and moved to Vermont, where her husband, Richard Tristman, had accepted a job teaching English at Bennington College. Preoccupied for a few years with raising two young children, Dorothy later found a part-time job teaching history at nearby Southern Vermont College. Although she had only a bachelor's degree in history, she had always found history an interesting subject and knew much more about it than did her students. Even so, she thought that graduate work in history would broaden her knowledge and provide her with the credentials for full-time teaching. Thus, she decided to enroll at the nearest university with a graduate history program: SUNY/Albany. But this time, she told herself, she would grit her teeth and bear the apolitical nature of the faculty. Then she began her first course—and met me.

For several years, our friendship deepened. Occasionally, she would stop by my office, and we would talk about everything from the state of the world to the state of the history department. When I realized that she had received an A in every graduate course she took, I suggested that she might want to apply for a teaching assistantship in the department, which she did, successfully. After one semester at this job, however, she phoned me to ask about an awkward situation that had developed. The faculty member to whom she had been assigned had demanded that she deliver graded exams on the night before Christmas, in the middle of a snowstorm. As he would not be on campus, he explained, she should leave them for safekeeping with the campus police. Was this normal, she asked, or a bit over the edge? I replied that it seemed rather extreme to me. In these circumstances, I suggested, the most useful course of action would be to deliver the papers, explain the situation to the chair, and ask him to transfer her to someone less demanding for the second semester. As I was going to need a teaching assistant that spring, she was welcome to suggest that she be transferred to me. In this fashion, Dorothy became my teaching assistant, much to our mutual satisfaction.

At this point, in the spring of 1979, our relationship began to move beyond friendship. I liked her very much, and it seemed clear that she liked me too. One day at lunch in one of the campus dining halls, I was expounding on some subject or other when I noticed that she had a strange, entranced look on her face. Realizing that she wasn't listening to what I was saying, I stopped and asked: "What's the matter?" "Oh, it's just that I find you very attractive," she said. A pause followed as I took that in. "What does that mean?" I asked. "Well, nothing, I guess," she replied, adding that she was happily married. As we had become pretty frank with one another, I explained that I was not happy with my own marriage. But, even so, if hers was solid, friendship was the only reasonable option. So we agreed that it didn't make sense to become more deeply involved with one another. We would just remain good friends.

That seemed a rational enough decision, but, of course, the boundaries of relationships are not so easily set. In addition to the magnetism we felt between us, there was now also the recognition that our strong feelings were mutual. What stood between us was marriage to other people, and neither of us felt enthralled by our spouses or by the institution of marriage. Day after day, Dorothy sat smiling up at me as I lectured in class about—among other things—Emma Goldman's famous essay "Love Among the Free." How long could we applaud this sentiment in the abstract and resist it for ourselves? One spring day, we decided to have lunch off campus at a nearby Japanese restaurant. With rain pouring down, we piled into my old car and drove there. When I pulled into the restaurant parking lot, there were no other cars around, and it was evident that the place was closed. Wiping the condensation off the windshield with my hand, I looked around as best I could and speculated on where else we might go to grab some lunch. Suddenly, Dorothy said: "Larry." "Yes," I said, still absorbed in the restaurant question. "Kiss me," she said. And so I did, although our seatbelts were rather confining. And that was it. From that time onward, we were no longer just good friends.

So where did that leave us? For a time we resisted discussing the issue with our spouses, for we weren't sure where things were leading. But, after a while, it was clear to us that our relationship was a very powerful one. We wanted to be with one another rather than with them. Dorothy's marriage, it turned out, had not been nearly as happy as she first asserted. And the more she thought about it, the less she liked it. In these circumstances, I asked her to come live with me. She, in turn, asked if she could bring her children with her. I agreed. And so we came to a decision: that June we would tell our spouses our plans and thereafter act on them. Having never quite mustered the courage in the past to leave Patty, I knew that this would be very difficult. But I was determined. After all, I had a responsibility not only to myself but to Dorothy. It was now or never.

But, once again, we found that these kinds of things are easier to plan than to implement. Breaking the news to Patty was an agony, and there was an additional agony in breaking it to Julia. And then there was the lingering torture of living with Patty for weeks before I made my departure. From Patty's standpoint, separation (and the inevitable divorce) would ruin her life. I tried to convince her that she was young (thirty-six years old), attractive, financially secure, and would certainly marry again—probably someone far more in line with her values and aspirations than I was. Furthermore, with divorce quite common, it was hardly the mark of shame that she considered it. But she didn't buy any of that and frequently burst into tears at her plight. I felt a strong sense of guilt, alleviated only when she would provoke me to anger by vindictive behavior, which wasn't very pleasant either. Even worse, as I made plans to leave, Dorothy decided—after broaching our plans to her husband—that she couldn't go through with it. Deeply distraught, she had begun seeing a psychiatrist, who convinced her that romance didn't last. "But what about love?" I asked plaintively. "What about love?"

Despite Dorothy's dramatic change of heart, I was determined to leave my marriage. And so I did at the beginning of August 1979. With Ben's help, I loaded my books, clothing, and a few pieces of furniture into his van, and we moved these items over to an inexpensive studio apartment facing Washington Park in downtown Albany. Located in a rather down-and-out building, the apartment was drab and exceptionally tiny, with an uncomfortable bed that pulled down from the wall. Meanwhile, Patty and Julia drove off to Cape Cod, where they shared the house that we had rented for our own vacation with her family.

For me, it was a grim summer and fall. My dealings with Patty remained very painful, and I continued to swing between feelings of guilt (when she appeared distressed) and anger (when she grew vindictive). Thanks to numerous tearful conversations she had with my parents, my friends, and colleagues, many of them became convinced that I was an absolute cad. She was so effective in giving them this impression that when the History Department held its annual party the chair did not invite me to it and invited her instead. Gossip began to circulate among faculty wives about how I had run off with a younger woman—though, in fact, Dorothy was two years older than Patty and, in any case, she was no longer part of my life. Feeling lonely, battered, and depressed, I lost at least twenty pounds.

Fortunately, my relationship with Dorothy slowly resumed. Some time that fall, quite unexpectedly, she phoned, asking me how I was doing. It was clear to me that, back in Bennington, she was not doing well at all. Her phone calls continued, usually made from a pay phone not far from her home. As the calls were lengthy, she often didn't have enough change to pay for them. When the time came to deposit additional money, she simply ran off rather than confront the operator. On one occasion, the operator rang me in irritation to ask who had just phoned, and—with far greater interest in protecting Dorothy than in filling the coffers of AT&T—I responded that I didn't work for the phone company. When I told Dorothy of this exchange, she was charmed by it. Once again we began to see one another. We even traveled down to New York City together for movies and a visit with her sister. Gradually, Dorothy made up her mind. She wanted to be free of her marriage and to be with me. As a result, she decided to move with her children to Albany.

We agreed that it would be best for everyone concerned if we did not live together right away. We found Dorothy a small apartment on the other side of the park from mine, and she and her kids moved into it on January 1, 1980. Although this meant that we could see each other much more freely than in the past, things were not easy in the following months. Dorothy had no savings or income, and her husband paid child support when he felt like it, in amounts that varied, and with checks that all too frequently bounced. Julia seemed to adapt reasonably well to the new circumstances, which included taking her out for dinner and playing games with her midweek, and bringing her to my place over weekends. But Dorothy's children, David and Jonah, did not adapt as well and acted out through boisterous behavior, fights, and smashing things. Dorothy's husband, Richard, did not help the situation. Although he lived only a fifty-minute auto ride away from Albany, he chose to see his children infrequently. Moreover, when he did see them they were the ones who had to travel. Eventually, while still teaching at Bennington, Richard moved down to New York City, which made visiting him even more problematic.

Nevertheless, some semblance of normality gradually resumed. In the summer of 1980, Dorothy, David, Jonah, and I moved into a relatively large apartment that bordered the east side of Washington Park. That fall, Dorothy started graduate classes at SUNY/Albany's School of Social Welfare, with the goal of becoming a social worker. Although she had received her master's degree in history the previous spring, the scarcity of college-level teaching jobs convinced her that further graduate work in that field was pointless. By contrast, her sunny, outgoing personality and the continued possibilities for employment in social work offered greater opportunities in this field. Meanwhile, I plunged into writing once more, with funding from a National Endowment for the Humanities fellowship. Although my relationship to David and Jonah was considerably less than ideal, our new living arrangements at least enabled me to exercise some authority now and then, which somewhat eased an otherwise chaotic situation. Patty, too, began to adapt to our separation, taking up jogging and starting to go out on dates.

With my personal situation stabilizing, I also found it possible to give renewed attention to political activism. In October 1980, increasingly attuned to the priorities of the local labor movement, I managed to get Albany UUP members to join a picket line set up by striking hotel workers at the Ramada Inn, located near the SUNY campus. However, I was more disengaged from the national elections, for I found it hard to believe that a centrist politician like Jimmy Carter could be defeated by a right-wing zealot like Ronald Reagan in the presidential race. Indeed, I was so blind to the disastrous turn to the Right then beginning in national politics that I ended up voting for a third-party candidate, Barry Commoner. Reagan's election triumph came as a shock to me, as it did to many other local peace and social justice activists. As an expression of our determination to fight back against Reagan and his Christian fundamentalist allies, hundreds of us turned out for a very lively rally that November, shortly after the election, to protest the appearance of the Rev. Jerry Falwell, founder of the Moral Majority, at Albany's Palace Theater. I was among the speakers at the event and was quoted in the press as asking if it was truly "moral" to incite "militarism, war, and hatred."

Thus, by late 1980, although my circumstances were hardly ideal, they had improved substantially over what they had been when I first arrived in Albany. Central to the change was the fact that I had dealt successfully with two of the key problems weighing on me in 1974: my job and my marriage. Grappling with both of them had been exceptionally difficult. But I had survived the experience. Now, with the issues of work and love resolved, it was time to get on with my life.

Joseph Tzvi Barnatsky and Dvorah Barnatsky in Russian Poland, late nineteenth century.

Abraham Barnett and Rose Barnett, circa 1911.

Leah and Joseph Wittner with their son, Jacob ("Jack") Wittner, circa 1911.

Rose Barnett, circa 1928.

Jack Wittner, February 1930.

Rose Wittner, with the author, August 1941.

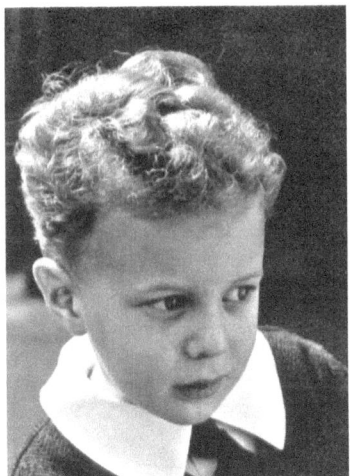

The author as a young boy, circa 1945.

The author in the playpen, June 1942.

Alpha Phi Omega visits McSorley's Old Ale House, Manhattan, fall 1958. The bartender sits in the foreground, while the author is in the background, sitting mid-table.

Mike Weinberg and the author (*left*) on the Brooklyn streets, about to depart "On the Road," June 1962.

Arriving for convocation ceremonies at Hampton Institute, Hampton, Virginia, September 1967. The author is wearing Columbia doctoral robes.

Speaking with sailors from the U.S. aircraft carrier *Midway,* at an antiwar coffeehouse, Yokusuka, Japan, January 1974. The author is seated on the far right.

Marjie Wittner, Julia Wittner, and Jack Wittner, late 1970s.

DSOC luncheon talk by Michael Harrington, with the author to his left and Bob Redlo (of the Amalgamated Clothing and Textile Workers Union [ACTWU]) to his right, Albany, New York, October 1982.

In the police van, having been arrested during a Free South Africa sit-in at the Federal Building, Albany, New York, January 1985. *Left to right:* John Funiciello (chair, Solidarity Committee), a local minister, and the author.

A support demonstration for ACTWU members outside the Lorbrook factory, Hudson, New York, May 1987. Gerry Zahavi and the author are holding the UUP banner.

Ben Barker-Benfield and the author on Cape Cod, summer 1988.

At the meeting with a delegation from the Conference on Peace Research in History and peace researchers from the Institute of General History of the Soviet Academy of Sciences, Moscow, July 1990. Ruzanna Ilukhina, who initiated the gathering, sits on the left. The author is on the right, under a picture of Lenin.

Dorothy Tristman, on the second floor of the Wittner/Tristman home, between a DSOC poster and the author's study, Albany, New York, late 1990s.

Peace Historians meet for dinner during the Hague Appeal for Peace conference, The Hague, May 1999. *Left to right:* Anne Kjelling (Norway), Peter van den Dungen (Britain), Charles Chatfield (United States), the author (United States), and Frances Early (Canada).

A TV reporter interviews the author amid the SUNY/Albany uprising demanding union recognition for the campus dining halls workers, Albany, New York, April 2000.

Solidarity Committee activists gather during the committee's annual Labor Day Picnic, Menands, New York, circa 2000. *Left to right:* the author, Jeff Levitt, John Funiciello, Doug Bullock, Dorothy Tristman, Tam Kistler, and Gus Santos.

Leading the singing of "Solidarity Forever" at the statewide UUP convention, Albany, New York, February 2001. *Left to right:* the author, Joe Lombardo, and Bill Scheuerman (UUP president). Photo courtesy Howard Cohn.

The Solidarity Singers perform at the Caffè Lena, the oldest operating coffeehouse in the United States, Saratoga, New York, November 2003. *Left to right:* Joe Lombardo, Bev Seinberg, the author, Dave Crump, and Jack Kilrain. Also performing, but not visible: Mo Hannah, Roger Allen, and Dave Pallas. Photo courtesy Howard Eskin.

On the lecture circuit, speaking at Georgian Court University, Lakewood, New Jersey, March 2004. Photo courtesy Joseph Sharp.

Leading the annual nuclear disarmament march through the streets of Hiroshima, August 2004. Holding the banner (*left to right*) are the author; an Australian antinuclear activist; Shigetoshi Iwamatsu, a former president of Gensuikin; and Gediminas Jancauskas, chair of the Lithuanian antinuclear group, Cernobylis. Photo courtesy Hidemichi Kano.

Receiving Upper Hudson Peace Action's "Peacemaker" award, Albany, New York, March 2007. *Left to right:* Dorothy, the author, and David Easter.

8

An Activist Academic, 1981–1989

During the early 1980s, my family life once again reached an even keel. Dorothy attended the School of Social Welfare, obtaining her master's degree in social work in 1982. After graduation she was employed for a time as a counselor at Albany's Planned Parenthood clinic and then became a full-time social worker for Parsons Child and Family Services, a local agency. While at social work school, Dorothy became caught up in the reevaluation counseling (RC) movement, which soon filled much of her free time. As RC viewed itself as a liberation movement, she began giving workshops on Living in the Nuclear Age, Combating Racism, and Preventing Burnout. Her sons, Dave and Jonah, attended the Albany public schools and, after a rocky time at first, adapted to the new environment. Julia continued to attend classes in Niskayuna but resided most weekends at our apartment in Albany, where she seemed to enjoy the urban experience. Often on a weekend morning we all went around the corner for a special breakfast at Cathy's Waffle Shop—a countercultural hangout that combined great food and a meeting place for local activists. On weekend evenings, we often drove over to the small Third Street Theatre in nearby Rensselaer to watch avant-garde movies.

Although life in downtown Albany could be stressful, it was also more interesting and more diverse than in the neighboring suburbs. This was especially true of our area of the city—just east of Washington Park—which was Albany's most bohemian and politically liberal area. Dorothy and I both decided that we didn't want racially or economically segregated lives, so it made sense to us to live downtown. Thus, when we decided to buy a house we looked for one in that area and eventually purchased one only a few blocks away on Irving Street. A charming, densely packed, one-block-long street of small, often-connected brick or wooden houses, Irving Street was the home of poor and working-class whites, poor and working-class blacks, and middle-class professionals. Our house, about a hundred years old, was what in Albany is called a row house (and in New York City a brownstone), and we decided to occupy two floors of it, renting out the third to a tenant. With the help of Ben and other friends, we piled our furniture and other goods into a van and in late August 1983 moved into our new residence. Dave and Jonah were as rambunctious as ever, and within thirty minutes Dave had smashed a hole in the living room wall. But things gradually settled down as we carved out a new life in our new home.

On campus, things continued much the same. Although my department—in the context of the Ph.D. crisis—had grudgingly come around to supporting my tenure, the conservative faction was determined that no more lapses of this kind would occur. Nor was there much support for affirmative action in a department that was not only almost entirely male but also, to the best of my knowledge, had never had an African American faculty member. These issues came to a head in March 1983 in a struggle over a contract for Iris Berger, a specialist on the history of Africa who had come to SUNY/Albany to head the Women's Studies Department. I first became acquainted with Iris in 1981 when I went to a gathering called to protest the arrival in Albany of the Springboks, a South African rugby team. Although I heard someone addressing the crowd, I couldn't see her. It turned out to be Iris, a tiny young white woman as well as a veteran political activist. Iris was also an excellent scholar, a fine teacher, and an exceptionally nice person, so there should have been no problem about her receipt of a contract in my department. But, of course, there was. A conservative colleague of mine, whom I shall call Kenneth Jones, went around talking heatedly of a "feminist plot." One of the documents in her file was mysteriously tampered with in a way clearly designed to damage her candidacy.

At the crucial department meeting, the official evaluation committee strongly supported giving Iris a contract, but Jones immediately retorted that if this occurred our jobs would be sacrificed to protect hers. A woman who teaches African and African American history courses and Women's Studies courses has a favored position, he maintained, and white men must protect their jobs. He was "a middle-aged white male with no official ties to minorities," he remarked, "and I am not inclined to put my own position up for Mrs. Berger's." Driving the point home, he urged us to look around the room, see that we were virtually all white men, and act accordingly. When some of my colleagues actually began to discuss whether or not their jobs would be jeopardized by hiring her, I interjected that this line of discussion was thoroughly improper and indecent. The only appropriate consideration was whether she was qualified for the job—which, of course, she was. Ben came to her rescue as well, noting that under the law we were supposed to welcome affirmative action. In the end, a solid majority supported giving her a contract. And, in later years, Iris went on to become president of the African Studies Association, vice president of the American Historical Association, a member of the editorial board of the *American Historical Review,* and perhaps the most eminent member of our department.

Not long after the department's conservatives failed in connection with the Berger case, they had greater success in undermining another job candidate whom they considered dangerous—only to be hoisted by their own petard. During the candidate's presentation to the department about his dissertation, he talked enthusiastically about how the radical organizers of New York City's Transport Workers Union had helped lift the city's subway workers out of the depths of poverty. I noticed that Jones's face had grown red and that he was crunching a metal ash tray in his hands, apparently as a substitute for the candidate's neck. He reminded me of Captain Queeg in *The Caine Mutiny.* And, sure enough, Jones soon led an angry verbal assault upon the poor fellow. Ultimately, this derailed the candidate and led to our giving the job to an apparently safer individual, Gerry Zahavi, who had done his dissertation on the defeat of unionizing efforts by an upstate corporation. Ironically, though, Gerry turned out to be more left-wing and activist-oriented than the candidate who was rejected. Indeed, Gerry's next research project focused on the invigorating roles that communists had played in American unions. Not surprisingly, the department conservatives, once they recognized their mistake, sought to sabotage him. But, given his strong record as a scholar and teacher, their efforts failed. And I acquired another interesting, activist colleague.

My own promotion to a full professorship came up in the 1982–83 academic year. By this point, I had three books in print (*Rebels Against War, Cold War America,* and *American Intervention in Greece*), had edited another book (*MacArthur*), and had written a very large number of articles and reviews. My service and teaching record was also very good, with large numbers of students crowding into my courses. Nevertheless, although I had a pretty unassailable case for promotion, negative comments about my "ideological" orientation cropped up in the letters of two of the outside evaluators. One charged that I was "a child of the 60s." Another complained that my *Cold War America* had "an unremitting revisionist tone." Even so, all six of the evaluators recommended my promotion, some of them quite forcefully. Much the same thing happened at the departmental level. Here a few conservatives sniped at my scholarship, charging ideological heresy, but without much effect on the final vote, which went heavily in my favor. Not surprisingly, then, my case sailed through the higher levels of the university, resulting in my promotion to professor of history in 1983.

Just as some faculty displayed political bias in evaluating me, so did some students. Endeavoring to be polite and reasonable, I avoided the sarcasm and nastiness that sometimes mar college teaching. Moreover, in the classroom I observed the norms of academic propriety—staying away from issues that went beyond the coursework and telling students at the outset that they were free to adopt any historical interpretation they pleased. Nevertheless, when teaching courses on social movements, modern U.S. history, and especially U.S. foreign policy, it is impossible to avoid tipping one's political hand. As a result, some students liked me immensely, while others—usually those desiring a glorification of U.S. foreign policy and wars—didn't like me at all. These two groups tended to balance out, so the overall student evaluations of my teaching were rather good. However, there was a noticeable division of opinion. Sometimes I would receive letters from former students saying that my courses were the most important that they had ever taken. Some other students—though not many—displayed considerable hostility.

On one occasion, in my foreign policy class, I noticed that a student asked a question in a very angry way. A few weeks later, during the midterm exam, he stormed out after only a few minutes, writing on the exam paper that he would have no trouble answering the questions but refused to dignify this pro-Communist course in that fashion. As he never returned and did not take the final exam either, I assumed that he had dropped the course. But, in fact, he continued his enrollment, and I had no alternative but to give him a failing grade. Thereafter, he began to send me very nasty letters, accusing me—among other things—of being a "gunslinger" for the department chair. By this time in my life, I had had enough experience of mentally ill people to know that there was something off about this fellow. And I was particularly concerned about his reference to guns. Even so, I offered to meet with him, but he just sent another hostile letter. So I called the campus medical office and the campus police. Neither proved helpful or gave me any information about this student. Ultimately, I learned through one of my colleagues, who had good contacts in the administration, that I was dealing with a Vietnam veteran who had been diagnosed as suffering from post-traumatic stress disorder and, in fact, resided in special housing for such persons.

Other hostility was less troubling. On the final day of my foreign policy course, as I was plunging into my concluding remarks, a couple of Marine Corps ROTC students rose to their feet, began singing "God Bless America," and marched contemptuously out of class. Thereafter, I called them in to my office, where Ben and I played good cop / bad cop with them. When Ben suggested that their military commander would not be pleased to hear of their disruptive behavior, they panicked. I suggested, in turn, that I would be willing to forget about the incident if they made a sincere apology. Not surprisingly, they fell all over themselves apologizing. On yet another occasion, someone wrote "Commie Kike" on my office door. I mentioned this to Dorothy, who responded dryly: "At least he could have written 'Democratic Socialist Kike'!"

Although, in my academic role I followed the norms of professional behavior, the early 1980s *were* a time of particularly intense political activity for me. Against the backdrop of the Reagan administration's nuclear buildup and loose talk of nuclear war, the worldwide struggle against nuclear weapons grew particularly intense, with millions of people mobilizing against the danger of nuclear annihilation. In Albany I gave occasional speeches deploring the nuclear arms race and participated in antinuclear demonstrations. When the great June 12, 1982, nuclear disarmament march and rally occurred in New York City—the largest political demonstration up to that point in American history, with nearly a million people—Dorothy, Julia, and I were enthusiastic participants. And there were lots of local antinuclear events, as well, usually linked to the nuclear freeze campaign. In October 1983, at an Albany freeze march—one of hundreds that occurred simultaneously all across the country—I chatted amiably with one participant who turned out to be the executive editor of Temple University Press, visiting his girlfriend in Albany. Within half an hour, we had made tentative plans for Temple to publish a revised version of my *Rebels Against War*. Who says politics and scholarship are antithetical?

In addition, I emerged as a key activist in the local labor movement. With Tim Reilly as president of the Albany chapter of United University Professions and Myron Taylor—another local activist, particularly on gay rights issues—as Albany UUP secretary, it was a great time to be serving on our campus union's executive board. I ran for vice president for academics—and won—serving in this capacity from 1983 to 1987. Working together, Tim, Myron, and I met regularly with President Vincent O'Leary in labor-management meetings. We also arranged to have UUP fund a variety of good causes and sponsor interesting speakers on campus, including (in 1985) Irving Howe, the famed author, literary critic, and democratic socialist. In addition, we brought UUP more firmly into the local labor movement. In 1983 Albany UUP turned out a reasonably strong contingent for the capital district's first Labor Day celebration in many years, which included a parade, rally, and picnic. At the state capitol, where the rally was held, I played guitar and helped lead the crowd in singing "Solidarity Forever." Later that fall, during a strike against the Greyhound corporation by the members of the Amalgamated Transit Union, we swelled the union picket line at the Albany bus terminal and managed to convince the SUNY/Albany student government to cancel plans to hire Greyhound buses to transport students downstate during the winter break.

Nor was that all. As local branches of a New York State Labor-Religion Coalition began developing, I was persuaded to serve as a co-chair of the capital district branch from 1982 to 1984. I represented the labor side of things while Ed Bloch—a regional staffer for the United Electrical Workers who took his religious faith quite seriously—served as the religion co-chair. Probably the Capital District Labor-Religion Coalition's most important venture was a protest march and rally that we organized in nearby Amsterdam, New York, where the Mohasco corporation was busy shutting down its rug-making operations, moving production elsewhere, and abandoning large numbers of unionized textile workers. With the support of local unions, we held the march and rally on a bitterly cold day during the winter of 1981–82. In addition, some of my union friends arranged for me to join the Labor Advisory Committee of the capital district branch of the New York State School of Industrial and Labor Relations, a component of Cornell University. This advisory committee—composed of local labor leaders—had a breakfast meeting once a month, and my service on it from 1983 to 1991 gave me some credibility with officials from the Teamsters, the Plumbers, the Sheet Metal Workers, and other local unions.

Although UUP was considerably wealthier and less endangered than most other local unions, we did need their support—and I secured it—during the 1985–86 academic year. With our state contract negotiations thoroughly bogged down, Tim suggested that some public protest would be useful. We had large banners made up ("Too Many Days Without a Contract: UUP") and hung them outside a few campus buildings—including the Social Science Building, where I managed to hoist one on a rope between my office and that of the History Department. Then we laid plans for a faculty-staff-community picket line outside the administration offices. As this protest would occur on campus, with no official authorization, we faced the prospect of the campus police being called in to disperse us. So we dispatched one of our executive board members to speak about this with the police, who were also union members (though of a different union). The police told her that although they would have to respond to an administration order, they would make sure to do it very slowly, taking at least half an hour for that purpose. That sounded good to us. In October we held the demonstration, which drew heartening contingents from other local unions, as well as our own, and never had to tangle with the police. Although I doubt this agitation had much effect, UUP did receive an excellent contract from New York State.

I was also involved in the struggle against South African apartheid. Intensely frustrated with the Reagan administration's sympathetic policy toward the apartheid regime, a Free South Africa movement developed in the United States. By having prominent individuals arrested for acts of nonviolent civil disobedience, it hoped to dramatize the apartheid issue and make it inescapable. In 1984 the campaign began in Washington, D.C., where politicians, labor leaders, and other well-known individuals courted arrest and—thanks to arrangements made in advance with the local prosecutor—were quickly released with no more than token fines. When the campaign hit Albany, the local Coalition Against Apartheid and Racism, a genuine force in our community, quickly approached local luminaries about their participation. However, as no advance arrangements had been made with law enforcement officials, people at the top of the local political, religious, labor, and educational hierarchies shied away from the project, for they faced the possibility of lengthy jail terms. Against this backdrop, I volunteered, for by this point I had some credibility as a labor leader. The Coalition accepted my offer, as well as the offers of nine others: some local ministers, a member of the city council, and John Funiciello, a Newspaper Guild delegate to the Albany Labor Council.

The event was extraordinarily dramatic. In mid-January 1985, as TV cameras whirred, the ten of us entered the local Federal Building and, when asked to leave at the time of closing, made short speeches, sat down on the floor, joined hands, and said a little prayer, led by one of the ministers. The police then arrested us and prepared to take us one by one—beginning with me—to the police van parked across from the building. It was a pretty tense moment, as two white policemen had recently killed a black resident of Arbor Hill, a local black ghetto, in his apartment, and the community was enraged at what it viewed as an act of police brutality. Furthermore, by this point it was getting dark and there were hundreds of militant demonstrators—about half of them African Americans—surrounding the Federal Building and chanting antiapartheid and antiracist slogans. As four policemen surrounded me and prepared to escort me through the crowd, one of them said to me: "Tell them everything's fine, OK?" "Don't worry about a thing," I answered, with more confidence than I felt. And then we plunged out the door. The crowd surged forward, with my incendiary labor crony, Bob Redlo, leading a chant of "Free Larry! Free Larry!" I flashed the crowd a big smile, and fortunately we continued through it without incident to the police van, where the police deposited me and then returned to the Federal Building for the rest of our crew. It was a stunning event—all of it broadcast live on local television stations.

Given what could have happened, things went remarkably well. Julia, who was in the crowd with Dorothy and friends, was just thrilled by the incident—or so a friend told me. Although the ten of us were taken to the police station and booked, we were charged with no more than a "violation" (equivalent to a traffic ticket). The next day, when I showed up at my office to prepare for my class, my department chair, Sung Bok Kim—to whom I hadn't said anything about my arrest plans—looked at me in astonishment. "You're out of jail!" he said, remarking that he had watched my arrest on television. "Yes," I noted, determined to soothe his anxiety; "it was nothing at all; just a violation." At our subsequent trial, the judge—citing what he claimed was a need to impose penalties for civil disobedience—sentenced us to fines of $100 each. But the Albany Labor Council, on a motion from Redlo, voted to pay my fine and John's. Also, of course, the antiapartheid struggle was becoming irresistible, and Congress, swept up in the spirit of the time, defied Reagan and passed legislation imposing sanctions on the South African regime.

About two years after this, I was arrested at the same site again—though with far less forethought. Outraged by U.S. military intervention in Central America—and particularly U.S. funding of the Contra war in Nicaragua—peace activists around the country were vigorously protesting government policy. In Albany an anti-intervention demonstration with a civil disobedience component was scheduled at the Federal Building. Dorothy and I both turned out for it and, agreeing that it was not practical for either of us to be arrested, decided to participate only in the large protest rally outside the building that would precede the arrests. Thus, when I looked around after the rally, I was surprised to discover that Dorothy was missing. "Where did she go?" I asked a friend. "I think she went into the building for the nonviolent civil disobedience," he replied. Peering through one of the building's glass walls, I discovered that, sure enough, Dorothy was inside. Now what should I do? Remaining outside while she was arrested seemed cowardly. So I rushed over to the building's door and, just before it was shut by the police, managed to push through it and join her. "I thought we decided not to do this," I said to Dorothy as we sat there, waiting to be arrested. "Well," she explained, "friends were going inside, and it seemed like the right thing to do." The judge, however, disagreed, and—noting that I was "a two-time offender"—doubled my fine.

Of all my political activities, however, the one closest to my heart—and certainly to my politics—was building a democratic socialist movement. In the mid-1970s, Michael Harrington and other veterans of the Socialist Party had created the Democratic Socialist Organizing Committee (DSOC) in the hope of popularizing democratic socialism. The dominant groups in the United States and the Soviet Union had long peddled the lie that one couldn't have democracy *and* socialism, and unfortunately much of the American public had come to believe that. Now, however, a movement had emerged to challenge that notion. The strategy was to appeal to democratic socialism's most likely supporters within America's broad democratic Left: labor, women's rights, racial justice, and peace activists. Furthermore, convinced that a key reason for the weakness of socialism in the United States was its linkage to a third party, DSOC sought to foster democratic socialism where these key constituencies were already located: *within* the Democratic Party. For me—long pining for a movement that embraced neither big business nor leftist revolution, one that rejected both capitalists and commissars—the goal and strategy of DSOC made perfect sense. So I joined DSOC in the late 1970s. Then, in December 1980, some friends and I, with the assistance of the DSOC national office (which provided us with a local membership list), organized a meeting of local DSOC members, most of whom had never met one another. It was genuinely exciting: Here was a group of predominantly young, talented, politically sophisticated people. If we worked together, we had a real chance to build a strong and effective democratic socialist presence in Albany. And that's what we did.

Chartered at the beginning of 1981, our Albany DSOC local grew rapidly. To my astonishment, I found it easy to get people to join it. By early 1985, we had 164 dues-paying members, a couple of dozen subscribers to *Democratic Left* (the DSOC magazine), and a total mailing list of some 200 people. As a percentage of the local population, we constituted perhaps the largest DSOC local in the United States. A membership survey that we did indicated that our biggest single constituency was composed of union leaders and staffers (18 percent), but we also recruited substantial numbers of social workers, college teachers, government employees, students, the retired, and the unemployed. Our ability to attract members, I think, reflected the fact that there were a lot of unaffiliated activists from the 1960s and 1970s who found democratic socialism compatible with their political beliefs. Furthermore, even when people did not have an activist background, democratic socialism—if defined as comparable to West European social democracy (rather than as a sectarian Left program)—could be quite appealing to them. Finally, our friendships, contacts, and credibility in the labor movement, in the racial justice movement, in the peace movement, and in other activist arenas made DSOC acceptable to numerous people who in other circumstances probably would have shied away from it.

It was also an exciting time for democratic socialism on the national and international levels. By the spring of 1981 DSOC—having grown by 60 percent over the previous two years—had 5,000 dues-paying members in fifty-one locals found in every state of the union except Nevada. DSOC's youth group had been established on seventy-five college campuses, and had become the largest left-wing youth organization since SDS. More than thirty DSOC members were holding elective public office, among them Congressman Ron Dellums of California and numerous state legislators from Maine to Georgia. DSOC also recruited presidents and/or vice presidents from some of the nation's major unions: the auto workers; the machinists; the state, county, and municipal employees; and the textile workers. Three DSOC members, in fact, sat on the AFL-CIO national board. And the progress continued. In March 1982 DSOC merged with the New American Movement—a smaller democratic socialist group—to form Democratic Socialists of America (DSA). With some 10,000 members, DSA was the largest democratic socialist organization to appear in the United States since the Socialist Party of the 1930s. As a member group of the Socialist International, DSA sent its leaders to international conferences, where they hobnobbed and served on committees with the leaders of the social democratic parties that governed or had governed most democratic nations. Furthermore, many of these parties seemed to be on the rise, with stunning social democratic election victories occurring during the early 1980s in Greece, France, Spain, Sweden, Australia, and elsewhere.

Although our progress in Albany was by no means as grand, it was exciting. We elected a small steering committee—on which Dorothy and I served— and plunged into an array of activities. Holding monthly business/membership meetings, we eventually decided to spice them up with featured talks on such topics as "Health Care and Capitalism." Beginning in May 1981, we started publishing the *Albany Anvil,* our Albany DSOC newsletter, carrying news of our activities and those of other social justice and peace organizations in the capital district. We also held a mass meeting on the SUNY/Albany campus, in which local labor, women's rights, and peace movement leaders assailed the Reagan administration's right-wing policies. Following up, we organized campus forums on such topics as "Socialism and the European Left," "Socialism and the American Radical Tradition," and "Prospects for the Democratic Left in America," as well as a debate on the subject of "Democratic Socialism vs. Capitalism." Drawing upon my campus and DSA contacts, I arranged to bring Michael Harrington to SUNY/Albany, where in October 1982 he addressed an exceptionally large, friendly audience in the Campus Center ballroom and then spoke to a smaller crowd at a DSA-hosted reception. Harrington also drew good TV, radio, and press coverage. Subsequently, I brought other DSA luminaries to speak at SUNY as well, including Barbara Ehrenreich, Noam Chomsky, and Manning Marable.

Probably our biggest outreach events were our annual Eugene V. Debs award dinners. Beginning in 1982 they honored outstanding local labor leaders (ACTWU's Bob Redlo in 1982; UUP's Tim Reilly in 1983; the American

Federation of State, County, and Municipal Employees' John Funiciello in 1984; and the Public Employees Federation's Doug Bullock in 1985) and at the same time provided the major funding for Albany DSA's activities. In organizing these dinners, our contacts with local labor leaders were particularly important, for unions dipped into their treasuries to buy blocs of dinner tickets for their members. The unions' purchase of these tickets also meant that although a portion of the 200 to 300 attendees at each dinner were DSA members or other local lefties, a substantial number of those in attendance were rank-and-file union members who throughout their lives had been thoroughly propagandized about the evils of "socialism." Consequently, through our speeches and behavior at these events, they received their first introduction to what democratic socialism really meant. I wondered sometimes what these textile workers, bus drivers, firefighters, clerks, and other poorly educated workers thought about what they heard at the Debs dinners or, for that matter, what they and other community residents thought about the large street sign outside the banquet hall: "Welcome, Democratic Socialists!"

DSA's New Year's Eve parties were considerably wilder. Held at our house, they soon became *the* place to be on that party-going evening and were attended by many DSA members who never appeared at our monthly business meetings. The featured attraction at each party was a madcap, satirical play, which began every year precisely at midnight. Written by Dorothy and by me, this musical comedy production—with partygoers pressed into starring roles on the spot—would lampoon political events (including DSA's activities) over the past year. With Warren Beatty's film *Reds* then popular among moviegoers, we began this series of plays with *Pinks: An Epic Drama of Love and Revolution*. Then, in subsequent years, we performed variants on this theme. Perhaps this song, sung by "Ronnie Richpig" in *Pinks II,* captures the irreverent flavor of these productions. Sung to the tune of "Chiquita Banana," it went:

> I am Ronnie Richpig, and I've come to say
> We're gonna stamp out pinkos, working people,
>   and gays.
> We're loaded with dough
> From the wealthy few.
> And if you don't like it
> Here's what we will do:
> We will put you in a prison
> On an unemployment li-ine
> Any way we can get to you
> We will find a way to screw you.

> Oh, this government's the product of reactionary
>   capitalist strata.
> So better stay away... all you DSAers!
> Bang, bang, bang, bang!

Of course, we also joked about our own events. Here, from *Pinks Go to Washington,* is a little spoof (to the tune of "Oh Holy Night") about our Debs dinners:

> Oh holy night
> The silverware is shining
> It is the night of Eugene Debs's birth.
> Long lay the world
> In corporate clutches pining
> 'Til he appeared and to socialism gave birth
> A thrill of hope
> The working class rejoices
> For yonder breaks
> A new and socialist dawn.
> Plunk down your cash,
> Oh hear the dreary speeches.
> The dinner has begun
> On the night when Debs was born
> Oh night divine,
> Oh night, oh night divine.

Our Albany DSOC/DSA leadership began with a steering committee, but we eventually added a secretary and a chair. Some of the most active leaders were Pat Malone, a retired state government budget officer who hosted steering committee meetings at his house; Ronnie Steinberg and Lillie McLaughlin, researchers at SUNY's Center for Women in Government; Gene Damm, a writer for the *South End Scene,* a community newspaper; Gary Dorrien, an Episcopal priest; Judy Ferraro, a teacher active in the Troy Labor Council; Bruce Miroff and Todd Swanstrom, SUNY political scientists; and Dorothy and me. Gary became chair of the group in early 1983 and, beginning in 1984, he and Dorothy served as co-chairs. I became the Albany DSOC/DSA secretary at a fairly early date and, much like an executive director, handled most of the group's organizational work. For the most part, it was a very congenial group of people, and whatever tensions emerged developed less from political or personal differences than from the heavy burden of work necessary to maintain an effective socialist political organization.

From 1981 to 1985 we were remarkably effective. We drew large crowds to many of our events, added substantially to union picket lines and to peace movement rallies, and publicized a variety of liberal-Left causes through the *Albany Anvil*. In addition, working in coalition with other progressive organizations, we helped to inject progressive issues into local Democratic Party politics. In 1982 John Dow, a former member of Congress who had been an early opponent of the Vietnam War, came to an Albany DSA meeting and appealed for our support in his political campaign, which focused on backing the nuclear freeze. Dow was challenging U.S. Representative Samuel Stratton, an exceptionally hawkish Congressman who had long represented the capital district, in the Democratic primary. Although, ultimately, Dow drew little more than 27 percent of the vote, it was the best showing yet by any of Stratton's opponents. In 1984 and 1986, we worked for Ed Bloch, a DSA member and the Democratic challenger to U.S. Representative Jerry Solomon, in an adjoining district. Although Ed, too, had little chance to win, particularly in Solomon's almost entirely rural, Republican bastion, DSA members threw themselves into his campaigns—raising money, posting signs, and distributing literature. Given the unpromising circumstances, Ed did reasonably well.

Our most exciting campaign, however, occurred in 1985, when, together with other progressive forces, we rallied behind Nancy Burton's reelection to the Albany Common Council from the Sixth Ward (where Dorothy and I lived). In a city controlled by a conservative Democratic Party machine, Nancy stood out as the fifteen-member Common Council's only independent, progressive legislator, as well as its only woman. She had participated in the January 1985 antiapartheid sit-in at the Federal Building, had sponsored a Freeze resolution (which somehow had passed in the Albany Common Council), and had sponsored South Africa divestment legislation (which had not). Having won the last Democratic primary (her first) against the machine candidate by only twelve votes, she came to an Albany DSA meeting that May and appealed for our support. We gave it to her and, among other things, provided the volunteers who staffed her phone banks for a two-week period. Meanwhile, the machine threw everything it had into defeating her—a young, attractive candidate (Mike Conners, son of the longtime state assemblyman from that district), endorsements of Conners by every local politician in the region, and constant (and vicious) political mailings. One day I heard a band going down our street and looked out to see Conners and a fleet of local officeholders knocking on every door and glad-handing the residents. How, I wondered, could we possibly win this one?

Nonetheless, I gave the Burton campaign my all, including mobilizing DSA members, gathering signatures, phoning, leafleting, and driving "our voters" to the polls. On election night that September, I served as a poll-watcher in the crucial First Election District (my own). Then, when the votes were finally counted, I sprinted over to the Burton campaign headquarters and called, breathlessly, for silence. Nancy, I announced to the crowd, had carried the First E.D. by an overwhelming margin. "That's it!" screamed her campaign manager. "Nancy's won!" And she had, with some 60 percent of the vote. As this was the hottest political story of the night in Albany, the TV cameras zoomed in on Nancy, who proceeded to thank three organizations for contributing to her stunning victory: the New Democratic Coalition (a reform Democratic group), the Eleanor Roosevelt Democratic Club (a gay-lesbian Democratic group), and Democratic Socialists of America. It was quite a night!

Despite some remarkable successes, however, Albany DSA had significant problems. For one thing, we were never able to mobilize more than a small portion of our membership for our activities. This is fairly common among social movement organizations. And it was even truer of DSA, which nationwide suffered from what its New York leaders called "the bagel problem" (and others called "the doughnut problem"). This boiled down to the fact that our members were often active in all sorts of other groups (e.g., labor, women's rights, racial justice, and peace) and didn't seem willing to put the time into what should be uniting them: a democratic socialist movement. Thus, there was a hole in the middle—where we were. But *why* did that hole exist? Why weren't more people willing to move beyond their paper memberships in DSA and put in the time necessary to build a democratic socialist movement? The answer, I think, is because it was so difficult, at least compared to working for a variety of more popular, more feasible, single-issue causes. And this, in turn, reflected socialism's broader problems in American life: the racial, ethnic, and religious divisions that undermined class consciousness; the strength of American capitalism; and the discrediting of "socialism" because of the horrible example provided by the Soviet Union and other Communist nations. In short, a socialist movement failed to mobilize activists not because they thought socialism was a bad idea, but because they considered it a very remote possibility in the United States.

In any case, by the end of 1985 I was pretty well burned out. I was not only exhausted by the demands of running Albany DSA, but also growing increasingly impatient and irritated with other people for not sharing more of the burden. And yet, if I did not do things, I complained to Dorothy, they were not going to get done. In response, Dorothy assured me that the organization could keep going without my being a martyr to the cause. But, if it couldn't, she added, perhaps it was time for it to fold up. More reassured by her first point than by her second, I discussed the issue with other steering committee members and then decided that, although I would continue to be an active member of Albany DSA, I would no longer serve as one of its leaders. Thus, with new officers and a new steering committee elected for 1986, I proceeded to end my leadership role. And by the end of that year, the organization was dead.

This disaster sparked a good deal of reflection on my part. Although there was some grim personal satisfaction in confirming how important my leadership was to Albany DSA's survival, I was nevertheless heartbroken by its collapse. Not only did all that effort I had put into it seem wasted, but I still believed in the cause of democratic socialism and thought that DSA provided the best possibility for attaining it in the United States. On the other hand, Albany DSA had contributed to a number of useful things, including popularizing democratic socialism, bolstering progressive causes, and assisting liberal-Left candidates. Furthermore, although Albany DSA was dead, DSA continued on the national level. Finally, Albany DSA had brought together dozens of local labor activists, most of whom found their way into another organization with much the same political perspective, the Solidarity Committee of the Capital District.

The Solidarity Committee began in November 1983, when, in the midst of a bitter strike by transport workers against the Greyhound bus company, union members in the capital district organized a Greyhound Strikers Solidarity Committee. Determined to defeat the giant corporation, then demanding enormous givebacks from the workers, the committee staged large, pro-labor demonstrations at Albany's Greyhound terminal. When the company hired scabs to drive the buses, activists milled about in front of the moving vehicles, blocking their progress and, as the buses inched forward, draping themselves over the sides and over the front windshields. On one occasion when I was present, the police made two arrests for disorderly conduct. Ultimately, faced with this kind of spirited resistance in Albany and elsewhere, Greyhound was forced to agree to a settlement with the Amalgamated Transit Union. In turn, the Strikers Solidarity Committee—elated by the outpouring of union and community support—decided to form a permanent organization: the Solidarity Committee of the Capital District.

The Solidarity Committee brought together some very interesting and talented people. Its heart and soul was the charismatic John Funiciello, a hefty, bearded, public relations staffer for AFSCME who had gone through a variety of careers, ranging from lumberjack to journalist. Raised in a union household in New York's rugged North Country and largely self-educated, John reminded me—in appearance and political orientation—of an early twentieth-century IWW member. He also knew an enormous amount about labor and public policy. Other key figures in the Solidarity Committee included the brash Bob

Redlo, manager of the Hudson Valley Joint Board of ACTWU and president of the Hudson Labor Council; the feisty Doug Bullock, a NYS Labor Department employee active in the Public Employees Federation; the radical Fred Pfeiffer, a machinist and rank-and-file militant in the International Union of Electrical Workers; and the stalwart Art Fleischner, an organizer for the Service Employees International Union. I participated in the Solidarity Committee's early meetings, presided over by John at the AFSCME headquarters, but I was not yet a major player in this dynamic organization.

The new group proceeded to do the kinds of things that I had always thought the labor movement did—until, of course, I started attending Labor Council meetings. It revived the Albany area's Labor Day parades and picnics, organized a labor film series, and began publishing a monthly newsletter, *Solidarity Notes*, which it mailed free of charge to local activists. The Solidarity Committee participated in nearly every union organizing drive, strike, or contract struggle in the capital district—leafleting, swelling picket lines and leading chants, raising support funds, and sometimes working with the union leadership to plan strategy. Moving farther afield, it collected food and other desperately needed supplies for striking copper miners in Clifton, Morenci, and Ajo, Arizona, then battling against the powerful Phelps-Dodge corporation. In December 1984, to top off our work for the miners, John hopped in a large truck and drove thousands of miles to personally deliver the supplies to them. Indeed, no crusade for justice seemed too distant for the Solidarity Committee, which threw itself into workers' struggles from Guatemala to South Africa.

As there was a lot of overlap between the political perspective and the labor constituency of DSA and those of the Solidarity Committee, it was hardly surprising that, as I drew back from my leadership role in DSA, I began to play a larger role in the Solidarity Committee. In early 1988, when Fred no longer had the free time to serve as Solidarity Committee treasurer, I volunteered to take on the job. Given the Solidarity Committee's prestige in the Albany labor movement and activist circles, the treasurer position turned out to be pretty easy. All I had to do was to send out a yearly dues notice to sympathetic unions and activists and the money rolled in. This proved to be an important boost for the Solidarity Committee. With our financial base secure, we now could do lots more, including mail *Solidarity Notes* to a thousand people per month. We were in much better shape than most other local activist organizations, and many of them began to approach us for contributions.

Although Dorothy was far less involved in the labor movement than I was, she, too, ultimately came within the Solidarity Committee's orbit. Attending a play one night, I noticed that John Funiciello had just entered the theater with his wife, Stephanie. As I knew Dorothy had never met John, I pointed him out to her. Dorothy took note of him and remarked: "I know that woman he's with!" Dorothy and Stephanie had been classmates, decades before, at Hunter College. And now, through the Solidarity Committee, they renewed their friendship as they attended activities together. And so the Solidarity Committee gradually became an increasingly important part of both of our lives.

Despite the fact that the Solidarity Committee had strong support among union activists and many of their local leaders, the higher-ups in the labor movement—and particularly the officials of the New York State AFL-CIO—hated it. Part of the reason, I think, is that we embarrassed them by doing many of the things that they were supposed to do, but, in fact, neglected doing. Moreover, politically we were to their left—perfectly willing to excoriate corporate greed and U.S. foreign policy in the sharpest of terms. Perhaps most significant, though, we were loose cannons, union members out of their control; and for a union bureaucrat—or any bureaucrat—that is the worst crime of all.

Consequently, state AFL-CIO officials bad-mouthed us in private, and in public they demanded that the Albany Labor Council—to which we reported monthly as a standing committee—terminate our status as an official body of this AFL-CIO-chartered organization. The formal justification for this demand was that people who did not belong to AFL-CIO unions (e.g., members of the Teamsters and of the Student Association of the State University) participated in our meetings. Few, of course, viewed this as the real reason for the crackdown upon us. In any case, Tim Reilly suggested an ingenious way around the state AFL-CIO decree. If the Solidarity Committee couldn't be part of the Labor Council, the Labor Council should become part of the Solidarity Committee. So that's how we finessed the issue. Henceforth, like a few dozen unions in the area, the Albany Labor Council made annual dues payments to the Solidarity Committee. Meanwhile, the Solidarity Committee, though shorn of its official AFL-CIO status, continued to report to the monthly Labor Council meetings.

These connections in the local labor movement facilitated my support efforts for one of the nation's most dynamic but impoverished unions—the United Farm Workers (UFW). To assist the UFW, I brought its founder and president, Cesar Chavez, to Albany in 1987. Chavez, probably the country's most beloved labor leader, was then engaged in a nationwide barnstorming tour, stirring up publicity and raising funds for the UFW's table grape boycott. All I had to do to lure him to Albany was to raise $6,000. Drawing upon every union and campus contact I had, I somehow managed to do this and, at the same time, widely publicize his appearance and secure coverage of it by the communications media. To my delight, Chavez's visit to Albany that April was a great success, drawing lots of attention, media interviews, and a standing-room-only crowd to his major speech on the SUNY/Albany campus. Along the way, he and one of the UFW vice presidents, Artie Rodriguez, took a break at our house, where Chavez ate a macrobiotic lunch (which wasn't easy for me to obtain), chatted about his life and times, took a nap, and left me with a signed grape boycott poster as a souvenir. Although coordinating this whirlwind visit was exhausting, it was also very satisfying. Two years later, this visit was repeated, though on a smaller scale, by Artie, who—after Cesar's death—succeeded him as UFW president.

I became even more deeply enmeshed in labor movement activism through the work of UUP's statewide Solidarity Committee. Inspired by the Solidarity Committee of the Capital District, the UUP Solidarity Committee was organized in 1986, when Tim Reilly convinced the statewide UUP president, Nuala Drescher, that it would be a good idea to form a committee to make recommendations for UUP support of other union struggles. Creating this new committee was apparently regarded by Nuala as a means of heading off hasty, ill-considered financial contributions proposed on the floor of our statewide conventions. But, from Tim's standpoint, it provided a way to build a more militant, socially conscious union, and—with this in mind—he saw to it that Nuala appointed me as the first chair of the new committee.

I loved coordinating the UUP Solidarity Committee. For one thing, there was a committee budget, albeit not a very large one. Indeed, it never went above a few thousand dollars a year during my reign as committee chair. Furthermore, appropriations had to be voted on by the full committee, and all committee recommendations for financial contributions had to be approved by the UUP president. Nevertheless, as committee chair I could and did set the agenda, and almost invariably I secured what I wanted. This included not only financial contributions to struggling unions, but also the issuance of UUP statements and the mobilization of UUP members on their behalf. Furthermore, we backed all sorts of worthy causes with money, letters of support by the UUP president, and support resolutions by the delegates at UUP conventions. These causes were all part of the labor movement's social and political agenda, I argued, and—whether or not they were so originally—they were now.

The most satisfying of these UUP Solidarity Committee ventures—the epitome of my redistribution of resources from the professoriat to the proletariat—was support of the South African freedom struggle. At the time, there was a great deal of discussion in the union about divestment in companies with investments in South Africa and about boycotting their products. But these tactics didn't seem to me to be particularly useful, for UUP didn't own corporate stock, and its outlays for purchases of typewriters and other equipment were miniscule. But I hit upon an alternative idea. The almost all-black Congress of South

African Trade Unions (COSATU) was a key force in the antiapartheid struggle, and its strikes, all illegal, often led to the prosecution and imprisonment of its leaders by the apartheid regime. Was it possible, somehow, to fund COSATU? I contacted the American Committee on Africa, a leading organization in the U.S. antiapartheid campaign, and discovered that it was, indeed, feasible to get money through to the hard-pressed labor federation.

So—with the support of Tim, now statewide UUP president—I decided to move forward on this front. Establishing a UUP South Africa Labor Support Fund under the aegis of the UUP Solidarity Committee, I began to solicit contributions to it in 1987. To encourage such contributions, I arranged to have an article about the South African labor struggle, written by Iris Berger, published that December in the *Voice,* UUP's statewide newspaper. In the following years, having familiarized myself with the union situation in South Africa, I wrote another three articles for the *Voice,* lauding COSATU and reporting on the South African government's attempts to suppress it. One article was adorned with a wonderful photo of black workers engaged in a militant demonstration and doing the toyi-toyi (a South African protest dance). Meanwhile, I promoted our fund-raising campaign at UUP conventions, lobbied local UUP leaders for chapter contributions, and solicited funds from the general membership. Ultimately, we raised about $5,000—all of it dispatched, successfully, to COSATU.

Although this was not a large amount of money, it appears to have meant a great deal to the embattled South African labor movement. COSATU refused to accept contributions from the AFL-CIO, which it distrusted thanks to the cozy relationship the U.S. labor federation maintained with the U.S. government. But, for some reason, UUP had greater credibility and managed to forge close ties with COSATU. Sending his "revolutionary greetings" in 1988, COSATU's general secretary, Jay Naidoo, profusely thanked Tim for our early contributions and added that "we, in COSATU, highly appreciate your unprecedented opportunity to build relationships on the firm ground of international cooperation, as well as your gesture of solidarity with the struggle of the South African masses." Years later, when the apartheid regime had fallen and UUP's new president, Bill Scheuerman, traveled to South Africa to serve as an official observer in that nation's first free elections, he was astonished to find a car and driver waiting for him at the airport. It had been dispatched for him by COSATU, now the nation's thoroughly legal and very powerful labor movement. Looking back on my organizing of this South Africa labor support campaign, I think it was one of the best things I did in my life.

My political influence was enhanced by the fact that the local communications media sometimes asked me to comment on contemporary public issues. As a writer on peace movements, I was occasionally phoned for background information or for quotable comments by journalists who were covering peace demonstrations. Once, in my capacity as a foreign policy specialist, I was asked by the news staff at a local television station if they could videotape my comments upon a major world affairs speech, delivered that day by President Reagan. Because the call came in on a nonteaching day, when I was working in my office, garbed in a particularly disreputable, ratty old sweater, I suggested that the TV crew film me that afternoon, when I could arrange to look more presentable. But the TV staff insisted upon filming me immediately. So there I sat, critiquing the president as the cameras rolled. My only consolation was that it was doubtful that much, if any, of my commentary would appear on television that evening. Therefore, I was startled that night, as I sat before Pat Malone's television set, to watch a few minutes of Reagan's speech, a few minutes of my remarks in rebuttal, a return to Reagan's speech, and then a return to my critique. To my great amusement, that news segment came off looking like a debate between Reagan ("The Great Communicator") and me. And, for a stutterer, I didn't do so badly, either.

Even though working as a political activist took an enormous amount of time, I did not entirely neglect my role as a scholar. My book, *American Intervention in Greece, 1943–1949,* was published by Columbia University Press in 1982, and it was certainly my best work thus far—exhaustively researched, smoothly written, and tightly argued. Although it did not make as big a splash as I would have liked, it did receive some very positive reviews and probably resulted in my election that year to the national council of the Society for Historians of American Foreign Relations. In addition, a few years later it led to my speaking at a high-powered conference in Washington, D.C., sponsored by AHEPA, a Greek heritage organization, along with U.S. Senator Joseph Biden, U.S. Representative Pat Schroeder, military analyst Edward Luttwak, and Greek Ambassador George Papoulias. Meanwhile, in 1984 Temple University Press published the revised version of my *Rebels Against War*—a book that, despite its dated research and language (neither of which Temple allowed me to alter), continued thereby to stay in print for additional decades. Ironically, although my preoccupation with political issues led to a decline in my scholarly activity in the early 1980s, I received SUNY/Albany's Excellence in Research award in May 1985.

Serving on the national board of the Conference on Peace Research in History, however, provided a wonderful blending of the two. CPRH represented a true community of scholars—cooperative and supportive—and it was a pleasure to hang out with its participants at AHA conventions and at board meetings. Determined to put major peace proponents on the intellectual map, we came up with a plan to produce a *Biographical Dictionary of Modern Peace Lead-*

ers, with entries on leading peace campaigners from around the world. Harold Josephson, a gregarious, down-to-earth historian at the University of North Carolina–Charlotte, agreed to serve as editor in chief. I became one of three associate editors, supervising the preparation of over a hundred essays covering twentieth-century U.S. peace activists. Published by Greenwood Press, this 1,133-page book contained 750 biographical essays, written by 250 authors, on peace leaders from forty-one countries. It was a path-breaking work and received a prize from the Society for Historians of American Foreign Relations as the outstanding book that appeared in 1985 on peace movements and/or internationalism. In addition, noting the popularity of the film *Gandhi,* we decided to put together a shorter inspirational book, *Peace Heroes in Twentieth-Century America,* that we hoped would be read by college students. Chuck DeBenedetti, who suggested the venture, was tapped for the editing job, and I contributed a chapter on one of my heroes, Eugene Debs. In 1986 Indiana University Press published the first edition. As these and other projects of ours were collective ventures, we donated all the royalties to CPRH.

In 1984 I took on a CPRH project of my own: serving as coeditor of our scholarly journal, *Peace and Change.* This role was considerably less glamorous than it might seem. The journal, then headquartered at Kent State University, had a rather grubby-looking format, was always in financial trouble, and had a confusing division of editorial responsibilities between a CPRH editor (in this case, me) and an editor from the other sponsoring group, the Consortium on Peace Research, Education, and Development. Although the shared editorial responsibility lightened the burden of each editor's work, it also allowed things to fall through the cracks and often kept me in the dark as to when articles and reviews would appear in print. Furthermore, I learned how utterly irresponsible some academics could be after they had agreed to review manuscripts or books for publication. Fortunately, though, by this point in my career I did have many useful contacts that I could call upon for these purposes or ask to submit articles to the journal. Furthermore, it was a treat to edit short autobiographical articles for publication by my former mentor, Merle Curti (then in his eighties), and by my more recent champion, Arthur Ekirch. Even so, when my editorial stint came to an end in 1987, I was happy to turn over the job to someone else. I had had enough of editing other people's work and was itching to do more research and writing of my own.

In fact, the most ambitious research and writing venture of my career was already shaping up. It began in late 1985, when CPRH's Charles Chatfield, who had long been working to spread our peace researcher network to Europe, announced plans for a small European-American Consultation on Peace Research in History, to be held during the following summer, in Schlaining, Austria. This was particularly appealing to Americans, for the conference was to be convened in a genuine castle, now operated by the Austrian Peace Research Institute. Recognizing the competitive nature of the situation, I realized that what I needed to secure my participation was to think up a new, exciting project on which I could present a paper. But what would that be? With antinuclear activism convulsing the globe, the answer came to me fairly quickly. I would write a paper on the history of the world nuclear disarmament movement. Given my prominence as a historian of peace movements and the fact that no one had ever done a study like that before, my application for the conference was accepted, and I started work on the paper in January 1986. As there was an enormous amount to read, I began with published sources and—despite what I soon recognized as the vast nature of the nuclear disarmament campaign—managed to put together a lengthy paper. That summer I continued the research while traveling in Europe.

But Dorothy and I also turned the trip to Europe into a vacation. Unlike me, she had never visited that continent, so we planned more than a month's travels to numerous countries. Beginning in Paris, though, we found we had very different traveling rhythms. I was a dogged tourist, determined to see and do everything possible. Dorothy, on the other hand, liked to sit around and read. Even when I dragged her out of our Paris hotel room (where she was happily ensconced with a book) to see the art at the Louvre, she eventually broke away from my stalwart march through its galleries to find the café, where she settled down at a table with a cup of coffee and a paperback. Nevertheless, we had a wonderful time. In Paris we flitted about among the gargoyles on the top of Notre Dame. In Amsterdam we visited with George Berger, who, ever the eccentric, filled his bathtub with an unlikely stew of water, dirty clothes, and yeast, which he claimed cleaned the clothes by devouring the dirt. In Geneva we took a boat across the lake to the Castle of Chillon, immortalized by Byron's graffiti. In Venice we visited open-air markets and gobbled incredibly fragrant, juicy peaches as bees hovered drunkenly in the air.

Venice was also the place where we encountered the Italian Communist Party (PCI). By the time we reached that city, even I—after viewing thousands of paintings of the Madonna and child—was growing bored with conventional tourism. One day, as we wound our way through Venice's crooked streets, we were pleased to see a poster announcing a Festival of *Unita,* the newspaper of the PCI. Although I had always had a negative view of Communist parties, the PCI was certainly the best of the lot, for it had long ago broken with the Soviet model, committed itself to electoral politics, and developed a mass, popular base in Italian life. As the poster was in Italian, we couldn't decipher it very well, but it did seem to announce the performance of a play that afternoon and a musical event that evening—both in one of Venice's major squares. Naturally, we were curious. So we headed off in the afternoon to see the play, which, as best as I could understand the title, dealt with something Red ("Rosso"). When we got to the square, all we saw was a tiny stage (adorned with red hammers and sickles) in the middle of it, with an audience of women and small children. Then the play, performed with puppets, began. Although it was in Italian, I soon recognized it: *Little Red Riding Hood!* Laughing hysterically, we decided to return that evening. When we did, the square was packed with thousands of people, talking vibrantly to one another, picking up food at concession stands, and looking quite apolitical. Suddenly, the lights flashed on a large stage and a slickly dressed young man stepped to the fore. Announcing something in rapid-fire Italian, he put the first song on the record player: "Blue Suede Shoes," blasted out at top volume by Elvis Presley. Every young pointy-shoed guy and ponytailed gal immediately began frenetically rocking and rolling, while pudgy, middle-aged mamas and papas looked on or minded the *bambini*. And so the evening went. For people raised on sinister images of the Red Menace, it was almost unbelievable.

From Venice, we moved on to the CPRH-sponsored conference at Schlaining, located in Austria's Burgenland region. Charles Chatfield had done an excellent job in organizing it, pulling together an all-star cast of peace researchers not only from the United States but also from Western Europe, Eastern Europe, and elsewhere. Many were very interesting people. A Hungarian, Ferenc Köszegi, had organized the first independent peace group in his Communist country. Ralph Summy, born in the United States, had relocated to Australia in the 1960s after his work for Boston SANE had rendered him politically suspect. Subsequently, he became a prominent Australian peace activist and peace researcher. On most days we gathered in the Castle Schlaining to present our papers, and the discussion was lively.

Fortunately, there was also plenty of time for banquets and tourism. One evening the whole gang of us set off by bus to a local vineyard, where wooden tables and benches had been set up outdoors to enable us to sample the "new wine." Joined by some local peasants, we downed bottle after bottle and were soon lifting our voices in songs from our respective countries, some of them quite political. Fritz Klein, an East German historian attending the conference, was suspicious of us until that evening, but—as he later remarked—finally recognized that our criticisms of Communism did not mean that we were fans of the Reagan administration. Harold Josephson, recently recovered from heart bypass surgery and having the time of his life, asked one of the peasants what the delicious spread was on the crackers that we were devouring along with the wine. "Pig fat," answered the peasant. "Pig fat," shrieked Harold. "I'm eating *pig fat?*" Both Dorothy and I, who preferred to flavor our tourism with political/intellectual activism and our political/intellectual activism with tourism, found the weeklong conference a wonderful combination of the two.

As things turned out, the Schlaining conference had some important consequences. It cemented ties among leading European, American, and Australian peace researchers, most of whom met there for the first time. The conferees also agreed on a broad definition of peace research in history: the study of the historic causes and consequences of violent international conflict and of the historic search for alternatives to such conflict. Furthermore, Charles and Peter van den Dungen (a lecturer in Peace Studies at the University of Bradford in Britain) drew together fifteen of the most significant papers (including mine) into a book, *Peace Movements and Political Cultures,* which was published by the University of Tennessee Press in 1988. The book was dedicated to Chuck DeBenedetti, a past president of CPRH. During the Schlaining gathering, Chuck had suffered from headaches and upon his return home was diagnosed as having a brain tumor. Within months, he was dead at the age of forty-four.

Another consequence of the conference was that, having received a lot of compliments on my paper, I decided to move forward with a major study of the history of antinuclear activism. While in Europe, I had done some preliminary poking around—interviewing a few individuals (such as Mient Jan Faber, the head of the powerful Dutch Inter-Church Peace Council) and looking at some archival collections (such as those located in the Peace Palace at the Hague). But now I realized that the time had come to get serious about this project, which, I increasingly saw, was going to be enormous. After all, it involved a study of hundreds of organizations and millions of people over roughly half a century. Moreover, I wanted to look at the issue of the movement's effectiveness, and that would entail plowing through a vast quantity of government records and interviewing government officials. What a job! To cover come of the costs of the research, I secured a small grant from SUNY/Albany and, to free me from teaching responsibilities, I landed an American Council of Learned Societies/Ford fellowship for 1987–88. Plunging into the manuscript research, I began gathering copious quantities of material. Even then I saw that I was only scratching the surface of what should and could be done.

My research for this book, which I now called *The Struggle Against the Bomb,* took me far and wide. I drove up to Canada, to McMaster University, to look at the Bertrand Russell and Vera Brittain Papers. I flew to Britain to look through the records of the prime minister, the Foreign Office, and the cabinet, located at the Public Record Office in Kew, just outside of London. I flew to Chicago to go through an assortment of files by atomic scientist and world government groups. I drove down to the Swarthmore College Peace Collection to examine the records of numerous peace organizations. I examined the papers of an array of U.S. government officials, traveling to the Truman Library in Independence, Missouri; the Eisenhower Library in Abilene, Kansas; the Kennedy Library in Boston; and the National Archives in Washington, D.C. I also flew to diverse cities to interview leading nuclear disarmament activists, including E. P. Thompson, the leader of the European Nuclear Disarmament campaign.

One of the more memorable research trips occurred in July 1989, when Julia and I flew out to California to look at the Leo Szilard papers (in San Diego) and the Norman Cousins papers (in Los Angeles). As Julia had not yet entered college, her research skills were minimal. But, if properly directed, she could take good notes, and it was fun working with her. While in San Diego, we also had the chance to visit with the Zwanziger family, whose members I hadn't seen for decades. Dorothy and Jonah joined us in Los Angeles, and then we all drove up the California coast to Big Sur. Julia really liked it there, but, unfortunately, we had already made plans to move on north, to San Francisco and then up the California and Oregon coasts to visit with Mike Weinberg in Corvallis. So that's where we headed, driving through redwood forests and along ocean-pounded shores on the way.

Once in Corvallis, Julia and I researched the Linus Pauling papers at Oregon State University while Dorothy and Jonah, after a few days hanging around Mike's place, returned to Albany. A couple of times we tried to attend a performance by the musical group Balafon, whose centerpiece was an instrument of the same name (a sort of African xylophone), but we never managed it. However, during the final days of our trip, Julia, Mike, and I headed off in his car to an environmentalist festival, in an old growth forest. It turned out to be quite a scene, with an assortment of countercultural types lying about on blankets, smoking pot, playing music, and bathing nude in a local stream. Julia had missed the late 1960s, but now she finally had her chance to see it. And that evening, serendipitously, who should appear on the festival stage but Balafon. As their music rang out into the night, Mike, Julia, and I joined the rest of the crowd in a wild, frenzied dance.

Of course, Dorothy and I also managed to carve out some vacation time with neither scholarship nor politics playing a prominent role. At a fairly early date we began renting a cottage for a week or two in the Wellfleet area on Cape

Cod. Here we combined hanging out on the beach, reading novels, eating dinners at interesting restaurants, and attending plays, lectures, and concerts in the evenings. Julia, Jonah, and Dave joined us there on occasion. We also took a trip up to Nova Scotia, whose highlight—after fairly conventional ocean vistas and bland, English-style food—was a visit to the city of Halifax, where Dorothy nearly underwent a meltdown under the impact of some very spicy Indian food. On the long drive back home, I noticed a sign for the town of Springhill and suddenly remembered the grim ballad "The Springhill Mine Disaster." So we found the Cumberland mine, now turned into a tourist site, and—attired in appropriate slickers and boots—plunged into its dark depths with a guide, a former miner. Posted in the miners' dressing room was the original handwritten version of the song, written by Ewen McCall, and mailed to the miners by his partner, Peggy Seeger.

On another occasion—a few years before my research trip to the West Coast with Julia—Dorothy and I explored San Francisco, watched the sun go down over dinner at Nepenthe's on Big Sur, and drove up the coast for her first meeting with Mike in Oregon. About a decade before, Mike—fascinated by water ever since our thirst-inducing ordeal in the Grand Canyon—had begun studying watershed management at Colorado State University. When he and dozens of other students sought to bring food to the embattled Indians at Wounded Knee, South Dakota, they were arrested by federal marshals and indicted by a Nixon administration grand jury for conspiracy to cause a riot under what was then popularly known as the "Rap Brown Act." However, thanks to the efforts of the ACLU and the incompetence of the government attorneys, the charges against them were dismissed. Thereafter, Mike obtained employment in Oregon managing water resources for a group of farmers and was delighted to renew contact with me and to meet Dorothy. The three of us had a wonderful time together, whether whitewater rafting or lolling about in his backyard hot tub. Over dinner one evening at a local restaurant, Mike and I swapped stories of our rambunctious past, turning us all so hysterical that the other diners on the scene swiftly departed.

Meanwhile, as I had predicted, Patty was once more on her feet and thriving. After dating a number of eligible bachelors, she decided to marry Reinhard Sidor—a recently divorced German-born chemist. Although Reinhard was an amiable person and not a conservative ideologue, he voted Republican, worked as an industrial hygienist for General Electric (the capital district's major corporation), and consistently defended corporate positions—for example, GE's claim that its dumping of PCBs in the Hudson River had no harmful consequences. After their marriage, Patty—along with Julia—moved into his nineteen-room, eight-bedroom mansion, located in an exclusive area of Schenectady known as "the GE Plot." The large carriage house behind it was used to store their surplus furniture. They had a great deal of it, especially after Patty decided to acquire a new set of furniture to go along with her redecoration of the main house. When I stopped by to pick up Julia, I would glance occasionally at the magazines on their coffee table, such as *Fortune* and *Business Week*, featuring stories like "What Will the Environmentalists Try to Scare Us with Next?" Delighted with her large modern kitchen, Patty threw big dinner parties and seemed quite happy with her new life. This time, at least, she had chosen well.

I do not know what Julia thought of the disjuncture between Patty's life and my own, for she was not very self-disclosing and probably didn't want to take sides. Nevertheless, she seemed to handle these circumstances reasonably well. In middle school and in high school, she proved an excellent student. Even though she was diminutive and shy, her gentle and cooperative nature served her nicely among more aggressive students who otherwise might have bullied her. Indeed, the toughest girl in her high school warned others that they had better leave Julia alone or they would have to reckon with *her*. For a time, Julia didn't have much of a social life, but this changed during her senior year of high school, when she met Bob Hughes, the son of a history teacher at Schenectady County Community College. The two of them quickly formed a little dyad and became inseparable. When Julia and I were in California doing research, she frequently moped about, missing her new boyfriend. I wasn't entirely happy about their intense relationship, for, based on my own experience, I thought she might be falling in love too early. So I looked forward to her developing a broader social life after the fall of 1989, when she started attending classes at Brandeis University. But, in fact, she didn't. Although she supplemented her excellent academic work there with new friendships, when it came to boyfriends her heart belonged to Bob.

Dave and Jonah continued to provide us with some anxious moments, but eventually they simmered down. For years, through their frequent horsing around, they managed to destroy many a piece of household furniture. As late as the summer of 1986, Dorothy and I were awakened in Paris by a phone call from Dave, announcing that he had totally wrecked Dorothy's car. In addition, Jonah fell in with some tough kids at his high school who were engaged in a variety of criminal enterprises. When two of them came around to our house, I confronted them and told them to get the hell off my front steps and never come back again; to my relief, they departed peacefully, though not without a lot of nasty snarling. But after Dave's departure for Bennington College—which he could attend free of charge, thanks to his father's employment there—he became caught up in college life. A few years later, Jonah also headed off to Bennington. Here Dave exhibited genuine talent in art; Jonah, in music. Thus, by the end of the decade both were losing their rough edges and emerging as more or less normal college students.

Dorothy and I, sometimes accompanied by Julia, paid frequent visits to my father and Marjie, with whom we continued to get on very well. After the mid-1970s, when my father had retired, the two of them had become confirmed "snow birds," spending the warmer months in an apartment in Westchester (within range of Marjie's daughter and her family) and the colder months in an apartment in Century Village, a senior citizens' housing development in Deerfield Beach, Florida. Marjie, particularly, enjoyed life in Century Village, where there was a small, aging group of "progressive" residents who organized lectures by left-wing speakers. In these rather Popular Frontish circles, my father sometimes raised embarrassing questions. "If Eastern Europe is such a paradise," he would ask, provocatively, "why are so many people trying to leave it?" Usually very good-natured, Marjie would grow upset about this kind of thing, complaining that my father was becoming a red-baiter. Often I was called upon to settle political conflicts between them, and I sometimes felt like a United Nations diplomat, trying to mediate a dispute between East and West. Most of the time, though, we sat around their Westchester apartment, ate the strange meals that Marjie prepared, and played lengthy games of Scrabble—games that either Marjie or I almost invariably won.

With Dorothy largely cut off from her circle of friends at Bennington and my friendships thinned out somewhat by my divorce, we acquired many new friends in Albany. Some of them came from the ranks of our associates on the Solidarity Committee. But there were numerous others, including Bill Gulla and Judith Rubenstein, two socially conscious social workers who moved into the capital region; Leon Van Dyke, a founder of The Brothers, a defunct local activist group reminiscent of SNCC and the Black Panthers; Raffi and Aliza Sulkowitz, an Israeli couple who had come to the United States to escape their country's wars; and Paula Maute, another local social worker. On campus, my friend Myron Taylor died unexpectedly in 1989, but I picked up new friends, including Sucheta Mazumdar and Vasant Kaiwar, very erudite and left-wing Indian historians who became members of my department; Colia Clark, a dynamic former SNCC worker who taught African American Studies; and Bruce Miroff and Todd Swanstrom, political scientists previously active in our DSA group. I also retained relationships, usually by mail but sometimes through visits, with a far-flung network of friends, including Howie Schonberger, Blanche

Cook, Ted Lieverman, Sandi Cooper, Paul Metzger, David Schalk, and Mike Weinberg. In the Albany region, Ben and I remained particularly close, and I was delighted that he and Dorothy got on well.

In the circles that Dorothy and I frequented, discussions of gender roles and changes in marital status seemed fairly common. Probably for this reason, some of us got together to form a men's group. Bill first broached the idea to me, and I rounded up a group of other Albany-area friends to participate in it as well: George, Todd, and Bruce. Meeting every few weeks, we discussed our childhoods and assorted aspects of our personal lives. Although George dropped out at a fairly early stage, the rest of us continued meeting and found our friendships developing accordingly. Bill, especially, proved a warm and excellent host and arranged for breakfasts, parties, and even dance lessons at his house for us and the women in our lives. I tried playing tennis with Todd, but he was much too good at it, making our games lopsided and predictable. Fortunately, Bill and I had about the same skill level, and almost every game was lengthy and hard-fought. Sometimes, in fact, our tennis sets dragged on endlessly. As the years went by, the four of us never really explored our lives very deeply. But we did have a good time together.

Often my social life intersected with my intellectual and political concerns. In 1987 Ralph Summy and his son, Gil, arrived from Australia, and—during their stay at our house—we enjoyed seeing the sights, discussing writing projects, and gabbing about political activism in our respective countries. In the fall of 1989, when Leon Van Dyke became a candidate for the Albany school board, he pressed me into service. Although Leon didn't have much of a campaign effort going, his past activism with The Brothers had made him a well-known figure in the African American community. Thus, it was an interesting and unusual experience to accompany him to campaign events. Once, with an amplifier tied to the roof of my car, we used it as a sound truck, wending our way through the blighted streets of Albany's black wards. As I chauffeured, Leon—with microphone in hand—blithely outlined his political message to the city's impoverished black residents, many of whom came up to the car to shake his hand and cast an occasional look at the strange white guy driving him around.

Music also became an increasingly important part of my life. Thanks to DSA meetings at the home of Pat Malone, I became acquainted with Roger Allen—a former Nebraska farm boy, now a carpenter—who was married to his niece. Roger was a terrific musician and, learning that I played the guitar, suggested that we get together with other musicians he had come across to jam. And so we did, meeting first at one another's homes and, later, as other performers joined us, at the Albany Friends Meeting House. Coincidentally, in the mid-1980s two DSA members, Bob Andrews and Peg Wilson, decided to put together a singing group to perform songs at political gatherings. This Occasional Chorus, to which I was recruited for singing and sporadic backup on the guitar, gave some spirited performances at peace movement and labor movement events. Once, as we were about to lead a union crowd in labor songs on the steps of the New York State Capitol, the head of the local musicians' union demanded to see our union cards. Fortunately, I had my UUP card to show him—although I don't think he found that entirely satisfactory.

Overall, by the end of 1989 my life was going very well. Although Dorothy and I—disillusioned with the institution of marriage—did not bother to get married, our relationship remained very strong. Furthermore, my job was reasonably secure, my scholarship was flourishing, my political activities were numerous, my daughter and Dorothy's sons had gone off to college, my friends were plentiful, and I was exploring new aspects of my life. Politically, of course, the situation was far less satisfying, for the social and political gains of previous decades, under challenge by right-wing forces, were being dismantled by the Republican Party. The 1960s, I realized sadly, really were over, and the obstacles to creating a just and peaceful society were far greater than I had ever imagined. But I remained hopeful that the political tide would turn and that the march of progress would be resumed. On most days my energy felt boundless. And I was never bored. My major regret was that there was not enough time in the day to do everything I wanted to get done.

9

A National and International Figure, 1990–2001

Beginning in the early 1990s, my prominence as a historian, coupled with my research on the history of the world nuclear disarmament movement, led to my playing a growing national and international role. I had presided over a nationwide (albeit small) scholarly organization in the past (the Conference on Peace Research in History) and had participated in the 1986 conference at Schlaining that had brought together European, American, and Australian peace researchers. But, starting in 1990 my national and international activities rapidly escalated—spurred on not only by my work as a historian, but also by the broader surge of social, political, and economic developments that was knitting together groups and peoples around the world. As a result, without dropping my activities in the Albany area, I took on a range of new ventures on the national and international stage.

This new trend in my life was exemplified by a research project that emerged in connection with the work of Soviet scholars. With the advent of Mikhail Gorbachev's liberalizing leadership in the Soviet Union, researchers at the Institute of General History of the Soviet Academy of Sciences seized the opportunity to contact CPRH and inquire if we would like to work with them on producing an anthology of major writings on world peace. As this book, tentatively entitled *Peace/Mir,* would be the first Soviet work to break out of the straitjacket of Marxist-Leninist orthodoxy and provide Soviet citizens with genuinely peace-oriented essays, we found the idea very appealing. Determined to proceed with the project, Charles Chatfield—after numerous attempts—managed to secure a grant from the United States Institute of Peace that would fund our travel to Moscow for a lengthy conference with the Soviet participants. Although I had avoided traveling to the Soviet Union—both because I disliked the regime and because I didn't want to give any ammunition to my critics—

this seemed like too good an opportunity to miss. Consequently, I decided to join other prominent CPRH scholars—Charles; Sandi Cooper, a specialist on European peace movements; Carole Fink, a historian of European diplomacy; and David Patterson, a historian of the U.S. peace movement and the deputy historian at the State Department—on our very own mission to Moscow. We would be accompanied by Dorothy and David's wife and son.

Thus, we ended up living and working in Moscow from June 22 to July 2, 1990. Arriving at Shermetyevo airport, Dorothy and I almost didn't make it past the scowling armed guard at the entry booth, apparently because we arrived some hours earlier than expected. But a phone call to the Institute put things right. Along with the rest of our delegation, we were soon ensconced in the Academy Hotel—a dingy, decrepit place with sour-faced women grudgingly doling out limited supplies of toilet paper on each floor and serving what passed for food in a very tiny cafeteria. For most of our stay, there was no hot water in the rooms. When David complained to the ubiquitous woman in charge of his floor that his bathroom lacked a toilet seat, she just shrugged. In addition, with his suitcase lost by Aeroflot, poor David—a rather formal person—had no change of clothes for the entire period and fell back on wearing his son's Snoopy T-shirt. Needless to say, it was virtually impossible to buy any replacements for the missing items or almost anything else. One supermarket we entered had nothing but powdered milk, located on a shelf in the corner. But we found lots and lots of Lenin pins that could be purchased, and very cheaply too. So this, I thought to myself, is the mighty Soviet Union—the great hope of all progressive humanity.

Although I arrived with the expectation that we would be pressed to accept the official Soviet view of things, I could not have been more wrong. For the most part, our hosts and the Soviet graduate students who guided us around Moscow were sharply critical of Soviet life. Treated to several days of complaints about the Soviet Union, Dorothy finally asked one of the women students what she liked about it. The young woman shrugged and replied: "Nothing." Not even Gorbachev's glasnost and perestroika inspired much enthusiasm. Gorbachev, one of them told us, was "just another Communist." Faced with this attitude and with a rather mindless glorification of American capitalism, our U.S. delegation eventually found itself striving for some balance, pointing out that things *were* changing for the better in the Soviet Union and that robber baron capitalism wouldn't serve the Soviet people well either.

Actually, we got along very nicely with our Soviet hosts. Meeting in a conference room at the Institute (where I sat uncomfortably under a picture of Lenin), we agreed upon a broad range of essays for *Peace/Mir*. In the evenings, we had dinner at their rather modest apartments, participated in large banquets, or were escorted to cultural events. On one afternoon we were supposed to visit Tolstoy's estate at Yasnaya Polyana. Instead, though, we were dragged off to visit a local Russian Orthodox church complex, much to my dismay. Not long after that, to wrap things up, a small Soviet delegation—headed by the Institute's Ruzanna Ilukhina—met with us in the United States at Rutgers University. Here we renewed our friendships, put the finishing touches on *Peace/Mir,* and discussed plans for its publication. However, by the early 1990s, when it was finally published in the United States and Russia, the Soviet Union had ceased to exist. As a result, the anthology was no longer extraordinary in either country. On the other hand, we did have an impact on our Russian counterparts—or so Ruzanna told us. In fact, she said, she took inspiration from us when—together with thousands of others resisting the attempted coup by the Communist Old Guard in 1991—she stood defiantly in front of Moscow's government buildings bearing a sign that read "Soldiers, Don't Shoot Your Mothers!"

Other projects, too, began taking on international dimensions. In July 1990, on my way home from the meeting with our new friends in Moscow, I stopped off in London to do research for *The Struggle Against the Bomb.* Sitting in the Public Record Office and examining the newly opened prime minister's records, I was startled to discover a folder of documents showing that in the late 1950s cabinet-level government officials had launched a conspiracy to undermine Britain's Campaign for Nuclear Disarmament (CND). Moreover, it seemed likely that documents indicating all kinds of improper and illegal government actions were stored in the following folders, which—in sharp contrast to the government's standard thirty-year declassification practice—were marked "Closed for the next 100 years." Although the research room was cold, sweat began pouring down my face. Should I bring those documents lying before me up to the front desk to be photocopied? I had better not, I concluded, or they might be locked away once more where no outsider would ever see them. So I spent the rest of the day copying them by hand and then spiriting away the copies to my hotel room.

Fortuitously, the next day I was scheduled to interview CND's chair, Monsignor Bruce Kent. Therefore, at the end of the interview, I mentioned the folder of documents illustrating the British government conspiracy. With his eyes brightening, Bruce suggested that I write up something on the issue and then he would have it placed in the *Guardian,* Britain's best newspaper. Eager to combine historical and political issues—and particularly when the combination would expose government misconduct—I was elated. Thus, immediately after my return to the United States, I dashed off an article on the conspiracy and mailed it to him. Unfortunately, though, Bruce couldn't deliver on the *Guardian*. Instead, he placed the article in *New Blackfriars*—a Dominican journal that, from the standpoint of publicizing the conspiracy, was considerably less satisfactory. I did have the consolation, though, of receiving a very nice letter on the article from E. P. Thompson—a prominent British historian and the leading figure in the European Nuclear Disarmament campaign—who praised it lavishly. The article was also reprinted in Britain's *Catholic Herald* and, more than a decade later, I did a follow-up story on the affair ("A Hot Day at the PRO") for *Peace and Change*.

As the research and writing of *The Struggle Against the Bomb* progressed, I began to look around for a publisher. Normally, it would not have been very difficult to find one, for I was a heavily published author and a reputable scholar. The problem was that I was convinced that I was onto a major issue with a very important story to tell—one that required *three* volumes. Oxford University Press claimed to be interested in a trilogy, but at this point would give me a contract for only the first volume. Contracts for the second and third volumes, the Oxford editor told me, would depend upon how well the first one sold. While considering this, I consulted with Marty Sherwin, a historian at Tufts University, whose path had crossed mine thanks to our common peace research interests. As the editor of a Nuclear Age series for Stanford University Press, he asked whether I would give Stanford a try. I did, and with his help secured a contract from Stanford for publication of cloth and paperback editions of each of the three volumes. The die was cast.

Other aspects of my life also were going very well. During the early 1990s I was physically fit, intellectually alert, and in many ways at the peak of my abilities. If the small house Dorothy and I lived in was relatively shabby, clogged with books and papers, and in a chronic state of disrepair—including the roof, which often sprang leaks—that was mostly because the two of us were burning the candle at both ends. Writing, activism, and teaching crowded my days from morning through night. I learned the advantage of doing two things at a time, such as performing calisthenics while listening to the National Public Radio news. When friends commented on how frequently they saw me on television or in the press taking part in a rally or a demonstration, I joked that some people spent their lives watching events, while others spent their lives participating in them.

It was an intense existence, sometimes dizzying, filled with plenty of hopes and friends. Until the late 1990s, the men's group continued, as did my very enjoyable—though usually exhausting—tennis games with Bill. In addition, the Solidarity Committee continued to pull interesting people into our orbit. Dorothy and I also made a number of new friends, including Jim Collins (a left-wing SUNY anthropologist) and his wife, Fiona Thompson, then finishing up her Ph.D. dissertation. Noticing that Dorothy and I kept bumping into one of my teaching assistants, Elizabeth Griffin, and her partner, Andy Feffer (a Union College historian), at interesting film showings, we began socializing with them, a practice that produced a warm relationship. In May 1991, when Dorothy organized a fiftieth birthday party for me at the local Friends Meeting House, it was packed with celebrants. Under the tongue-in-cheek title of "Fifty Years of Un-American Activities," we put up a display of photos chronicling my life and times, as well as portions of my FBI file. As friend after friend arose to recount incidents from my life, it was quite embarrassing but also poignant and enjoyable.

Taking a leap into the unknown, I even became a vegetarian. Ever since childhood Julia had refused to eat meat, chicken, or fish. Furthermore, by the late 1980s Dorothy had pretty much screened meat out of her diet for health reasons and suggested on occasion that I do the same. Thanks to these pressures—plus some uneasiness about the slaughtering of animals and a recognition of the need to conserve grain for humans (rather than shovel it into cows to produce Big Macs)—I gradually cut back on meat consumption. But I didn't turn strictly vegetarian until 1990, when I saw the film *The Cook, the Thief, His Wife, and Her Lover*—a very powerful allegory about the wanton destruction of life through greed and gluttony. After that, I simply decided to stop eating meat, chicken, and fish. This proved remarkably simple—at least when there was something else to eat.

Dorothy was also thriving. In the late 1980s, she had left her job at Parsons to become a school social worker in the Albany-Schenectady-Schoharie BOCES system, which provided special education for emotionally and physically handicapped students. Although all social work jobs were difficult and underpaid, at least this one followed the school calendar, which provided for plenty of days off, including the entire summer. It also gave her union representation and contracts, factors which markedly improved her salary, benefits, and job security. In addition to this paid employment, she also worked diligently as the area reference person for reevaluation counseling (RC). Convinced that social and political transformation required the elimination of individual "patterns" (what others would call neuroses), she devoted an enormous amount of time to RC counseling, classes, and workshops.

Despite our busy professional lives, Dorothy and I managed to find time for a variety of recreational pleasures. Together with friends, we went to dinner at foreign or vegetarian restaurants, saw avant-garde films at the Spectrum

Theatre or at the university's Page Hall, and attended folk music concerts. Although most of the latter occurred at two local coffeehouses—the Eighth Step (in Albany) and the Caffè Lena (in Saratoga)—numerous musicians (including Pete Seeger, Arlo Guthrie, Odetta, Charlie King, and Holly Near) came through our region and performed at a variety of venues. One of the most enjoyable musical events, the Old Songs Festival, occurred over the last weekend in June and, as that roughly coincided with Julia's birthday, we made it a tradition to bring her (and eventually Bob) there. Another tradition we developed was to drive out to Bennington, Vermont, to hike around amid the gorgeous fall foliage. During the summer months we continued to rent a cottage (at times with friends) for a week or two on Cape Cod. But sometimes we headed off to vacations on the West Coast, where we often visited Mike.

There were, however, sadder developments. During the late 1980s, the *Bangor Daily News*—seizing upon my old friend Howie Schonberger's public criticism of U.S. intervention in Nicaragua—published the charge, attributed to one of his colleagues at the University of Maine, that Howie was a Communist who persistently worked for the defeat of the United States. When the newspaper refused to retract the statement, even after his colleague denied making it, Howie sued the paper for libel. In a much-publicized court case, the jury ruled in Howie's favor and awarded him a princely sum, which he promptly announced would be shared with the Nicaraguan people. Unfortunately, however, the judge intervened and drastically reduced the settlement. Later, in October 1991, while jogging in Madison, Wisconsin, during a conference of historians in that city, Howie keeled over and died of a heart attack. Like me, he was fifty years old. The last time I had seen him was in the summer of 1990, when he was attending an institute at West Point to prepare for the military history course he had begun teaching. On one of his days off, he drove up to Albany for a visit, and we traded jokes about the irony of the situation. That's how I remember him, vibrant and undaunted, laughing until the tears rolled down his cheeks.

Four years after Howie's untimely death, his wife, Ann, invited me to come to the University of Maine and deliver what had become the annual Schonberger memorial lecture. I did so, speaking on "The Worldwide Struggle Against the Bomb." At the invitation of one of Howie's friends on campus, I also addressed the Socialist and Marxist lunch series on the subject "Has the Time Come for a World Government?" These events—underscored by a vigil with Ann alongside Howie's grave—led me to reflect on my own life and mortality.

There was ample reason to do so. In 1992, at forty-four, my sister, Debbie, committed suicide by taking an overdose of sleeping pills. Plagued with severe asthma, Debbie had continued to be medicated with heavy steroids year after year. As a result, she experienced the worst of both situations: she was physically sick and, all too often, mentally unbalanced. With her life blighted by illness and her mind deranged by steroids, Debbie apparently concluded that life was no longer worth living. Her untimely death was very disturbing and came as a particular blow to my father, who was eighty-four years old at the time.

His health, too, had begun to deteriorate. After tearing some ligaments in a fall, he was forced to use a walker or a wheelchair, making it very difficult to get around or even to go out to eat in a restaurant. As his asthma grew worse, he took heavy medications, including steroids, which clearly impaired his mental functioning. In the past, when we sat down for a game of Scrabble he was usually able to keep within a reasonable distance of Marjie and me. Now he couldn't manage more than the simplest words. In addition, he sometimes experienced blackouts or seizures. Even his usual good humor disappeared; he spoke less and, when he did, more gloomily. After a time, his speech largely came to a halt as well, for—to facilitate his breathing—the doctors gave him a tracheotomy, inserted a tube in his throat, and put him on a respirator.

The situation was clearly approaching a crisis. In 1993 I drove numerous times to the Westchester hospital where my father was kept alive on the respirator, and I sat by his bedside as he lay there unconscious. At one point, I told him that he had been a wonderful father and that I would never forget him, but I doubt that he heard me. Although Marjie's health held up fairly well, on one occasion that year she became sick, too, and was placed in a hospital bed a couple of floors below him. In these circumstances, Julia and I drove there to visit the two of them. Watching my father, unconscious, with tubes and fluids running in and out of him as oxygen was pumped into his lungs, was very difficult. At one point, Julia—always quite sensitive—stood up shakily and announced that she was going out to get some fresh air. But she didn't make it out of the room before, barely supporting herself on one of the walls, she began to crumple to the floor. I grabbed her unconscious body and hollered for the nurse, who managed to revive her quickly. On the trip back, Julia and I joked bleakly about the fact that three Wittners had almost ended up in the same hospital. How long could this situation continue?

Not long, as it turned out. Marjie adamantly refused to let my father die—even though it was clear to all of us, including her, that that was what he wanted to do. Didn't my father have a living will, I asked. And, if so, shouldn't she inform the doctor of his wish not to be revived? She thought he did have such a will, she said, but couldn't find it. Eventually, though, she did. And then, on the morning of July 24, 1993, she phoned to say that he had died of respiratory failure a few hours before. He was eighty-five years old. Marjie indicated that she had donated my father's body to a local teaching hospital and had no plan for a funeral. Furthermore, she said, she saw no reason for us to rush down to Westchester to visit her. Even so, Dorothy, Julia, and I insisted upon driving to see her that same day. Marjie didn't object, but upon our arrival she insisted—very bizarrely—on taking us out to shop at a local discount store. Never a person to show depression, Marjie apparently used the shopping as a way to avoid thinking or talking about my father's illness and death, which, in fact, had a devastating effect on her. Her health and mental condition deteriorated dramatically, and within a short time after her return to their apartment in Florida she died.

Although I continued living much as I had before, these events had a substantial impact on me. For one thing, I had a very strong sense that I was the last of my childhood nuclear family. In fact, I had a vivid dream in which I saw a photographic display, showing four cameo frames, with three pictures blotted out and only my own remaining. Complementing this view of myself as the last of the Wittners was my recognition that I was no longer in the middle generation, between my parents and my child, but a member of the older generation. Through death, I had become an elder. But, of course, one never escapes the influence of the past, and particularly those with whom you establish emotional bonds. As I had told my father, I would not forget him, for I loved him, and in a number of ways he was the parent with whom I most identified. Thus, I took his ashes—which had remained in a box on my mantelpiece since being shipped to me from the hospital—and brought them down to a quiet spot on the Hudson River. There, in a little ceremony of my own, I scattered them over the river that flowed ceaselessly past the city in which he had been born and raised.

Fortunately, even in the midst of death, life continues. In 1993 Julia finished up at Brandeis, graduating magna cum laude. Having as little vocational sense as I did, she had majored in English and written her senior honors thesis on an obscure British poet. When questioned about what she planned to do about post-college employment, she said she would like to become a professional writer. The problem with this plan was not only that she was a shy, nonassertive person, but also that she had never published anything. Consequently, I asked her if she would mind my contacting an individual whom I knew slightly (but had never met)—Murray Polner, the acting editor of *Fellowship,* the magazine of the pacifist Fellowship of Reconciliation (FOR)—to see if there was any chance of her working for him as an intern. To my surprise, she agreed. After I dropped him a note, as did Julia, he was happy to take her on. It proved to be an excellent arrangement. That summer she lived with other gentle young people in the FOR's decaying mansion on the banks of the Hudson, in Nyack, New York, and had a chance to do serious editorial work. That fall, the FOR hired her as assistant to the editor. Although it was not a full-time job, she earned enough to keep food on her table—and on Bob's, for that fall she moved in with him in New Paltz, where he was completing his senior year at the SUNY college in that town.

Julia liked the job at *Fellowship*—so much so that she decided to return to school and study journalism. Therefore, in the fall of 1994 she moved up to Syracuse, New York, where she enrolled in the Newhouse School of Journalism at Syracuse University. Bob went with her and, uncertain about what career path he should follow, found work as a mental health aide in a local hospital. On June 1, 1996, after Julia's graduation, they were married in a ceremony conducted in the large, verdant yards behind Patty's house and the adjoining one. Predictably, Patty and Reinhard wanted a lavish, fairly conventional wedding. But Julia and Bob insisted on a much simpler, unorthodox one. In the ensuing family conferences, Dorothy and I invariably backed the suggestions of the young couple, and ultimately the wedding ended up pretty much along the lines they wanted, with unusual speeches (e.g., mine was on the commodification of love under capitalism), vegetarian food, and spirited Renaissance dancing. Returning to Syracuse, Bob entered law school and Julia began working for Laubach Literacy International as an assistant editor for its adult literacy newspaper.

Locally, I continued my activist ventures. During the first part of the decade, I served as the vice president of the capital district's World Federalist group—helping to organize lectures, letter-writing to public officials, and joint banquets with the United Nations Association. Meanwhile, in my capacity as a UUP leader, I served as a marshal at a giant protest demonstration by public workers in downtown Albany in February 1991. Organized by UUP and other public sector unions, the demonstration was designed to stop layoffs and other attacks upon the state's work force. Standing on the wall of the State Capitol and using bullhorns, Doug Bullock (of the Solidarity Committee) and I had no trouble getting the throngs of marchers to chant "Tax the Rich! Tax the Rich!" Later that year, when the Graduate Student Employees Union—after years of legal barriers erected by the state—finally secured the right to a representation election throughout SUNY, I assisted the union's successful campaign for an affirmative vote by providing a statement lauding unionization. It ultimately appeared on posters all over the Albany campus.

Continuing my work as treasurer of the Solidarity Committee, I played a leading role in its assorted causes. In one of our most impressive actions, we lined up unions around New York State to oppose the state's proposed purchase of electric power from Hydro-Quebec, the giant corporation then destroying the habitat of the native peoples living around James Bay in Canada. Eventually, to our delight, the state refused to sign the contract. We also organized a major labor outreach event at SUNY/Albany. Under the new AFL-CIO leadership of John Sweeney and other reformers, the labor federation was far more open than in the past to working with groups outside its ranks, including prolabor faculty on the nation's college and university campuses. Accordingly, the Solidarity Committee put together a "Teach-in on the Labor Movement" that occurred in October 1997. Asked if he would like to deliver a speech at this event, Ed Cleary, the humdrum president of the New York State AFL-CIO, turned to one of his aides and barked: "What the hell is a teach-in?" As in the past, the State Fed proved totally uninterested and uncooperative. But the Solidarity Committee, its allies in local unions, and university faculty produced an impressive event with a good turnout.

One of my favorite Solidarity ventures developed out of my disgust at UUP's being forced to wage constant battles to save SUNY from the state budget cutters—who, like their national counterparts, had plunged the public sector into debt by cutting the tax rate for the wealthy. In response, I proposed that UUP initiate a campaign for progressive taxation. Accordingly, I asked a UUP public relations staffer to consider developing appropriate bumper stickers that could be distributed to drivers of cars around Albany, where they would be visible to the governor and state legislators. When she threw cold water on this idea, I brought it to the Solidarity Committee and proposed that we design and distribute our own bumper stickers with a simple message: "TAX THE RICH." Everyone agreed it was a great idea but wondered how many we could actually sell. Ultimately, we decided to be daring and order 250 of them. When they arrived in early 1996, with their bright red capital letters on a yellow background, they proved an immediate hit. Within a few weeks we had distributed our entire stock. Ultimately, we sold and distributed thousands.

Meanwhile, I was finishing up the first volume of my *Struggle Against the Bomb* trilogy. In the late 1980s, when I began my broad study of the worldwide nuclear disarmament campaign, I believed that it had been a failure. After all, despite the enormous antinuclear movement that had circled the globe, the Bomb had not been banned. And I wanted to understand why. But, as I dug into once-secret government and peace organization records, conducted interviews, and examined the memoirs of public officials, I began to realize that the antinuclear campaign had had a very important effect on international behavior—curbing the nuclear arms race and averting nuclear war. Here, then, was what I considered one of the most important and unnoticed stories of modern times. As a result, I worked zealously on the book—harder than I ever did in my life on a scholarly project—and in mid-1993 Stanford University Press published the first volume, *One World or None: A History of the World Nuclear Disarmament Movement through 1953*.

Unfortunately, the book had much less of an impact than I expected. The mass media, for example, did not bother to review it. Even so, I used whatever contacts I had to arrange to have it reviewed by publications other than the usual scholarly journals. This meant that the book did receive some attention among a small group of peace movement and political magazines. Fortunately, almost all the reviews were exceptionally favorable, stressing the path-breaking nature of the book, its extensive research, and the eloquence of its style. Unfortunately, though, Stanford did very little to promote it. This was reflected not only in the absence of reviews and ads in the major newspapers and magazines, but even in displays at scholarly conferences. When *One World or None* was awarded the Warren Kuehl prize of the Society for Historians of American Foreign Relations (SHAFR) as the outstanding book published in 1993 or 1994 on peace movements and/or internationalism, I attended the SHAFR convention, where the prize was presented to me at a very large banquet. Although I was the only prizewinner to be honored at the convention, Stanford—which had a bookstall at the event—did not bother to display my book.

Yet another sign of the subdued response to *One World or None* was the difficulty I experienced in securing fellowship funding after its publication. I had a sabbatical leave (i.e., one semester with full pay) coming up in 1994–95, and I hoped to supplement that with a fellowship from a major foundation, thus leaving me free to work on the remaining research and writing of volume two for the entire academic year. But despite my applications to a large number of foundations, none awarded me a fellowship. Admittedly, such funding is scarce, and only a minority of researchers receive fellowships to work on their scholarly projects. Nevertheless, I had managed to secure fellowships in the past and, also, was a highly regarded scholar who had just published an important book. Therefore, I suspected that the rejection of my fellowship applications resulted from the politically controversial nature of my findings. In any case, I once again decided that I wasn't going to "let the bastards get me down." If they wouldn't fund my research, I'd fund it myself. And so, forgoing half my salary, I took off the entire academic year to work on the second volume.

Weighed down by the combination of my father's death and the limited impact of *One World or None,* I decided to give myself a treat and attend the fall 1994 convention of the International Peace Research Association (IPRA) in Valletta, Malta. A number of CPRH luminaries—most notably Irwin Abrams— had been encouraging CPRH members to attend the gathering, meet with their overseas counterparts, and establish a Peace History Commission within IPRA. This idea, combined with the unique nature of that tiny and very unusual nation, appealed to me, and so I decided to attend the convention and to give a paper there on one aspect of my research. It proved an excellent decision. I had barely arrived, very jet-lagged, at my small hotel when I was rounded up, along with other peace researchers, and driven to a welcoming celebration in downtown Valletta. There we lined up in a narrow, ancient street and, preceded by a brass band, began a colorful march as local residents went wild, cheering and showering us with confetti. Arriving at the town square, we crowded around the central stage, where various dignitaries were assembled, including Malta's president, who welcomed us to his nation and lauded us as paragons of peace. Accustomed to a rather different sort of reception in our home countries, we could hardly believe it. Over the following days, the dazzled peace researchers (including outgoing CPRH president Jeff Kimball and his successor, Frances Early) had a wonderful time—gaping at ancient stone fertility goddesses, eating what looked like Big Macs (but were actually large buns filled with lima beans and ketchup), and establishing a Peace History Commission headed by Jeff.

The very different reception accorded peace-oriented historians in the United States was underscored only weeks later when a major controversy broke out over an exhibit at the Smithsonian Institution on the U.S. atomic bombing of Japan. With the fiftieth anniversary of the event approaching, the museum curators felt that the *Enola Gay,* the plane that dropped the atomic bomb on Hiroshima, could provide the centerpiece for a retrospective on the event. Accordingly, they drew up an exhibit script, with pictures, and submitted it to a distinguished panel of historians who modified it somewhat. Then they sent it out for public comment and all hell broke loose. Veterans groups and the Air Force Association (an industry lobbying group) vigorously condemned it as "anti-American." With the Republican Congress threatening an investigation and a cutoff of funding to the Smithsonian, Martin Harwit, the museum director, crumpled and ordered the exhibit transformed into a celebration of U.S. military might and of a uniquely virtuous United States while eliding all reference to the human cost of the atomic bombing.

In response, peace groups and historians fought back and demanded objective history rather than patriotic propaganda. As a leading writer on nuclear controversies, I was contacted by the Fellowship of Reconciliation and asked to participate in a small scholarly delegation that in mid-November 1994 met with Harwit and his aides. It included Barton Bernstein, Daniel Ellsberg, and Robert J. Lifton. We did our best to convince Harwit that the kind of exhibit the Legionnaires were demanding falsified the past, and I urged, as did others, that he restore to it the voices of those (including General Dwight Eisenhower) who had expressed misgivings about the bombing. But he seemed immovable. Later that day, our delegation went on to the National Press Club, where we spoke at a press conference comprised of newspaper, radio, and TV reporters from around the world. As a result, we appeared on a nationwide television broadcast that night. Barraged by historians and peace groups, Harwit finally made a small concession to them by lowering the casualty levels projected by U.S. government officials for an invasion of Japan.

That was the final straw. The veterans groups and their political allies forced his ouster, the exhibit was truncated into a cardboard cutout of the *Enola Gay*'s crew, and most of the U.S. communications media viciously berated historians for their alleged anti-Americanism. Nothing historians said seemed to have any impact on the widespread belief that the atomic bombing was a necessary and virtuous act. When I gave a talk on the Smithsonian controversy to a local meeting sponsored by World Federalist Association and the United Nations Association, I challenged this unreasoning faith by pointing out to the irate veterans in the audience that the justification for dropping the Bomb was dubious, for (1) How could one say with certainty what would happen if a particular act (in this case, the dropping of the atomic bomb) did not occur? and (2) it seemed fairly clear that they—the men in the foxholes—had already won the war. But they continued to insist that they *knew* that the atomic bombing was necessary. When an article on my talk appeared in a local newspaper, a right-wing talk show host devoted hours to denouncing me. His denunciation, in turn, inspired threatening messages left on my answering machine.

The danger I faced as a public intellectual was also brought home to me when I became a potential target of the Unabomber. By early 1996 this violent opponent of modern technology—who specialized in mailing out bomb-laden packages—had successfully killed three people and injured twenty-nine others. That spring, however, after a very extensive manhunt, the FBI arrested Theodore Kaczynski, a mathematician who was held in custody awaiting trial as the Unabomber. I didn't give much thought to the case until an FBI agent phoned and told me that my name and address had been found among Kaczynski's papers. What, she asked, did I think was the reason for that? Initially, I could think of no reason for it at all. But soon I figured out the connection. A year before, in my capacity as a writer on resistance to one form of technology (nuclear weapons), I had been phoned by a science reporter for the *San Francisco Examiner* and asked to comment on the Unabomber case. I had provided the reporter with a few critical statements, and these appeared in his article in that newspaper. Not surprisingly, someone clipping stories on the bombings—such as the Unabomber—would have taken note of my remarks. What was disturbing was that Kaczynski had gone out of his way to locate my office address, thus laying the groundwork for mailing me a package. In fact, as the FBI agent warned me, maybe he *already* had mailed one to me and it had not yet arrived. She urged me to keep on the lookout for suspicious packages—and I did, alerting the department secretaries, who sorted our mail, to watch out for them as well. None ever arrived.

Fortunately, I didn't have to sit around long awaiting the arrival of a bomb, for that May I headed off to Berlin. Carole Fink of CPRH had helped put together a conference, sponsored by the German Historical Institute, in that city. As the conference focused on events in the turbulent year of 1968, I had initially resisted participating, observing that the nuclear disarmament movement was at a low ebb at that point. In response, Carole ingeniously argued that I could present a paper on the disintegration of the movement. So—in the midst of a rather high-power intellectual assemblage—that's what I did. Although I knew few people at the conference, it was enlivened by tours of the city, including a visit to the remains of the Berlin Wall and to key sites of West Berlin's youthful "revolutionary" activism of 1968. After the conclusion of the conclave, I spent a few days at the rural home of my fellow peace researcher, Günter Wernicke, just outside the city in what had previously been East Germany. I had met Günter, a left-winger happy with neither the old regime nor the new one in the East, at the IPRA conference in Malta. He was the only survivor of the Humboldt University history faculty, who had been replaced by West German academics after German reunification. Together with his girlfriend, Günter and I toured portions of the once-forbidden East Germany, including the Sachsenhausen concentration camp. We also discussed the possibility of drawing on recently opened East German Communist party records and Stasi files for my *Struggle Against the Bomb* trilogy.

When traveling, I almost invariably resisted going to Third World nations, as I did not want to play the role of a comfortable tourist in the midst of their massive poverty. But in 1997, UUP offered to fund my participation in a fact-finding trip to the *maquiladoras*—the giant, foreign-owned manufacturing plants in northern Mexico that employed a million people. And this was too interesting and unusual an opportunity to resist. Sponsored by the New York State Labor-Religion Coalition, the trip took some fifteen labor and religious activists across the border in a small van into Nuevo Laredo and other border towns that November. Our tour leader was Marta Ojeda, a former *maquiladora* worker who had gone underground to save her life in the aftermath of a bitter strike and was now executive director of the Coalition for Justice in the Maquiladoras (CJM). Although the corporate authorities barred us from entering the *maquilas*, we met with the workers in their homes. Located in the impoverished *colonias*, these homes were made of cardboard and tin, lacked heat, light, and running water, and were built on a vast wasteland of garbage, barbed wire, and chemical effluents. This pathetic existence was not the workers' choice, of course, but was forced on them by their miserable wages, which averaged about twenty-five dollars a week—paid by the world's largest and wealthiest corporations, many of them American. Although most of our group remained in good spirits, I felt sickened and depressed.

Back in the United States, we were supposed to spread the word on what we had seen in Mexico, and I did my best. I wrote up an op-ed piece for the Albany *Times Union*, but that newspaper refused to print it. However, I did write a strong article that was published in my union newspaper and contributed photos to a good centerfold on the trip that appeared in the *New York Teacher*. Occasionally, I gave talks on the plight of Mexico's *maquiladora* workers, as did Marta, who traveled up to Albany to speak in one of my classes and to address the statewide UUP convention. Some years later, when my friend Rosemary Hennessy, of the SUNY/Albany English Department, made a similar UUP-funded trip, with Marta as guide, she was even more profoundly affected by it than I was. Ultimately, with my support Rosemary convinced UUP to donate thousands of dollars to CJM ventures, served as a UUP representative on the CJM executive board, and devoted her future research and writing to exposing corporate exploitation in the *maquiladoras*.

In January 1998 a delegation reunion took place in Syracuse, where a short film on our trip, made by one of the participants, was screened. This documentary certainly brought back memories of our time in Mexico. It included an interview with me in one of the *colonias* as I shivered in the cold. Fortunately, the film concluded with a more upbeat scene, in which another UUP member and I led the Mexican workers in the singing of "Solidarity Forever." As I drove home that evening along the New York State Thruway, it suddenly occurred to me that, with my life as a channel, a connection had developed between the ghetto radicals of Poland, the social justice activists of the United States, and the insurgent workers of Mexico. And this, in turn, was part of a larger pattern. When the would-be masters of the world had slaughtered the European Jews and others who had stood in their way, they had assumed that they would secure a "final solution." But, against all odds, the struggle for equality continued.

I almost didn't participate in any of these controversies, conferences, and events, for in the mid-1990s my health underwent a dramatic turn for the worse. Ever since the 1960s I had noticed that my skin would break out in hives from the cold. I didn't pay much attention to this until the summer of 1994, when Mike Weinberg and I, on a brutally hot day, took some time out to go tubing down the Esopus Creek in the Catskill Mountains. As the creek was very cold, I wasn't at all surprised that my body became covered with red hives. But I was concerned about the fact that I started shaking with cold, eventually undergoing uncontrollable spasms—so much so that I began to fear that if my tube tipped while I plunged through the rapids, I might not be able to swim out of the swirling water. As a result, Mike and I called it a day and got out of the creek. As I warmed up again, I felt much better. But I retained a sense that I had better avoid situations in which my body temperature dropped dramatically.

The situation reached a crisis point in 1995. That summer, Bill Gulla and his new partner, Liz Gath, a physician, joined us for a week in renting a cottage in South Wellfleet on Cape Cod. I took long walks on the beach, but, determined to be prudent, was careful to stay out of the ocean. However, on one of our last days there—a glorious sunny afternoon with a perfectly blue sky—I couldn't resist the allure of the water. And there was no one else around to urge caution upon me. Consequently, I plunged into the surf and was soon having a great time. Even so, I decided not to press my luck. After about ten minutes I came back to the beach, covered with hives. Here I dried myself off, lay down on my blanket, and waited for the sun to warm me up. But I felt very cold and experienced some spasms. Even worse, I started to see flashes of light. I was either about to experience a divine visitation or pass out. Recognizing that the latter was more probable, I headed up the dune to our cottage. Usually, I had little difficulty with the return walk, but this time I was forced to sink down onto the sand several times along the way. Eventually, I made it to the back porch and slumped into a chair. Dorothy, reading in another room, asked me how the beach was, and I told her that I was shaking with cold. Alarmed, she got me into bed, threw blankets over me, and—when I still complained of the chill—jumped into bed with me. Warm and cozy, we both dozed off.

Only afterward did I learn how serious this situation had become. Awakening from my afternoon nap, I felt just fine, and so Dorothy and I went out to dinner. We were both relaxed and reading novels when Liz and Bill returned. "Where was my attending physician when I needed her?" I joked with Liz. "I almost fainted!" Then I told her the story of that afternoon's events. When I finished, she turned to me and said: "Larry, you didn't almost faint; you almost *died*!" That got my attention. It seemed that my body had been going into anaphylactic shock, with my blood leaving my heart and brain for my extremities. With Liz insisting that upon my return to Albany I consult my doctor about this condition, I did so and was told that it was vital to keep myself warm. In this connection, plunging into cold water was the worst thing I could possibly do. As a result, I dropped swimming from my life, gave away my cross-country skis, and bought long underwear and woolen socks to get myself through Albany's icy winter months. For a time, at my doctor's recommendation, I even carried an Epi-pen, giving me the ability to inject myself with epinephrine in the event that I started going into shock.

Ironically, when I had another health crisis the following year, it was for a totally different reason. Throughout the summer of 1996, I suffered from pains in my outer calves, and my doctor gave me a prescription for ibuprofen. When I asked him if there would be any side effects, he said it might upset my stomach somewhat and I should take the medication with meals. I did so over the following three months. Then, in late October I was at a buffet brunch at a friend's house when I suddenly felt a very powerful pain in my stomach area. In fact, it was so bad that, as sweat poured out of me, I leaned desperately on the wall and began sliding to the floor. Of course, friends immediately noticed this and insisted that Dorothy rush me to nearby Albany Medical Center. For the rest of the day, as I experienced excruciating pain, alternating with heavy doses of morphine, the doctors gave me x-rays but couldn't figure out what was wrong. Then they finally had me stand up for an x-ray, and they discovered that I had a perforated ulcer through which the hydrochloric acid from my stomach was pouring into my chest cavity. Explaining the situation, a doctor asked me if I wanted the necessary microsurgery. "*Yes!*" I said, writhing in pain. Was I ready for it now, he asked. "*Yes*," I said, "*do it!*" Never was there a more eager patient. When I awakened, my stomach lining was sewn up and numerous tubes were carrying fluids in and out of me.

For a time, I recuperated at the hospital. The worst part of it was not the set of tubes running from my stomach, through my throat, and coming out of my nose—though that was pretty bad—but the constant yammering of the television set in the room. My roommate, whom I never saw, had TV shows on day and night, depriving me of sleep and all concentration. In desperation, I repeatedly complained about it to the hospital staff. But nothing seemed to work. Apparently, television-watching is viewed as a constitutional right in the United States. Certainly the hospital staff couldn't seem to understand why I wanted to forgo it. Ultimately, though, in response to my complaints, I was transferred to a double room with no roommate—though, of course, the television set was blasting away. My first act there was to crawl out of bed, slowly and painfully, and turn it off. After a week, I was allowed to go home and hobble around there while convalescing. Then, miraculously, I was perfectly fit once again. Later tests revealed that there had been (and remained) nothing wrong with my stomach. Ibuprofen had simply burned a hole through it. Needless to say, I never used it or comparable medications again.

Despite these distractions, in the final days of December 1997 the second volume of my trilogy—*Resisting the Bomb: A History of the World Nuclear Disarmament Movement, 1954-1970*—was published in cloth and paperback editions. This time, harboring no expectations that the publisher would do much to promote the book, I took matters into my own hands, contacting numerous newspapers and magazines in an effort to stir up reviews. My greatest success along these lines came when I spoke with Colman McCarthy—a pacifist writer for the *Washington Post* with whom I had had no previous acquaintance—and convinced him to write a review for that newspaper. But there were other breakthroughs as well, including reviews by the *Philadelphia Inquirer,* the *Progressive,* and the National Catholic News Service. As the book also drew good coverage in peace movement and scholarly publications, it ultimately secured some fifty reviews—almost all of them exceptionally favorable. Although writers of popular novels, cookbooks, or exercise manuals would consider this a pathetic record, I was cheered by the fact that, to some degree at least, I had broken out of the academic ghetto. Dorothy and I also organized a book-signing party at a local bookstore, and it was fun to host it as friends and local activists stopped by to celebrate and to purchase copies of both published volumes.

With the Peace History Commission now in operation, I decided to give a paper at a session it was sponsoring at an IPRA conference in Durban, South Africa, in June 1998. Not only had I enjoyed the past IPRA conference in Malta, but I was also intrigued by the prospect of seeing the new South Africa, liberated from apartheid and now ruled by the African National Congress. Although I knew fewer people at this conference than at its predecessor, it did prove interesting for a number of reasons. Roaming the streets of Durban, visiting one of Gandhi's early ashrams, exploring new housing developments, watching Zulu dancers, and listening to speeches by descendants of Gandhi and the ANC's Albert Luthuli provided memorable experiences—considerably more exciting than those provided by, say, American Historical Association conventions in Cincinnati. Also, my paper—on a small, international nuclear disarmament march of 1960–61 that had somehow managed to wend its way for months through East European Communist nations—attracted one of the participants on the march, Nils Petter Gleditsch, who was now editor of the *Journal of Peace Research,* published by the Peace Research Institute of Oslo. This inspired Gleditsch, upon his return to Norway, to write a newspaper column on what I had discovered about the march and its reception by Communist governments.

Eager to do widespread research for the third and final volume of *The Struggle Against the Bomb,* I applied for a substantial grant to cover the costs of research travel from an unusual source—the Nonprofit Sector Research Fund of the Aspen Institute—and received it. Together with smaller grants, this enabled me to travel to the Jimmy Carter and Ronald Reagan Presidential Libraries to examine U.S. government documents, to plow through the files of peace groups at the Swarthmore College Peace Collection, and—most exciting of all—to conduct more than a hundred interviews. The interviews with U.S. peace movement leaders proved very interesting and sometimes a lot of fun. During 1998 and 1999, I was delighted to have the chance to converse with leading activists, including Randy Forsberg, Sandy Gottlieb, Helen Caldicott, John Isaacs,

Randy Kehler, Jeremy Stone, Bernard Lown, Bob Musil, and Frank von Hippel. As might be expected, we usually got on very well, and sometimes, as in the case of interviews with Peter Bergel and Judy Lipton, our meetings ended up with meals at their homes. I had a wonderful time interviewing Michael Foot, a longtime antinuclear activist and a former leader of the British Labour Party. Sitting in his backyard in Hampstead, sipping a glass of wine, watching the sun go down, and listening to him talk of British disarmament policy, Labour Party leader Neil Kinnock (one of Foot's protégés), Indian Prime Minister Rajiv Gandhi, and Gorbachev, I thought, "How can life be any better than this?"

Other interviews took me a bit beyond my usual comfort zone. For example, I interviewed a range of former top-level U.S. government officials from the Carter, Reagan, and Bush administrations, including Caspar Weinberger, Zbigniew Brzezinski, Paul Warnke, Frank Carlucci, Richard Perle, and James Baker III. As I had expected, Weinberger was not particularly friendly or informative. Brzezinski, too, began our conversation in a rather curt and arrogant fashion, but eventually—as I fed him some intelligent questions—grew more talkative and less cantankerous. Perle, who had provided much of the brainpower behind the Reagan administration's hawkish policy, surprised me with his thoughtful and candid responses to my queries. James Baker, who struck me as a particularly smooth operator, must have sensed my political orientation from the questions I asked, for he finished up by saying: "I want you to understand, we secured peace through strength!" Tactful to the end, I avoided commenting on this point but merely thanked him for his observations, whereupon Baker repeated the message, this time more sharply: "We had peace through strength!"

The most revealing of the interviews with former policy makers was probably the one with Robert ("Bud") McFarlane, Reagan's former national security adviser. Other administration officials had claimed that they had barely noticed the nuclear freeze movement. But when I asked McFarlane about it, he lit up and began outlining a massive administration campaign to counter and discredit the freeze—one that he had directed. At this point in our conversation, his secretary buzzed to remind him that he had another important appointment coming up soon. My heart sank at the thought that his flow of revelations was about to be shut off. But McFarlane briskly informed her that she should reschedule the other appointment, for he was having a very important conversation. And so he continued, and I learned a lot about the administration's battle against the freeze.

A month later, I interviewed Edwin Meese, a top White House staffer and U.S. attorney general during the Reagan administration. When I asked him about the administration's response to the freeze campaign, he followed the usual line by saying that there was little official notice taken of it. In response, I recounted what McFarlane had revealed. A sheepish grin now spread across this former government official's face, and I knew that I had caught him. "If Bud says that," he remarked tactfully, "it must be true."

I also had plans for extensive research in Europe during May and June 1999. As my top priority was gaining access to newly opened Soviet records and interviewing leading Russian antinuclear activists, I arranged for the assistance of a well-informed Russian scientist, obtained a Russian visa, and located housing in Moscow. But that spring the U.S. military attack upon Yugoslavia shattered my plan, for it inflamed popular Russian sentiment against the United States. A Russia specialist on my campus informed me that although he spoke Russian fluently, had a Russian wife, and had been hired to work at a Russian institute, he had canceled his travel plans. When I hesitated to follow his example, he warned me that on a Moscow street I might well be accosted by an angry Russian, surrounded by an irate crowd, and—while sputtering in English—have my jaw broken. Stubborn as ever, I e-mailed my Russian assistant (who, as a prospective paid employee, had much to gain by my traveling to Moscow) and asked him what he thought. He replied that our interview prospects were drying up, that someone had fired a grenade at the U.S. embassy that very day, and that it would be best if I didn't come there. With great reluctance, I canceled this component of my travel plans, although I did manage to hire a young Russian scholar to do some archival research for me.

The rest of my European research went very well. In May 1999 I flew off to the Hague Appeal for Peace conference—a commemoration of a major peace gathering a century before. Sponsored by the International Peace Bureau and other major peace organizations, it brought together thousands of peace activists from around the world to discuss their work and their priorities. CPRH (now renamed the Peace History Society) played a role in it, sponsoring scholarly panels, including one in which I gave a paper. In addition, as the event brought together peace movement leaders from around the world, it was ideal for interviews, and I scurried about eagerly, conducting them with leading activists from Japan, Germany, Norway, Britain, and the United States. From there, I traveled on to Germany, where Günter had set up a series of interviews for me with former leaders of East Germany's Communist-dominated peace groups and a former East German diplomat. Among them, a strong atmosphere of gloom prevailed. One leader of an "official" peace group, referring to his independent peace movement rivals and to the collapse of the Communist regime, told me, bitterly: "You won. The peace movement won!"

Then it was back to Western Europe. Returning to the Hague, I interviewed a former Dutch prime minister, Ruud Lubbers, who had been in the thick of the

1980s Euromissile crisis, and then met up in Amsterdam with an old friend from my Vassar days, Paul Metzger. Paul had had serious health problems in the past year, and I had suggested that he join me on some of my European travels. In Amsterdam, we did some socializing with old friends. After that, we hopped on a train to Geneva, where Paul explored the old League of Nations buildings while I interviewed several key peace movement leaders, including Colin Archer, the savvy secretary general of the International Peace Bureau, and plowed through that organization's extensive files. Returning briefly to Amsterdam, where I said goodbye to Paul, I did some research at the International Institute for Social History and then headed on to London for more interviews, including a nice chat with Bruce Kent and his activist wife, Valerie Flessati, at their home.

On my last full day in London, I interviewed Mary Kaldor, a vibrant figure in the European Nuclear Disarmament (END) campaign, at her office in the London School of Economics. She not only provided me with fascinating information but also reminded me that she had some material I might want to see. This turned out to be an entire file cabinet full of END records, including correspondence among its top leaders. Although she had to head off to a meeting and dinner with a group of East European activists, she offered to have me stay in her office, read the END files, and use her photocopying machine. How could I resist? But there were problems. A heavy rainstorm hit, and water began pouring through the light fixture and portions of the ceiling. Determined to persist, I moved the records to a dryer spot, turned off the sodden lights, and worked feverishly. As the sky darkened, however, I could barely see the files. At around 9:30, Mary returned, accompanied by about a dozen loud, bohemian-looking men who crowded into the office. Enough! Even scholarly research has its limits! The next day, I was winging my way back to the United States with a suitcase full of taped interviews and photocopies of documents.

Although I was certainly a fanatical researcher, I continued to explore other, quite different aspects of life, especially music. At some time during the 1990s, the Occasional Chorus disappeared, mostly because its two central figures moved out of the area. But a variety of organizations continued to crave music with a message. Consequently, in the latter part of the decade I found myself, along with a few friends (with whom I now gathered at the Albany Friends Meeting House to play and sing songs), being pulled into peace and social justice gatherings to perform appropriate music. Soon we had a full complement of performers: Roger Allen, now a state trooper, on guitar, harmonica, and mandolin; Dave Pallas, a psychiatrist, on bass; Dave Crump, operator of a diesel truck repair shop, on guitar and vocals; Jack Kilrain, a prison librarian, on Irish drum and vocals; Joe Lombardo, a systems analyst for the courts, on guitar and vocals; and me, on guitar and vocals. As our musical debut—at a May

Day celebration in Troy, New York, on May 1, 1999—neared, I chose a name for us: the Solidarity Singers.

And so the Solidarity Singers began to perform social protest songs at an array of local events: Labor Day picnics organized by the Solidarity Committee; fasts for social justice organized by the Capital District Labor-Religion Coalition; gatherings of peace activists sponsored by Upper Hudson Peace Action; and Martin Luther King Jr. Day celebrations in black churches. Probably our most unusual venue was the Albany garbage dump. Asked to play environmental songs by organizations sponsoring an expansion of the state's bottle-return law, we performed them for the attendant mass media while standing in front of an enormous pile of garbage. With the gigs rolling in, Roger—always more musically ambitious for me than I was—suggested that I switch to playing banjo, for we had lots of guitar players. Reluctantly, I did, although without much skill and only with considerable effort. Aesthetically, we were definitely not the best musical group in the region. But we were pretty good at stirring up audiences and getting them singing. Furthermore, what we lacked in musical artistry, we made up for in the strength of our political message and our resounding voices. As listeners often told us, we were powerful.

Meanwhile, Dorothy and I finally got married. For a time we had drifted along without giving marriage much thought, except occasionally in the context of how it might affect our health insurance or taxes. There was something enjoyable about living together, unmarried, and getting along well—a subversive model for others, as well as a provocation to the self-appointed guardians of moral propriety. Furthermore, both of us had had more than enough trouble in our previous marriages and weren't in any hurry to hop on board the marriage train again. Even so, many of our friends simply assumed that we were married; so were we really setting an example of love among the free? Also, as we had lived together happily for about two decades, marriage seemed unlikely to change our relationship for the worse. Consequently, one day in the summer of 1999, when Dorothy—joking around—got down on her knees and proposed to me, I responded by saying: "OK, let's do it!" At first, she thought I was joking too. But then she decided: why not? As a result, in a ceremony witnessed only by our friend Colia Clark and Dorothy's son Jonah (back in Albany to study for his master's degree in education), we were married by an official at the Albany City Hall on August 31, 1999.

To celebrate, we organized a big party at the Friends Meeting House that October. Enlivened by poems, anecdotes, and songs by friends, the event went off very well. At Dorothy's suggestion, we performed a little love song—so corny that one member of the audience broke into laughter at the presumed joke. Then we followed that with a raunchier one ("Rollin' in My Sweet Baby's Arms"), accompanied by instrumentalists from the Solidarity Singers. What really brought down the house, though, was a song written and performed for the occasion by Julia and Bob—"Twenty Years of Living in Sin"—which concluded by suggesting that we had finally become conservatives.

Needless to say, that was not at all true. I recognized, of course, that the political revolt of the 1960s had ended and that powerful forces stood in the way of further advance. And I had long ago given up on voting for quixotic third-party candidates. Even so, whatever political concessions I made were more tactical than reflective of a fundamental shift in political orientation. I remained a democratic socialist and determined to act upon my beliefs. Indeed, by this time I was deeply enmeshed in another tumultuous campaign—to unionize SUNY/Albany's dining halls.

Thanks to a union-organizing drive among some 500 food service workers at SUNY/Albany by Local 471 of the Hotel Employees and Restaurant Employees (HERE), more than 70 percent of them signed union authorization cards in the spring of 1999. After an independent arbitrator certified that a majority of workers desired union representation, University Auxiliary Services (UAS)—the board selected by the SUNY/Albany administration to manage campus facilities—promised that June to recognize the union. Then it promptly forgot about this agreement and contracted out management of the dining halls to the Sodexho-Marriott Corporation.

Sodexho-Marriott, a giant multinational firm and the largest investor in private (i.e., profit-making) prisons in the United States, apparently viewed the campus dining halls as part of its slave labor complex. Taking control on July 1, 1999, it refused to recognize the union and launched a campaign to deprive food service workers of the few benefits they had enjoyed. The company stripped workers of hundreds of hours of accumulated sick time and quadruped their health insurance premiums. As workers were paid only six to seven dollars an hour, many had no choice but to opt out of Sodexho-Marriott's expensive health care plan. Facing reduced benefits and deteriorating working conditions, the number of regular employees plummeted. Because of the now chronic understaffing, most workers put in twelve-hour shifts. Workers were told that they could not discuss job conditions among themselves or with others. And when some dared to wear "Union Yes" pins, Sodexho-Marriott managers ordered them to remove these traces of resistance. Despite the efforts of HERE Local 471, the workers grew increasingly demoralized.

Although I had gravitated toward dealing with national and international issues, there was no way that I could ignore these events on my own campus. In fact, I was fuming at managerial arrogance, as were others. Therefore, I joined with student groups, community organizations, and other campus unions in publicizing and protesting Sodexho-Marriott's antilabor practices. Gradually, a coalition—the Student-Labor Initiative (SLI, pronounced "sly")—was forged, with its key conspirators meeting in my office. One of our first ventures was a joint rally sparked by the Graduate Student Employees Union. At my instigation, my own union, United University Professions (UUP)—the largest on the campus—repeatedly condemned the behavior of Sodexho-Marriott in communications with its members, in resolutions, and in labor-management meetings. Our executive committee, which for years had held luncheon meetings in a small campus dining hall, voted to bring its own food to such gatherings rather than patronize an antiunion company. However, despite these early protests, the assorted campus managers—the administration, UAS, and Sodexho-Marriott—resorted to every possible excuse to evade the issue of the mistreatment of food service workers.

By the spring of 2000, it could no longer be evaded. On April 4, thanks to a plan I helped to craft, activists from a variety of campus unions posted signs and distributed thousands of leaflets to people entering the dining halls during the lunch hour. The leaflets not only exposed the disgraceful behavior of Sodexho-Marriott; they also asked the diners to wear "Union Yes" pins as an act of solidarity with the food service workers. To our surprise, almost everyone seemed supportive and reached for a button. Within twenty minutes we had distributed our entire stock of a thousand "Union Yes" pins and were resorting, in desperation, to a fast-dwindling pile of "Dump Sodexho" stickers. In one dining hall, the delighted workers surged out of the kitchen and donned the forbidden pins themselves. Meanwhile, student activists—who had been very mysterious about their plans for that day—poured into university president Karen Hitchcock's office and staged a sit-in. As I denounced Sodexho-Marriott in front of the Campus Center on a bullhorn, I could see and hear the crowds on the other side of the campus—including workers, students, and police—milling about outside the administration building. It was quite a scene.

The smooth university managers and their public relations flaks had lost control of the situation, and after that they never quite had it again. Local newspapers and television stations suddenly discovered the dining halls issue, much to the administration's regret. Rally followed rally. Although I was concerned at times that the student sit-in's sensational aspects and complicated legal aftermath were diverting attention from the underlying issues, I need not have worried, for Sodexho-Marriott came up with new outrages to fan the flames of discontent. Within days the company—which had failed numerous Health

Department inspections of its campus facilities in the past—produced an outbreak of e-coli on the campus. This led to a shutdown of one campus dining hall and to further embarrassing coverage in the mass media. For the first time, I began to think, "We're going to win!"

The pressures on the administration now mounted rapidly. In early May, when university president Hitchcock arrived to open the annual campus fountain ceremony, students greeted her with a chorus of boos. Meanwhile, UUP called for Sodexho-Marriott's contract to be terminated—a demand echoed by the College Council, the Solidarity Committee, and other organizations. Prodded by unions, state legislators now began to ask the administration what the devil was going on at SUNY/Albany. President Hitchcock, in turn, appointed a university committee to examine the dining halls issue. Although the committee was only supposed to deal with the quality of food, the labor issue also made an appearance. Everyone, it seemed, wanted a "fresh start," and Sodexho-Marriott, by this point, seemed unlikely to provide it. In June the administration terminated its contract with that corporation and appointed a search committee for a new food service provider.

But would this new contractor accept fair labor standards? Our campaign had so shattered managerial confidence that the new company had no alternative. During the search process, the anxious SUNY/Albany administration, roused from its torpor, told prospective contractors that the union issue had to be settled, for it did not want a repetition of the labor troubles of the past year. Consequently, in July, when a new food service provider for the campus was chosen, its parent organization immediately faxed a letter to HERE Local 471 declaring that it recognized the union. Furthermore, the food service workers fired by Sodexho-Marriott were rehired and contract negotiations began. Within a fairly short time, the company and the union agreed to a contract providing for substantial wage increases, with the highest (a 33-percent raise) going to the most poorly paid workers; free medical insurance; pensions funded entirely by the company; and the restoration of seniority, sick days, and personal days that workers had built up over years of employment but had lost under Sodexho-Marriott's reign of terror. It was a terrific victory.

For years thereafter, whenever I saw one of the dining halls workers on campus, I thought: "There's another person who finally can afford to take her kids to the doctor, have their teeth fixed by a dentist, take them on a vacation, and maybe even send them to college." I couldn't have been happier.

The Solidarity Committee was particularly adept at pushing beyond Establishment complacency. In 1998 one of our members, Fred Pfeiffer, went to a meeting of government officials who planned New York State's celebration of

Martin Luther King Jr.'s birthday—which over the years had grown ever more devoid of social significance—and proposed adding a labor component to it. Impossible, he was told. "That would be taking sides!" King, of course, did "take sides"—that of the poor and the oppressed. Indeed, he was assassinated while supporting the unionization of sanitation workers in Memphis. And so we decided to ignore the official festivities and to organize a celebration of Martin Luther King Jr. and the labor movement. Held at a large African American church on King's birthday, in January 1999, it proved to be a very well-attended, inspiring gathering, with free food, speeches, and music. Eventually, attracting the cosponsorship of the Coalition of Black Trade Unionists, the Labor Council for Latin American Advancement, and assorted unions, it turned into an annual event.

Meanwhile, ventures with a broader focus tugged at my life, including a Citizens Panel on Ultimate Weapons. Having met Robert J. Lifton, the distinguished psychiatrist and author, during the Smithsonian controversy, I had followed up a few years later by urging him to take the lead in reviving public interest in nuclear disarmament. Therefore, I was not totally surprised when he faxed me a letter inviting me to his Upper West Side Manhattan apartment for a December 1998 meeting, which he said was designed to bring together key people in an effort to focus public attention on nuclear dangers. I was very happy to accept, both because I believed in the cause and because, living in Albany, I had long felt somewhat isolated from prominent New York City intellectuals. When I arrived at his apartment, however, I was disappointed to discover that there were over a hundred people present and that the event was simply a fund-raiser for a Lifton antinuclear project: a Citizens' Panel on Ultimate Weapons. Even so, I made the best of it, taking a seat to listen to the featured address by Jonathan Schell, a famed author, on the reviving nuclear menace. Part way through his talk, Schell remarked: "You know, recently I have been reading some remarkable books, the first two volumes of *The Struggle Against the Bomb*." Lifton immediately piped up: "The author, Larry Wittner, is sitting right over there!" Immediately, all eyes were upon me, and I sputtered a few words. After the talk I was suddenly surrounded by a coterie of interested people. I also spoke at length with Schell and suggested to Lifton that I would be delighted to help out with the Citizens Panel. "You will soon receive an invitation," he said. And I did.

Thereafter, from February 1999 to early 2001, the small Citizens Panel met periodically in midtown Manhattan at John Jay College. The meetings were hosted by the Center on Violence and Human Survival, run by Lifton and Chuck Strozier, a prominent psychiatrist and author, and drew together a wonderful assemblage, including Lifton, Strozier, Schell, Richard Falk, Saul Mendlovitz, Todd Gitlin, and Rolf Ekeus (Sweden's ambassador to the United Nations). At times, we were joined by others, including Richard Barnet, Stephen Cohen, Katrina vanden Heuvel, and Bob Musil (executive director of Physicians for Social Responsibility). Our discussions were always on a very high level—sometimes, I thought, a little too high to be practicable—and I certainly enjoyed them, as I did the opportunity to meet face to face with some of the world's most outstanding activist intellectuals. Although we failed to stir up a tidal wave of popular concern about the reviving nuclear arms race, we did manage to organize a large conference, "The Second Nuclear Age and the Academy." Held in mid-November 2000 at the Graduate Center of the City University of New York, it attracted a reasonably good audience and a stellar cast, including UN Secretary General Kofi Annan. Lifton and Strozier also managed to obtain foundation funding that provided for eight small fellowships to young faculty who would develop courses on the nuclear menace. And I managed to get Schell to participate in a panel on nuclear weapons that I organized at the American Historical Association convention of January 2000—a panel that also included presentations by Randy Forsberg, Vladislav Zubok, and me.

International ventures also absorbed a great deal of my time. In 1998 I became chair of the Peace History Commission (PHC) of the International Peace Research Association (IPRA)—an organization with great possibilities but which had very little structure and no dues-paying members. However, with the assistance of Anne Kjelling, the secretary of the PHC and the head librarian at the Norwegian Nobel Institute, I began to lure peace historians into participating in scholarly panels at the forthcoming IPRA conference in Tampere, Finland. Many of these historians would then go on to present papers at a Peace History Society (PHS) conference that, at my suggestion, Anne had scheduled right after that at the Nobel Institute in Oslo. Thanks largely to my ability to draw on a broad range of contacts I had developed over the years among peace researchers and to the work of Anne and Scott Bills (then president of PHS) in organizing the Oslo meeting, both conferences attracted widespread participation.

Indeed, both gatherings—held in August 2000—proved very successful and enjoyable. At Tampere dozens of peace historians made presentations and attended a PHC dinner, which I organized in an effort to provide the group with the social interaction necessary for a viable organization. On one interesting evening, we joined other IPRA conferees on a boat trip to an island in the Bay of Finland. Here, after a buffet supper and a performance by a Swedish polka band, the women headed off to the sauna. Then it was the men's turn. I arrived at the sauna a bit late, and by the time I entered the steamy room, dozens of the world's most prominent peace researchers were sitting on tiers of benches—nude, throwing dippers of water on the hot bricks, beating themselves with clusters of birch leaves, and laughing heartily. Then, periodically—and still nude—they ran out the door, raced down the dock, and leapt into the bay. Things were a bit more formal at the Nobel Institute, where we felt in awe of the eminent recipients of the Peace Prize who had once graced its halls. Even so, we managed to break away from giving papers to wander around Oslo's port area and attend a spirited banquet at a local restaurant, where after dinner I led the assemblage in singing peace ballads. I was a bit apprehensive when one of the other diners in the restaurant—a big, husky fellow—strode over to my table to speak with me. But I needn't have been; after all, this was Scandinavia. He simply thanked me for the wonderful songs.

The following year, I traveled to China. This trip, too, developed thanks to my network of scholarly contacts. Ever since I had met Mark Selden during my Fulbright year in Japan, he and I had kept up occasional correspondence, in part because, as an Asia specialist, he was a very useful person to consult in connection with my research on antinuclear activism in Japan and China. In 2000 he asked me if I would like to give a paper, comparing the Japanese and American nuclear disarmament movements, at a symposium he was organizing at the University of Science and Technology in Hong Kong. Focused on twentieth-century wars in Asia and resistance to them, the conference would be funded and hosted by the university's Social Science Department, chaired by Alvin So. It was too good an opportunity to forgo, so I flew to Hong Kong. There I saw Mark for the first time in almost three decades and also met other scholars, often activist intellectuals, including Marilyn Young of New York University and Yuki Tanaka of Hiroshima City University. Although the subject of the symposium was pretty grim—millions of lives lost in imperialist and racist wars—we did manage to break away on occasion and see aspects of the city, which was now under Chinese Communist rule. We walked around inside a giant Buddha, located the site of a notorious Japanese prison, and met with activists from a leading workers' rights group. Ultimately, a revised version of my paper appeared in a book edited by Mark and Alvin entitled *War and State Terrorism*, with a promotional blurb on the cover by Noam Chomsky.

Other old friends also crossed my path. At a statewide UUP convention in the fall of 2000, one of the delegates sat down next to me and greeted me by name. As he did not look at all familiar, I asked, "Do I know you?" "Well, you should," he replied. It turned out to be a friend from my Vassar College days, Howard Cohn, now shorn of his enormous beard and lengthy hair. Howard had also been purged by Vassar's Mossbacks. Since then he had been largely underemployed—including his work now on a part-time basis at SUNY/Purchase. As we traded stories on the whereabouts of friends in the Vassar diaspora, Howard remarked that he still got together with a number of them. So that November, when Dorothy and I were down in Manhattan for the Second Nuclear Age conference, Howard invited us to meet them at a party at his West Side apartment. And there, suddenly, almost three decades later, were Mel Rosenthal, as eccentric as ever; Linda Pommer, still charming but without her husband, Dick, who had died years before; and Erika Franke, now an architect with a husband and children. Fortunately, none of them had become a stockbroker or a religious fundamentalist. Howard did me another good turn by bringing his camera to the next UUP convention in early 2001, where the Solidarity Singers performed labor and peace songs, and snapping lots of photos of us in action. Once again I came away with a strong sense that, despite all the misery our masters could inflict upon us, the human spirit managed to survive.

These continuities with the past were supplemented by new possibilities for the future. In June 2000, Julia and Bob used the occasion of our annual attendance at the Old Songs Festival to report that she was pregnant. How could this be? I wondered. She was still a little girl in my mind. And she was certainly easy to take for one, for she was diminutive and certainly looked very youthful. But, in fact, she was twenty-nine years old and, together with Bob, had decided that it was time to have a child. So, as they returned to their lives in Syracuse, I waited nervously for the childbirth, expecting that something just had to go wrong. But it didn't. On Christmas Day, Julia gave birth to a baby boy, Benjamin Wittner Hughes. At five pounds and fourteen ounces, he was a tiny thing, with red hair and bright blue eyes. Surveying this small bundle of life, which I could easily hold in my hands, I could hardly believe it. Not only was my little daughter a mother, but I was a grandfather. And who knew what this tiny child, already kicking and yowling, would do when he grew up and confronted the world.

10

Growing Old, but Not Gracefully, 2001–2011

As people age, they usually lose their youthful exuberance—indeed, grow gloomier and more pessimistic. One reason for this, I guess, is that their glands start pumping out lower levels of adrenalin, thus reducing their energy level. Also, they begin to recognize their mortality. They develop aches and pains, grow ill and more fragile, and contemplate the deaths of their friends, their relatives, and themselves. In addition, people who work at transforming the world often begin to recognize that it really hasn't changed very much. War, injustice, and ignorance persist, however much individuals may throw themselves into attempts to abolish these negative aspects of human existence. At worst, they conclude that they have failed. At best, they find, the social gains have not matched their hopes.

I could certainly see these factors operating in my own life. Although I continued to do calisthenics and to stay reasonably fit, I entered my sixties in 2001, and over the ensuing decade there were signs of a slow erosion of my physical and mental stamina. For some reason, my asthma actually disappeared. Nevertheless, my allergies and sensitivity to cold grew worse, my hair and beard turned quite gray (and increasingly white), and I experienced new, inexplicable bodily aches. Even the wild mop of hair on my head, a characteristic feature of mine that I always enjoyed, began to thin out—though I started with so much that this change was not very noticeable for some time. Meanwhile, old friends startled me by suddenly dying, including Tim Reilly and Paul Metzger.

It was also disturbing to experience the new climate of political reaction—fostered by religious fanatics, unscrupulous businessmen, and right-wing communications media and symbolized by the startlingly regressive policies of the Bush administration. Immense tax cuts for the rich, the destruction of social welfare programs, the assaults on affirmative action and abortion rights, the abandonment of environmental regulations, the scrapping of nuclear arms control and disarmament treaties, and the reckless plunge into militarism and war were enough to disturb anyone, and certainly more than enough to depress an activist whose political beliefs went in the opposite direction. I had never really thought that there would come a time when the U.S. government would be working to destroy the public school system, to privatize the prisons, the armed forces, and social security, and to brazenly defend its widespread use of torture. But that time had come. It was almost enough to undermine whatever remained of my Enlightenment faith in reason and human progress.

But not quite. After all, I was a stubborn cuss with plenty of psychological calluses derived from past defeats. Also, I had a good sense of history, which led me to conclude that today's conventional wisdom is tomorrow's discarded tradition. And so, like many others, I persisted.

In 2001, when the film *Bread and Roses* came out, Dorothy and I thought that its screening would provide a useful way to call attention to the exploitation of workers, particularly workers of color. Directed by the British filmmaker Ken Loach and starring Adrien Brody and Pilar Padilla, it was a very powerful drama portraying the successful struggle of 50,000 downtrodden immigrant janitorial workers in Los Angeles for union representation. To get the film shown commercially, we bombarded Albany's best movie house, the Spectrum Theater, with petitions, as well as promises to mobilize a substantial union constituency to see it. But nothing seemed to work. So, once again, the Solidarity Committee went forward on its own. We obtained a copy of the film through one of my fellow UUP members, Tom Hoey, who had a friend working for the distributor; rented Page Hall, a very large auditorium on campus, for an evening; and worked zealously at selling tickets, with the proceeds earmarked for striking furniture workers.

Our plan for the screening of *Bread and Roses* was almost derailed when just three weeks before it the terrorist attacks of September 11 occurred. These were so shocking and seemed so all-absorbing that all other issues were simply marginalized. Furthermore, in the Albany area, as elsewhere, the events of 9/11 generated an extremely nationalistic, intolerant environment. Television stations showed endless scenes of the twin towers collapsing, politicians whipped up enormous fears of internal attack, American flags appeared everywhere, pledges of allegiance were restored at public gatherings (including union meetings), and dissident groups faced a very inhospitable environment. In these circumstances, we wondered if anyone would attend our event. Finally, miraculously, some 400 people turned out to see the film.

Another unexpected development was my receipt of funding to complete the writing of *Toward Nuclear Abolition,* the final volume in my *Struggle Against the Bomb* trilogy. Once again, I had applied to numerous foundations for fellowships and—despite the rave reviews drawn by the first two volumes—was turned down repeatedly. Curiously, though, the United States Institute of Peace (USIP), a U.S. government-funded entity established during the Reagan years, made me a finalist. Accordingly, in early 2001 I flew down to Washington, D.C., for an interview. A friendly staffer told me that in the past, with the USIP board dominated by Reagan and Bush appointees, "you never would have gotten through the front door." But retirements and the advent of Clinton appointees had opened up a window of opportunity. As things turned out, my interview came late in the day and the committee chair, Seymour Martin Lipset—a very distinguished political scientist, now well on in years—dozed off. As a result, another committee member took charge of the situation, and this probably worked to my advantage. She was much younger, with a crew cut, no makeup, and steel-rimmed glasses. At the end of the interview, we stood around chatting about peace movement leaders we both knew. I returned from Washington convinced I had done well. And I had. The USIP offered me a modest fellowship for the spring of 2002. Also, within a brief time, the MacArthur Foundation awarded me a research and writing grant that brought me up to full salary for that semester. Now all I had to do was finish the book.

It wasn't easy. Although I was a ferocious writer with a very high level of motivation, at the beginning of February 2002, when I began the fellowship, I still needed to fill some research gaps dealing with the Clinton era and had about eight hefty chapters to write. To complicate the situation, I had to be "in residence" at the USIP, meaning that I had to work at the USIP headquarters in Washington, D.C., and reside in that city for the next four months. It was a strain to live apart from Dorothy and my friends, so I commuted to and from Albany every other weekend—a practice that absorbed a lot of time. Also, perhaps because of the contrast between sitting at a USIP desk hour after hour and then walking vigorously a mile or so back to my tiny Washington apartment on cold, blustery nights, I strained my leg muscles (or perhaps my ligaments), which made getting about very painful. On the other hand, living a monkish existence and working seven days a week from nine to nine, I got an enormous amount of writing done. Also, I conducted some additional interviews with Washington officials and nuclear disarmament activists and had the good fortune of being afforded full access to the extensive files of Daryl Kimball, who had led Washington antinuclear lobbying for some years and was now executive director of the Arms Control Association. As a result, when I left Washington at the end of May, the book manuscript was virtually finished.

I was barely back in Albany when Bob, Julia, and Benjamin moved to Niskayuna, about a half hour's drive away from us. Before leaving Syracuse, Julia—determined to spend more time with Benjamin than afforded by full-time employment—had proposed to Laubach Literacy that she work part time, but that religiously based nonprofit company, despite its professed concern for family values, refused to consider it. So she quit her job and did freelance editorial work from her home. Meanwhile, Bob graduated from law school and accepted a position clerking in the New York State Appellate Court in Albany. Their move to the capital district facilitated our seeing them on a more regular basis. Benjamin, nearing three years of age, was delighted and turned Dorothy and me into his abject slaves—reading him stories, playing banjo for (and sometimes with) him, and catering to his every whim. Sometimes he gave us a friendly bite. Soon, however, he had a rival for our attention, for on March 28, 2003, Julia gave birth to a second child, Elizabeth (Betsy) Hughes, who weighed in at six pounds one ounce. A power struggle ensued, but eventually Betsy learned to hold her own. Overall, grandparenting proved to be a lot of fun.

New friends also came into our life. Some were from nearby Union College, where my activist buddy and fellow historian, Andy Feffer, now divorced, married one of his colleagues, Michelle Chilcoat, thereby bringing her and a number of other interesting faculty members (including Megan Ferry and Daniel Mosquera) into our circle. Gathering together at movies or over coffee, we enjoyed many a lively discussion about culture and politics. In addition, we became increasingly friendly with Said Shah, who raised issues of global poverty and promoted the worldwide Social Forum movement at meetings of the Solidarity Committee, and with another couple we had known for some time, Paul Tick and Agnes Zellin, both increasingly caught up in a rising tide of local peace activism. Allen Ballard, an unusually congenial member of my department who decades before had played a key role in opening up the admissions process for racial minorities in the City University of New York, also entered the ranks of our friends.

Meanwhile, as the Bush administration used the public hysteria over the terrorist attacks of 9/11 to lay the groundwork for a disastrous invasion of Iraq, friends and I—like many other people around the world—did our best to head off the looming war. At SUNY/Albany I joined with a small, ad hoc group of concerned faculty and students to sponsor an October 2002 antiwar teach-in. Although I doubted that many people would show up for the event on our normally placid, apolitical campus, we decided to go for broke by reserving the largest room at the university, the Campus Center Ballroom. And that proved a good decision. Some 600 people—many from the community—packed the hall and vigorously applauded an array of speakers. Addressing this unusual assemblage, I warned that the real danger of the moment was a "return to the simple-minded, militaristic nationalism that has brought massive, terrible destruction to the people of this planet." Given the fact that this event was addressed by the Albany area's academic experts on the Middle East, U.S. foreign policy, and presidential power, the mass media should have given it some thoughtful attention. But, in fact, the coverage was terrible. The local Fox News station, which showed pictures of the gathering, avoided broadcasting a word that we said. Instead, it flashed pictures of burning flags on the screen—its own creation, of course—and interviewed a critic of our talks.

With the mass media trumpeting the Bush administration's case for war, there was not much we could do to stop the militarist juggernaut, but we certainly tried. On February 10, 2003, in conjunction with teach-ins on dozens of campuses around the state, we organized another large event at SUNY. Then, on February 15 Dorothy and I joined hundreds of Albany residents on board a "Peace Train" to New York City, where hundreds of thousands of Americans—battling bitter cold, penned arbitrarily behind barricades, and subjected to police assaults—participated in an enormous antiwar demonstration. This event was part of the most massive outpouring of antiwar sentiment in human history, "The World Says No to War," in which some 10 million people around the globe participated in protests against war with Iraq. In mid-March, paired with a prowar speaker, I delivered a critique of the administration's case for war at an auditorium packed with students at nearby Bethlehem High School. Although U.S. military forces invaded Iraq the following day, our group of concerned SUNY/Albany faculty and students met again on March 22, decided to dig in for the long haul, and formed a new organization to sustain our efforts, SUNYA Peace & Justice. However, as a wave of patriotic propaganda engulfed the nation, the situation looked bleak.

Against this unpromising backdrop, *Toward Nuclear Abolition*—the final volume in my *Struggle Against the Bomb* trilogy—was published by Stanford University Press during the summer of 2003. Although I worked once more at encouraging individuals and publications to give it some public attention, the results were very disappointing. No newspaper in the United States reviewed the book. It was also ignored by virtually every other mass communications medium. About the only exception was WAMC-FM, a local public radio station, which broadcast an hour-long live interview with me. To be sure, *Toward Nuclear Abolition* did receive reviews in many scholarly journals, most peace movement publications, and a few political magazines. And these reviews were spectacular. But such publications reached relatively few people. Once again, I came away with the sense that I had produced a very important book—probably the best that I had ever written—and it had been blacked out by the mass media.

Fortunately, I began to find ways to break through the media blackout. That summer, I wrote a number of Op-Ed pieces and e-mailed them off to the nation's major newspapers. The results were discouraging. None accepted them, and most didn't even bother to respond. But in the past I had placed a few opinion pieces in the Albany *Times Union* (which had a paid circulation of about 100,000), so I fell back on that publication and, in conjunction with the anniversary of the Hiroshima bombing, it accepted my latest offering. Then, at the suggestion of a friend, I sent the same piece to the website *History News Network*. In response, the editor, Rick Shenkman, ran it and suggested that I send other short articles directly to him. Given my lack of success with mainstream publications, I began doing so later that month, and he invariably published them. This enabled me not only to place articles on a website that attracted some 300,000 readers a month, but also to arrange to have these articles republished by other websites, including the left-wing ZNet, the libertarian LewRockwell.com, truthout, the Huffington Post, and others. Without consulting me in any way, other electronic and print publications picked up and ran my Op-Eds on their own. My ability to reach a mainstream audience was enhanced when PeaceVoice, operated by Tom Hastings of Portland State University, began syndicating my Op-Eds to newspapers in small cities and towns. Generally, I produced about one article per month. For the most part, I dealt with nuclear weapons issues, but sometimes I wrote on other foreign and domestic policy concerns.

I supplemented this outreach effort with speaking engagements, mostly on the theme of my *Struggle Against the Bomb* trilogy: "How Peace Activists Saved the World from Nuclear War." Often initiated by me—but sometimes in response to outside invitations—these lectures occurred on numerous college and university campuses, including those of Amherst College, Siena College, Swarthmore College, Georgian Court University, Colgate University, Rutgers University, Columbia University, Princeton University, Wittenberg University, the University of California/Berkeley, and the University of New Mexico. Unfortunately, none of these talks drew vast crowds, nor did the many lectures I gave for peace groups and citizens organizations in scattered cities and towns. But they put me in direct contact with members of the public and enabled me to reach them with an empowering message: that the staunch efforts of average people had curbed the nuclear arms race and prevented nuclear war. Many people—particularly those already active in peace organizations—were thrilled to learn this and told me so. And it was a thrill for me to meet them, as well as to give the talk at the United Nations, where it was sponsored by the UN's NGO Committee on Disarmament.

The leadership of the peace movement recognized the significance of what I had to say. Consequently, Colin Archer, the secretary general of the International Peace Bureau (IPB), invited me to address a Europe-wide conference titled "Towards a World without Violence." Organized by the IPB (the worldwide federation of peace groups) and the Fundacio per la Pau (a Catalan peace organization), it was scheduled to be held in Barcelona in mid-2004. I sprang at the offer—both because I welcomed the opportunity to present my research findings at a large international peace movement gathering and because I wanted to see the city of Barcelona, immortalized in George Orwell's *Homage to Catalonia*. So, accompanied by Dorothy, I set off for that city in late June. There we explored Barcelona's fascinating streets, architecture, and vistas, went out to lively dinners with Colin, Bruce Kent, and other peace movement leaders, and participated in about five days of peace-oriented lectures, panels, plays, dances, and songs. I gave a short speech to a plenary session of about 800 people on "Civil Society and Disarmament" and my standard "Saved the World" address, supplemented by pictures of the nuclear disarmament campaign.

That June I flew off for another round of speeches in Japan. Takao ("Taka") Takahara (director of the International Peace Research Institute, at Meijigakuin University, in Tokyo) and Yuki Tanaka (a peace researcher at the Hiroshima Peace Institute of Hiroshima City University) had both extended speaking invitations to me. Taka also arranged for me to give some talks sponsored by Gensuikin (the Japan Congress Against Atomic and Hydrogen Bombs). Eventually, I commenced a whirlwind of activities in Japan. In late July I flew into Hiroshima, was housed at the luxurious Rihga Royal Hotel, and made a presentation on my research (as did three other guest scholars) at the Hiroshima Peace Institute. I finished up my first day with a dinner in honor of our scholarly group at the mayor's mansion, hosted by Hiroshima's mayor, Tadatoshi Akiba. On the following day, we placed a wreath at the cenotaph commemorating the victims of the atomic bombing and gave our talks (with mine on the *Enola Gay* controversy) at a large public symposium, after which I raced by taxi to the airport to catch a plane to my meeting with Taka in Tokyo. The trip to the airport was a nightmare, however, as a major typhoon was sweeping into Hiroshima and my flight was grounded. I was supposed to deliver my lecture at Meijigakuin the next day. How was it possible for everything to pan out? Miraculously, I got to the airport just in time to catch the last flight out of the city. And so off the plane flew, its wings shuddering dangerously in the high winds but eventually bearing me safely to Tokyo.

In that city, Taka took charge of things, housing me in the university's guest house and introducing me at a university symposium, where I gave my "Saved the World" address. I barely had time to catch my breath before I was picked up the following morning and escorted to the headquarters of Gensuikin. Ever since its founding in the mid-1960s, when non-Communists (particularly the Japan Socialist Party and the unions) had revolted against the party-line tactics of Communists within Japan's nuclear disarmament campaign, Gensuikin had been one of two major disarmament groups in Japanese life. Now, with the decline of the Socialists and the unions, it had fallen on leaner days, but it still maintained a significant staff, a network of local groups, and a variety of peace and antinuclear activities. After a lengthy discussion with Gensuikin leaders—ranging from my *Struggle Against the Bomb* trilogy, to the state of the movement in the United States, to the prospects for defeating the Bush administration in the forthcoming U.S. elections—I was freed up for a little political tourism that afternoon. Unfortunately, the museum devoted to the 1954 *Lucky Dragon* incident (in which a U.S. H-bomb test had irradiated Japanese fishermen) was closed. But it was possible to visit the controversial Yasukuni Shrine, which housed a militarist exhibit beloved by Japanese right-wingers and the Japanese prime minister. So a young Gensuikin staffer, with some uneasiness, escorted me there. After that we headed back to Gensuikin headquarters, where I gave my "Saved the World" address once again.

The next day, together with a Gensuikin delegation, I returned to Hiroshima by train for a series of events in commemoration of the atomic bombing of that city. At first I felt a bit like a parasite—lodged (though in much less splendor than previously) and fed by my hosts. But they made good use of me. Kevin Martin, executive director of Peace Action, was supposed to fly in from the United States and address a press conference organized by Gensuikin. But Kevin's passport had not been renewed in time, and I was startled to learn that I was filling in for him. Thus, on August 4, together with a survivor of the Chernobyl disaster, I addressed a gaggle of reporters from the *Asahi Shimbun* and other major newspapers, who probed my thoughts on the current state of the nuclear disarmament movement. (If only the U.S. press showed a fraction of their interest!) Then my Gensuikin hosts and I piled into a taxi and headed off to the starting point of the annual nuclear disarmament march through the city's streets. Arriving there, I asked where in the long march column they would like me to stand. "Why, right in the front," they said. "You're leading it!" I grasped one end of the demonstration's large antinuclear banner, also held aloft by a former president of Gensuikin, and our crowd of thousands paraded through downtown Hiroshima—preceded by a sound truck, escorted by the city police, and cheered on by the local populace.

More events followed in Hiroshima, including the opening of Gensuikin's massive world conference (in which I sat with several dozen other dignitaries on stage), the delivery of another "Saved the World" lecture to a gathering of Gensuikin activists from around the nation, a talk to the Hiroshima Association for Nuclear Weapons Abolition on Article 9 of the Japanese constitution (which bans the maintenance of military forces and war), attendance at the annual August 6 peace ceremonies sponsored by the city of Hiroshima, a lantern-floating ceremony along the Ota River in honor of those annihilated in the atomic bombing, and a sizzlingly hot day with Kevin (who had finally arrived) touring Miyajima Island. But I think I shall best remember leading the nuclear disarmament march through the city streets. It seemed a particularly appropriate follow-up for the little boy in elementary school who, more than half a century before, had been ordered by the authorities to hide under his desk from nuclear war.

I also would have liked to follow up my *Struggle Against the Bomb* trilogy with an abbreviated version of the work, for I realized that a short paperback without footnotes or other scholarly apparatus had a better chance to reach college students and the general public. Thus, in December 2003, when my Stanford editor suggested that I write this abbreviated version, I enthusiastically endorsed the idea and drew up a proposal for it. In turn, she promised to take the proposal to the Stanford editorial board in January. At this point, however, she stopped answering my e-mails, and ultimately I grew tired of contacting her about it.

Meanwhile, I turned to other writing projects. This included putting together an article ("The Power of Protest") summarizing the trilogy that appeared in the *Bulletin of the Atomic Scientists,* an article on the *Enola Gay* exhibits that appeared in *Social Alternatives* (an Australian journal), a lengthy article comparing peace movements in East and West that appeared in *Archiv für Sozialgeschichte* (a publication of Germany's Friedrich Ebert Stiftung), and an article on world antinuclear activism for *Nonviolent Alternatives for Social Change* (a UNESCO anthology). As usual, there was plenty of writing to do—if I could find time to do it.

As if this wasn't enough to keep me busy, the Solidarity Singers were also flourishing. Over time we grew better—a result not only of practicing occasionally but also of adding two talented women to the group: Bev Seinberg (a copy editor) and Maureen ("Mo") Hannah (a college teacher and psychologist).

Drawing upon traditional folk melodies, I wrote a number of songs that we performed, including "Back Again" (a jaundiced look at some of the top officials in the Bush administration). With great energy, we performed our music at labor, peace, and other political events. We even performed on the stage of the Cohoes Music Hall (a famed site of nineteenth-century concerts and vaudeville routines) and at the Caffè Lena (the oldest continuously operating coffeehouse in the United States). Once, barely keeping our balance, we performed on the back of a flatbed truck as it rumbled down one of Albany's main thoroughfares as part of the capital district's annual Labor Parade. Hillary Clinton was among the flock of political dignitaries waving to us from the reviewing stand. Probably our most appreciative audience was at McGregor Prison—a grim, medium-security facility topped with coils of razor wire—where the downtrodden inmates not only sang along with us fervently but also gave us a standing ovation.

As news of our performances reached two leaders of the Peace History Society, Wendy Chmielewski and Scott Bennett, they proposed that the Solidarity Singers serve as the centerpiece of a large reception that PHS would sponsor at the annual convention of the American Historical Association. In January 2004 most of the group traveled to Washington, D.C., where—at the main convention hotel—we performed a full range of peace and social justice songs, the words of which we projected on a screen to facilitate audience participation. If there were government agents present at this event, I hope they didn't miss "George Dubya" (written by me and sung to the tune of "Jesse James"):

> George Dubya was a boy, a Texas good ole boy.
> He robbed the election train.
> He gave to the rich, and he stole from the poor—
> Greedy hands, with no heart and no brain.
>
> CHORUS:
> His daddy had the wealth, to keep him in good health,
> A family pedigree.
> But he couldn't get enough of that million dollar stuff,
> So he's robbing from you and from me.
>
> Young Dubya he arose, with cocaine up his nose.
> He wanted lots more money to command.
> So daddy fixed things right, to feed his appetite
> And made him a Texas oilman.
>
> For a time young George was pleased, he drank and took his ease,
> He partied with the bankers and magnates.

But that proved just a bore, he wanted even more,
He wanted the whole United States.

He wrapped himself in Jesus, and in our country's flag,
The rich poured millions into his campaign.
And when that didn't fly, he fixed things on the sly,
And robbed the election train.

Now there's tax breaks for the wealthy, and wars of every kind.
They loot our treasury.
Then he tells us that the government can't help the rest of us.
He's robbing from you and from me.

This song was written by hard-workin' folks
As soon as the thievery began.
Don't you trust that oily guy, with dollar signs for eyes.
He's just a robber man.

Of course, unlike George Dubya, I still had to earn a living, and this entailed work of a more mundane kind at SUNY/Albany. By this point, teaching my courses—on the history of U.S. social movements, the history of U.S. foreign policy, and international history—was pretty easy. Also, on student evaluations of teaching, I drew reasonably good grades. Even so, it was discouraging to read student papers, to observe the overall decline in literacy, and to realize how little many students had learned in my courses and in others. Student mastery of new electronic gadgetry had advanced remarkably, but overall student knowledge seemed to have dwindled. Also, most students appeared less engaged than in the past with confronting the major problems of the modern world. Occasionally, to be sure, students with a broad social consciousness—usually older and more thoughtful than most of their classmates—would stop by to talk with me about issues of substance. But many students—and particularly the undergraduates—on my campus struck me as cynical and uninteresting.

Nevertheless, teaching was more enjoyable than other university chores. Usually I stayed as far away as possible from committee and administrative work, but in 2001 my friend Iris Berger was elected department chair, and it was hard to resist her entreaties to accept some responsibilities along these lines. And so I served two dreary years as the History Department representative on the College Council and a good part of another chairing a search committee. Such searches, though, were important, for my department was made up overwhelmingly of aging white males. Thanks to Iris's tactful persistence—and to continued pressure for affirmative action from Ben and from me—this pattern shifted significantly. Soon there were many young women—and not all white, either—moving up the departmental ladder. Meanwhile, in 2006, responding to new pleas from Iris, I became the department's director of graduate studies.

Yet I had no intention of being buried under piles of university memos. I served on the steering committee of our local Peace Action group (ably led by two Quaker activists, Pat Beetle and David Easter), continued work on the Albany UUP executive committee, and participated in meetings of UUP's statewide Solidarity Committee. At one of UUP's statewide conventions, I successfully championed the passage of a resolution endorsing Peace Action's Campaign for a New Foreign Policy. At another I made an impassioned speech that helped turn the tide in favor of an antiwar resolution and of our union's financial support of U.S. Labor Against the War. In the spring of 2005, in conjunction with the nuclear Non-Proliferation Treaty review conference at the United Nations, I pulled together a coalition of capital district peace and religious groups that sponsored a Nuclear Abolition Week, with dozens of talks (many by me), film showings, and other presentations focused on the necessity for nuclear disarmament. Randy Forsberg flew in from Boston to serve as the featured speaker at our largest public meeting, at nearby Siena College, and I escorted her there, as well as to a meeting with the editorial board of the Albany *Times Union*. On May 1 many of us piled into chartered buses that transported us to an international nuclear disarmament march outside the United Nations.

As in recent decades, the Solidarity Committee of the Capital District provided a focal point for many of my local activities. Unfortunately, it did not seem to pick up many new young members. Moreover, the Capital District Area Labor Federation (established by the AFL-CIO as a new level of labor bureaucracy) revived the chilly attitude of labor officialdom toward Solidarity's operations. Even so, by this point the Solidarity Committee's veterans were old friends who worked together smoothly and efficiently, whether in swelling picket lines, turning out its monthly newsletter, or planning the annual Martin Luther King Jr. Labor Movement Celebration. Furthermore, the dues from union locals and activists continued to flow in. Reviving the Solidarity Committee film series, Dorothy, Tam Kistler, Jon Flanders, and I showed movies with prolabor, anticorporate, women's rights, racial justice, and antiwar themes to an audience that packed the Bricklayers' Local 2 union hall. Later, with Trudy Quaif replacing Tam, we screened them at the local Unitarian Society hall.

Meanwhile, after a lull in activism on the SUNY/Albany campus, our SUNYA Peace & Justice group sprang back to life during the 2005–6 academic year. Beginning with a film and speakers on the growing oil crisis, we finished things off with a meeting of well over 200 people who turned out to hear Michael Klare lecture on oil and U.S. foreign policy. Once a fraternity brother of mine at Columbia College, Michael now directed the Five College Program in Peace and World Security Studies at Hampshire College, wrote on military affairs and resource issues for the *Nation,* and was well known for his many powerful books, such as *Blood and Oil.* Although we had gotten on badly during our college years, our relationship had improved thereafter until, by this point, we were on the same wavelength.

In the fall of 2005, my longtime activity in the peace movement—combined with my prominence as a writer about it—led to my election as an at-large member of the Peace Action national board. Although Peace Action was the largest peace organization in the United States, with about 100,000 members and about a hundred chapters, it was not as influential a force in U.S. life—or even within the peace movement—as these numbers might suggest. Not only were its finances precarious, thanks to a substantial debt and to an inadequate dues structure, but there existed numerous other national and local peace organizations—a situation that kept the overall movement fragmented and drained off potential members and resources. Even so, Peace Action had inherited the mantle of mass organizations like SANE and the Freeze (which, in 1987, had merged to form it) and, after a lull during the 1990s, had undergone a substantial revival. Thus, from my standpoint, it provided the best opportunity for developing a broadly based, effective national peace organization. As a result, I was delighted—and flattered—to be asked to serve on the Peace Action national board.

But what could I do to assist the organization? Attending Peace Action board meetings in late 2005, I got on well with the other board members and renewed my acquaintance with its executive director, Kevin Martin. Even so, I realized that I had no special talent for dealing with the board's major tasks, such as fund-raising. Eventually, however, when plans for Peace Action's fiftieth anniversary celebration (scheduled to occur in 2007, based on SANE's founding in 1957) were discussed, I conceived the idea of putting together a book for the occasion. Titled *Peace Action: Past, Present, and Future,* it would comprise essays written by SANE, Freeze, and Peace Action leaders, as well as by some friendly politicians. I discussed this idea with Glen Stassen, a board member and holder of a chair in Christian ethics at Fuller Theological Seminary, and we decided to work together on the project as coeditors. Glen also agreed to raise enough money so that 2,000 copies could be purchased from the publisher and then sold by Peace Action to anniversary celebrants or distributed free of charge to members of Congress and the press. At the suggestion of David Cortright and with the enthusiastic backing of the Peace Action leadership, we secured a contract for the book from Paradigm Publishers—a new high-quality publishing house—and began lining up contributors.

Ironically, in early 2006, on the very day I mailed off a signed contract to Paradigm Publishers, my editor at Stanford University Press suddenly revived her proposal that I write an abbreviated version of my *Struggle Against the Bomb* trilogy. In these circumstances—with one book project just beginning, numerous listserv and website article opportunities open to me, more political activities than I could handle, a full-time teaching job, and my department's graduate directorship in the wings—it was tempting to tell her to forget it. But the fact was that I did think that a short version of the trilogy would serve a useful purpose. Besides, when did practical considerations ever play a role in my life? So I told her I'd write it.

During the reign of George W. Bush there were more important things to worry about. Here was a president who was undermining the hard-won rights of workers, racial minorities, and women, who had thrown open the nation's natural resources to corporate plunder, who was subverting cherished civil liberties, who was placing public schools and social welfare institutions under the control of fundamentalist fanatics, and who had plunged the United States into vastly destructive, costly, and unnecessary wars. And the U.S. public reelected him (and his shock troops in Congress) in 2004. Naturally, I felt more than ever like an outsider. Of course, I recognized that there were large numbers of Americans who didn't approve of this lurch to the Right and, indeed, were resisting it. But it was impossible not to feel politically besieged.

This siege acquired a personal dimension when I discovered that I had been placed on the hit-list of David Horowitz, a former left-wing extremist who had gone on to become a right-wing extremist. The first tip-off appeared in late 2004, on FrontPageMag.org, one of his numerous well-funded websites. Here—amid ads for luxurious right-wing retreats, T-shirts that suggested gunning down leftists, and books equating liberalism with treason—was a slashing attack on my *Toward Nuclear Abolition*, written by one of Horowitz's acolytes at the U.S. Naval War College. Then, in March 2005, while doing a search on the web for the latest reviews of this book, I came upon a reference to myself on another Horowitz website called *Discover the Networks*. In this alleged "Guide to the Political Left," I found "profiles" of forty historians—among them, me. This lengthy sketch of my life was replete with false statements and innuendoes. Most disturbing (aside from the awful photo accompanying it), this public denunciation depicted me as enmeshed in these shadowy "Networks" of "terrorists," "totalitarian radicals," and "anti-American radicals."

Was this rubbish worth responding to? Initially, I was inclined to think that it was, especially as the keepers of this website claimed that it was being consulted by millions of visitors. On the other hand, would I not be squandering my time, psychological energy, and financial resources in making the case, legal or merely public, that I was an unlikely participant in an anti-American, terrorist conspiracy? Surely Horowitz's use of this website to denounce Jimmy Carter, Bill and Hillary Clinton, John Kerry, and the Ford, Rockefeller, and MacArthur foundations as part of the same gigantic conspiracy would convince reasonable people that he was either a lunatic or a scoundrel. I also recalled Dwight Eisenhower's remark that one should "never get in a pissing match with a skunk." So I decided to just ignore his campaign of political vilification.

Nevertheless, it was chilling to see how far Horowitz's unscrupulous behavior carried him. Drawing on over $14 million in support from right-wing foundations, he established a front group, Students for Academic Freedom. Although he had not been a student for about forty years, he continued to control this group and to use it as a springboard to charge that there was a left-wing reign of terror on the nation's college campuses that monopolized faculty positions and abused conservative students. Soon, at the behest of Republican legislators, twenty-five state legislatures and the U.S. Congress were considering Horowitz's misnamed Academic Bill of Rights, legislation that would give the government the power to patrol political expression on campus. Most faculty and civil libertarians, including me, were appalled by Horowitz's reckless charges and behavior, and the ACLU, the American Federation of Teachers, the American Association of University Professors, the National Education Association, the United States Student Association, and other respected organizations banded together in defense of intellectual freedom. Nor did Horowitz's wild contentions hold up under scrutiny. Taking the issue of student political intimidation seriously, the SUNY board of trustees surveyed the sixty-four campuses (with 400,000 students) under its jurisdiction, only to find that not a single student had filed a complaint along these lines.

But Horowitz had found his niche. Rolling in right-wing largesse, he paid himself well over $300,000 a year for his work as a thought controller and pulled in an additional $200,000 or so annually from his lavish speaker's fees. In early 2006 he followed up with the publication of *The Professors: The 101 Most Dangerous Academics in America*. On its cover, the book proclaimed: "Terrorists, racists and communists—you know them as The Professors." According to the book, they were also "murderers, sexual deviants, anti-Semites, and al-Qaida supporters." Furthermore, Horowitz insisted, these 101 were just "the tip of the iceberg," for there were at least 50,000 other faculty members just as dangerous—all part of "a shocking and perverse culture of academics who are poisoning the minds of today's college students." Despite the fantastic nature of these charges, Fox News and other right-wing communications media gave *The Professors* an enormous buildup, and it became an immediate best-seller. For some reason—perhaps because I was not important or flamboyant enough—I did not make the list of the 101 Evil Ones. Joking with friends, I promised to keep on trying. Even so, the whole thing was disgusting and said a great deal not only about Horowitz but also about the narrowing range of intellectual freedom in the United States.

There were other depressing trends as well. As my friends aged, a number of them became seriously ill, including Ben, Mike, Charles Chatfield, Ralph Summy, and Günter Wernicke. Although they survived, their precarious health and evident mortality weighed upon me. Also, I felt uncharacteristically helpless in these circumstances. Unlike political issues, which could be addressed through action, declining health was a natural part of the human condition and, at best, could be alleviated temporarily by medical treatment. In addition, interpersonal tensions began to disrupt the Solidarity Singers. In the past, I had never quite fathomed why successful musical groups split up. Now, however, watching how people working closely together got on one another's nerves, I began to understand the phenomenon. When we performed, people still told us that we sounded great—better than ever, in fact. But it became more and more difficult to pull the group together for rehearsals, and we performed on fewer occasions.

Fortunately, there were also some positive developments. By 2006 polls on the Iraq war and on the Bush administration's other policies showed a sharp falling-off in public support. As a result, my once dangerously dissident views seemed more and more mainstream. Furthermore, faced with strong opposition from academic and civil liberties groups, Horowitz's "Academic Bill of Rights" lost momentum, with some states rejecting it outright, others leaving it in limbo, and none adopting it. In addition, there seemed to be some loosening in the mass communications media blackout of dissident opinion. My HNN article—"Have Peace Activists Ever Stopped a War?"—was picked up by numerous media outlets, including the Organization of American Historians' radio program "Talking History" (broadcast not only throughout the United States but also, via the Voice of America, around the world). Another Op-Ed piece that I did for HNN, on the Bush administration's nuclear deal with the Indian government, led to interviews on a number of radio programs, domestic and foreign. When the Democrats captured both houses of Congress in the midterm elections of 2006, it was clear that the political tide was turning.

Closer to home, there was plenty to celebrate. My relationship with Dorothy had survived marriage and, indeed, was remarkably free of whatever conflicts that had existed in the past. Our children were also doing well. And my grandchildren, Benjamin and Betsy, whom I saw almost every week, were bubbling with life and absolutely irresistible—though I am quite biased on that score.

As for me, I found myself busier than ever with professional and political activities. Both the Peace History Society and the Peace History Commission of IPRA had undergone a decline, and I sought to give their new leaders a hand with reviving them. In late March 2007 Upper Hudson Peace Action held an anniversary dinner at which I was one of three honorees. Probably because the featured speaker at the dinner was U.S. Representative Dennis Kucinich, it drew a very large crowd and raised thousands of dollars for the organization. In May 2007 I kicked off a roundtable discussion of the U.S. peace movement's efficacy on a widely read website, *Foreign Policy in Focus*—to the evident dismay of some movement leaders, who apparently felt that I was encroaching upon their organizational turf. Although at times it occurred to me that I could afford to retire, I wondered: "Why should I? I'm happy enough doing just what I'm doing."

But I guess one should always prepare for the worst. In June 2007, just as *Peace Action* was about to appear, I found I wasn't feeling up to par. Thinking that I might be suffering from an early stage of Lyme Disease (which had become common throughout the Northeast), I made an appointment with my doctor. After confessing that he was puzzled by my symptoms, the doctor arranged for blood tests, x-rays, and CT scans. Within hours of the x-rays and scans, he phoned me at my office to tell me the bad news: I had tumors throughout my liver, my adrenals, and the lymph nodes of my abdomen. It looked like an advanced stage of cancer, possibly colon cancer. What a shocker! I barely had time to speak with him at his office and to consider the situation before Dorothy phoned to ask about the tests. Although I tried to delay such a discussion until I arrived home, my tone of voice must have given me away. She insisted that I tell her immediately, which I did, and she was even more stunned than I was.

Coming down with cancer seemed like a particularly foul blow. After all, I should have been at very low risk for it. None of my immediate family had ever contracted cancer. I had never smoked and rarely drank. I exercised regularly. And I had an unusually healthful vegetarian diet. People considered me exceptionally vigorous and healthy. So why me? Our (admittedly uninformed) conclusion was that the cause was probably environmental. After all, we lived in a world that increasingly was becoming a toxic waste dump.

Anyway, the immediate problem was getting the cancer diagnosed and treated. My primary care physician put these matters on what seemed like a rather slow track, but a former student of mine, Andy Coates (now a physician), and a cousin of mine, Hernan Rincon (also a physician), recommended moving more rapidly. Consequently, I was admitted quickly to St. Peter's Hospital, in Albany, where tissue samples were taken and I was diagnosed as having non-Hodgkin's lymphoma. Informed of this, Andy said: "Good!" This kind of cancer, it seemed, had a higher cure rate than many others. My oncologist, pointing to my age and the advanced nature—Stage IV—of the cancer, rated my chances of a cure at 30 to 40 percent. A quick trip to Sloan-Kettering in New York City confirmed the diagnosis; however, the lymphoma specialist there said that I had about a 50-percent chance of survival.

And so, starting in July 2007 I began seven three-week cycles of chemotherapy. The procedure was certainly no fun, particularly during the first cycle, when I suffered from nausea, weakness, and the collapse of my white blood cell system, 90 percent of which was destroyed by the chemo. As a kind of Pascal's gamble, I also began weekly sessions of acupuncture with a former Yale graduate student in Chinese history, and Reiki with a medical doctor who also advised me on complementary medicine. Although I resigned my department's graduate directorship and took a medical leave for the fall semester, these treatments—plus imbibing lots of medications and supplements—kept me busy. And then there were also commitments I couldn't ignore: writing student recommendation letters, participating in graduate student exams, and writing or revising small articles. Furthermore, political work kept intruding, including a rabble-rousing defense of democracy at Rensselaer Polytechnic Institute, where the campus president had abolished the faculty senate; acceptance of an award for "progressive activism" at a local Citizen Action banquet; and campaign work for Doug Bullock, my Solidarity comrade who was running for a seat in the Albany county legislature—and miraculously won it. Friends urged me to engage in lots of rest, enjoyment of comic films, "visualization" of the cancer's demise, and strolls in the sunshine. But there seemed little time to do any of this.

The irony of the advice to keep myself in a blissful state of mind was brought home to me in the opening weeks, when it seemed that my health insurance wouldn't cover the thousands of dollars in medical bills I was racking up for the diagnoses and conventional medical treatment. (I didn't even bother to try to obtain coverage for the acupuncture and Reiki.) Making anxious telephone calls and visits, I shuttled back and forth between my insurance provider and the hospitals, trying, without much effect, to convince the former to cover the very substantial costs. This mini-trauma occurred just as Michael Moore's wonderful documentary *Sicko* opened in movie theaters across the country, and for a time it looked like I might end up in the same situation as the other pathetic Americans whose health care providers had abandoned them. But, finally, after weeks of worry, I was assured that the bulk of the conventional medical costs would be covered. Whew!

The silver lining to all of this (aside from shucking off the graduate directorship) was the outpouring of support from friends and associates. Ever since my rather lonely childhood, I had felt insecure about my popularity. But the onset of cancer convinced me that I really had quite a fan club. Dorothy, of course, was terrific, fanatically determined to keep me alive. But what was really unexpected was the large number of people who contacted me, expressed their love and admiration for me, and told me how much they wanted to see me pull through this latest crisis. In fact, so many people e-mailed, wrote, or phoned, wanted updates on my condition, and even visited me that on occasion I longed for more time for solitude, reading, and writing.

Aside from the chemo, one of the worst things was having to cancel a number of planned activities. These included promotional work for *Peace Action,* as well as numerous scheduled talks around the country. Nevertheless, accompanied by Dorothy and a carload of other local peace activists, I did drive to the Alhambra Ballroom in Harlem for a very large, lively Peace Action anniversary celebration, where I autographed copies of *Peace Action*. Also, I felt well enough to appear at an Albany book reception, sponsored by Upper Hudson Peace Action, on July 31. There, amid a substantial turnout (prompted by the appearance of the new book, but mostly I think by the desire to show support for me as I wrestled with death), I gave a little speech about the history of SANE, the Freeze, and Peace Action and talked about my long-term involvement in the peace movement. I also sold (and autographed) numerous books, thereby raising some useful money for the local and national organizations. Naturally, I was delighted by the political impact and touched by the level of personal support.

After a five-month ordeal, the chemotherapy finished up in early December 2007. And it was none too soon. By this point, the chemicals had produced neuropathy in my legs and hands; furthermore, I was urinating blood. But the good news, conveyed to me by my oncologist on December 20, was that the cancer was gone. All I had to do was to recover from the side effects of the treatment—and, of course, to avoid a recurrence of the lymphoma. I immediately began making plans for a return to teaching, for lectures, and for new writing and political projects. On balance, it was a remarkable comeback from the most advanced stage of a deadly cancer. As Dorothy pointed out, this latest crisis was consonant with a recurring theme in my life: reaching the brink of disaster and then somehow escaping it.

One of my first postcancer activities involved giving a talk at Yale University to a high-powered conference of scholarly specialists on the nuclear arms race. Invited by Ernesto Zedillo, the director of Yale's Center on Globalization, I was happy to discuss the history of the world nuclear disarmament movement with this eminent assemblage. Curious, though, as to why the participants referred to him as "President Zedillo," I eventually figured out that he was actually a former president of Mexico. Another indication of Yale's linkages with power came when our gathering of several dozen scholars moved to a large ornate hall to attend a lecture—a featured part of the conference—delivered by Ted Turner, the media mogul. Although I appreciated Turner's disdain for nuclear weapons and war, I found the contrast between the wise-cracking, unsophisticated Turner and the far more knowledgeable audience striking. I suppose I shouldn't have been surprised, though. After all, courting the wealthy is how the major private universities have built up their massive endowments.

Even public universities like my own had few scruples when it came to obtaining money. For the past few years a group of wonderful young activists on the SUNY/Albany campus, Students for Workers' Rights, had been agitating for a nonrenewal of the university's exclusive contract with the Coca-Cola company. Charging massive violations of human rights by this giant corporation, they pointed especially to Colombia, where it colluded with right-wing paramilitary groups that had kidnapped, tortured, and murdered union members at one of its bottling plants. These students, led by the valiant Jackie Hayes, were participating in the worldwide Killer Coke campaign, which had already gotten dozens of colleges and universities to sever their contracts with the company in the hope of convincing it to mend its ways. At SUNY/Albany, Students for Workers' Rights did everything that a serious, responsible campus organization should do—distributed literature; invited speakers to campus; circulated a petition signed by 1,200 students; lined up the support of leading campus groups, including the Graduate Students Organization and, with my assistance, United University Professions; and met repeatedly with University Auxiliary Services, our old antagonist from the days of the dining halls' unionization. All, as it turned out, to no avail. In mid-May 2008, as students were heading home and faculty were scattering to the winds, UAS announced that it was signing a ten-year contract with Coca-Cola. According to the UAS board president, John Murphy, the giant corporation had offered more lucrative terms than its competitors, and therefore "it would be fiscally irresponsible for us not to recontract with Coke." Once again, money talked and the people walked—or, less metaphorically, were kidnapped, tortured, and murdered.

Nor was all going well within the campus chapter of United University Professions. In the aftermath of the socially conscious leadership that Tim Reilly and Myron Taylor had provided, more conventional, personally ambitious types came to the fore. With a vision limited to administering the UUP contract, they showed no interest in the conditions of the broader society, of workers generally, or even of other unions. Thanks to my decades of participation in the chapter executive committee, these new leaders did not usually challenge me directly. But gradually they narrowed the room for action, finding ingenious technical reasons to block social solidarity, such as opposing UUP contributions to strike funds, cozying up to campus management, and wasting time on trivia.

The epitome of this type of humdrum leadership was reached with the ascent to the chapter presidency of a campus librarian, whom I shall call Martha. When she insisted that she needed time off from her campus employment to attend properly to union business, the union agreed to pay 40 percent of her university salary. Meanwhile, she turned executive committee meetings into lengthy monologues in which she discussed her vacations, meals, and suntan; bragged of her friendship with campus administrators; and complained about how hard she was working for the union. Increasingly, union action or inaction depended upon what Martha would or wouldn't accept. Even worse, observing this sorry state of affairs, people with a broad social vision abandoned the executive committee while people content with mediocrity and autocratic rule joined or remained. Gritting my teeth, I remained, convinced that I could accomplish more on the inside than on the outside. But it was a struggle.

Things came to a head in the fall of 2009. In September, Chartwells Corporation, which had been brought in to settle the SUNY/Albany dining halls controversy a decade earlier, suddenly announced that it would no longer accept Local 471 (now affiliated with SEIU) as the collective bargaining agent for the hundreds of food service workers. Company officials claimed that the reason for this action was that a rival union claimed jurisdiction. But the real reason appears to have been that Local 471's new business agent, Amanda Lefton, had been filing grievances against Chartwells for failing to pay raises in accordance with the union's contract, and the corporation—seizing upon a battle between two nationwide unions, SEIU and UNITE-HERE—decided that this conflict provided a good opportunity to create a union-free environment. As I had played a key role in the earlier unionization of the dining halls, Amanda, a former student of mine, contacted me in an effort to obtain support from the campus chapter of UUP. That seemed perfectly reasonable to me.

But it seemed quite unreasonable to others. At the next chapter executive committee meeting, when I raised the issue of UUP support for the embattled dining halls workers, Martha immediately intervened. She said that she couldn't touch this issue because she served on the board of UAS, and acting on it would be a "conflict of interest." Thinking fast, I countered that as chair of our chapter's Solidarity Committee, I would be happy to meet with the workers and report back on the situation to the executive committee. The executive committee approved this plan, and I booked a room on campus, in the name of Albany UUP, for such a meeting and notified the dining halls workers accordingly. Shortly before the meeting, I received a phone call from Martha, who furiously berated me because, as she said, the administration had given her enormous flak about the scheduled gathering. She went on to say that she had personally canceled the booking for the room and warned me never to dare to take such action again. As there was no way to tell the workers of this startling development before our meeting, I met them outside the locked room. Then we walked downstairs to a campus lounge, where they regaled me with stories of recent misdeeds by Chartwells and of the impossibility of rectifying their grievances without union representation.

Even worse followed. After I e-mailed a report on the meeting to the executive committee, Martha sent out a follow-up message implying that this report had imperiled UUP's use of the campus e-mail system, and that henceforth no one should use e-mail to discuss the dining halls situation. Although I expected trouble at the next executive committee meeting, I was unprepared for the severity of the attack in which Martha and her cronies ranted on at great length about the difficulties I had caused her and (supposedly) our union. At one point in the meeting, she threatened to have me expelled from the executive committee. In response, I pointed out that as a union we should stand up for workers' rights, and that I had been authorized by the executive committee to hold the meeting. Another executive committee member, Sally Knapp, responding to Martha's claim that only she could book a campus meeting room for a UUP committee, piped up to say that her committee had always booked campus meeting rooms on its own. Nevertheless, it was a very ugly confrontation, with obvious ramifications. I was now under the gun not only of the university administration and a giant corporation, but of my own union leadership.

Fortunately, though, I had allies. A few members of the executive committee, including my friend Jim Collins, spoke up in my defense at the meeting, while others commiserated with me privately. When Martha asked another executive committee member, Tom Hoey, to replace me as chair of the Albany UUP Solidarity Committee, he stoutly refused. Unwilling to be silenced or intimidated, I spread the word to a campus- and Albany-wide constituency about the dining halls situation. I also publicized a forthcoming support rally, organized by Local 471, in front of the Campus Center (the site of the main dining all). The rally drew a lively, substantial turnout, with speeches by Local 471 leaders and by members of the university community, including me. In my remarks, I denounced Chartwells and its (unnamed) campus "sycophants." Although Chartwells threatened to fire any employees participating in the rally, a small group did so anyway, and one worker—a courageous black woman—gave a wonderful speech. Somewhat later, at the only Albany UUP membership meeting of the semester, some UUP members took to the microphones to deplore the fact that our union was not backing the dining halls workers.

Martha and the other top chapter officers, embarrassed by the continuing controversy, did their best to sidetrack it, but without much success. Refusing to meet with Amanda, they instead organized an executive committee meeting to hear representatives of both SEIU and UNITE-HERE. In this fashion, they adopted the company line that the central issue was a dispute between two unions rather than management's decision to terminate union representation. Nevertheless, at the meeting, spokespersons for Local 471 proved very impressive, while the spokesperson for UNITE-HERE had to confess that he had never met with any of the workers whom his union claimed to represent. Finally, in December, after the National Labor Relations Board officially informed Chartwells that union charges against the company had merit, Chartwells surrendered, once more accepting union representation by Local 471.

Although Martha and other Albany UUP officials never acknowledged their betrayal of the university's lowest-paid workers, their hold on power was slipping. Probably out of a mixture of embarrassment and sympathy, the chapter executive committee voted to nominate me for statewide UUP's highest award, for service to the union and to the labor movement. In the spring of 2010, at a statewide convention, I received the award amid applause from the assembled UUP delegates. That October, when the SUNY/Albany president, George Philip, announced plans to scrap language departments and other humanities programs—leading to nationwide and worldwide condemnation—these same Albany UUP leaders maintained a remarkable public silence, despite the administration's clear disregard of the tenure and job security of their own union members. In this context, a Union Democracy campaign, with my strong support, began mobilizing to elect a new, more committed union leadership.

Things also livened up in the long somnolent Albany Labor Council. In March 2011, a group of Solidarity Committee stalwarts were elected as its top officers. As a result, I became the new executive secretary of the Albany County AFL-CIO.

Meanwhile, the peace movement continued to tap much of my energy. At the May 2008 national board meeting of Peace Action, I groaned inwardly when an outside consultant kicked off the event by having us group ourselves by our identification with specific vegetables. But, fortunately, we soon got down to the more practical business of building an effective campaign against militarism. Probably because I asked some pointed questions about why Peace Action was losing members, I ended up as the new chair of the board's membership/

affiliation committee. I promised to do my best in this capacity, and in subsequent months began to brainstorm with other Peace Action leaders about what could be done with our very limited resources. For the most part, peace activists are unusually independent types, and therefore it was not always easy to get them moving in the same direction. Even so, we made some progress in implementing more effective membership recruitment practices, developing closer cooperation between the national office and regional affiliates, and in adding new members and affiliates. In 2010, Peace Action grew by more than 4,000 members.

Other peace groups also sought my assistance. In July 2008, at the invitation of Bruce Kent, I flew to Britain to give a talk on the history of the nuclear disarmament movement to the national council meeting of the Campaign for Nuclear Disarmament. I found it a very appreciative audience and was delighted to meet a new generation of CND leaders, as well as to learn that, thanks to CND's leadership in the tumultuous campaign against a new nuclear weapons system for Britain, this flagship of the worldwide struggle against the Bomb was growing once again. Somewhat later, the National Priorities Project, a Massachusetts-based think-tank that did wonderful work illustrating the imbalance between military and civilian spending, recruited me for its national board. Over time, it seemed, I had become not only a scholarly specialist on the peace movement but also a useful participant in its leadership.

In August 2008, however, I was back in my scholarly role as I took part in a conference in Prague on European protest movements during the Cold War. Invited to give a keynote address to the gathering—sponsored by the European Union, the University of Heidelberg, and the Charles University—I lectured on European peace movements since 1945. In addition, I heard numerous intriguing speakers, among them leaders of the "Prague Spring" of 1968, and became acquainted with many lively people, among them Martin Klimke, one of the young organizers of the conference, and Bernardine Dohrn, a former leader of the Weather Underground whose husband, Bill Ayers, was fast becoming the bogeyman of the 2008 Republican presidential campaign. Although I never had any sympathy for the "revolutionary" beliefs and tactics of the Weather Underground, the Bernardine Dohrn of 2008 struck me as a level-headed, decent person.

Dorothy accompanied me to Prague, for we thought it would be a good idea for her to see the home of her grandfather (Edward May) in nearby Jablonicz, from which her mother, aunt, grandmother, and other family members had fled after the Nazi takeover of the late 1930s. The problem was that we had no idea where the house was located—not even an address or a street name—or even the certainty that it still existed. But we hired a young guide, fluent in Czech and English, to assist us, and—with the aid of a picture of a nearby church drawn by Dorothy's cousin—I discovered the area of the town in which it had been located. So one morning off we drove with our guide into the Czech countryside and, miraculously, found not only Jablonicz but also the church. Walking down a nearby street, Dorothy said: "There it is!" It was a large house, with "E. May" carved into the stone. After taking numerous pictures, our intrepid guide suggested that we try to enter and proceeded to ring the doorbells. Two Czech teenagers opened the door, and when our guide explained Dorothy's connection to the building, they suggested that we go on upstairs. There we met an aged woman who had known Dorothy's uncle (Erich May, now deceased) many years ago, and Dorothy, almost dumbstruck, did her best to question her about how things had fared over the past seven decades of Czech independence, Nazi occupation, Soviet domination, and the new Czech Republic.

As if this was not emotionally draining enough, the next day we took a tour of nearby Theresienstadt, which, in the Nazi era, housed both a grim Jewish ghetto (a "gift" from the Führer, who had Czechoslovakia's entire Jewish population rounded up and confined there) and a more conventional concentration camp, with the usual torture and mass murder. The death rate in both was astronomical. One of Dorothy's aunts, incarcerated there as a teenager, had managed to survive, although her aunt's father, a famous sculptor, had perished. It was a rushed, expensive tour. I joked that first they murder the Jews, then they charge the survivors lots of money to visit the places where they killed them. Along the way, Dorothy looked around for a model of the camp that she understood the Nazis had ordered her great uncle to sculpt. In the late afternoon, when we were both feeling emotionally frazzled, our guide announced that we would now visit the crematorium. By this point, Dorothy had had it and wanted to stay outside. But, as in the case of museums, I was determined to have us see it all. So we did. And right next to the crematoria stood the model of the camp, sculpted by her great uncle before his untimely death. Alerted to its significance, everyone in our tour group snapped pictures of it.

There were other travels—to Sydney, Australia, to address a plenary session of the International Peace Research Association; to Basel, Switzerland, to speak at the world congress of International Physicians for the Prevention of Nuclear War; to Washington, D.C., to give a talk at a scholarly gathering hosted by the German Historical Institute; and to Juneau, Alaska, to make a presentation to the annual conference of the local World Affairs Council. Most of my travels were to cities around the United States—including Salt Lake City, Seattle, Tacoma, Portland, Poughkeepsie, Olympia, Buffalo, and Boise—where

I addressed campus and local peace groups, usually connected with Peace Action, on nuclear disarmament-related themes. I often arranged to have copies of my new book, *Confronting the Bomb* (the abbreviated version of my *Struggle Against the Bomb* trilogy), displayed, which resulted in book-signings at the end of the events. Sometimes during these jaunts I appeared on radio or television programs.

Of course, all of this public speaking represented a sharp break with my shy, stutter-plagued childhood. And I still was not entirely comfortable with it. Speaking before an audience—or even doing the necessary socializing with strangers that accompanied these talks—clashed with my inclination to steer clear of situations like these. Even so, I felt strongly that I had something of significance to say and was determined to say it. Also, my experience with arrests, blacklisting, investigations by intelligence agencies, tear gas attacks, and threats of violence over the decades put my embarrassment at a lack of speech fluency into perspective. After all, was it really that important? The upshot was that I no longer resisted going on the road as a public speaker and sometimes did a fairly good job of it.

Travels of a more sentimental kind occurred in June 2008, when Mike Weinberg and I celebrated fifty years of friendship by revisiting Columbia University, where we had first met. And so we drove from Albany down to New York City and, after miraculously managing to find a parking space on the corner of West 116th Street and Broadway, proceeded to stroll around the Columbia campus—two elderly, poorly dressed alumni commenting on how things had changed and reviving memories of their youthful hijinks. Then we huffed and puffed with our suitcases down Broadway to a budget hotel we had found on the internet. Unfortunately, the hotel turned out to be a flophouse, with a tiny room that featured rickety bunk beds, a peeling linoleum floor, a total absence of towels, and no chairs. However, people can adapt to almost anything—or at least Mike and I can. After washing, I dried myself with a clean pair of socks (though Mike preferred his sheet), and sat on the closet floor (with the door open). Laughing hysterically, we had a wonderful time—including that evening, when we went on a radical walking tour through Lower Manhattan.

The next day, we visited the Brooklyn neighborhoods of our childhood. At Mike's old apartment house, we explored changes in the nearby streets and managed to enter the building by helping some elderly Russian émigrés up the front steps and following them through the door. When we got to my neighborhood, it was clear from the signs and the people on the streets that the area was now heavily Hispanic, African American, and Syrian. Kids were playing happily in the schoolyard of my old haunt, P.S. 217, but there were lots of security warnings on the school doors, as well as on my former apartment house. I rang the buzzer repeatedly for the apartment building's security guard, but no one responded. Then I tried turning the doorknob and found that the door wasn't locked. So we strolled about, visiting the hallways and cellar hideaways of my youth. As I wanted to see the backyard, I managed to throw open the bolt of a door leading there. Heading down the stairs, I heard Mike call out: "Larry, I think you set off an alarm." Sure enough, all hell was breaking loose in the building. So we retreated fast to the front door and the freedom of the outside world.

Driving off quickly to elude any possible pursuers, we recalled that Dorothy had warned us: "Hey, guys. Don't get in any trouble. You always seem to do that when you get together." In rejoinder, I had remarked: "How could we possibly manage that this time?" And now, it occurred to both of us that we might be arrested for breaking and entering—and we might have to phone Dorothy to have her bail us out of jail. More laughter followed. Yes, we really were troublemakers—even in our old age.

11

In Retrospect

Although I sprang back from the cancer and chemotherapy of late 2007 with renewed teaching, speaking, writing, and troublemaking, I did become more thoughtful. After all, near-death experiences do lead people to reflect upon the meaning of their lives. And I have done some thinking about mine. What do all these experiences that I have recounted—and others that I have not—add up to? Indeed, do they add up to anything?

I believe they do.

Despite the fact that much of human existence is made up of relatively mundane activities, it seems clear that, at least some of the time, people search for a deeper meaning. After all, we have a short span of life on this ancient planet without apparent purpose. On some occasions, life is characterized by misery, and—as we age—it is always concluded by bodily decay and death. To give meaning to this inexplicable and sometimes painful existence, people have invested themselves in a variety of broader, transcendent projects, among them vast religious and philosophical systems.

Looking back at my own life, I believe that I have found meaning in it by working to foster social justice and world peace. At a fairly early age I recognized that I could contribute something useful along these lines, for—despite flaws in other areas (for example, as an athlete)—I possessed considerable intellectual ability. Thus, like the great and daring thinkers of past centuries whose lives I so admired, I became an activist intellectual, plunging into the public controversies of my time in an effort to alleviate the human condition. Did I measure up to their example? No, for I lacked their extraordinary abilities. But I did my best with what I had. Did I really believe in utopia? No, although I found utopias appealing as examples of alternative thinking. Like the Enlightenment *philosophes,* I did believe that reason and knowledge could help light the way to a better world.

I did not come to this position through a sudden political or intellectual conversion but—as these memoirs indicate—over time. It reflected a combination of my family background, the political and intellectual milieu in which I found myself, and my own experience. Even so, my core political convictions were largely formed by the time I was in my twenties, and they have directed and shaped much of my life ever since.

Given the general consistency of these convictions, some observers might conclude that I am not a particularly introspective person. And they would not be entirely wrong. I have always been rather impatient with the intellectual hairsplitting that often is found in academia, as well as with the factionalism and sectarianism that often have characterized the far Left. Recognizing the direction in which I wanted the world to go, I usually have avoided agonizing over details. Instead, my standard approach has been: We've known for years what needs to be done; let's just get on with it!

But I will admit that occasionally I have had my doubts. As a believer in political, social, and economic democracy, I've wondered: Why do the masses (and not only the economic elites) harbor ancient prejudices or sometimes support reactionary politicians? As a believer in reason, I've wondered: Why do so many people cling to supernatural beliefs? As a believer in workers' rights, I've wondered: Why do many union members and leaders lack a broad social vision? As a believer in democratic socialism, I've wondered: Why do social democratic parties sometimes betray their principles? Finally, as a believer in the need to end war, I've wondered: Will people ever be ready to abandon the practice of mass killing and treat one another decently? Perhaps the misanthropes are right, and human progress is only an illusion.

And yet, upon reflection, I don't think so. Over the course of history, there are heartening indications that people of goodwill and determination have made headway in pulling humanity out of the nightmare of ignorance, superstition, slavery, tyranny, exploitation, and militarism that has characterized the past. In my own lifetime I have seen courageous people topple dictatorships, shatter systems of racial oppression, roll back corporate domination, bring an end to unjust wars, and avert a nuclear holocaust. And I am confident that efforts to extend human progress will continue, as will the sense of meaning such efforts bring with them.

In addition to meaning, however, people seek community, as well as the friendships and love that go with it. Anxious to transcend their individual isolation, they reach out to others, in the hope that others will reach out to them. Of course, we can never experience the totality of the lives of other people. Nor can they totally experience ours. Ultimately, we do not really want to merge our individual selves with others, for too much loss of self can be stultifying—so much so that we conclude, with Sartre, that Hell is other people. Even so, individuals do crave community and seek it within families, nations, and groups based on ethnicity, religion, race, and gender. One of the worst punishments meted out to prisoners is solitary confinement.

Through my involvement in movements to change the world, I found my own community—not only friends and lovers but also millions of good people in nations around the globe. Martin Luther King Jr. called it "the beloved community," and although it has not always lived up to this idealized description, it has often inspired and sustained me. Of course, when I became an activist intellectual, I did not do it with the intention of finding a community. Instead, my activism was sparked by a sense that some things were seriously wrong with the world and therefore should be changed. And so I became a social critic—a dissident—a role that added to my sense of myself as an outsider. Over time, however, I discovered that there were millions of other outsiders, too. And many of them were interesting, lively, warmhearted people. Thus, without abandoning my position as an outsider in the broader society, I became a member of a smaller but vibrant community: those who dared to challenge injustice and cruelty. Hopefully, that community has somewhat improved the human condition. I know it has enriched my life.

So that is my story—ranging from the vicious, bloody pogroms of Eastern Europe to the turbulent social struggles of modern America. Would my nineteenth-century forebears have recognized a trace of themselves in me? Perhaps so, perhaps not. But, as a historian, I do think there is a certain logic to how I ended up: an outsider, chipping away at the irrational customs and practices of the past in the belief that, eventually, a new and brighter day might dawn. Some have characterized this stance as a recipe for suffering, even for martyrdom. But, as I hope I have shown, although this role is certainly not free of adversity, it can also be interesting, exciting, and deeply satisfying. Thus, as I confront the approach of death, either sooner or later, I do not believe that activism has blighted my existence. Instead, I know that I have really lived.

Other Books by Lawrence Wittner

As Author

Rebels Against War: The American Peace Movement, 1941-1960. New York: Columbia University Press, 1969. Revised, expanded edition published as *Rebels Against War: The American Peace Movement, 1933-1983.* Philadelphia: Temple University Press, 1984.

Cold War America: From Hiroshima to Watergate. New York: Praeger Publishers, 1974. Revised, expanded edition. New York: Holt, Rinehart & Winston, 1978.

American Intervention in Greece, 1943-1949. New York: Columbia University Press, 1982.

One World or None: A History of the World Nuclear Disarmament Movement through 1953. Vol. 1 of *The Struggle Against the Bomb.* Stanford, CA: Stanford University Press, 1993.

Resisting the Bomb: A History of the World Nuclear Disarmament Movement, 1954-1970. Vol. 2 of *The Struggle Against the Bomb.* Stanford, CA: Stanford University Press, 1997.

Toward Nuclear Abolition: A History of the World Nuclear Disarmament Movement, 1971 to the Present. Vol. 3 of *The Struggle Against the Bomb.* Stanford, CA: Stanford University Press, 2003.

Confronting the Bomb: A Short History of the World Nuclear Disarmament Movement. Stanford, CA: Stanford University Press, 2009. A Japanese-language edition will be published by Horitsu Bunkasha (Kyoto) in 2011.

As Editor

MacArthur. Englewood Cliffs, NJ: Prentice-Hall, 1971.

Biographical Dictionary of Modern Peace Leaders. Associate editor, with Harold Josephson, Sandi E. Cooper and Solomon Wank. Westport, CT: Greenwood Press, 1985.

Peace/Mir: An Anthology of Historic Alternatives to War. Coedited with Charles Chatfield, Ruzanna Ilukhina, Kyril Andersen, Sandi E. Cooper, Alexei Filitov, Carole Fink, and Victoria Ukolova. Syracuse, NY: Syracuse University Press, 1994. Russian language edition: *Mir/Peace. Al'ternativy voine ot Antichnosti do knotsa mirovoi voiny. Antologiia.* Moscow: Nauka Press, 1993.

Peace Action: Past, Present, and Future. Coedited with Glen H. Stassen. Boulder, CO: Paradigm Publishers, 2007.

Index

Page numbers in *italics* indicate photographs. The acronyms LW and DT stand for Lawrence Wittner and Dorothy Tristman, respectively.

1984 (Orwell), 36

Abrams, Irwin, 201–2
Academic Bill of Rights (proposed legislation), 235, 236
academic life: blacklisting, 116, 117–18, 124; crisis in job market, 116, 124, 129–30; McCarthyism's effects on, 58, 71. *See also* faculties; intellectual freedom; intellectual life; politics, academic; tenure
Academic Marketplace, The (Caplow and McGee), 58
Adelphi University (Long Island, New York), 76–77
affirmative action, 106; at SUNY/Albany, 162–63, 231–32
AFL-CIO, 170, 179, 199–200; Albany County, 137, 177, 232, 243. *See also* Albany Labor Council (Albany County Central Federation of Labor, AFL-CIO)
AHEPA (Greek heritage organization), 180
Ahmed, Eqbal, 115–16
Air Force Association, 202
Akiba, Tadatoshi, 227
Albany, New York, 161–62. *See also* labor movement, in Albany; State University of New York at Albany (SUNY/Albany)
Albany Anvil (DSOC newsletter), 170, 173
Albany Labor Council (Albany County Central Federation of Labor, AFL-CIO), 137, 168, 176, 177, 243
Albany Times Union, 232; Op-Ed pieces for, 205, 226
Alexander II (czar), 2
Alexander III (czar), 2
Allen, Roger, 189–90, 211, 212

Allen Center (SUNY/Albany), 118, 131–32; closing of, 133, 134, 135
Alpha Phi Omega fraternity (Columbia College), 46–47, *152*; Columbia Arts Festival, 49–50; Intersession Orgy, 53–54; Ugliest Man on Campus (UMOC) contest, 46
Amalfi, Italy: sabbatical in, 110, 113–14
Amalgamated Clothing and Textile Workers Union (ACTWU), 137, *154*, 170, 176; demonstration for, *155*
American Committee on Africa, 179
American Federation of Teachers (AFT), 136
American Friends Service Committee, 96, 116
American Historical Association (AHA), 70, 99, 102, 180, 208, 217, 230
Amsterdam, Netherlands: sabbatical in, 114–16
Andrews, Bob, 190
Annan, Kofi, 217
antidiscrimination efforts. *See* civil rights legislation; civil rights movement; New York City Commission on Human Rights; New York State Commission Against Discrimination
anti-Semitism, 2, 7–8, 11–12, 134. *See also* Jewish people
antiwar movement. *See* Iraq, invasion of, protests against; peace movement; Vietnam War, protests against
apartheid: protests against, xv, *155*, 167–68, 173, 178–79; South Africa's liberation from, 208
Arbeter Ring. *See* Workmen's Circle (Arbeter Ring)
Archer, Colin, 211, 227
Armstrong, Samuel Chapman, 89
arrests, xv, *155*, 167–68
arts: enjoyment of, 49–50, 72, 80–81, 195–96
atheism: LW's views on, 28, 52
awards: Citizen Action, 238; James Madison High School English prize, 33; Society for Historians of American Foreign Relations, xvi, 201; SUNY/Albany Excellence in

awards (cont.)
　Research, 180; United University Professions, 243; Upper Hudson Peace Action "Peacemaker," 160, 237
Ayers, Bill, 244

Baker, James, III: interview with, 209
Balafon (musical group), 185
Ballard, Allen, 224
Barker, Charles, 99
Barker-Benfield, Ben, 131, 139, 156, 162–63, 165, 189, 231, 236
bar mitzvah: Jacob Wittner forgoes, 9; LW forgoes, 27
Barnard College (New York City), 51–52
Barnatsky, Aaron Lazer (great-uncle of LW), 4, 5
Barnatsky, Abraham (grandfather of LW). See Barnett, Abraham (grandfather of LW)
Barnatsky, Anna Mary (great-aunt of LW), 5, 6–7
Barnatsky, Chaya Sarah (great-aunt of LW), 5
Barnatsky, Dvorah (great-grandmother of LW), 1, 3, 5, 11, 149
Barnatsky, Joseph Tzvi (great-grandfather of LW), 1, 3, 5, 9, 11, 149
Barnatsky, Meyer (great-uncle of LW), 3, 4, 5
Barnet, Richard, 217
Barnett, Abraham (grandfather of LW), 3–5, 7, 9, 23, 149
Barnett, Anna Semiatitsky (grandmother of LW), 5–6; remarriage to Samuel Rosen, 6. See also Rosen, Anna Semiatitsky Barnett (grandmother of LW)
Barnett, Fanny (aunt of LW), 6
Barnett, Frances (aunt of LW), 6, 23
Barnett, Harold (uncle of LW), 6, 23
Barnett, Lena (Lipka) Schiff (grandmother of LW), 6, 7, 23
Barnett, Louise (aunt of LW), 6, 23
Barnett, Mildred (aunt of LW), 23
Barnett, Rose. See Wittner, Rose Barnett (mother of LW)
Baskin, Abraham, 5
Beetle, Pat, 232
Bennett, Scott, 230
Bentley, Eric, 49
Bergel, Peter: interview with, 209

Berger, George, 98, 107, 114, 115, 182, 189
Berger, Iris, 162–63, 179, 231
Bernstein, Barton, 202
Bialystok, Poland, 1, 2, 11
Biden, Joseph, 180
Bierman, Artie, 107
Bills, Scott, 217
Biographical Dictionary of Modern Peace Leaders (CPRH), 180–81
Birn, Don, 131
Birr, Kendall, 124, 125, 126, 132, 138
Black, Algernon, 84
blacklisting, academic, 116, 117–18, 124
Bloch, Ed, 166, 173
Bond, Julian, 93
Boy Scouts, 27, 104
Bozell, L. Brent, 71–72
Bread and Roses (film): Solidarity Committee's screening of, 222
Brock, Peter, 99
Brody, Jane, 33
Brooklyn, New York, 13–14, 28–29, 38, 43; revisiting, 246–47
Brown, LaVaughn, 67
Brzezinski, Zbigniew: interview with, 209
Bullock, Doug, 158, 171, 176, 199, 238
Bund (Jewish socialist organization), 2
Burton, Nancy: campaign for, 173–74
Bush, George W.: invasion of Iraq, 224–25, 236; protest song regarding, 230–31; regressive policies of, 221–22, 234
business: activism against, 108, 165–66, 175, 176, 199, 240, 241–43; LW's skepticism regarding, 34–35, 74; military's alliance with, 45, 103–4. See also specific companies
Byer, Stan, 137

Caffè Lena (Saratoga, New York), 159, 230
Caldicott, Helen: interview with, 208
Campaign for a New Foreign Policy (Peace Action), 232
Campaign for Nuclear Disarmament (CND, Great Britain), 193–94, 244
Capital District Anti-Nuclear Alliance, 137
Capital District Area Labor Federation (AFL-CIO), 232
Carlucci, Frank: interview with, 209
Carroll, Berenice, 99
Carter, Elmer H., III, 34
Carter, Jimmy: LW's views on, 146

Index

Center on Globalization (Yale University), 239–40
Central America: protesting U.S. intervention in, 168
Chambers, John, 135
Chartwells Corporation, protest against, 241–43
Chatfield, Charles, 99, 132, *157*, 181, 183, 236; as *Peace/Mir* editor, 191, 192, 193
Chavez, Cesar, 177–78
Chilcoat, Michelle, 224
childhood, 13–24, *151*; conventionality of, 38, 41, 43
Chmielewski, Wendy, 230
Chmielnicki, Bogdan, 7–8
Chomsky, Noam, 170, 218
Christians: Jewish views of, 28, 34
Citizens Panel on Ultimate Weapons, 216–17
civil disobedience, nonviolent: apartheid protests, 167; Central American intervention protests, 168; M. A. thesis on, 72–73. *See also* nonviolent resistance
civil rights legislation, 33, 45, 77, 83
civil rights movement, 89, 97; DT's involvement in, 142; LW's involvement in, 34, 44, 45, 59–60, 64–67, 85, 88, 89, 97, 100–101; research and writings on, 72–73, 98; at Vassar College, 100
Clark, Colia, 188, 212
Cleary, Ed, 200
Cliadakis, Harry, 131
Clinton, Hillary, 230
Coalition Against Apartheid and Racism (Albany), xv, 167
Coalition for Justice in the Maquiladoras (CJM), 204, 205
Coalition of Black Trade Unionists, 216
Coates, Andy, 237, 238
Coca-Cola Company: protesting SUNY/Albany's contract with, 240
Cohen, Stephen, 217
Cohn, Howard, 98, 218–19
Cohoes Music Hall, 230
Collins, Jim, 195, 242
Columbia University (New York City), 67, 69; Ph. D. study at, 75–77, 85–87, 88, *152*; political activism at, 44–46, 78–79, 99; revisiting, 246–47; summer teaching position at, 133; undergraduate study at, 39–61; Vietnam War protests at, 78–79, 81, 82–83, 85–86, 87, 88

Committee of Concerned Asian Scholars (CCAS), 119–21
Commoner, Barry, 146
Communism and Communists, 10, 25–26, 34, 74, 118; collapse of, 13, 210; Italian, 182–83; LW's views on, 58, 183. *See also* Marxist-Leninists
community, importance of, 88, 180, 250–51
concentration camps, 11, 204, 245
Conference on Peace Research in History (CPRH): as board member of, 99, 132, 135, 180–81; Russian trip, *156*, 191–93. *See also* European-American Consultation on Peace Research (Schlaining, Austria); Peace History Society (PHS)
Congress of Racial Equality (CORE), 59–60, 64–67
Congress of South African Trade Unions (COSATU), 178–79
Conners, Mike, 173
Conroy, Hilary, 99
conscientious objection, 93, 95
conservatives: at Hampton Institute, 89, 94; at SUNY/Albany, 125, 128, 132, 133, 138, 139, 162–63; at University of Wisconsin, 71–72; at Vassar College, 101–2, 110, 116
Contra war, U.S. funding of: protests against, 168
Cook, Blanche Wiesen, 99, 132, 188–89
Cook, the Thief, His Wife and Her Lover, The (film), 195
Cooper, Sandi, 99, 132, 189, 192
copper miners' strike (Arizona), 176
CORE. *See* Congress of Racial Equality (CORE)
Cortright, David, 233
Cronin, E. David, 71
Crump, Dave, *159*, 211
Cuban missile crisis, 71
culture, 1940s and 1950s, 16–17
Cumberland Mine (Nova Scotia), 186
Curti, Merle, 61, 70–71, 73, 85, 99, 181

Damm, Gene, 136, 172
dating, 51–52, 53–54. *See also* girls, early experiences with
DeBenedetti, Chuck, 181, 184
Degler, Carl, 75, 95, 101
Dellinger, Dave, 86
Dellums, Ron, 170

Democratic Party: bringing democratic socialist values into, 118, 169, 173; liberals in, 10, 13, 45; LW's identification with, 44. *See also* Johnson, Lyndon; Kennedy, John F.
democratic socialism, 36, 136; building movement of, 168–75; DT's involvement in, 142; European, 80, 169; LW's involvement in, 80, 86, 118, 131, 139, 213, 250. *See also* socialism and socialists
Democratic Socialist Organizing Committee (DSOC), 118, 168–75; luncheon, *154*
Democratic Socialists of America (DSA), 170–75, 176, 189
Dennis, Dave, 66
Dewey, Thomas E., 22
dining hall workers' disputes (SUNY/Albany), *158*, 213–15, 241–43
disarmament. *See* nuclear disarmament movement
dissertation, 85–87, 92
Dohrn, Bernardine, 244
Dorrien, Gary, 172
Dow, John, 173
draft, military: in Russia, 2, 4; in U.S., 79, 88, 93, 95
Drescher, Nuala, 178
DSOC. *See* Democratic Socialist Organizing Committee (DSOC)

Early, Frances, *157*, 202
Easter, David, *160*, 232
education: elementary school, 24, 35; high school, 28–29, 32–33, 35–36; junior high school, 24–26; pre-school and kindergarten, 15. *See also* Columbia University (New York City); University of Wisconsin at Madison
Ehrenreich, Barbara, 170
Eisenhower, Dwight, 35, 44, 202, 235
Ekeus, Rolf, 217
Ekirch, Arthur, 124, 129, 133, 181
Eleanor Roosevelt Democratic Club, 174
elections: Albany local, 173–74, 189; 1948 presidential, 21–22; 1960 presidential, 44; 1972 presidential, 115, 118; 1980 presidential, 146
Ellsberg, Daniel, 202
Enlightenment thought, 3, 42, 222, 249

Erasmus, Desiderius, 42, 43
Erasmus Hall High School (Brooklyn), 28
Eugene V. Debs award dinners (DSOC/DSA), 170–71
Eurich, Nell, 100
European-American Consultation on Peace Research (Schlaining, Austria), 181–82, 183–84, 191
European Nuclear Disarmament (END) campaign, 211. *See also* Kaldor, Mary; Thompson, E. P.
Evers, Medgar, 67

Faber, Mient Jan, 184
faculties: Hampton Institute, 89–90, 93, 94, 95, 96; in Japan, 119–20; SUNY/Albany, 128–30, 131, 132–34; Vassar College, 97–98, 100–103, 108–10, 111, 116–17, 130, 132, 218–19. *See also* United University Professions (UUP)
Falk, Richard, 217
Falwell, Jerry: protesting appearance of, 146
Feffer, Andy, 195, 224
Fellowship (magazine): Julia Wittner's work for, 198–99
fellowships and grants: American Council of Learned Societies/Ford, 184; difficulty obtaining, 201; MacArthur Foundation, 223; National Endowment for the Humanities, 98, 146; New York State Regents Teaching, 77; Nonprofit Sector Research Fund (Aspen Institute), 208; Truman Library research, 130–31; United States Institute of Peace (USIP), 191, 223
Ferraro, Judy, 172
Ferrell Committee, 132–33
Ferry, Megan, 224
Fields, Emmett, 132–33, 134, 137
Fifth Avenue Vietnam Peace Parade (New York City), 78
Fink, Carole, 192, 204
Fisher, Adrian, 59
Flanders, Jon, 232
Fleischner, Art, 176
Flessati, Valerie, 211
Fogel's bungalow colony (Catskill Mountains), 26–27
Foner, Eric, 44
Foot, Michael: interview with, 209

Index

foreign policy, U.S., 71, 119, 233; LW's classes on, 98, 124, 164, 231; media coverage of, 180, 225; protests against, 177, 232; USIA-sponsored lectures, 120, 121–22
Foreign Policy in Focus (website): peace roundtable, 237
Forsberg, Randy, 217, 232; interview with, 208
Fort Dix, New Jersey: antiwar rally at, 100
Frangos, George, 98, 130, 131, 134–35
Franke, Erika, 103, 219
Free South Africa movement, 167, 178–79; sit-in for, 155. *See also* apartheid
Freud, Sigmund, 42, 92
friendships: childhood, 17; at Columbia University, 40, 48; through CPRH, 99; at Hampton Institute, 90; high school, 29, 34; in Japan, 120, 122–23; in Albany, 131, 188–89, 194–95, 224; support during illness, 239; at Vassar College, 103, 107, 132, 219
Fundacio per la Pau (Catalan peace organization), 227
Funiciello, John, 155, 158, 167, 171, 175–76, 176–77
Funiciello, Stephanie, 177

Garfunkel, Art, 42
Gath, Liz, 206
Gay, Peter, 49
Genovese, Eugene, 102
Gensuikin (Japan Congress Against Atomic and Hydrogen Bombs), 227, 228, 229
Georgian Court University (New Jersey): speaking engagement at, 160
German Historical Institute, 204, 245
Gilbert, Paul, 47, 53
Gillin, Don, 117
Giovinco, Joe, 131
girls: early experiences with, 18–19, 30, 36, 38. *See also* dating
Gitlin, Todd, 217
Gleditsch, Nils Petter, 208
Goldman, Emma, "Love Among the Free," 143
Goldsmith, Gary (cousin of LW), 23
Goldsmith, Rhyna Murstein (cousin of LW). *See* Murstein, Rhyna (cousin of LW)
Goldsmith, Si, 23
Goldstein, Abe "Algie" (uncle of LW), 6, 23
Goldstein, Chester, 94–95

Goldstein, Frances Barnett (aunt of LW). *See* Barnett, Frances (aunt of LW)
Golembe, Andrea (niece of LW), 139
Golembe, Deborah Wittner "Debbie" (sister of LW). *See* Wittner, Deborah "Debbie" (sister of LW)
Golembe, Eddie, 106, 139–40
Goodman, Paul, 142; *Growing Up Absurd*, 42
Gorbachev, Mikhail, 191, 192
Gottlieb, Sandy: interview with, 208
Graduate Student Employees Union (SUNY/Albany), 199, 214, 240
Graff, Henry, 49
Gregory, Dick: 1968 presidential campaign, 96
Greyhound Lines, Inc.: strike against, 165–66, 175
Griffen, Clyde, 110
Griffin, Elizabeth, 195
Gulla, Bill, 188, 189, 194, 206
Gunty, Morty, 15
Guyot, Lawrence, 66

Hague Appeal for Peace conference, 157, 210
Hampton, Virginia, 90–91, 96
Hampton Institute (Hampton, Virginia): political activism at, 93, 94, 96; teaching position at, 87–88, 89–96, 152; Vietnam War protests, 89, 93, 97, 100
Hannah, Maureen "Mo," 229
Harrington, Michael, 118, 142, 154, 168, 170; *The Other America*, 46
Harwit, Martin, 202–3
Hastings, Tom, 226
Hayes, Jackie, 240
health issues: broken ankle, 72, 73–74; cancer, 237–39, 249; among friends, 236; sensitivity to cold, 205–6, 221; ulcer, 206
Heifitz, Bob, 90
Hennessy, Rosemary, 205
Herbert Lehman Fellowship in the Social Sciences and International Affairs, 77
Herblock (Herb Block, cartoonist), 35
HERE. *See* Local 471, Hotel Employees and Restaurant Employees (HERE)
Hillinger, Mike, 90, 94
Hiroshima, Japan, 227; nuclear disarmament march in, 160, 228–29
history, study of. *See* Columbia University (New York City), Ph. D. study at; Columbia

history, study of (cont.)
    University (New York City), undergraduate study at; publications; research, scholarly; University of Wisconsin at Madison, master's degree study at
history departments: SUNY/Albany, 124–26, 128, 130, 132–33, 137–39, 145, 162–63, 231–32; Vassar College, 101–3, 109–10, 116–17, 124, 125
History News Network (website), 226; article for, 236
Hitchcock, Karen, 214, 215
Hodges, Norman, 90
Hoeing, "Uncle" Fred, 24, 33, 34, 36, 45
Hoey, Tom, 222, 242
Hofstadter, Richard, 48; *Anti-Intellectualism in American Life,* 70
Holland, Jerome, 88
Hong Kong: speaking engagement in, 218
Horowitz, David, 234–36
Howe, Irving, 165
Hughes, Benjamin Wittner (grandson of LW), 219, 224, 237
Hughes, Bob, 187, 196, 198, 213; children of, 219, 224; marriage to Julia Wittner, 199
Hughes, Elizabeth "Betsy" (granddaughter of LW), 224, 237
Hughes, Sandy, 90, 96
Humphrey, Hubert: LW's support for, 44
Hydro-Québec: union opposition to, 199

Iatrides, John, 131
IBM Corporation: Vassar's confrontation with, 103–4, 108
Ilukhina, Ruzanna, 156; as *Peace/Mir* editor, 191, 192, 193
Institute of General History of the Soviet Academy of Sciences (Moscow), 156, 191
Institute for Policy Studies (IPS), 115–16
intellectual freedom: intrusions on, 110, 118, 124, 126, 234–36. *See also* academic life, McCarthyism's effects on
intellectual life: combining activism with, 58, 76, 88, 118, 119–21, 126, 180–81, 216–17, 249, 250, 251; LW's awakening to, 33, 38, 42–44. *See also* academic life
internationalism, xvi, 181, 201
International Peace Bureau (IPB), 210, 227

International Peace Research Association (IPRA): Malta conference, 201–2; South African conference, 208
In These Times (newspaper): discussion group based on, 136
Iraq, U.S. invasion of: protests against, 224–25, 232, 236
Isaacs, John: interview with, 208
Italian Communist Party (PCI), 182–83. *See also* Communism and Communists
Italy. *See* Amalfi, Italy
Iwamatsu, Shigetoshi, 160

James Madison High School (Brooklyn), 28–29
Jancauskas, Gediminas, 160
Japan: Fulbright lecturer position in, 117–24, 153; speaking engagements in, 160, 227–29
Jester (Columbia College humor magazine), 41
Jewish people: awareness of prejudice, 33–34; immigration to U.S. by, 4–5, 7, 10; LW's connection to heritage of, 28, 205, 251; persecution of, 2, 5, 7–8, 11–12, 134, 204, 245
jobs: at All-Rite Pen Company, 74; as camp counselor, 31, 38, 51, 52–53; as history reader, 77; with New York State Commission Against Discrimination, 51; as prune picker, 62–63; as stock boy, 50–51. *See also* teaching positions
Johnson, Glen, 103
Johnson, Lyndon: LW's views on, 77, 79, 93; Vietnam War policies, 78, 82–83
Josephson, Harold, 181, 183–84

Kaczynski, Theodore. *See* Unabomber
Kafka, Mark (cousin of LW), 22
Kafka, Reece (cousin of LW), 22, 25, 29
Kafka, Sidney (uncle of LW), 22
Kafka, Sylvia Rosen (aunt of LW). *See* Rosen, Sylvia (aunt of LW)
Kaiwar, Vasant, 188
Kaldor, Mary: interview with, 211
Kaplow, Susi, 136
Keenan, Mike, 137
Kehler, Randy: interview with, 209
Kempton, Murray, 35

Kendall, Richard, 125, 128–29, 132, 133, 134; faculty evaluation of, 137–38
Kennedy, John F., 45; assassination of, 77; civil rights policies, 67; LW's views on, 44; nuclear testing policies, 59
Kent, Bruce, 193–94, 211, 227, 244
Kilrain, Jack, *159,* 211
Kim, Sung Bok, 138, 168
Kimball, Daryl, 223–24
Kimball, Jeff, 202
King, Martin Luther, Jr., 251; antiwar activities, 82; assassination of, 94, 96, 216; 1968 presidential campaign, 93–94; Solidarity Committee of the Capital District's labor celebrations of, 212, 215-16, 232
Kirk, Grayson, 88
Kistler, Tam, *158,* 232
Kjelling, Anne, *157,* 217
Klare, Michael, 233
Klein, Fritz, 183
Klein, Steve, 82
Klimke, Martin, 244
Knapp, Sally, 242
Köszegi, Ferenc, 183
Kroll, Judy, 98
Kucinich, Dennis, 237
Kyoto, Japan: Fulbright lectureship in, 122

Labor Council for Latin American Advancement, 216
labor movement: in Albany, 137, 168, 176, 177, 232, 243; demonstrations for, 146, *155*; Japanese, 122; Jewish, 2; LW's involvement in, 137, 139, 165–66, 177–78, 199–200, 243, 250; musical events for, 190; Polish, 11. *See also* union activities
Laubach Literacy: Julia Wittner's employment at, 199, 224
Lefton, Amanda, 241, 243
left-wing politics: democratic socialism and, 118, 173, 175; LW's views on, 45–46, 58, 124, 177, 250; at University of Wisconsin, 71; at Vassar, 97–98. *See also* Communism and Communists; Marx, Karl; Marxist-Leninists; New Left
Lerner, Gerda, 76
Leuchtenburg, William, 75, 76, 86, 87, 92

Levitt, Jeff, *158*
Levy, Marjorie. *See* Wittner, Marjorie Levy (second wife of Jacob Wittner)
liberals: in Albany, New York, 161; at Columbia University, 58, 76; in Democratic Party, 10, 13, 45; democratic socialism and, 173, 175; in Madison, Wisconsin, 69, 70; in New York City, 10–11, 13, 22, 35; at SUNY/Albany, 118, 124; at Vassar College, 97, 101, 110, 116, 125
Liddy, G. Gordon, 97
Lieverman, Ted, 99, 103–4, 115–16, 132, 189
Lifshitz, Selig (great-great uncle of LW), 3
Lifton, Robert J., 202, 216
Link, Arthur, 130
Lipkin, Ben (uncle of LW), 23
Lipkin, Louise Barnett (aunt of LW). *See* Barnett, Louise (aunt of LW)
Lipset, Seymour Martin, 223
Lipton, Judy: interview with, 209
Little World of Don Camillo, The (Guareschi), 25–26
Loach, Ken, 222
Local 471: Hotel Employees and Restaurant Employees (HERE), 213–15; Service Employees International Union (SEIU), 241-43
Locke, John, 42
Lombardo, Joe, *159,* 211
Lorbrook factory (Hudson, New York): demonstration at, *155*
Lown, Bernard: interview with, 209
Lubbers, Ruud, 210–11
Lucky Dragon incident, 228
Luthuli, Albert, 208
Luttwak, Edward, 180
Lynd, Staughton, 102

MacArthur, Douglas: research on, 92, 98–99
Malone, Pat, 172, 189
Manhattan, New York, 14
maquiladoras: research trip to, 204–5
Marable, Manning, 170
marriages: to Dorothy Tristman, 212-13, 236–37; to Patricia Sheinblatt, 73, 74–75, 84–85, 106-8, 141–46, 147
Martin, Kevin, 228, 229, 233
Marx, Karl, 42, 115

Marxist-Leninists, 58, 80, 118, 119, 136. *See also* Communism and Communists; left-wing politics
Maute, Paula, 188
May Committee, 132
May Laws (Russia), 2
Mazumdar, Sucheta, 188
McCall, Ewen, 186
McCarthy, Colman, 207–8
McCarthy, Eugene: 1968 presidential campaign, 103, 139
McCarthyism, 34, 35, 36, 44, 70; effects on academia, 58, 71
McClellan, Jim, 137
McDonald, Angus, 120
McFarlane, Robert "Bud": interview with, 209, 210
McGovern, George: 1972 presidential campaign, 115, 118
McGregor Prison: Solidarity Singers' performance at, 230
McLaughlin, Lillie, 172
McSorley's Old Ale House (Manhattan), 46, *152*
media: commenting for, *158*, 179–80; coverage of Chavez in Albany, 177–78; dissident opinion blacked out, 225, 226, 236; LW's skepticism regarding, 34–35; Smithsonian atomic bomb controversy in, 202–3
Meese, Edwin: interview with, 209–10
Mendlovitz, Saul, 217
men's group (Albany), 189, 194
Metzger, Paul, 97, 129, 132, 135, 189, 211; death of, 221
military, the: business's alliance with, 45, 103–4. *See also* draft, military
Mill, John Stuart, 42
Mills, C. Wright, 48–49; "Letter to the New Left," 58; *The Power Elite*, 45
Mirer, Freddy, 29
Miroff, Bruce, 172, 188, 189
Mohasco Corporation: protest against, 166
Mohr, Walter, 54
Molin, Alma, 101, 117
Moore, Ronnie, 59–60, 64–66
Moos, Malcolm, 75
Morgan, Bob, 47
Moses, Bob, 66
Mosquera, Daniel, 224
Mossbacks (Vassar College faculty), 101–2, 218

Murphy, John, 240
Murstein, Anna Mary Barnatsky (great-aunt of LW). *See* Barnatsky, Anna Mary (great-aunt of LW)
Murstein, Frances (cousin of LW), 7, 23
Murstein, Rhyna (cousin of LW), 7, 23
music, 189–90, 196. *See also* singing
Musil, Bob, 217; interview with, 209
Muste, A. J., 78, 86

Nadler, Charlie, 44, 81
Nagata, Toyoomi, 122–23, 127, 129–30
Naidoo, Jay, 179
National Committee for a Sane Nuclear Policy. *See* SANE
National Defense Education Act (NDEA) loans, 37–38
National Education Association (NEA), 136
National Lead Industries (Albany, New York): protest against, 137
National Negro Congress: research on, 98
National Priorities Project: as board member of, 244
Negotiations Now! (antiwar movement), 82
Netherlands, the. *See* Amsterdam, Netherlands
Neustadt, Richard, 45
New America (Socialist Party newspaper), 80
New American Movement: DSOC's merger with, 170
New Democratic Coalition, 174
New Left, 81, 109; LW's views on, 122, 125, 126. *See also* left-wing politics
New Year's Eve parties, DSA's, 171
New York City Commission on Human Rights: Jacob Wittner employed by, 83
New York Post (newspaper), 35
New York State Commission Against Discrimination: Jacob Wittner's employment at, 19–20, 33–34, 74, 83; LW's summer job at, 51
New York State Labor-Religion Coalition, 166, 204
New York State School of Industrial and Labor Relations: Labor Advisory Committee, 166
Nicholas I (czar), 2
Nixon, Richard: LW's views on, 44; 1968 presidential campaign, 93, 97; resignation of, 125; Watergate scandal, 115

Index   263

Nolan, Michael, 17
nonviolent resistance, 72–73, 86, 167. *See also* civil disobedience, nonviolent
Norton, Eleanor Holmes, 83
Novack, David, 98, 103, 109, 118, 132, 134
Nuclear Abolition Week, 232
nuclear disarmament movement: in Albany area, 137, 175, 217; in Europe, 204, 211; freeze campaign, 165, 173, 209–10, 233; in Great Britain, 193–94, 244; in Japan, 218, 228–29; LW's involvement in, 44–45, 204, 216–17, 239–40; opposition to testing, 58–59; protests, 137, *160,* 165, 216, 232; research and writings on, 191, 203; speaking engagements for, 226–28, 244, 246. *See also* publications, *Confronting the Bomb;* publications, *The Struggle Against the Bomb* (trilogy)
nuclear war, 35, 71, 86

Occasional Chorus, 190, 211
Ojeda, Marta, 204, 205
Old Songs Festival (New York), 196, 219
O'Leary, Vincent, 137, 138, 165
Olsen, Don, 101, 110, 116, 117, 124
Organization of American Historians (OAH), 70, 236
outsider, feelings of being, xvi, 16, 17, 18, 27, 29; overcoming, 67, 85, 251

Pale of Settlement (Russia), 2
Pallas, Dave, 211
Papoulias, George, 180
Paradise Now! (play), 80–81
Patterson, David, 192
Peace Action: award from, 237; as board member of, 233–34, 243–44; Campaign for a New Foreign Policy, 232; celebrations, 212, 239; speaking engagements for, 246
Peace Action: Past, Present and Future (Peace Action), 233–34, 239
Peace and Change (CPRH journal), 181
Peace and Freedom Party (PFP), 93–94, 96
Peace Heroes in Twentieth-Century America (CPRH), 181
Peace History Commission (PHC, IPRA), 201, 202, 208, 237; chairmanship of, 217–18

Peace History Society (PHS), 210, 217, 230, 237
Peace/Mir (Chatfield and Ilukhina, editors), 191, 192, 193
peace movement: anthology on, 191, 192, 193; Communist collapse and, 210; democratic socialism and, 170, 173, 175; DT's involvement in, 142; in Europe, *157,* 181–84, 191, 204, 210, 227; history of, 71, 184; intellectuals' involvement in, 180–81, 217; LW's involvement in, 118, 176, 179–80, 182, 236–37, 239, 243–44, 249; musical events for, 190, 211–12, 218; protests, 78, 146, 168; research and writings on, 85–87, 93, 99, 124, 135, 194, 201–2; in Russia, *156,* 191, 192, 193; Smithsonian atomic bomb controversy and, 202–3; speaking engagements for, 227, 244, 246; at Vassar College, 103–4. *See also* social justice movement; SUNYA Peace & Justice group (SUNY/Albany); Vietnam War, protests against; *and individual peace organizations*
Peace Movements and Political Cultures (CPRH), 184
"Peace Train" (Iraq war protest), 225
PeaceVoice, 226
Pendleton Act of 1883, 76
Pentagon: 1967 march on, 93
Perle, Richard: interview with, 209
Pfeiffer, Fred, 137, 176, 215–16
Phelps-Dodge Corporation: strike against, 176
Philip, George, 243
Phillips, Wendell, xv
picket lines. *See* union activities, picketing
Pioneer Youth Camp (New York), 38
pogroms, 2, 5, 11
Poland. *See* Bialystok, Poland
police brutality, 167; protest against, 78
political activism: in Amsterdam, 114–15; at Hampton Institute, 93–94, 96; in Japan, 119–21; LW's, 58–60, 67, 124, 136, 146, 165–80, 190, 199, 222, 232–33, 238; at SUNY/Albany, 136, 138; at Vassar College, 97–98, 100–101, 103, 108–9. *See also* intellectual life, combining activism with; Vietnam War, protests against
politics: academic, 101–4, 108–10, 116–18, 124–26, 129–30, 132–34, 137–39, 162–63, 240–43; LW's, 33–36, 45–46, 58, 59, 77–80, 164, 250; reactionary, 221–22; in Wittner family, 10, 22, 83. *See also* Democratic Party;

politics (cont.)
    elections; left-wing politics; Republican Party; right-wing politics; Socialist Party
Polk, George, 131
Pollak, Peter, 136
Polner, Murray, 198
Pommer, Dick, 98, 219
Pommer, Linda Nochlin, 98, 219
Poor People's Campaign, 94
Poughkeepsie, New York, 96–97
poverty, 45, 46, 78; protests against, 88, 97; in Tokyo, 120–21
prejudice. *See* civil rights legislation; civil rights movement; racism
publications: *American Intervention in Greece, 1943-1949*, 163, 180; *Biographical Dictionary of Modern Peace Leaders* (associate editor), 180–81; *Cold War America*, 115, 122, 129, 130, 133, 163; *Confronting the Bomb*, 246; "Have Peace Activists Ever Stopped a War?", 236; letter to *New York Post*, 35; *MacArthur* (editor), 99, 130, 163; "MacArthur and the Missionaries," 98–99; "On Conscientious Objection," 93; *One World or None* (trilogy, v. 1), 200–201, 216; op-eds, 205, 226; *Peace Action: Past, Present and Future* (editor), 233–34, 239; *Peace/Mir* (editor), 191, 192, 193; *Rebels Against War*, 92, 98, 99, 130, 133, 163, 165, 180; *Resisting the Bomb* (trilogy, v. 2), 207–8, 216; *The Struggle Against the Bomb* (abbreviated version), 229, 234, 246; *The Struggle Against the Bomb* (trilogy), 184–85, 193–94, 200–201, 204, 207–11, 216, 223, 225–27; *Toward Nuclear Abolition* (trilogy, v. 3), 223, 225–26, 234

Quaif, Trudy, 232
Quinlan, Lawrence, 97, 99, 100

racism, 92; in Hampton, Virginia, 91, 96; protests against, xv, 88, 128, 167
Rand, Ayn, 45
Randall, John Herman, Jr., 87
Randall, Mercedes, 86–87
Randolph, A. Philip, 78
Raskin, Paul, 134
reading, love of, 16, 21, 24, 26, 27, 32, 48, 85, 186, 206, 239

Reagan, Ronald: hawkish policies of, 209; LW's views of, 183; protests against, 146, 165, 170; South African policy, 167, 168; world affairs speech, 180
recreation activities. *See* arts, enjoyment of; singing; tennis playing; travel
Redlo, Bob, 137, *154*, 167, 168, 170, 175–76
reevaluation counseling (RC) movement: DT's involvement in, 161, 195
Regents Scholarships (New York State), 37
Reilly, John "Tim," 136, 165, 166, 170, 177, 178, 179, 240; death of, 221
Reinartz, Kay, 131
religion: LW's views of, 27–28, 34, 52
Republican Party: challenges to social gains, 45, 190, 235; in Congress, 202, 234; in New York City, 13; in Poughkeepsie, New York, 96–97; presidential elections and, 22, 44, 244; Sheinblatt family's preference for, 74; Wittner family's preference for, 10, 22. *See also* Bush, George W.; Nixon, Richard; Reagan, Ronald
research, scholarly, 117, 180; on civil rights movement, 72–73, 98; on McArthur, 92, 98–99; U.S. intervention in Greek civil war, 130–31, 163, 180. *See also* fellowships and grants; nuclear disarmament movement, research and writings on; peace movement, research and writings on; publications
Rice, H. Dustin, 46
Ridgway, Sara, 103
right-wing politics, 109; attacks on intellectual freedom by, 235–36; challenges to social gains, 190; George W. Bush administration's, 234; LW denounced by, 203; Nixon administration's, 44, 97; Reagan administration's, 146, 170
Rincon, Hernan (cousin of LW), 237
Roddman, Philip, 33
Rodriguez, Artie, 178
Rosen, Anna Semiatitsky Barnett (grandmother of LW), 6, 7, 22–23
Rosen, Dorothy (aunt of LW), 7, 16, 22
Rosen, Samuel (grandfather of LW), 6, 7, 22–23
Rosen, Sylvia (aunt of LW), 7, 16, 22, 25
Rosenthal, Mel, 98, 99–100, 107, 219
Rothschild, Joseph, 45
Rubenstein, Judith, 188

Russell, Bertrand, 130; autobiography of, 109
Russia, 210; Jews in, 1–5, 11; peace movement in, *156*, 191, 192, 193
Rustin, Bayard, 142

sabbaticals: in Amalfi, Italy, 113–14; in Amsterdam, Netherlands, 114–16
SANE, 44, 183, 233, 239
Santos, Gus, *158*
Sanya section (Tokyo), 120–21
Sarafis, Marion, 131
Sartre, Jean-Paul, 251
Saunders, Leonard, 25–26
Sayre, Wallace, 75
Schalk, David, 98, 101, 110, 125, 132, 189
Schell, Jonathan, 216, 217
Scheuerman, Bill, *159*, 179
Schonberger, Howie, 90, 93, 94, 129, 132, 188; *Aftermath of War*, 92; death of, 196
Schroeder, Pat, 180
SDS. *See* Students for a Democratic Society (SDS)
"Second Nuclear Age and the Academy, The" conference, 217
Seeger, Peggy, 186
Seinberg, Bev, *159*, 229
SEIU (Service Employees International Union), 241, 243
Selden, Mark, 120; *War and State Terrorism*, 218
September 11, 2001, attacks, 222, 224
Shah, Said, 224
Shaw, George Bernard, 52
Sheinblatt, Joseph (father of Patricia), 74; death of, 75
Sheinblatt, Molly (mother of Patricia), 74
Sheinblatt, Patricia "Patty." *See* Wittner, Patricia "Patty" Sheinblatt
Shenkman, Rick, 226
Shenton, James, 57–58, 75–76, 77, 133
Sherwin, Marty, 194
shyness, xvi, 25, 29, 38, 48, 51, 72
Sicko (documentary, Moore), 238
Sidor, Patricia "Patty" Sheinblatt Wittner, 186–87, 199
Sidor, Reinhard, 186–87, 199
Simpson, Alan, 97, 100, 104, 108, 116
singing, 25, 53, 140, 165, 218; in Japan, 120, 123; with Mexican workers, 205; no stuttering during, 20; political activism and, 132, 165, 218. *See also* Occasional Chorus; Solidarity Singers
Smithsonian Institution: exhibit on atomic bombing of Japan, 202–3
SNCC. *See* Student Nonviolent Coordinating Committee (SNCC)
Snyatyn, Ukraine, 7–8, 11–12
So, Alvin, *War and State Terrorism*, 218
social democracy. *See* democratic socialism
socialism and socialists, 10, 46, 174; Jewish, 2, 3–4; University of Wisconsin club, 71–72; U.S., 80, 169. *See also* democratic socialism
Socialist Party, 80, 118, 142, 170
social justice movement: LW's involvement in, 45, 146, 170, 204–5, 249; at SUNY/Albany, 176, 232–33. *See also* peace movement
Society for Historians of American Foreign Relations (SHAFR): award from, xvi, 201; as board member of, 180
Society of Orpheus, 54–57
Socrates, 43
Sodexho-Marriott Corporation, 213–15
Sohyo (Japanese labor federation), 122
Solidarity Committee of the Capital District, *158*, 199, 243; copper miners, 176; dining halls issue, 215; film series sponsored by, 176, 222, 232; and friends, 188, 194–95; James Bay project, 199; Labor Day picnics, *158*, 176, 212; LW as treasurer, 176; Martin Luther King, Jr. Labor Celebrations, 215–16, 232; origins and early activities, 175–77; relations with AFL-CIO, 177, 200, 232, 243; *Solidarity Notes* (newsletter), 176, 232; SUNY/Albany teach-in, 200; Tax the Rich campaign, 199, 200; World Social Forum, 224.
Solidarity Singers, *159*, 211–12, 213, 219, 229–30, 236
Solomon, Jane (daughter of Marjorie Wittner), 106
Solomon, Jerry, 173
Solomon, Steve, 106
South Africa. *See* Free South Africa movement
Soviet Union. *See* Russia
Spectator (Columbia College newspaper), 41–42, 45, 52, 77
Spinoza, Baruch, 42, 43
Spock, Benjamin: 1968 vice-presidential campaign, 93–94, 96

sports. *See* tennis playing
"Springhill Mine Disaster, The" (song, McCall), 186
Stassen, Glen, 233
State University of New York at Albany (SUNY/Albany): budget cuts at, 133, 200; Coca-Cola contract protest, 240; dining hall workers' disputes, *158,* 213–15, 241–43; faculty of, 128–30, 131, 132–34; LW's teaching position at, 124–26, 127–35, 163–65, 231–32, 238; saving Ph. D. program at, 128, 132–33, 134, 138, 162. *See also* Allen Center (SUNY/Albany)
Steinberg, Ronnie, 172
Stern, Lilo, 98
Stone, Edward Durrell, 127
Stone, Jeremy: interview with, 209
Stratton, Samuel, 173
Strozier, Chuck, 216–17
Student-Labor Initiative (SLI, SUNY/Albany), 214
Student Nonviolent Coordinating Committee (SNCC), 65, 66–67
students: evaluations of LW by, 110, 117, 164–65, 231–32; Japanese, 119–20; at SUNY/Albany, 131, 231
Students for Academic Freedom, 235
Students for a Democratic Society (SDS), 80, 88; at Vassar, 97, 103
Students for Workers' Rights (SUNY/Albany), 240
Studies on the Left (New Left, journal), 58, 71
stuttering, xvi, 15–16, 31, 48; overcoming, 20, 98, 180, 246
Sulkowitz, Raffi and Aliza, 188
Summy, Gil, 189
Summy, Ralph, 183, 189, 236
SUNYA Peace & Justice group (SUNY/Albany), 225, 232–33
Swanstrom, Todd, 172, 188, 189
Swarthmore College Peace Collection, 86
Sweeney, John, 199

Takahara, Takao "Taka," 227, 228
Tanaka, Yuki, 218, 227
Taylor, Myron, 165, 188, 240
Taylor, William, 71
teaching positions: Adelphi University, 76–77; Columbia University summer session, 133; Fulbright lecturer, 117, 124; at Hampton Institute, 87–88, 89–96, *152;* student evaluations of performance, 110, 117, 164, 231–32; SUNY/Albany, 124–26, 127–35, 163–65, 231–32, 238; Vassar College, 95, 96–111, 116–17
tennis playing: Jacob Wittner's, 9, 18, 20; LW's, 18, 189, 194
tenure: denied at Vassar, 109–10, 116–17, 124, 125; granted at SUNY/Albany, 133–35, 138, 162. *See also* academic life
Thayer, Julie, 99, 103, 115
Thomas, Norman, 78, 86
Thompson, E. P., 185, 194
Thompson, Fiona, 195
Thüsen, Joachim von der, 98
Tick, Paul, 224
Tokyo, Japan, 118–22
Tolles, Frederick B., 99
"Towards a World without Violence" conference, 227
travel, 245–46; camping and canoeing trips, 81, 104–6, 205–6; to Cape Cod, *156,* 185–86, 196, 206; childhood, 26–27; to Europe, 182–84, 204, 210–11, 217–18, 227, 244–45; to Hong Kong, 218; to Japan, 117–24, 227–29; to Malta, 201–2; to Mexico, 204–5; to Nova Scotia, 186; post-graduation road trip, 60, 61–67, *152;* revisiting Columbia University, 246–47; to Russia, *156,* 191–93; to San Francisco, 107, 186; to South Africa, 208; to West Coast, 185, 196
Trilling, Lionel, 48
Tristman, David (son of DT), 146, 161, 162, 186, 187–88
Tristman, Dorothy Axelrad (DT, second wife of LW), *157, 158, 160;* DSOC/DSA activities, 170, 171–72, 174; employment, 161, 195; finding ancestral home, 244–45; friendships, 188–89; LW's cancer and, 239; marriage to LW, 212–13, 236–37; in peace movement, 142; protest activities, 165, 168, 225; in reevaluation counseling movement, 161, 195; relationship with LW, 142–46, 190; Solidarity Committee activities, 176–77, 222, 232; trips, 182–84, 185–86, 192–93, 227
Tristman, Jonah (son of DT), 146, 161, 162, 185, 186, 187–88, 212
Tristman, Richard (former husband of DT), 142, 145, 146

Index

Trotsky, Leon, 109
Trotskyites, 136
Truman, Harry S., 22
Turner, Ted, 240

Ukraine. *See* Snyatyn, Ukraine
Unabomber: LW becomes target of, 203–4
union activities: democratic socialism and, 170–73, 175; LW's involvement in, 109, 232–33; picketing, 78, 146, 166, 173, 176, 232; for SUNY dining hall workers, *158*, 213–15, 241–43. *See also* AFL-CIO; labor movement; Solidarity Committee of the Capital District; United University Professions (UUP)
United Farm Workers (UFW), 177–78
United Nations: Non-Proliferation Treaty review conference, 232; speaking engagement at, 227
United Nations Association, 203
U.S. Defense Department: Jacob Wittner's employment with, 106
U.S. Federal Bureau of Investigation: spying on LW, 94–95
U.S. Information Agency (USIA): talks sponsored by, 121–22
United University Professions (UUP), *159*; as board member of Albany chapter, 136–37, 165–66, 199, 232, 240–43; CJM support, 204, 205; dining hall workers' disputes, *158*, 214–15, 241–43; progressive taxation campaign, 200; protests by, 146, *155*, 166; statewide and Albany chapter Solidarity Committees, 178–79, 232, 242
UNITE-HERE (union), 241, 243
University of Wisconsin at Madison: master's degree study at, 60–61, 69–73
USS *Midway*: sailors from, 120, 121, *153*
utilitarianism, study of, 42
utopias, 35–36, 44, 249

Van den Dungen, Peter, *157*, 184
Vanden Heuvel, Katrina, 217
Van Doren, Charles, 49
Van Dyke, Leon, 188, 189
Vassar College (Poughkeepsie, New York): faculty of, 97–98, 100–103, 108–10, 111, 116–17, 130, 132; firings at, 109–10, 132, 218–19; IBM confrontation, 103–4, 108; LW's teaching position at, 95, 96–111, 116–17; political activism at, 97–98, 100–101, 103, 108–9; tenure denied to LW, 109–10, 116–17, 124, 125
vegetarianism, 195
Vietnam War, protests against: at AHA meeting, 102; in Amsterdam, 114–15; at Columbia University, 78–79, 81, 82–83, 85–86, 87, 88; at Hampton Institute, 89, 93, 97, 100; in Japan, 119–20; at SUNY/Albany, 128; at Vassar College, 103
violence: in high school, 32; racist, 67; threats toward LW, 203–4, 246. *See also* pogroms; police brutality
Vlanton, Elias, 131
Voice (UUP newspaper), 179
Voltaire, 43
Von Hippel, Frank: interview with, 209

Walden Two (Skinner), 43–44
Wallace, George: 1968 presidential campaign, 93
Wallace, Henry, 22
Walters, Vernon, xvi
War and State Terrorism (Selden and So, editors), 218
Warnke, Paul: interview with, 209
Washington, Booker T., 89
Watergate scandal, 115
Watson, Thomas J., Jr., 103
Wechsler, James, 35
Weinberg, Michael, 107, 132, 189, 236; in Army National Guard, 79; camping and canoeing trips, 81, 104–6, 205–6; at Columbia University, 40, 43, 48, 51, 53; in Oregon, 185, 196; as Peace Corps volunteer, 80, 82–83; political activism, 58–60, 78; post-graduation road trip, 60, 61–67, *152*; revisiting Columbia University, 246–47; Society of Orpheus and, 54–57; at Wounded Knee, 186
Weinberg, Sydney, 81–82
Weinberger, Caspar: interview with, 209
Weinstein, James, 136
Wernicke, Günter, 204, 210, 236
Williams, William Appleman, 71
Wilson, Peg, 190
Wittner, Abraham (great-grandfather of LW), 7–8

Wittner, Bernard (uncle of LW), 8, 23
Wittner, Deborah "Debbie" (sister of LW), 19, 30, 78, 84; birth of daughter Andrea, 139; illness, 139–40; marriage to Eddie Golembe, 106; suicide, 196–97
Wittner, Derek and Barbara (friends), 82
Wittner, Estelle "Stella" (grandmother of LW), 8
Wittner, Harold (uncle of LW), 8, 9, 23
Wittner, Jacob "Jack" (father of LW), 7, 8–11, *150, 154*; death of, 197–98; employment, 9, 14, 19–20, 33–34, 51, 74, 83, 106; influences on LW, 18, 20, 34, 35, 37; marriage to Rose Barnett, 9–11, 30–31; polio attack, 8–9; remarriage to Marjorie Levy, 83–84, 188
Wittner, Joseph (grandfather of LW), 8, 13, 23–24, *150*
Wittner, Joyce (cousin of LW), 23
Wittner, Julia Rachel (daughter of LW), 140–41, *154*, 195, 196, 197; in Amalfi, 113–14; in Amsterdam, 114–15; birth of, 108; children of, 219, 224; college, 187, 198; at demonstrations, 165, 167–68; employment, 198–99, 224; father's remarriage, 213; in Japan, 118, 123; marriage to Bob Hughes, 199; mother's remarriage, 186–87; parents' separation and divorce, 144, 145–46, 161; travels with LW, 185, 186
Wittner, Lawrence S. "Larry" (LW): photos of, *151, 152, 153, 154, 155, 156, 157, 158, 159, 160*
Wittner, Leah Heller (grandmother of LW), 8, 9, *150*; LW named for, 13
Wittner, Leonard (cousin of LW), 23
Wittner, Marilyn (aunt of LW), 8
Wittner, Marjorie Levy (second wife of Jacob Wittner), 83–84, 106, *154*, 188, 197, 198
Wittner, May Markman (aunt of LW), 23
Wittner, Murray (uncle of LW), 8, 9, 15, 23
Wittner, Patricia "Patty" Sheinblatt (first wife of LW), 124; in Amalfi, 113–14; in Amsterdam, 114–15; dating LW, 52–53, 57, 61; employment, 140; family of, 72, 74–75, 85, 88, 142; in Hampton Institute graduate program, 91, 94; in Japan, 118, 119, 123; marriage to LW, 73, 74–75, 84–85, 106–8, 141–44; pregnancy and motherhood, 107–8, 110; remarriage to Reinhard Sidor, 186–87, 199; separation and divorce from LW, 144–47

Wittner, Rose (great-aunt of LW), 8
Wittner, Rose Barnett (mother of LW), 6–7, 74, *149, 150, 151*; death of, 83; financial worries, 31–32; as housewife, 14, 19; illness, 30–31, 37, 38; marriage to Jacob Wittner, 9–11
Wittner, Sara (great-grandmother of LW), 7–8
Wohl, Tony, 101
Women's International League for Peace and Freedom (WILPF), 86–87
Workmen's Circle (Arbeter Ring), 10; summer camps, 20–21
World Federalist Association, 199, 203
"World Says No to War" protests, 225
World War I: fate of European Jews during, 11
World War II: fate of European Jews during, 11–12, 245
writing, love of, 14, 16, 24, 26, 33, 48, 49. *See also* publications; research, scholarly

Yakubian, Sue, 82
Yale University, 239–40
Young, Marilyn, 218
Yugoslavia: U.S. attack on, 210

Zacek, Joseph, 125, 128, 129, 132, 133, 137
Zahavi, Gerry, *155,* 163
Zedillo, Ernesto, 239–40
Zellin, Agnes, 224
Zubok, Vladislav, 217
Zwanziger, Daniel (cousin of LW), 23, 81
Zwanziger, David, 23
Zwanziger, Eve (cousin of LW), 23
Zwanziger, Frances Murstein (cousin of LW. *See* Murstein, Frances (cousin of LW)

www.ingramcontent.com/pod-product-compliance
Lightning Source LLC
Chambersburg PA
CBHW030309080526
44584CB00012B/495